What is the power of ABHIJNA?
Who were the BENJEES?
What is an ETHERIC BODY?
What was ORPHISM?
Who was CORNEILLE QUIRADELLI?
What is the MEMPHITE DRAMA?
What was MARK TWAIN'S connection to the psychic?
What is TELEGNOSIS, the PARABRAHM,
the HUGIN and MUNIN?

It's all in the book for reference and pleasurable skimming,
the book for wonder and enlightenment—

THE NEW
STEINERBOOKS DICTIONARY
OF THE PARANORMAL

THE NEW
STEINERBOOKS
DICTIONARY
of the
PARANORMAL

by

George Riland

WARNER BOOKS

A Warner Communications Company

Warner Books Edition

Copyright © 1980 by Rudolf Steiner Publications.

This Warner Books Edition is published by arrangement with Steiner Books, c/o Virginia Barber Literary Agency, Inc., 44 Greenwich Avenue, NY, NY 10011.

Warner Books, Inc., 75 Rockefeller Plaza, New York, N.Y. 10019.

(w) A Warner Communications Company

Printed in the United States of America

First printing: July 1982
10 9 8 7 6 5 4 3 2 1

Library of Congress Cataloging in Publication Data

Riland, George.
  The new Steinerbooks dictionary of the paranormal.

  1. Psychical research—Dictionaries. 2. Occult
sciences—Dictionaries. I. Title.
BF1025.R5 1981   133'.03'21   81-16280
ISBN 0-446-97010-7 (U.S.A.)   AACR2
ISBN 0-446-37360-5 (Canada)

Preface

After many years of publishing the rarest, most important, and finest books in all the related fields of the supernormal, this publisher had increasingly grown aware that the time was ripe for the appearance of a truly superior dictionary on these subjects. However, it is easier to recognise the time and the need for a superlative dictionary than to bring it to fruition. For not only must it be up-to-date and comprehensive, but also it had to be well-written and genuinely to demonstrate an unusually broad reach of erudition. With our reputation throughout much of the world for the excellence of our books, nothing less than the publication of an exemplary dictionary would do. It is therefore with a feeling of pride that we now present, finally, *The New Dictionary of the Paranormal, Psychic, Mystic, Occult*. We do so with the belief that *The New Dictionary* possesses the scholarship and scope, the depth and richness, the uniqueness in dimension, plus the technical aids and innovations, that will make it the standard reference for everyone interested in this field.

But since a dictionary must speak for itself, here are its facts. Firstly, *The New Dictionary of the Paranormal, Psychic, Mystic, Occult* with close to 2800 entries represents the largest number ever displayed in such a dictionary. Secondly, the list has been chosen with uncommon deliberation from every age, from every nation, and from numerous smaller cultures past and present. The extent of information which is available to the reader is thus exceptionally comprehensive and instructive. Thirdly, and further increasing the scope of information, there are a great number of entries with articles of ency-clopedic length. The criteria determining these longer articles were these: (1) importance of the entry in its own right; (2) historic impact; (3) germinal influence; (4) combinations of these factors. Fourthly, there are a wealth of cross-references. Moreover, in each case every cross-reference markedly fulfills the purpose of expanding the initial entry which has been looked up. Fifthly, all entries are defined to be understood; for unlike some books and dictionaries in this field, this dictionary scrupulously avoids opaqueness and imprecision; rather, in *The New Dictionary*, particular care has been exercised to present all information with clarity, precision, factuality, and specificity. And where these standards have been impossible to follow, owing to the limitations of the available data, this fact itself is clearly stated.

What has guided the creation of this dictionary throughout has been a strict attention to the methodology of the scholar. In conse-quence, and sixthly, the definitions and articles in this reference work exhibit the scholar's devotion to setting out the complexity of a topic; that is, of offering to the reader the pros and cons for all those entries where this type of evaluation is warranted. Seventhly, because of the vast literature this book embodies—not only geographically and his-torically, but in the multi-disciplines it surveys, (religion, philosophy, myth, literature, art, science, the mystic, and the many components of the supernormal) the inquirer is not left wondering or puzzled about relationships or sources: identification of the origin or origins at the beginning of entries are always given when necessary. As with several other of the above facts, this feature is unique in dictionaries of this specialty. Eighthly, and an outgrowth of the preceding, the number of fields of knowledge this dictionary incorporates far ex-ceeds any other such dictionary ever published. Ninthly, although this book is a dictionary, the assemblage of so varied a body of data— ancient, past, and present, in one volume, very strikingly reveals to a contemporary audience (what was a commonplace in earlier periods) the existence of that underlying unity which binds the diversity of all our cosmic phenomena, whether material, biological, or supernormal. Again, this latter aspect is a first, a distinctly new orientation, not found in similar dictionaries.

We hope it obvious by now that we have published a dictionary in which the word "new" lives up to its many meanings, among which are "original" and "superior." As a consequence of this fresh ap-proach to our material; we have taken into account the fact that the occult, the psychic, the mystic, and the paranormal have enjoyed a checkered career in the history of mankind—variously honored, obeyed, condemned, and hunted. And since, therefore, its colossal quantity of data exhibits different degrees of merit, it seemed the time had come to introduce into a dictionary a presentation strengthened by newer insights and some assets of today's perspective. Concomitantly, inasmuch as ours is a period when a number of the social sciences have grafted elements of the supernormal into their disciplines; when there has been an unprecedented resurgence of interest in the supernormal on the part of the public, the universities, and the arts; it is unquestionably necessary to have a first-rate dictionary on the subject.

All of which now brings us to a word about the author. *The Dictionary of the Paranormal, Psychic, Mystic, Occult* was written by George Riland. What the dictionary has become—in concept, in richness, in authority, and felicity of language is totally owing to his labors. That he shared the same sense of perfection with this publisher was evident from the beginning. But even more, George Riland is among those authors who help to make publishing, despite its many pitfalls, a rewarding art and business. Though recognising that the present book is certainly more than the reference work this publisher envisioned in the beginning, at this point both publisher and author are as one in the awareness that the ultimate judgment now belongs to the public.

Aa

A. Historically "A" has been at the head of all known alphabets, for example, the Semitic *aleph* (from a symbol denoting the head of an ox), the Greek *alpha*, the Latin A. Utilized as a letter of occult power, it has been part of many mystic formulae; and having the numerical value of one, it often symbolizes the universal "all" and the Godhead.

Aaron. The founder and head of the Jewish priesthood, who with his brother Moses led the Israelites out of Egypt, became in Christian symbolism a redeemer, a sacrifice, who acted as an intermediary between man and God and thus represented a type of Christ.

Abhijna (Buddhism). Among the southern Buddhists this power, which takes any form at will, has five elements: seeing at any distance, hearing at any distance, reading thoughts, knowing a person's spiritual state, and perceiving a person's former lives.

Abhinavagupta (fl. A.D. 1014). An eminent Hindu philosopher, ascetic and mystic who conceived siva (q.v.), the I (or consciousness), and the All, as the same entity. His concept of freedom (*svantantrya*) represents the I as possessed with the power of objectivity, freedom, and strength.

Abracadabra. A charm, incantation or magical word used to ward off misfortune, harm, or illness, particularly when written on an amulet in a mystical design. Said to be formed from the letters of Abraxas (q.v.). In modern times it has evolved to "hocus pocus," signifying a false magic.

Abraham (Judaism). The founder of Judaism and the Hebrew people, and the ancestor of the Mohammedans through Ishmael, was one of the great mystics of antiquity, and one of the founders of the concept of a universal god. Devoted to his mystical revelation of a supreme being who created the universe, he journeyed to a new land, Canaan, and was willing to sacrifice his only son, Isaac, to God when so commanded. Abraham's influence on Judaism, Islam, and Christianity has made him an enormously important figure and was one of the profoundly evolutionary events in the history of mysticism, religion, and man's ethical development. The story of Abraham's willingness to sacrifice his only son to God has been the source of many paintings and philosophical conceptions.

Abraxas. A term with a number of meanings. For some it has signified the Supreme Deity and the Godhead of all deities; it has been associated with Mithras (q.v.); for the ancients, the seven letters of Abraxas was a mystery symbol of the God in whom adhered the whole power of the 7 planets known to them and also of the year of 365 days—the year as eternity.

Absent Healing. Healing through the intercession of a healing medium (often but not always assisted by a dedicated group), with spirit doctors on behalf of patients who have no direct contact with the medium. Patients may not be aware that they are being treated.

Absolute, the. Ultimate ground of all reality—Brahma, God. It is the Absolute with which all mystics unite in an ecstasy of oneness. However named, the Absolute, therefore, is the universal foundation of all mysticism; also of religion and much of the occult.

Abulafia, Abraham ben Samuel (1240–1291). One of a number of important Hebrew scholars living in Spain. He contributed his wide knowledge to an enrichment of the intellectual content of the Cabala, particularly in incorporating the historic strain of mysticism in Judaism. His theories of emanation and metempsychosis (qq.v.) and his ideas on number and letter symbolism made him one of the central figures in the development of the Cabala.

Academia de Estudo Psychicos "Cesar Lombroso." This Academy for psychical research is in Sao Paulo, Brazil. Established 1919.

Acarya (Buddhism). A spiritual teacher or guide.

Acharya. A Hindu religious teacher. One who knows both the rules and the sacred writings of the Hindus, and is generally dedicated to preserving the ancient traditions. Applies also to illustrious and learned persons.

Adam Kadmon (Judaism). Meaning "first man," the archetypal man, who became in the ancient mystical writings of the Israelites the paradigm of the divine power emanating from God—the *En Sof* (q.v.) which made unformed substance into the form of man. This is the usage in the Cabala. It also has important meaning in the tradition of the Golem (q.v.).

Adams, Evangeline (1872–1932). One of America's most famous astrologers who more than anyone else made of astrology both a serious and a popular subject in the U.S. Many of her clients were among the world's great. Her books are still read and studied. (See: *The Bowl of Heaven, Astrology, Your Place in the Sun*)

Additor. A modified ouija board (q.v.) with a little hollow box and pointer. The box is supposed to conserve psychic power, as would a cabinet used for materialization phenomena.

Adept. An occult title representative of the highest attainment on this earth by an Initiate, with conscious and complete mastery of psychic powers. Sometimes associated with the Great White Brotherhood (q.v.) who are supposed to exert a guiding influence over mankind. The highest stage of Yoga (q.v.). Theosophists understand it to be the passing of the fifth stage of initiation.

Aditi (Hinduism). Refers to the boundless heaven which is "free, unbounded," representing infinity. Represents also Deva-Matri, Mother of the Gods.

Adonai. From early days the Hebrews have substituted the sacred name of God, Jehovah, by using *Adonai* when reading the sacred books both aloud and silently. The Tetragammaton—IHVH—is "the incommunicable name," also spelled JHVH, JHWH, YHVH, YHWH (the four letters of Jehovah). This tradition of mystic letters impregnated the whole Cabalistic and occult tradition.

Advaita-Vadins (Hinduism). A very important aspect of the whole evolution of Hindu doctrine, for the adherents represent the workers against twoness and they are the dedicated followers of the doctrine of universal unity.

Adventist. One who believes in the second coming of Jesus the Christ.

Aeon. Among the ancient Greeks this term referred to either an indefinite or infinite period of time. Therefore, existence that endures forever. It was adopted by the Gnostics (q.v.) in its latter sense to represent those eternal beings or manifestations which emanate from God.

Aesch Mezareph. A term meaning purifying fire. It is the name of a book taken from the "Kaballah Denudata" of Knorr Von Rosenoch that incorporates both alchemical and Cabalistic information. It was translated in 1714, and is considered so informative that recently it has been reprinted.

Aesha (Zoroastrianism). This power represents the culmination of intense spiritual development, for it is nothing less than the power of wishing personified.

Aeshm or Aeshma (Zoroastrianism). One of the important demons in Zoroastrianism, the demon of rage. It also represents "rage" abstractly. In the Book of Tobit, a book of the Apocrypha (q.v.), he is designated Asmodeus.

Aesir. The greater gods of the Scandinavian pantheon which included: Odin, Frigga, Balder, Thor, Tyr, Vali, Vidar, Bragi, Hodur, Hermdo, and Loki (qq.v.). They inhabited the heavenly city of Asgard.

Affair of the Poisons. At the end of the 17th century France was swept by an epidemic prosecution against practitioners of witchcraft, sorcery, and poisonings. The mania began with a scandal at the court of Louis XIV when the Marquise de Brinvilliers was accused of poisoning her father and brother and sentenced to death in 1676. The notorious Brinvilliers trial attracted attention to other mysterious deaths in which poison was found to be involved. Thus attention became focused on the spiritual seances, fortunetelling, and the use of love potions which, having become a fad in high Parisian society, inevitably attracted quack practitioners who engaged in the selling of poisons. When a number of these quacks were arrested, they furnished the police with a list of their clients—who in the main were guiltless—and accused them of complicity in their crimes. The fortuneteller La Voisin, whose clients were all among the first families of France, was burned as a poisoner and sorceress in 1680. At the scandal's height, charges of witchcraft and intercourse with the devil became common accusations, bringing in its wake the *chambre ardent* (burning court) to judge cases of poisoning and witchcraft. The Affair of the Poisons, in its intensity and affect on the popular imagination, rivaled the witchcraft trials then occurring throughout Europe and New England.

Affinities. According to reincarnation theories, one person's destiny may be bound to another's throughout many earth lives. If they are fond of each other, an extremely close bond of affection is said to be formed which transcends death and the possible alternation of sex. These two persons are then said to be "affinities."

Afflatus. Inspiration drawn upon. An aura of divine origin.

Afreet (Arabic). In Arabic mythology, he represents variously a powerful evil jinni, a demon, or a monstrous giant. Among the ancient Egyptians he was one of the many evil powers they feared.

Agent. In psychical research, one who acts as the transmitter in telepathic communications.

Agna (African). Smooth glassy fragments found by the Ivory Coast natives of West Africa, to which they attribute supernatural powers, they are among the most mysterious objects found on earth. Though scientists have known about them for more than a hundred years—calling them "taktites"—and know they come from outer space (some of them as old as 35 million years), no theory accounts for their source. Taktite fields are found in many parts of the earth, from Australia through Asia, Europe and the Americas. Strangely, both the West Africans and the aborigines of Australia perceived their uniqueness, giving them supernatural qualities and using them in magic rites.

Agni (Buddhism-Hinduism). A term meaning fire and representing the most important of the Vedic gods (primarily the god of the altar fire), he designates a trinity which joins the lightning and the sun. He is the mediator between the gods and men.

Agnishwattas (Hinduism). A class belonging to the solar ancestors as contrasted with the lunar ancestors. The Agnishwattas are our solar spiritual-intellectual traits, our inner teachers, which guide us to become fully self-conscious of our godhead.

Agnostic. Scepticism of the unknown. One who denies the possibility of proving or disproving anything beyond material phenomena.

Agrippa von Nettesheim, Heinrich Cornelius (1486-1535). During his relatively short life, this extraordinarily talented man who was a profound mystic, occultist, physician, orator, statesman, ambassador, and religious reformer, served kings and emperors, but courageously defied both crown and church in defense of his principles. In 1510 his *De Occulta Philosophia*, a significant defense of magic, demonstrates how man may use magic to come to a knowledge of nature and God. He also wrote another important work proclaiming the need to return to the simple and primitive doctrines of the Christian Church. Though imprisoned several times for his beliefs, his life and work have had a tremendous influence through the years.

Ahankora (Hinduism). The egoistical principal in man which develops the concept of the "I" as being different from the universal one-self.

Ah Puch (Mayan). In the mythology and art of Mayan culture in Central America, he was the god of death who ruled the underworld.

Ahriman (Zoroastrianism). Chief of the fallen angels (also Angra Mainyu q.v.), the principal of evil, or the Devil to the Persians and Chaldeans in the religion of Zoroastrianism. He and the other Cacodaemons were expelled from heaven for their sins, tried to settle on earth, were rejected, took residence in the space between the earth and fixed stars, and find their pleasure in injuring humanity. Ahriman is opposed to Ormuzd or Ahura Mazda (q.v.), the creative and benevolent being.

Ahura Mazda (Zoroastrianism). In the Persian dualism, he was the creative and benevolent being heading the good spirits—also called Ormuzd. His name means sovereign knowledge. Some six attendant deities accompany him, the Amesha Spentas (q.v.). Though these are abstract qualities, they have become personalized: Vohu Manah (good thought), Asha Vahista (highest righteousness), Haurvatat (salvation), Ksat hiara Vairya (divine kingdom), Spenta Armaiti (pious devotion), and Ameratat (immortality).

Ain-Soph (Judaism). The supreme source of wisdom. The hidden First Cause in the ancient Hebrew mysteries from which emanates the Sepiroth. (See: Cabala)

Akashic Records. This term refers to the cosmic picture gallery and record of every thought, feeling and action since the world began. Those possessing psychic vision can read and translate the world's history from the Akashic Records. Often advanced as an explanation of clairvoyant and psychometric perceptions. Somewhat akin to the idea of Cosmic Consciousness (q.v.). Yogis believe that this record can be contacted when in certain psychic states of consciousness.

Aksakov, Alex N. (1832-1903) Pioneer spiritualist and psychic researcher of Russia, an Imperial Councillor to the Czar. Was greatly influenced by Swedenborg and A. J. Davis. Translated many important works of psychical research.

Alaya (Hinduism). The universal soul, the source of all beings and things.

Albertus Magnus, Saint (c. 1200–1280). The foremost scholar of his time, this German monk—called *doctor universalis*—because of his unparalleled knowledge of philosophy, theology, and science, was also an eminent mystic, and a student of the occult, alchemy, and magic. He was, in addition, a great teacher (Saint Thomas Aquinas studied under him); emissary of several Popes; Bishop of Regensburg. He was the flower of Medievalism, a universal man, master of all knowledge, champion of Aristotle and science; but also, when the occasion demanded, an awesome magician who could suddenly produce gardens and orchards and create a mechanical man akin to the Golem (q.v.).

Alchemy. The ancient art which sought to transmute base metals into gold had its roots in China and Egypt, and reached its highest development in Alexandria from which it passed to the Arabs and through them to Europe in the Middle Ages. Although Neo-platonism, magic, astrology, mysticism, medicine, esoteric doctrines of the Near East, Pythagoreanism, and Orphism were elements in the corpus of the highest forms of Alchemy, mainly its adherents were engaged in experiments with metals and other chemical materials to convert base metals into gold. In its noblest practice it was a way, also, of purification and liberation (to restore the earth to its original likeness). It was a way, also, of strict spiritual discipline by which the alchemist transmuted himself from illusion to reality. The concept of the philosopher's stone, the *elixir vitae*, the preparation of which demanded the seeker's scrupulous attention to a very complex formula, was not only capable of making base metals into gold but also of restoring youth to man. While many quacks and villains used alchemy to dupe the rich and mighty, there were also Geber, Zosimus, Paracelsus (qq.v.) etc., proving that men of the highest integrity practiced the craft. And it was out of the alchemical experiments of these men and others that the science of chemistry was born.

Alexander of Abonuteichus. Born in Abonuteichus, on the south shore of the Black Sea (the modern Inebolu), in the 2nd century A.D., Alexander was a famous mystic, psychic, diviner and prophet of Asclepius. Declaring his oracular shrine at Abonuteichus to be a new manifestation of the god Asclepius—of which he was the appointed prophet, he and his shrine became famous throughout both the Roman peninsula and their Near Eastern provinces. Aside from the great repute of his oracles, he also held yearly ceremonies for his numerous disciples. Although these observances were analagous to the Eleusinian mysteries in form and in ritual, they were, however, rooted in the myth of the god Asclepius—both in his chthonian divinity— the rites of the snake, and in his celestial divinity—those expressed in divination, the healing arts, and many earthly ills (shipwreck, plagues, etc.). Following Alexander's death, somewhere near the end of the 2nd century A.D., his shrine and his cult survived and flourished for many years. Since, however, he and his shrine were new evocations of the divine spirit to his contemporaries, (unlike such historic shrines, for example, as Ammon, Delphi, Olympia, Dodona), and also as a result of his wide fame, he was an easy target for criticism. Even so eminent a writer as the Greek satirist Lucian in his "Alexander the Quack Prophet"—after first acknowledging that he was an extraordinarily gifted individual, then goes on to charge him with every "black" crime on record. Lucian calls him a "pederast," a "prostitute," and one steeped in "deceit, trickery, lying, sharp practices," a daring schemer, unparallelled faker, and one who "lived in a way that outdid all the notorious evildoers of history." Historically, this is a classic example of a rationalist, narrow-minded attack on a person of outstanding psychic, mystic, and spiritual abilities. The change in our present outlook was helped by the vision and wisdom of such persons as Wm. James, Wm. McDougall, Jung, Eileen Garrett, and Freud (qq.v.) in earlier years; more recent investigators such as Rhine, Castaneda, Robert Ornstein (qq.v.), etc., have authenticated the fact that genuine psychics do possess paranormal talents.

Al-Farabi (870–950). Arabian philosopher who has been ranked with Aristotle as one of the greatest of all teachers. He sought for the common elements of God, soul, time, and space among the diverse philosophies of Greece. But he was chiefly influenced by Plotinus' concept that the world and belief in it emanated from God, and by Aristotle's concept that there was a Prime Mover of the universe—that the world had no beginning in time and could not have preceded God who was the prime mover. Al-Farabi was also a noted musicologist (Dervishes in the East can still be heard singing his chants); he was, too, a Utopian whose *Model City* projected his desires for the heavenly city on earth.

Al-Kindi (d. 873 A.D.). One of the great Arabian philosophers whose work in physics, mathematics, and astronomy was utilized for centuries. He served both as a tutor and astrologer to the court, and was one of the great influences in Arabian astrology. He was an eminent Neo-Platonist and Neo-Pythagorean, and considered the theory of emanations as essential to the life of man, since through this process man became free and immortal though his body remained subject to the influence of the stars.

Allah (Islam). The "One" who is the all-knowing and the omnipotent God, who superseded the many nature-spirits once worshipped by the Arabs. It was the great mystic enlightenment of Muhammad (q.v.)

which gave this vision of the "One," the creator and all-powerful ruler of the universe, to the Arabian people.

Althanor. An occult hill with a well, mainly mist-surrounded; possessing magical symbols and the power to relieve drought in the surrounding countryside. The word also was used by alchemists to mean moral and philosophical alchemy.

Alzen-Myoo. The Japanese Buddhist divinity who exemplifies sexual love transformed into a love for enlightenment. He wears a liou in his hair, has three eyes and a fierce countenance, all representing the suppression of carnal desires.

Ambrose, Saint (A.D. 340?–397). Bishop at Milan, one of the eminent doctors and important mystics of the Roman (imp.) Catholic Church. His earnest instruction of the people coupled with his honesty, wide learning, and oratorical talents, gathered many converts to his orthodox Catholicism, from the lowliest to the Roman Emperor, but most notably Saint Augustine (q.v.). The body of his writings, broad in scope, contains many important theological works which reflect his mysticism. He also initiated the Ambrosian chant, and his hymns have become the standard for the Western Church.

Amen, Amon. One of the chief deities in ancient Egyptian religion, initially a deity of reproductive forces who developed into Amen-Ra, he was united with the sun, and became "the father of gods, creator of men," with the other gods partaking of his being. Later the Mediterranean world identified him with Jupiter in Jupiter Ammon.

American Institute for Scientific Research. Founded by Dr. Hyslop in New York (1906) to investigate abnormal psychology and psychical research. This last section later became known as the American Society for Psychical Research (independent).

American Psychical Institute and Laboratory. Founded by Dr. Hereward Carrington (q.v.), the noted American researcher in New York, 1920. Many scientists of international repute were on the advisory council.

American Society for Psychical Research (A.S.P.R.). Founded Boston 1885, dissolved and re-established under Dr. Hyslop (q.v.) (American Institute for Scientific Research [q.v.]), its publications are "Proceedings" and "Journal."

Amesha Spentas. The 6 archangels in Zarathustra's teachings.

Amida, Buddha. In Japanese Buddhism, the supreme Buddha of the Jodo sect (q.v.). Having performed good deeds for others through many reincarnations, he created a Blissful Realm for all who recited his name—"Buddha Amida"—in perfect faith.

Ammonius Saccas (c. 160–242). This self-educated laborer from Alexandria founded Neo-platonism (q.v.), which played an immensely important role in Western philosophy and mysticism. He left no writings, and practically nothing is known about his doctrines. But his illustrious pupils, notably Plotinus (q.v.), developed his theories and through them he influenced subsequent philosophy.

Amnesia (Spiritualism). A gap or loss in one's memory. It often occurs during trance states of mediums, the amount of material forgotten depending upon the depth of trance in each case.

Amshaspands. The 7 Amshaspands of ancient Persia are analogous to the 7 Devas of India, the 7 great angels of Chaldea, and the 7 archangels of the Christian Apocalypse.

Anaesthesia. Loss of the sense of feeling, which is exhibited sometimes by mediums in the trance state, has often been demonstrated. The extent varies from slight to complete loss of sensation. Anaesthetics have been used to induce clairvoyance, notably nitrous oxide in experiments conducted by Dr. N. Jeans, while peyote and mescalin are utilized by certain Amazonian tribes.

Analgesia. Loss of feeling, insensibility to pain (See: Anaesthesia)

Ananda (Hinduism). An epithet of Siva which has the meaning "Joy, Happiness." It has evolved into a suffix for many Hindu teachers' names. In Buddhism, it was the name of Buddha's personal attendant and beloved disciple.

Ancestor Worship. Since the earliest ages man almost everywhere, in one form or another, engaged in the worship of the spirits of dead relatives. Believing that the soul survives death and that this soul-spirit could cause havoc, mankind made sure it was placated. Generally the father was the recipient of the fullest reverence. Although most religions do not promulgate ancestor worship, some did, for example: the African Bantu, the Polynesian islanders, the ancient Chinese and other Asian people. The ancient Egyptians, aside from their elaborate funerary ritual (See: Book of the Dead), practiced a form of ancestor worship.

Angel. In the Jewish, Christian, Mohammedan, Indian, and other theologies, and in the mystical and occult traditions, a supernatural messenger of God. Angels as emanations of God, belong to any of the orders, but mainly to the lowest order of the celestial hierarchy. But as the ninth and last of the orders, angels play a vital part in man's destiny, in the realms of both the material and the immaterial. Satan and his companions are "fallen angels." In ancient Greece, Hermes, messenger of the gods, was called Angelos. In Homer and Plato, Iris and Hermes are the divine *angeloi*. In Gnostic and Neoplatonic systems they are important. Among the Chaldeans and Hebrews, they were connected with the planets; their names had magic virtues. Angels were worshipped in ancient Egypt and Asia Minor. (See: Spheres)

Angra Mainyu (Zoroastrianism). The absolute power of evil and supreme ruler of all evil and unclean spirits who fought relentlessly for the souls of human beings against the victory of Ahura Mazda (q.v.). He later evolved into Ahriman (q.v.). Christianity represents this universal power of Evil by the name of Satan.

Animal Worship. Among most of the early cultures of mankind the animal formed so vital a part of the diet, so central a part then of life and death, that the animal seemed a divine aspect of the universe. Often elaborate rituals preceded the hunt. Animals were acknowledged to be superior to men in some powers—in fertility, in speed, in strength— and therefore were regarded as a symbol for these powers. Extending this veneration to all animals (especially snakes, bulls, and birds), early cultures adopted prayer rituals and built temples in their worship. The Egyptian bull, Apis; the Greek eagle of Zeus; the early Buddhist, and American Indian snakes; the Aztec and Toltec Quetzalcoatl bird; and, in a sense, the Christian "Lamb of God" are some examples of animals raised to divinity. There has also been a widespread belief in animal transformation or lycanthropy (q.v.).

Animism. One of the oldest of man's abiding beliefs, and quite probably originating in the Paleolithic age. It means a belief in a soul or spirit inhabiting living things and inanimate objects, and in a future state belonging to a separately existing immaterial soul. Such concepts as mana, oranda, and manitou (qq.v.) embody the spiritual nonpersonal quality which animists conceive to be present in the universe. Most likely the difference between the dead and the living, and such phenomena as sleep, trance, dreams, strange encounters, and clairvoyance phenomena seemed evidence that each person possessed a phantom life as well as a physical. It had been suggested by Alex Aksakov (q.v.) in his counter theory to spirit survival that the medium's spirit is alone responsible for such phenomena; Eileen Garrett (q.v.) held somewhat the same judgment. Ancestor worship and animism are interrelated. In ancient China and Egypt it was believed that souls linger near the scene of their former lives, needing respect and sustenance. It is also an aspect of nature worship, and a belief in the gods and godlings of polytheism, as well as the evil spirits of demonology.

Ankh. A figure like a cross, having a loop instead of an upper vertical arm, which was used in ancient Egypt as a symbol of life—perhaps the life that follows death, since it frequently appears in tomb sculptures and paintings as symbolizing life's triumph over death. Having recently become a very popular adornment, it has been supposed to represent the union of male and female principles, the origins of life, the four winds, rain-bringers and fertilizers. Called also *ansate cross, crux ansata, key of life.*

Anthropoflux. The researches of E.K. Muller, Engineer of Zurich and Director of Salus Institute for Nervous Disorders, demonstrated the existence of an emanation from the human body which can decrease the resistance in an electrical circuit. These experiments were verified by Professor Farny of the Zurich Polytechnicum, who coined the term. He established that the maximum emission is from the inner surfaces of the left hand fingers. It also appears in the breath. (See: Emanations)

Anthropomancy. In divination it refers to the use of human entrails which were usually those of sacrificed virgins or children.

Anthropomorphic. The conception of Deity in the form of a man.

Anthroposophy. Literally, knowledge concerning man. Rudolf Steiner (q.v.) described it as "a path of knowledge leading from the spiritual in the human being to the spiritual in the universe," also as "knowledge produced by the higher self in man." In the latter sense he equated it with "the science of spirit," as the name of his teachings, particularly after 1900. The term itself however had been used much earlier, but in a somewhat different sense; it was first used in English by Thomas Vaughan (1622–1666) (q.v.), the English alchemist, Rosicrucian and Theosophist, in his *Anthroposophia Theomagica,* 1650.

Anubis. In ancient Egyptian religion—the son of Osiris who together with Toth conducted the dead to the Netherworld. Here Anubis weighed their hearts to ascertain the elements of truth and right as their souls were considered by the 42 judges and given a failing or passing status in their further journey to eternal life. Represented as dogheaded, he was later identified by the Greeks with Hermes.

Anupapadaka (Hinduism-Buddhism). Term used in Buddhism to represent the original or root from which the Hierarchy of Buddhas of various grades issue in mystical evolution. The center of any organic existent is an anupapadaka divinity. Consequently, it is the mystical word for expressing the doctrine of the "inner god."

Anuttara samya Ksambodhicitta (Buddhism). This immensely complex linguistic embodiment incorporates into one concept a very important multiple aspect of achieving the spiritual crown: for it means no less than the "most-perfect-knowledge-mind."

Aornarssuk. Among the Eskimos a protecting spirit possessed with much beneficent power.

Apocalypse. Refers to a revelation or unveiling of mysteries. Though mainly it applies to the book of *Revelation,* New Testament, there was much apocalyptic writing among the ancient Jews. Some of the sibylline oracles were used by Jewish and Christian occultists, since they contained ancient prophecies and occult insights from Babylonia, Egypt, Greece, and Roman Italy.

Apocrypha. In the occult tradition they have the Greek meaning of "hidden," that is, spiritual writings too sacred or mysterious for the uninitiated, and not included in the canonical books of the Hebrew Old Testament. But they have been part of all Christian translations of the Bible (Vulgate, Coverdale, etc.) except in England since 1826. The Apocrypha have been very important in the whole tradition of the occult, especially such works as *Tobit, Baruch, Prayer of Manasses*, and *Esdras*.

Apocryphal. Of unknown or doubtful authorship.

Apollo. In ancient Greece the most Greek and most significant of all the gods, his powers increased through the years till they dominated and overshadowed all their divinities. Most famous as the god of oracles, of music and poetry, he was also the protector of villages and streets and also of colonies; god of vegetation, of ceremonial purification, of healing; the sender and stayer of plagues as well as sudden death; god of law and philosophy; the divinity, too, of radiance and light, and identified with the sun god Helios. There were numerous statues of Apollo everywhere, large and small, the most famous being sculpted by Praxitiles. At famed Delphi, Apollo was the chief god of the oracle. The Romans adopted him as a god of healing, but chiefly as the divinity in control of oracles and prophecies. His most representative symbols are the bow, the lyre, and the laurel. The notion of Apollo has had an enormous influence in the arts, philosophy, and morals of Western culture. (See: Apollonian and Dionysian)

Apollonian and Dionysian Duality. Initiation into the mysteries by two different paths. The Apollonian oracle had a purely Hellenic character; the Dionysian, being cosmopolitan, combined both Eastern and Western wisdom. The Apollonian looked outward, the Dionysian inward. The antithesis of style developed by the Greeks stems from these two divinities of art, Apollo and Dionysos.

Apotheosis. Mythology, religion and nations record great men who have been so admired they have been deified, which is the meaning of this Greek word. Alexander was considered the son of the Egyptian god Ammon. In China, Confucius has been deified, and Buddha has been apotheosized in many lands. Among the Egyptians the Pharoahs were god-kings, as also among the Romans were their emperors, beginning with Augustus. The Incas also deified their kings.

Apotropaism. One of the oldest of all magical rites which goes back to the most primitive years of mankind: the prevention of evil through carefully elaborated observances. Blood, vegetation, noise, incantation, dancing, mystical rituals etc. were utilized; often these included using the blood of a victim. From this very ancient practice has proliferated a vast array of practices in magic, the occult—in the use of amulets, charms, and many household objects; and, accordingly, the dominance of witchdoctors, shamans, medicine men, sorcerers, etc.

Apparition. A supernormal appearance which suggests the presence of a person living or dead. From extensive research, it would appear to be of most common occurrence when special anxiety and the desire to send an urgent message concurs with physical extremity on the part of the agent. (See: Ghosts)

Apports. In spiritualism, the production of objects and the seeming penetration of matter: one of the most astounding examples of physical phenomena. According to spirit communicators, objects are first "dematerialized," then reassembled in the seance room. The apporting of human beings is termed "transportation" (q.v., and see Mrs. Guppy). Some of the most astonishing apport cases were received through the mediumship of Mme. d'Esperance (q.v.).

Apsaras (Hinduism). Angels who are divine water nymphs; often depicted dancing at a stream or waterfall. Applies, generally, to any figure of an angel in art form.

Aquarian Age. An astronomical epoch which will be occasioned by the entry of the Vernal equinox into the constellation Aquarius in about A.D. 2740. This is due to the phenomenon of precession, a very slow revolution of the pole of the earth around that of the ecliptic once every 26,000 years, changing the relationships of the signs to the constellations. Therefore approximately 2,000 years are spent by the vernal point in each constellation. As the present epoch is towards the end of constellation Pisces, this is taken by many as showing a special esoteric link with the past 2,000 years of Christianity, and it is said that we are on the brink of a new age which will be characterized by the astrological qualities of the sign Aquarius.

Aquarius (Astrology). Astrological sign; (Jan. 21–Feb. 19); symbol, man pouring water; ruling planets, Saturn and Uranus; qualities—cautious, prudent, noble, progressive, mentally acute, intuitive, psychic, inquisitive, generous, cosmic, modest; but can be lazy, erratic, unreliable, too self-interested, subservient to others' opinions. Many astrologers consider this the finest of all twelve signs because of the range of its talent and genius.

Arahant (Buddhism). The designation of the disciple who has followed the eightfold path to enlightenment. In Hinduism, by the name of Arhat, it is the appelation of a deserving, worthy person.

Aralu. In Babylonian religion this was the underworld or home of the dead. Seven doors framing a hole in the earth comprised the entranceway.

Arcana. That which is hidden. Mysteries and secrets.

Archangel. Chief of a host of heavenly angels. Hebrew archangels are: Samael (Satan), Prince of the Evil Spirits and Death; Gabriel, Prince of Fire; Rahab, Prince of the Sea; Dumah, Prince of Gehinnon (q.v.); Ridiah, Prince of Rain; Lailah, Prince of Night and Conception; Michael, Prince of Israel; Raphael, Prince of Healing; Uriel, Prince of Light. Christianity accepted Michael, Gabriel, Raphael, Uriel, Satan, Jophiel, Zadkiel. The Mohammedans took into their scriptures Gabriel, Michael, Azreal, and Israfel.

Aries (Astrology). Astrological sign; (Mar. 22–April 20); symbol, the Ram; ruling planet, Mars; qualities—ambitious, sincere, industrious, courageous, pioneering, idealistic, high-spirited, loyal, generous, determined, energetic; but can be completely self-centered, unfeeling, and over-involved in projects.

Ariola, Pepito. Spanish musical prodigy introduced in 1900 to the International Psychic Congress by Professor Richet. Although Pepito was only three and a half, it is claimed his tiny hands grew as he played the piano, enabling him to stretch full octaves.

Aristotle (384–322 B.C.). Greek founder of the Peripatetic school of philosophy who, along with Plato, was ultimately the most important source of a number of the great mystics in the Western world and among the Arabs. Aristotle was a pupil of Plato, but his contributions in logic, metaphysics, biology, ethics, politics, and aesthetics make him one of the greatest intellectual figures in the history of mankind. He believed in a primordial principle to which "the gods" were subordinated. His "unmoved mover" was often adopted by thinkers and mystics as a distinguishing quality of God. Aristotle's influence in every aspect of human religious and intellectual development has been unparalleled in human history, continuing into the present.

Arithomancy. Divination by the use of numbers. Among the ancients, and extensively expanded by Pythagoras, it represented the correspondence and relation that existed between the gods and numbers. Very important to the subsequent development of mathematics.

Arjuna (Hinduism). Although he is the chief hero of the *Bhagavad-Gita* (q.v.), his career also encompasses many adventures in which the bravery of this Pandu prince, son of Indra, are illustrated.

Ars Geomantica. Or Art of Punctation, a method of divination involving the throwing of grains, dice or coins, known since the thirteenth century. Once very popular but considered inferior to its eastern counterpart, the *I Ching* (q.v.).

Arts, Black. Derived from the practice of painting images of the Devil in black, it means sorcery in general or the imaginary power of performing wonderful feats by means of assistance and help from evil spirits or the Devil. (See: Black Magic)

Arysophic. The Christo-Germanic grail myth which was an elaboration of blood mysticism, only for elite Aryans. This authoritarian-fascistic doctrine was a spiritual order for "the fraternity of Knights-Templar," whose members predicted a bloody Last Judgment while the grail grew and flourished in the pure souls of the noblest elite Aryans. In Germany, from the turn of this century to the end of World War II, this form of blood mysticism enlisted a large number of followers.

Asana (Hinduism). The third stage of Yoga. The assumption of bodily postures to assist the development of certain thoughts. There are eighty-four postures.

Asanas (Hinduism). The postures utilized mainly during meditation in the Hatha-Yoga school. Though five are generally enumerated, there are numerous variations. Fundamentally it means "to sit quietly."

Ascendant. Astrologically, the degree of ecliptic longitude rising in the east at any given time. Said to be of special significance for any person or thing which comes into being at that moment.

Ascetic. A hermit. Austere, self-denying and self-disciplined.

Ashipu (Babylonian). A class of priests who were the exorcists and prominent in all the ceremonies involving magical control of nature. Also, they were the "witch doctors" who restored the sick to health by driving out the demons, the causes of all illness, from the bodies.

A.S.P.R. American Society for Psychical Research (q.v.).

Aspects. Astrologically, angular distance between celestial bodies as viewed from the earth. Various angles are said to promote harmony or discord between planetary principles.

Asports. Apport phenomena in reverse; objects disappear from the seance room and reappear elsewhere. (See: Apports)

Assisi, Francis of (1182–1226). One of the great Christian mystics and religious revolutionaries—founder of the Catholic order of Franciscan Friars. He was born to wealth, soldiered, and lived a gay, worldly life. But illness and a profound mystic experience determined him to imitate Christ, give away his wealth and inheritance, and live as a beggar. He preached an ecstatic message of self-sacrifice, attracted massive crowds, and won disciples. In 1208 he founded a brotherhood devoted to chastity, obedience and poverty. In 1224 he had a transcendent mystical experience and bore the stigmata of Christ. He was canonized in 1228. See *The Little Flowers of St. Francis*, a classic of Western mysticism, which also contains revelations of his humility, his love of man and of a love for nature so deep he even preached to the birds his divine message. His life has impressed itself on the whole range of Western thought and behavior.

Assyrian Religion. Derived from the Babylonians, but their god, Assur, was superior to the former deities. Assur's wife, Belit, was often considered the counterpart of Astarte (q.v.). The cosmology, astrology, divination, ritual, and ceremonial were replicas of Babylonian practice.

Astorte. A goddess, also known as Astoreth, and Ishtar, worshipped by the Canaanites and Phoenicians, and representing, most likely, both the oldest and most universally worshipped of man's deities—the all-important-life-giving fertility need of humanity. Religious prostitutes catered to her temples, for her cult-images were nakedly sexual. She was the most universally worshipped of Semitic deities. Among the Greeks she can be seen reflected in Aphrodite.

Astral, The. A common abbreviation for the astral sphere or plane of the spirit world.

Astral Body In Hinduism. It is the model-body, the linga-sarira (q.v.) on which the physical body is built. Being the vehicle of the prana or life-energy, it is the container of all the energies descending from the pranic stream. Theosophists, developing this concept, believe the matter of the astral body to be finer than that of the physical; the seat of desires, emotions; able to separate from the physical body in sleep, through drugs, and accidents—during which period it is sensitive to the thoughts and apparitions of the dead and dying. Clairvoyants, being able to penetrate the astral world of our bodies, are able to tell the state of a person's development from the appearance of his astral body. At death, the elementary matter of the astral body arranges itself into 7 concentric sheaths. By evolution the grosser sheaths wear away and eventually the body passes from the astral world to the mental. But those who know can prevent this gross arrangement of the astral body and live almost in the same way in the astral world as they did in the physical. Among Spiritualists, it generally designates the etheric body or double (q.v.).

Astral Light. According to the Hindu concept, it is considered the carrier of the cosmic siva or cosmic life-energy. Among Theosophists, it represents an invisible region surrounding our earth, and is both the storehouse of all the energies of the cosmos, and the "picture-gallery" of whatever takes place on the astral and physical planes.

Astral Plane In Theosophy. It means the plane occupied by the recent dead and non-human nature spirits or "elementals" (q.v.). This world is central to the destiny of man, for here he purges his grosser desires and evolves to higher planes. For Spiritualists, it is often synonymous with the etheric plane (q.v.); also, their "summerland" where the inhabitants live in a world of their own creations—their thoughts.

Astral Projection. The freeing of the astral body from the physical body so that the former is able to move by itself—even through solid substances. In death the etheric body is totally separated from the physical body, but in sleep and astral projection one is awake in sleep and aware of the soul and spiritual life in the supersensible world.

Astral Shells. An occult idea that the etheric body at death is soon discarded, leaving an inner astral or spirit body which continues. The discarded etheric vehicle may continue to manifest dimly on earth with a repetitive, mechanical intelligence responsible for hauntings and some apparitions.

Astrological Medals. Using astrological and alchemical symbols. These charms and amulets were worn in Western Europe during the later Middle Ages to ward off evil.

Astrological Symbols. See Symbols of Astrology.

Astrology. Began as one of the two important methods of ancient divination. Initiated by the Babylonians, expanded by the 2nd century B.C. Greeks, it was enriched in detail and usage by the ancient Egyptians, Hebrews, Arabs, and medieval Europeans. Founded on the influence of the stars and planets, astrology is a highly sophisticated occult science predictive in many areas. For individuals, by using an ephemeris to cast a horoscope, the astrologer obtains a constellation of the zodiac in the 12 mundane houses which shows the relative positions of the planets and signs at a particular time, making it possible to describe a nativity or the favorable times for actions.

Astromancy. Divination from the stars.

Asura (Hinduism). While in its earliest meaning it designated the "spiritual, divine," already in the most ancient parts of the Rig-Veda it meant the Supreme Spirit. Later it came to refer to Indra, Agni, Varuna and others in the highest hierarchy of the gods. Strangely, however, as Hindu religious thought developed, the appellation "Asura" changed its meaning to an extreme degree and denoted a demon, or an enemy of the gods.

Asvagosha. Hindu scholar (c A.D. 100), who was converted to Buddhism and is reputed one of the principal founders of Mahayana Buddhism—author of *Buddha Charita*, a basic Mahayana text.

Aswattha (Hinduism). The mystical Tree of Knowledge, the mystical Tree of Cosmical Life and Being, symbolized as growing in a reversed position—the branches pointing downward and the roots upward. It is the branches that signify the visible cosmical universe, while the roots indicate the invisible world of spirit.

Atharva, Atharvan (Hinduism). The fourth Veda. Containing as it does magic spells, for the most part in ancient days it bore the stigma of being apocrypha. But in time its immense popularity with the people persuaded the priests (atharvans) to make it canonical. Thereafter the atharvans, by calling the fourth Veda the Atharud-Veda, adopted it as their own and proclaimed themselves the sole authority in the use of these magic practices.

Atlantis. One of the greatest of the mysterious legends of the past, 10,000 years old, that finally is being investigated by a competent staff of researchers. Atlantis is reputed to have been a civilization that sank to oblivion in the Atlantic about 10,000 years ago. Plato's reference to the destruction of this highly advanced culture stimulated numerous theories, investigations, and books. Considered to be a powerful kingdom that once dominated the Mediterranean lands, it is believed to have been an ideal commonwealth in Plato's description. During the medieval era, it was accepted as a true history, and since that time has stimulated and interested men like Montaigne, Voltaire and countless others; but present explorations may definitively reveal the truth.

Atman (Hinduism). While this term has several meanings, in its profoundest sense it means *self*, pure consciousness, the "universal selfhood," which is the same in each individual entity whether organic or inorganic. With a capital "A" in Hindusim, it means the Great Self, identifiable with Brahma the Creator; yet capable of being split into individual egos, or invisible "Higher Selves"—spelt with a small "a."

Atmosphere. Any peculiar quality detected in surrounding conditions is often described as atmosphere by mediums and psychics. There is evidence that a special atmosphere or aura surrounds all living bodies. (See: Aura and Dr. Kilner)

At-onement. Realization of the essential unity with God, the Great Spirit.

Atonism. The worship of Aton (Aten), the sun's disc, inaugurated by the Pharoah Amenhotep IV, is considered the first example of monotheistic religion. During his reign (1375–1458 B.C.) the vast army of Egyptian gods was declared dead, but upon his own death the priests immediately restored the old gods and wiped out this epochal experiment in monotheism.

Atsiluth (Judaism). In the Aggadah (q.v.), in reference to the mystic emanation that proceeds from God to the highest beings (seraphim, angels, etc.). This is the concept of the "first world," in the Cabalistic tradition.

Attraction, Law of. More commonly spoken of as "like attracts like" (q.v.) on the mental level.

Aubert, George. French pianist-medium who claimed to play under control of classical composers. He was investigated in 1906 by the Institut Generale Psychologique in Paris, where he played a Mozart sonata perfectly while blindfolded, and his ears were plugged with tubes from two gramophones playing separate music simultaneously.

Auden, Wystan Hugh (1907–1973). English-American poet, playwright, essayist, and mystic. After leaving Oxford in 1928 he taught school briefly, but also published his first volume of poetry. By 1937 he was the leading poet in England and famous in America, receiving as evidence of his gifts King George's Gold Medal for poetry. In 1939 he emigrated to the United States where he became a citizen in 1946, and the winner of the Pulitzer Prize for poetry two years later. Transcending his early Marxist and Freudian influence, he became a socially oriented Christian with extraordinary fidelity to his moral principles. His mysticism was a subject he would not discuss, but those who knew him well understood this aspect of his life. Auden has been a major influence in the work and lives of many English and American poets.

Auditor. A therapist of the Scientology system.

Augurs. In ancient Rome the priests who interpreted the auspices—that is, the movement of birds, the movement of animals—and who interpreted the significance of thunder and lightning. Those signs which were on the augur's left or east side were favorable, while those on the west side were ill-omened.

Augustine, Saint (A.D. 354–430). Bishop of Hippo and one of the four great fathers of the Latin Church, this eminent Christian mystic and philosher is considered by many to be second only to St. Paul (q.v.) in his influence on Christiantity. At the age of 28 he came to Rome from his native Numidia, successfully taught rhetoric there, and studied the works of Neo-Platonism. Following a mystical experience, which gave him an awareness of God (whom he named the "changeless light" found within oneself), he forsook his belief in Manicheanism (q.v.) and became a Catholic, being baptized by St. Ambrose (q.v.). In 387 he returned home where he lived a monastic life; but a few years later, against his will, he was chosen to be a priest then advanced to bishop. His *Confessions*, a classic of Christian mysticism that was enormously influential; his *City of God*, a work of transcendent religious significance; his *On the Trinity*, and numerous other works, retain their importance. For they possess a quality of style, philosophical insight, religious perception and mystical relevance that mark Saint Augustine as one of the towering figures of Western culture.

A-U-M. See Om

Aura. A field of energy radiation that emanates from animate and inanimate bodies, in multi-colored, brilliant, or dull colors, expressing the character or quality of the person or thing. To the person who is psychically sensitive, the aura reveals a person's character, the state of his spiritual and mental development, also the impending changes in these latter, and the condition of his health. In Hinduism, it is considered a magnetic-electrical energy of the mind and spirit that can be used for life-giving, for healing, or conversely for producing death. It has been reported by some to be a light flowing from the eyes, heart, tips of the fingers, or other bodily features. In Christianity Christ, St. Paul, and many of the saints and mystics have emanated auras. But all through the history of man witness of this phenomenon has come from India, Japan, Egypt, Greece, Mexico, Peru, Europe, in their paintings and in their writings. According to Theosophists, there are a number of auras a person possesses: health, vital karmic, animal soul in man, character, spiritual.

Automatic Painting and Drawing (Spiritualism). Artistic expression without the medium's conscious volition, sometimes in complete darkness and at great speed. The results vary much in quality and subject: hieroglyphs, visions (see William Blake's work), departed relatives, and guides have all been depicted. Remarkable evidence has come through this means, usually termed "psychic art."

Automatic Speaking (Spiritualism). Impulsive speech without conscious volition, either in trance or the waking state. Retention of consciousness is possible but unusual.

Automatic Writing (Spiritualism). Scripts produced without the control of the conscious self. A very common form of psychic activity. Usually the hand of the medium is controlled and writes at a furious pace without pause for thought, often in an unfamiliar handwriting. The medium can be conscious and otherwise engaged mentally in reading or conversation while the writing progresses. The scripts sometimes exhibit a knowledge far exceeding that of the medium. It has been used in the past as a means of divination.

Automatism. Functioning of the body, not under control of the conscious self. Can be either subconscious self or a discarnate entity. It embraces automatic speaking, writing, drawing, painting, playing musical instruments, and dancing. Sensory automatism would include clairvoyance, clairaudience, and crystal gazing (qq.v.).

Automatist. Properly the medium or operator in any automatism, but is usually meant to describe an automatic writing medium.

Autoscope. Any mechanical means whereby communication from unknown sources may reach us. Planchette, ouija board (qq.v.), table, etc.

Avatar (Hinduism). In the Sanskrit it means descent, so that in Hinduism the various incarnations of Vishnu (q.v.) represent the passing down of a celestial energy, the incarnation of deity on earth.

Avicenna (979–1037). The greatest of the Arabian philosophers, born in Bokhard, he early demonstrated his genius in every area of knowledge, and at 17 his wide medical learning enabled him to cure the Sultan of Bokhard. About 100 works are accounted to his name. In his view God created intelligence or soul, which emanate from him to earth in huge chains. His great work on mysticism, *Philosophia Orientalis*, is lost, but his influence on Arabian and European mysticism and alchemy was profound.

Awareness. An exalted state, an expansion of consciousness in which one becomes aware of higher powers or the presence of protective entities. Meditation is often practised as a means of its attainment.

Ba'al Shem Tob (Israel ben Eliezer) (c 1700–1760). Founder of modern movement of Hasidim, he opposed the rationalism of the Talmud. Born in Poland, with no taste for formal education—preferring to roam the woods rather than to learn in school—he was considered dull-witted by his teachers. But this "ignoramus" became a noted judge, an excellent physician, an important prophet, and father of a profound development in Judaism. For Ba'al Shem Tob—pure rapture, miracles, an immediate approach to the Messiah, an emotional exaltation in prayer, and communion with God through ecstasy was the mystical way to the true life and the wholly God-steeped religion. Although he was branded heretical, his seminal message prevailed, growing increasingly influential.

Baalism. A great Near Eastern nature religion, highly developed by the Canaanites or possibly the Phoenicians, who believed that the copulation of Baal and Astarte brought fertility to their lands each spring. The chief divinities were El, father of the gods; Asherah, the mother-goddess; Baal who controlled the weather; his consort, Astarte, the goddess of fertility; and Mot, the god of death. The rituals, ceremonials, and worship were pointedly sexual. Baalism had a powerful influence on the Hebrew, Greek, and Roman religions, also the development of the occult in both the East and West.

Babism. The doctrine of a mystical religious sect which broke away from Mohammedanism in 1844. It taught, among other tenets, that God is unknowable; that prophecy continues till the end of the universe; that each divine prophet has foretold his successor; and that numbers have supreme mystical importance, notably the number "19," for it is the "number of unity." The mystic significance of numbers pointed to the Bab's successor—the Bab being the leader of the sect—and the term meaning "gate," the receiver of divine revelation. Babism was founded by Mirza Ali Mohammed of Shiraz. He was influenced by Sufism and Gnosticism (qq.v.). (See: Bahaism)

Baby, Water. In American Indian mythology, it represents the belief that there are a race of small persons who dwell in the water. Called "water babies," they are, however, considered to be malevolent spirits and most definitely to be avoided.

Bacon, Roger (c 1220–1292). One of the extraordinary universal scholars of his age, Bacon was a teacher at Oxford and a Franciscan monk, and, too, an eminent scientist in his period. He was, besides, a great Aristotelian in an era of Plato, Platonism, Neo-Platonism, and Augustinianism. Yet he was a profound devotee of alchemy, astrology, and the occult. His remarkable experiments and expertise in magic won him the title *doctor admirabilis*. His great works, encyclopedic in scope, are *Opus Majus, Opus Minus,* and *Opus Tertium.*

Bahir. Written by the early Cabalists, it was claimed to be a source-book that was produced in the Mishnaic period, the period of the development of the oral laws, which is the earliest period in Hebrew history. Actually, however, the Bahir was written at a much later date.

Bahism. Originally Islamic, a development of Babism (q.v.). Bahaists believe in the unity of God and his Prophets, that Divine revelation is continuous, that all mankind should be united, and that this will be achieved only through a Chosen Mouthpiece.

Bakdhi (Zoroastrianism). This term, one of man's most universally perceptive and most consulted about in divination, augury, astrology, ESP, etc., means in this ancient Persian religion a person's Lot, his Fate.

Bakira. In Japanese Buddhism, he is one of the twelve heavenly generals, and, as such, commands an army of 7,000 followers. He also protects the 84,000 pores of the skin against disease-carrying demons.

Balam (Mayan). God of agriculture, guardian of cornfields and villages, who walks in the air and whistles, and is a deeply-feared specter in the night.

Balam, Chilam (Mayan). This set of books containing some of the history and mythology of the Mayans was later copied into Spanish. It has been a source book of Mayan mythic practice, revealing the universality of man's supernatural responses.

Balder or Baldur. The ancient Norse god, son of Odin and Frigga (qq.v.), who was the god of light, joy, kindness and wisdom. The wicked Loki (q.v.) tricked Hodur (q.v.) into killing Balder with mistletoe. When he arrived in Hades, Hel, its reigning goddess, agreed to free him if all things and beings on earth wept for him, but again Loki's cunning intervened. Therefore, Balder will be released from Hades only on the great day of Ragnorak (q.v.).

Balfour, Earl of (1848–1930). President of S.P.R. in 1894. He wrote "Ear of Dionysius," an important case of cross correspondence.

Balzac, Honore de (1799–1850). One of France's greatest novelists, who mirrored the complete culture of his time in his world famous series of novels "La Comedie Humaine." He was a student of science and a noted realist. But what has given his work an extraordinary richness of scope and its universal appeal was his profound insight into the mystic relationship of man to the cosmos and his awareness of the psychic dimensions of mankind and the mysterious dimensions of existence. See *Seraphita, La Recherche de l'absolu*, and his short stories.

Band, Psychic (Spiritualism). A peculiar sensation of pressure often felt around the head during phases of mediumistic development. Other sensations like tickling and cobwebs on the face denote psychic operations by unseen workers. The presence of specific entities are often sensed by the signal touch which is characteristic of that personality. Psychic perfumes and lights are used in the same way. A group of spirit helpers often describe themselves as a "band."

Band, Spirit (Spiritualism). A group of spirit people working with a medium to achieve a definite purpose or phase of mediumistic activity. There is usually a "doorkeeper" who safeguards the medium's body from the spirit side, the chief guide or control who gives instructions to the leader of the circle and others of the "band" who are co-operating at the time. A medium may exhibit many forms of mediumship and there is usually a specific entity in charge of each form; a spirit doctor for healing, and so on.

Bangs Sisters. The Misses Lizzie and May Bangs of Chicago, mediums who specialized in direct writing, drawing and painting ink messages produced in sealed envelopes. In some of their spirit portraits, colors were precipitated on the canvas in eight minutes by daylight.

Banshee. In Irish and Scottish folklore, a female spirit who keens and wails beneath the windows of a house to warn the family of a coming death.

Baphomet. An idol supposedly worshipped by the Templars (flourished in Europe 1118–1308) in the form of a head. Variously described as the head of Muhammad, a symbol of gnosticism, or a form combining aspects of a dog, bull, ass, and goat, these exhibited many esoteric symbols. It was also described as the deity of the Sorcerers' Sabbath.

Baraduc, Hippolyte. French psychic researcher who experimented with thought photography. He claimed to have proved that something misty and vaporous leaves the human body at death. Inventor of the Biometer. He published several books.

Baraduc's Biometer. Constructed by Baraduc to measure nervous force and unknown vibrations connected with the human body.

Barddas. This is an ancient collection that elaborates but a small portion of the Celtic occult teachings and the Celtic mysteries. The pre-Christian Celts of Brittany, Cornwall, Wales, Ireland, and Scotland possessed a body of mythic and occult knowledge of great antiquity; and though some of this material has been collected, particularly as it is related to Egyptian and Greco-Roman influences, much is past recovery—particularly the Druidic elements.

Barrett, Francis. An English student of the occult. He wrote an interesting work on the subject: *The Magus, or The Celestial Intelligencer* in 1801.

Barrett, Sir William Fletcher (1845-1926). Professor at the Royal College of Science, Dublin. Noted psychic researcher. In January 1882 he called a conference at the British National Association of Spiritualists and inaugurated the Society of Psychical Research. He also provided the impetus for the formation of the American Society of Psychical Research (q.v.) during his visit in 1885. His final conclusions were summed up in a paper to the S.P.R. (Proceedings, Vol. XXXIV, 1924). "There is evidence for: 1. The existence of a spirit world. 2. For survival after death. 3. For occasional communication with those passed over." He wrote many books of his experiences.

Barrow. Primitive man buried his dead in barrows, under slabs of stone representing a room (dolmens q.v.). This was at some distance from the settlement or village, for the souls of the dead were both sacred and feared. The buried souls of the dead were tremendously important in the mythology, religion, magic, and mystery religions of all ancient people from China to Egypt, from India to all the cultures of ancient America.

Basilideans. Followers of the Cabala (q.v.). It was a gnostic sect with esoteric doctrines derived from a disciple of the Apostle Peter, that flourished in Alexandria from the second century. Initiates developed through the grades of the material and intellectual to a culmination in the spiritual.

Basilisk. In Roman and Greek mythology this fabulous creature, a small serpent which came from a cock's egg hatched by a serpent and named the "Kinglet," could kill by its mere look or breath. Also called a cockatrice, and probably derived from the Egyptian Cobra, it was much feared. As a consequence, a massive mythology developed around this marvelous creature, which was further expanded by Aldrovand in the 17th century.

Bat Kol (Judaism). Meaning "Daughter of the voice," that is, the voice of God. It was the Bat Kol the Israelites heard at Sinai at the time Moses received the Ten Commandments. At all extraordinary times in the history of Israel, and also to Rabbinic sages at times of great decisions, it is the Bat Kol that is heard. Jewish legend, the Cabala, and miracle working Rabbis are infused with this voice of God.

Beans. Used by Romans in funeral feasts, supposing them to harbor the souls of the dead. Pythagoras and Plato condemned bean-eating, since it corrupted the truth of dreams.

Bearded Demon. The demon who teaches the secret of the Philosopher's Stone. So named owing to his remarkable beard.

Bellow, Saul. (1915–   ) America's foremost novelist and Nobel laureate was born in Canada, but when nine his family moved to Chicago where he studied at the University of Chicago and went on to graduate work at Northwestern and Wisconsin. In his very first novel, The Dangling Man, Saul Bellow intensely explores a young married man who is struggling to find both the economic means to exist decently and the intellectual-emotional-spiritual framework that will nurture and support a meaningful life. Another theme which throughout his writing underlies and molds his vision of humanity is the awareness that men's lives are determined by luck. It is particularly well stated in his novel The Victim by his character Kirby Allbee who explains to the protagonist, Asa Leventhal, that there is definitely such a thing as being cursed by evil luck, and when Leventhal scoffs at this drunkard's cop-out for his weaknesses and failures, Allbee replies: "You haven't been touched. Wait till you're touched. . . . you've been luckier than I." Though Bellow has brought to his artistic talents an unusually rich complex of skills, he has never lost his passion for exploring man in society, man always laboring and fighting to solve the great hard difficulties of existence. This constant passion has enabled him to infuse all his writing with a special reality, every element of man's reality: whether it is material, social, psychological, emotional, intellectual, or spiritual—he endows it with a striking radiance and often a transcendence because of his strong dedication to his work. While his picaresque novel Augie March created a much-imitated style of writing and Henderson the Rain King was a bold departure in scene and treatment, both exhibit man's eternal need for experiencing and testing life on that deep gut level that truly gives satisfaction and fulfillment to life. For Bellow, man not only has a desperate need to come to terms with himself, but just as desperate is the need to come to terms with his relationship to the universe. Evidence for the constancy of this vision is found everywhere in his writing—in his short stories, his novels, his criticisms, his essays. It should not have come as a surprise, therefore, to so many of his admirers, that at the crest of his maturity he has announced his admiration and belief in the spiritual insights of the noted founder of Anthroposophy, or Spiritual Science, Rudolf Steiner (q.v.).

Belomancy. An ancient Chaldean form of divination by arrows which was practiced by the Greeks and later the Arabians. Divination by arrows utilizes the same principle used in the divination form of Rhabdomancy (q.v.).

Benbine Table of Isis. The symbolism of this table reflects important dimensions of Egyptian occult influences, being designated by some as the altar Plato himself used upon initiation into Egyptian cosmic wisdom. Referred to as the "Isiac Table"—having once been owned by Cardinal Bembo (d. 1547)—and now in the Museum of Antiquities Turin, it has been studied by many occultists.

Benjees, The. A people of the East Indies who are among those who worship the Devil.

Bergson, Henri (1859-1941). Noted French philosopher, one who believed that the true nature of reality could best be understood by the factor of intuition—which is superior to intellect, for it gives an awareness of the life-force, the operative force in all becoming. Furthermore, it is responsible for a sense of the true reality of time.

Berigard of Pisa (1578?-1664). This important French alchemist lived most of his years in Pisa, Italy. Through a lifetime of devotion to the secrets of alchemy, he added to the development of scientific knowledge owing to his intimate knowledge of the chemicals he worked with. He was a professor of natural philosophy at the University of Pisa.

Berkeley, George (Bishop) (1685-1753). Eminent Irish philosopher who denied the reality of matter. Existence was not possible, he maintained, which was not either conscious spirit or the ideas of which such spirit is conscious. This synthesis of subject with object asserts that mind alone is the ultimate reality. Nature, by this reasoning, is conscious experience forming symbols of divine universal intelligence.

Bernadette, Saint (1843-79). The grotto at Lourdes in France where thousands of Christians from all over the world have experienced to one degree or another the healing power of this French girl bears silent but eloquent witness to her mystical and visionary experiences. Bernadette Soubirous in apparitions saw the Virgin Mary at a grotto near Lourdes; and though the sceptical, the curious, and persons of power disturbed or derided her in her lifetime, she escaped to a convent in 1866, and lived to learn of the vindication of her reported revelations.

Bernard of Clairvaux, Saint (1090?-1153). A colossus of his age and one of its most commanding and powerful heroes, who dominated Popes, Emperors and Kings, brilliant scholars, the Church and the masses, he was also a man of such humility, humaneness, charity, saintliness, added to the gifts of being a profound mystic and a proven worker of miracles, that in himself he embodied the ideal of his era. Born into the nobility and educated for a career of eminence, he forsook worldly power, entered the abbey of Citeaux in his native France in his 22nd year and expanded it into 68 other monasteries throughout Europe. His miraculous cures, the incredible eloquence of his preaching, the logic, clarity, and beauty of his writing, and the charisma of his saintly character brought him to the attention of emperors and popes. Tireless in his love of the Church, he made and unmade Popes, Kings, and scholars; he launched vast crusades; stopped pogroms against the Jews; and won the faith of immense numbers to the moral radiance of Christ. His works, large in output and scope, went through numerous editions; his mystical writings profoundly influenced the years after his death. *On the Steps of Humility* and *Pride, Imitatio, On the Love of God, Against Abelard*, and his famous *Letters*, justify, among other extraordinary appelations, the name of the Mellifluous Doctor.

Bernstein, Morey. American businessman, author and hypnotist who, through the technique of hypnotic regression, claimed to have produced evidence for a former incarnation of his subject as "Bridey Murphy." Recordings were made of the actual statements made during the experiments, but a full investigation revealed his work to be fraudulent.

Besant, Annie (1847–1933). English atheist, radical, socialist, Theosophist, writer, propagandist, occultist, Indian nationalist, and orator, she went from one movement to another in her search for human enlightenment. She worked with many of the great figures of her time (Bradlaugh, Shaw, Blavatsky, Steiner, Nehru, Gandhi), and was always one of the leaders of any movement she adopted. She discovered Krishnamurti and declared him the world's new Messiah. She believed that in her previous reincarnations she had been an Indian, Hypatia, and Giordano Bruno. She died in the belief that she would be shortly reincarnated and would return to the mission designated for her by the occult hierarchy.

Besterman, Theodore (b. 1904). Lecturer for University of London, officer of the Society for Psychical Research. Author of many important works on psychic research.

Bestiary. Animals in the Neolithic age and even earlier have played a monumental part in man's affairs—religious, mythological, spiritual, and occult. A bestiary is a compilation of tales about animals and their magical marvelous, and spiritual significance for man. The Greek original of these collections, written by a Christian in the 2nd century A.D., which interprets scriptural doctrines, is the source of all the European translations in the Middle Ages. It had a marked influence on the development of the occult.

Bezalel (Judaism). In the Talmud, this artist-craftsman made the omnipotent Ark of the Lord for the Tabernacle in the Wilderness; for Bezalel knew the awesome mystery-of-mysteries—he knew how to arrange the letters by which heaven and earth had been ceated. For the Cabalists this was proof, from the Talmud itself, of the vast powers inherent in the proper arrangement of Hebrew letters. (See: Cabala).

Bhagavad-Gita. The profound Hindu philosophical drama, which is one of the most basic elements of Hinduism, is a part of the great Indian epic *Mahabarata*. On the realistic level, it tells the story of Arjuna's doubts about the humanity of attacking an army composed of many of his kinsmen and respected wise men. On the spiritual level, Krishna appears on the battlefield and in response to a recital of Arjuna's fears and anxieties, teaches him the way of Being on earth. He explains to him the eternal permanence of "body," despite seeming death; the absolute necessity of "action"; the nature of God and the understanding of his "meditating on me with wholehearted yoga"; the elements of the "divine properties" and the method to achieve them; also the difference between the latter and evil persons. Krishna tells him, finally, he must always under all circumstances follow "thine own duty born of thine own nature . . . becoming the ETERNAL, serene in the SELF." The *Bhagavad-Gita* has been translated into most of the languages of the world.

Bhagavat. In Hinduism, the Venerable, the Adorable, the Lord.

Bhakti. Hindu emotional practice for the maintenance of a personal relationship with God. Exposition in *Bhagavad-Gita* (q.v.).

Bhakti Yoga. A branch, or one of the seven paths of Yoga. The way of devotion and affectionate attachment.

Bhikkhu (Buddhism). A term which originally referred to a beggar, but later the name for the followers of Buddha who had left worldly life.

Bhikshu (Hinduism). A beggar who lives on alms. He is a Brahmana in the fourth and highest stage of his religious life.

Bhrigu (Hinduism). One of the great Vedic seers. He was the founder of the Bhrigus.

Bible and Number Wisdom. The numbers used in the Bible are considered to have a purpose and have been used to divine God's ultimate intentions. Some occultists use them as a method of attaining spiritual power. The number 3, for example, which is an important figure in the Bible, relates to three elements: The Old Testament; The Gospels; and The Revelation of St. John (Apocalypse). Further, there is the matrix form of the Trinity—The Father, Son, and the Holy Ghost. The New Testament contains a trinity of the Gospels, the Epistles, and Revelation of St. John. There were three Magi, who brought Gold (the wisdom of the Gods), Frankincense (the virtues of man), and Myrrh (the realization of human immortality). And the life of Christ is a trinity of Baptism, the Transfiguration and the Resurrection. Two, four, seven, and twelve are additional numbers that represent important elements in the Bible. There is the contrast between the two teachings of Elias and Moses; four—the sign of the Cosmos and Creation—the earth being formed on the fourth day; the four Evangelists Matthew, Mark, Luke, John; the seven Elohim that created Heaven and Earth; seven stages in the passion of Christ; the twelve Apostles of Christ; and the symbolical twelve gates of the Holy City described by St. John.

Billet Reading. A form of mediumship. It takes the form of a public demonstration; the audience writes—on pieces of paper or billets—messages to their departed friends. These are gathered and placed before the blindfolded medium. The heap of folded slips are not only read, but answered. Facts of evidential value to the writers are also given.

Bilocation. Being present in two places at once. Histories of the saints abound in this phenomenon, which in Spritualism is attributed to the separation and separate appearance simultaneously of the double, or etheric body. (See: Astral Projection)

Biofeedback. The ability of the mind to control involuntary bodily functions which heretofore had been achieved only by trained yogins and other Eastern ascetics (fakirs) and adepts. Dr. Neale E. Miller, one of the foremost researchers in this new science, has demonstrated that properly trained individuals can control their high blood pressure, their heart beat, certain brain rhythms, etc. (See: *Visceral Learning: Toward the Science of Self-Control*).

Biological Phenomena. In recent years increasing scientific evidence that psychic power can cause the accelerated growth of plants, the rapid curing of animal wounds, and psychic healing has been reported, notably by Dr. Sister M. Justa Smith (q.v.). Of course, psychic healing is a well-known phenomenon; but we now know that some persons induce healing because of a remarkable quality of energy which they are able to utilize in the cure of many illnesses.

Bio-magnetism. Animal magnetism. Mesmerism (q.v.).

Biometer of Baraduc. See Baraduc

Birds, Flying. In the ancient Near East, in ancient China, in ancient Greece, and, most especially, in ancient Rome divination from observing flying birds was a highly developed magical art, and part of an augur's range of skills. For alchemists, the image referred to the crystallization of sulphur.

Birds of Hermes. Hermes was one of the few Greek gods whose bird, the cock, was attributed to him long after his emergence in the pantheon of Greece. For the alchemists it became a symbol for the primitive, archetypal substance.

Birth (Spiritualism). A spirit entity's assumption of a new outward form; in our world, the physical body. At death the spirit leaves the physical body and remains clothed in the etheric body (q.v.), which corresponds to a birth into a new state of existence. There would appear to be many such births, judging from communications, including the possibility of reincarnation, or being reborn on earth.

Bishamon. In Japanese Buddhism he represents one of the seven Gods of Luck. Most often he is portrayed with a spear in his right hand, a temple or pagoda in his left, and angrily stands upon a demon who symbolizes the powers of evil.

Black Box. See Delawarr camera.

Black Fire. Since God was for many Jewish philosophers incomprehensible, the Cabalists used the term to mean ultimate inspiration and insight. Mystics of the East and West have conceived the same notion in terms like "uncreated light" and Ruysbroeck's (q.v.) "dark night of the soul."

"Black Hawk." Red Indian control of English medium Evan Powell, and one of the few guides who has succeeded in establishing evidence of his former earth existence through his Illinois statue and an autobiography—The *Life of Ma-Ka-Tai-Me-She-Kia-Kiak*, or *Black Hawk*, written in 1834.

Black Magic. The use of supernatural knowledge in order to achieve evil results. The petitioning of diabolic and infernal powers to aid this achievement is one of the most ancient of occult practices. From the ancient Egyptians, Persians, Greeks, and Hebrews, and in almost all the primitive tribes and cultures of past and present all over the world, the use of Black Magic has flourished. In Europe's Middle Ages it reached its zenith, drawing on the whole past tradition for its materials. Essentially, Black Magic aims to gain limitless power over gods or God, demons, and men. Some texts which contain formulas, or grimoires, give detailed information and methods. Some of the powers who have been worshipped in Black Magic are: the Source and Creator of Evil, Satanas, Belial, the Devil, Set, Ahriman, the Greek "Python," the Jewish "Serpent," Baphomet of the Templars, and the Goat-deity of the Witches' Sabbath. One of the most popular methods used by sorcerers and witch doctors in their practice of the art is the fashioning of a waxen image, in the likeness of the party to be assailed, and upon this figure are heaped curses, torture by knives, nails, pins, or sharp instruments, and, finally, it is stabbed in the heart. Necromancy, the raising of the dead to inflict evil, was also widely popular in the past.

Black Mass. Initially an idealistic protest against the Roman Catholic Church in the Middle Ages by such groups as the Cathari. Believing in a dualistic universe, in which God ruled over spiritual affairs and Satan over matter (adopted from Gnosticism and Manichaeism), their aim was perfection through ascetism. They disapproved, therefore, of the Church's sanctioning of marriage, calling it the Synagogue of Satan—since sex and marriage in the world was Satan's domain. The inevitable conclusion followed: the Mass of the Church and its rituals were profane. Those who burlesqued this avowed profanity instituted what came to be called the Black Mass, for their ritual was blasphemous and obscene. It was often presided over by a renegade priest, who used a valid consecrated host. Sometimes a woman's naked back served as the altar. The incantations and spells used in the service derive from Arabic, Gnostic, and Cabalistic sources; the Pater Noster is recited backwards to invoke the Devil; a drawn circle protects the leader or adept; the blood of animals such as the sacrifice of a cat may be used; the pentacle, signs of the zodiac, alchemical symbols, and dark eerie lights all add their effects to the service. In modern times Aleister Crowley (q.v.) was one of the foremost figures in the re-establishment of the practice of the Black Mass, which has markedly increased in adherents.

Blackwood, Algernon (1869-1951). One of England's most noted writers in the sphere of the weird and the supernatural. His career as a farmer and hotel owner in Canada, and his years as a reporter for the New York papers the *Sun* and *Times* gave him both the background and the literary experience for his many books and stories. (See: *Empty House, The Centaur, Shocks, The Doll and One Other*)

Blake, William (1757-1827). English artist, poet, visionary, mystic, inventor, and prophetic thinker. Born in London, son of a hosier, he was apprenticed to an engraver and attended the Royal Academy. His engravings and drawings are at once striking, powerful, and richly symbolical; his poetry is fresh, profound, and lyrical; his mystical and religious writings rank with those of the major mystics and prophets. Although ignored in his lifetime, considered mad by some, by the end of the nineteenth century his work was heralded for its incomparable originality. He has had a marked influence on such diverse personalities as the Rosettis, G.B. Shaw, and Allen Ginsberg. See: *Songs of Innocence, Songs of Experience, The Marriage of Heaven and Hell, The Book of Thel,* and, especially, *There Is No Natural Religion,* and *All Religions Are One.*

Blavatsky, Mme. Helene Petrovna (1831-1891). Russian born. With Col. H.S. Olcott, she founded the Theosophical Society. The society had its first headquarters at Adyar in India. Not only did she live a mysterious and extraordinarily adventurous life, but her talents as a leader, a medium, and a writer won her many important disciples such as Annie Besant, Rudolf Steiner and Krishnamurti. Wrote *The Secret Doctrine, Isis Unveiled.*

Blue. Colors clairvoyantly perceived have a generally recognized significance. Usually connected with the aura, they have been experimentally verified by an increasing number of researchers recently.

Pale blue is supposed to be the color of healing and spirituality. (See Colors)

Bodhi. In Buddhism—Enlightenment.

Bodhi-Dharma. Semi-legendary founder of Zen Buddhism in Japan; a sect which developed a new branch of Mahayana Buddhism.

Bodhi Tree, or Bo-tree. The tree under which Gautama Buddha attained his mystic enlightenment at Buddha Gaya. It is a kind of fig tree, popularly called pipal tree.

Bodhisattvas. Northern Buddhist conception of High Beings who sacrifice their attainment of Nirvana in order to incarnate as saints, out of compassion for mankind.

Bodies. A term having different shades of meaning in the various supernatural disciplines. Basically, its most common meaning is the separation of "bodies" from the physical body. (See: Astral *Body*, Astral Projection, Astral Shells, Double, Etheric *body*)

Bodin, Jean (1529–1596). French political philosopher, lawyer, religious humanist, and occultist. He won enormous fame in his lifetime for his original and humanistic writings on economics and political philosophy. His religious toleration elaborated in his book *Heptaplomeres* was so liberal it had to wait until 1841 for publication. His famous *Demonomaie des Sorciers* is a defense of sorcery, proclaiming the notion that spirits communicate with mankind, and describes the whole range of Black Magic (q.v.) in much detail. His fame in many areas of learning made him an influential occultist.

Boehme, Jakob. (1575–1624). A shoemaker with but a few years of schooling, Jakob Boehme's writings (he wrote 29 books and tracts) have had an astonishingly far-reaching influence on some of the greatest minds in the Western world. His lifetime was comparatively short but this mystic-spiritual-philosophic genius had a Faustian fecundity. He perceived that the polar structure of existence was the heart of the matter; that unity emerged from duality and trinity. In a remarkable mystical experience came the revelation that in "yes and "no" all things consisted." His great speculative problem, consequently, was to show how yes and no, good and evil, dark and light, came from the living heart of reality; his cardinal religious deduction, again, explained how the dualities of life were reconciled in spiritual unity. The Romantic Age, Hegel, Schopenhauer, Nietzsche, Bergson, Heidegger, George Fox, Berdyaev, Tillich merely indicate his range of influence.

Bogle (Bogey, Bogie). In Scottish mythology and in northern England, bogles and variants of this name were much feared by the people. They were harmdoing specters, goblins, and frightful phantoms. Bogie-man in our culture, American, has evolved from this term.

Boirac, Emil. French Rector of Dijon Academy. Studied animal magnetism and exteriorization of sensitivity. His book: *Our Hidden Forces* was awarded the Emden prize in 1917 by the French Academy of Sciences.

Bonati. A Florentine astrologer who lived in the 13th century, he was an innovator in predictive astrology. So prophetic were his predictions that he won many important converts to astrology. His works were published in Germany in 1491 under the title *Liber Astronomicus*.

Bond, Rev. Frederick Bligh (b. 1864). Excavator of the lost chapels of Glastonbury Abbey. Ecclesiastic, archaeologist, architect, editor of A.S.P.R. Journal. Author of many books based upon automatic writing in collaboration with John Alleyne (q.v.) and Hester Dowden. Also conducted experiments in thought photography with Mrs. Deane. Outlined his conception of immortality in *Journal of A.S.P.R.*, 1929, "Athanasia."

Book Bahir. The medieval Cabalists of Spain and Provence, believing that God was in all creation, yet outside it, named him *En Sof*, "Without End." Rabbi Azriel ben Menachem of Catalonia wrote the Bahir in 1240. It was one of the three enduring treatises of Cabalism.

Book of the Dead. Guidebook for the ancient Egyptian in his journey through the underworld, containing prayers and exorcisms to be used by the pilgrim-soul with which to pass the tests to gain his new life. It also contained the magic, ritual, and myth of the period. Copies were placed in the tomb of the dead or inscribed or painted on the wall for immediate reference when necessary. Dating from the period earlier than 3,000 B.C., the original book of 200 chapters went through several revisions—the Heliopolitan, the Theban, and the Saite—this last during the Ptolemaic period. The British Museum possesses the world's finest collection of the Theban edition. "Per em hru," the Egyptian title, means "coming forth by day."

Book Tests. Experiments designed to exclude the possibility of telepathy in a medium's communications. Usually the spirit communicator, in answer to a question, indicates a certain line of a page in a specified book accessible to the sitter and gives the appropriate text which can afterwards be verified.

Bosanquet, Bernard (1848–1923). English philosopher and mystic who was a memorable teacher and influential guide to many thinkers, notably William James (q.v.). Not only was he a leading British thinker, but his determined desire to lead an ethical and moral life led him to resign his distinguished posts at Oxford to engage in the human task of bringing his large gifts to a wider audience; in consequence, he became an active member of the London Ethical Society and the Charity

Organization Society. These were positive demonstrations of Bosanquet's philosophy, for he believed man must abandon himself to something larger than himself if he is to achieve a catharsis and self realization—the cosmic drama directed by the Absolute—which is the only means to experience a cosmic, mystical oneness. (See: *Value and Destiny of the Individual*)

Boston Society for Psychical Research. Founded May 1925 by Dr. Walter Franklin Prince, formerly Research Officer of A.S.P.R. It issues bulletins and books.

Bozzano, Professor Ernesto (b. 1862). Noted Italian psychic researcher. He wrote many books and articles on the subject.

Bradley, Francis Herbert (1846–1924). The greatest logician in modern British philosophy, he demolished the assumptions of Hegelian utilitarian, and hedonistic ethics, an achievement which compelled materialism and empiricism to abolish a number of their concepts. But this notably brilliant thinker found his own logic turned against himself, forcing him in later years to abandon some of his own theories. With the growth of enriching wisdom, he finally crowned his estimable career by acknowledging the depth of Plato's genius and adopting a platonic mysticism. His *Appearance and Reality* (1893) is one of the epochal books of modern philosophy.

Bragi. Ancient Scandinavian god, father of poetry, eloquence and the giver of wisdom, and he who welcomed the mighty dead upon their arrival in Valhalla. The "Bragi-cup" was ceremoniously drunk at feasts and funerals.

Brahamanic Trinity (Hinduism). The Father, Nara (Eternal Masculine); the Mother, Nari (Eternal Feminine); and the Son, Viraj (Creative Word).

Brahma. Hindu verbal image of the Sacred, the Creator or most High God. Identified also with the Atman or Great Self, differentiated into separate egos.

Brahma-yoni (Hinduism). The term "yoni" means the female organ. Consequently, Brahma-yoni has the meaning of the holy, or the worshipful female organ of Brahma which, both as it exists alone or together with linga (the male penis), is an object of worship by the Saktis. The word also refers to a sacred mountain cleft through which religious devotees pass to acquire spiritual worth.

Brahmaeva idam visuam (Hinduism). "Brahman, indeed, is this world-all." Considered by many to be one of the famous core insights in Hinduism, since it prefigures the central cohesive and endlessly generative sperm of Sankara's Vedanta. This passage was first stated in the Mundaka Upanishad 2.2.11. Once elaborated, it influenced the whole of Hinduism and many thinkers in the East and West who have shaped man's deepest insights.

Brahmana (Hinduism). A member of the noblest Hindu caste, having as his chief duty the study and teaching of the Vedas (q.v.), and religious ceremonies.

Breathing. Some consider the control of breathing of prime importance, regarding breath the king of the senses. The Hindus have made it an essential element of their training, seeing breath as divine and engulfing the whole universe; emphasizing that all things live, move, and exist because of the Divine Breath within them. By cultivating the habit of silence, looking within, the individual faculties develop, bring one in resonance with the universe, and as the breath becomes regulated the individual begins to see and contact the fundamental truths of existence. Finally, silence, the control of breathing, and concentration, function together. Science has corroborated the significance of breathing techniques in the astounding facts of Yogis. It is also well-known that control of breathing is essential to some forms of meditation, and in demonstrations of levitation.

Breezes. Cool currents of air combined with a drop of temperature is a well-known phenomenon in physical seances, although the reason for it is unknown. Apparitions are notoriously chilly.

Brendan son of Finnloga (c 484–c 578). Irish Saint and hero of a famous legendary voyage "Voyage of Saint Brendan" in the Atlantic. He was abbot of a monastery in Galway. The saga of his fabulous voyage, written in the 8th century, was one of the most popular of its age, being translated throughout Europe. The richness and accuracy of all its details (positive description of the continent of America, for example), its narrative power, and its spiritual and mystical qualities were much admired and much imitated.

Bridget of Sweden, Saint (c 1300–1373). This Swedish nun, after raising a large family, and separating from her husband, devoted herself to her true vocation—her mystic insight into God and the future. She founded an order, and her book of *Revelations,* which was widely read, reveals her numerous visions and prophecies.

British College of Psychic Science. Now dissolved, founded in London in 1920 by J. Hewat McKenzie and his wife for the sustained study of mediumship and for the assistance of researchers.

British Journal of Psychical Research. The official organ of the National Laboratory of Psychical Research, replaced later in 1926 by "Proceedings" and bulletins.

British Spiritualists Lyceum Union. See Lyceum.

Britten, Emily Hardinge (1823–1899). English medium who developed in America. One of the best attested cases of spirit return was given through her mediumship when the mail steamer *Pacific* sank, and one of the crew possessed her in trance and disclosed the tragedy before it was generally known. She was threatened with prosecution, but her story turned out to be true. Founded and edited the Spiritualist paper *Two Worlds* and wrote many books.

Broad, Professor C.D., Litt. D., F.B.A. President of S.P.R. 1935–36 and 1959–60, famous philosopher, outspoken in his criticism of science's neglect of psychical research. While admitting the existence of psychic phenomena, he thinks that none of them entails, though a few of them suggest, more than the persistence of a limited portion of an individual's mind after the death of his body.

Brotherhood of the Common Life, The. This extraordinary religious community which had a wide effect and influence on Christian movements and developments throughout Northern Europe was inaugurated by Gerhard Groote (q.v.) in the 14th century at Deventer in Holland. Groote was influenced by the great mystic Ruysbroeck (q.v.); was the creator of the *devotio moderna* and claimed author of The Imitation of Christ. And through these loftly spiritual directives he turned The Brotherhood of the Common Life toward a heightened spirituality and a realistically practical, down-to-earth, truly brotherly religious movement that yet ascended to a reawakened Christian mysticism.

Browne, Sir Thomas (1605–1682). One of the great physicians of England and also Europe, and among the most widely educated men of his age, he was also a literary genius—one of the superb English prose writers, and an important mystic. His *Religio Medici* reveals his private religious faith; his *Hydriotaphia: Urn Burial, Vulgar Errors*, and *Christian Morals*, are marvelous reading, informative and historically important in the domain of ideas and occult information. He was, however, opposed to witchcraft.

Buber, Martin (1878–1965). His philosophy of dialogue—the I-Thou relationship, has been most influential in 20th-century thought. His books and lectures on the Hasidim have advanced this communal mysticism of East European Jewry from a minor sect to a major mystical movement. God for Buber is the eternal Thou to whom one can talk but not talk about. As a seminal figure, he has influenced modern philosophy, ethics, Christianity and mysticism. *I and Thou, The Tales of the Hasidim, For the Sake of Heaven*, and *Hasidim and Modern Man* reveal his scope.

Buchanan, J. Rhodes (1814–1899). American scientist whose theory of the psychic faculty of sensitivity—psychometry—asserted that all substances gave interpretable emanations; that the world's history was entombed in the present.

Buddha (c 563 B.C. c 483 B.C.). In Sanskrit—"The enlightened one." An extraordinary mystic and teacher who developed one of the world's noblest, purest, and most profound ethical and religious systems. Born near Nepal, a prince at birth—Siddartha Gautama—he enjoyed the luxury and power of his position, and was carefully sheltered from the pains and realities of life. Not until he was 29 did he witness human misery; but this experience moved him so deeply he thoroughly abandoned his manner of existence, transforming himself into a penniless hermit and a wanderer in search of true wisdom. After years of testing both the insights of holy men and absolute self discipline, he found his own way—"the great enlightenment"—while meditating beneath a bo tree, in reward for his holy dedication and asceticism. Becoming a teacher, he gathered disciples, the first Buddhist monks. Further, by converting his influential family, he quickly won important adherents. Most importantly, it was in the manner of his living and the method of preaching his vision that he taught his disciples the humanistic procedure by which to spread his message. In his old age, his holy detachment brought him the further epithets of Bhagava (lord), Togatha (he who has come), and the Buddha (the enlightened one). See: Buddhism. It is interesting that of all the supreme mystic teachers of mankind Buddha's life, taken all together, was the most comfortable, the most satisfying, and the most triumphant in winning converts during his own years on earth.

Buddhagosha (Buddhism). Meaning "Voice of Buddha," and a name, therefore, utilized by several Buddhist writers. The most renowned, author of the *Visuddhimagga* and other writings, and the foremost of all Hinayana expositors, was born in North India early in the fifth century A.D.

Buddha Vasra-Sattua (Hinduism). Vasra symbolically means "thunderbolt," but in its literal sense it means penis; however, both meanings are essential to its full understanding. For Sattua refers to the essence of all being. The full explication, therefore, develops the insight that Buddha, possessing the virility of the penis and the explosive power of the thunderbolt, has an infinite driving force.

Buddhism. The religion based on the teachings of Gautama has today probably 750 million nominal followers. Gautama was a Hindu revolutionary of 560 B.C., born into an age of preoccupation with Yoga techniques, and with the oral tradition of the *Upanishads* (q.v.) and the Vedas as background. He saw the necessity for a personal practical application for the alleviation of suffering and endeavored to set an example. There are no contemporary writings; the Pali Buddhist canon is the earliest (probably 80 B.C.)—in which there are suspected interpolations. Gautama's modifications of Upanishad teachings, so far as we know, may be summed up as: seeking the Self (Atman), removal of passion, moderation, abandonment of asceticism and the

Hindu caste system. At a council (Patni, 270-240 B.C.) under King
Asoka, Buddhism split into two main divisions, known today as the
northern Mahayana and the southern Hinayana. The latter, at that
time a majority, excommunicated the former, but now the position is
reversed and Mahayana (Great system) holds sway over most Buddhists. They both tend to monasticism, which is the negative side of
Gautama's teaching, though the north is less rigid and employs the
idea of Bodhisattvas, reincarnations of Buddha. The Buddhist "eightfold path" is: right views, right resolve, right speech, right conduct,
right livelihood, right effort, right mindfulness, right concentration.

Buddhism (In Japan). Came from Korea in A.D. 552, establishing itself
firmly in the 7th century and throughout the next three centuries, it
was much influenced by Chinese Buddhism. Continual antagonism between Buddhism and Shinto, the native religion, was eventually re-
solved in the creation of Ryobu Shinto—"Shinto with two faces"
which incorporated aspects of Buddhism. Bushido, the faith of Japanese chivalry, was strongly flavored with Zen Buddhism. Over the
years Buddhism, like Shinto, developed a number of separate sects,
the most important of which are Zen, Tendai, and Shingon; others are
Sanron, Hosso, Kusha, Jodo, Shin, and Nichiren. However, there is a
mutual reverence among all sects of Japanese religion for each other's
divinities and temples. The dominant influence is Mahayana Buddhism which has superseded its early rival, Hinayana (qq.v.). There are
many magic rituals popular with the masses in Japanese Buddhism.

Buddhist Mystical School. A form of Mahayana Buddhism. Its adherents conceive the nature of the universe as consisting of 6 Great Elements—earth, water, fire, air, space, and consciousness, which designate the "Six Great Originations." The activity of the universe is embodied in the "Three Mysteries"—Action, Speech, and Thought. Its
character is represented by "Four Circles"—the four-fold perfection
of the character, form, name, and function of things.

Bulfinch, Thomas (1796-1867). His famous *The Age of Fable* (1855) established him at once as a popular American writer of classic knowledge in the area of mythology, his fame being secured by the publications *The Age of Chivalry* (1858) and the *Legends of Charlemagne*.
These three books published in one volume as *Bulfinch's Mythology*
tell of the Greek and Roman gods, of Egyptian and Oriental divinities,
and the ancient sagas of the North. Its popularity has increased over
the years, for it is a delightful amalgam of magic, the occult, ancient
legend, and both historic and prehistoric myth.

Bulwer-Lytton. Edward George Earle Lytton (1803-1873). Versatile
writer who succeeded at many forms of literature, but most popularly
and enduringly as a novelist. At an early age he became interested in
mysticism and the occult, which throughout his life remained a continuing and expanding pursuit. *A Strange Story*, for example, contains

the vivid portrait of Margrave, a character modeled on D.D. Home, (q.v.) the famous medium, and Bulwer-Lytton's friend of many years. This writer's profound knowledge of psychic-spiritual-mystical-occult phenomena can be discerned in many of his literary creations. (See: *A Strange Story, Zanoni, The Last Days of Pompeii, Rienzi*)

Butterflies. In many Japanese legends and folk-tales the butterfly is the beautiful, beneficent insect who either represents the souls of the beloved dead or is a messenger of the nether world who carries away the spirit of the humane and saintly dead.

Byssus. The extraordinary linen used to wrap the Egyptian dead was for use in the underworld. It was so miraculously fine and durable, (since the souls were to live forever—see *Book of the Dead*) the ancient Greeks and Romans copied it to use as a costly fabric.

Cc

Cabaclo. In Brazil this cult-group worships Indian and African gods. Cabaclo represents an aspect of Negro non-Christian American religion, mythology, and the occult.

Cabala. One of the great systems of mysticism. Excepting the Torah and Talmud, no body of thought has so long engaged the mind and affected the masses of the Jewish people as the Cabala. Although based on Jewish doctrine, it has taken important elements from gnosticism, Neo-Platonism, and oriental mysticism, making it a work ripe with profound philosophical, spiritual, and practical insights—alike for Jew and Christian. The Zohar, central book of the Cabala, was compiled and written by Moses de Leon in the 13th century. Teaching a way that leads to a oneness with God, the Cabala describes ten intermediary emanations: Crown, Wisdom, Intelligence, Loving-kindness, Power, Beauty, Eternity, Majesty, Foundation, and Kingdom.

Cabinet. A small space, usually enclosed by a curtain, in which most materialization mediums claim to condense the psychic energy necessary for a manifestation. Not all mediums have considered it necessary. Some sit inside, others outside the cabinet.

Cabiri. Though these were not Greek deities but gods of Phrygian origin who promoted fertility, their importance to Greek religion is attested by their connection with the worship of Demeter, Dionysius, and Hermes; their identification with the Corybantes and Curetes; their widespread influence throughout Greek worship, being associated with Chthonian powers (underworld gods), and their incorporation into Orphism. Later the Cabiri were often confused with the Dioscuri—Castor and Pollux.

Caduceus. The symbolic staff carried by the Greek god Hermes (given to him by Apollo) and the Roman god Mercury. These were the messengers of the gods, but had the further attributes of being the gods of eloquence, science, invention—also of roads, commerce and cunning. Two snakes are curled around the staff with two wings at the top. Early in Babylonian history the symbol of two intertwined snakes made its appearance, and it is related to the numerous serpent symbols of fertility, sun-gods, wisdom, and healing found in the history of the mythic, psychic, and occult. In Hinduism it represents the Yogic psychic channels of man's body.

Caelestis. A name given by the Romans to the Carthaginian goddess Tanit whose statue was brought to Rome and a shrine built to her on the Capitol. Her name was sometimes given to Aphrodite and Diana, and, owing to astrological influence, to the constellation Virgo.

Caesarius, Saint. One of the earliest exorcists in the history of the Roman Catholic Church. The physician to King Theodoric was assaulted at home by invisible demons who bombarded him with stones hurled from the ceilings. Only the official exorcism of Saint Caesarius obliterated the malevolent agents of Hell, proving that holy Christians have divine powers from God against these evil demons.

Cagliostro, Alesandro, Conte (1743–1795). Extraordinary and significant psychic who was influential in spreading throughout Europe an advanced knowledge of psychic phenomena. Born Giuseppe Balsamo in Italy, with a mercurial mind and an insatiable curiosity, he traveled in Greece, Arabia, Persia and Egypt. Returning home, he married Lorenza Feliciani. Now began his amazing career of traveling through Europe—organizing many Freemason lodges and utilizing his knowledge of alchemy, medicine, mesmerism, magic, and the occult; being received in the highest society and aristocratic circles—particularly at the court of Louis XVI of France; and winning numerous disciples by his charismatic display of occult wisdom. Unfortunately, a scandal at the French court caught him in its net, and though he was acquitted, he was banished. Forced to return to Rome in 1789, the Inquisition charged him with sorcery and sentenced him to death. The sentence, however, was commuted to life imprisonment. And he died in a dungeon. Few men have made the impact on their own time and on the imagination of subsequent generations as Cagliostro.

Caitanya (Hinduism). The state of superconsciousness close to the essential core of the Absolute Spirit.

Calabaza. Among the Peruvians, throughout the tenth to the eighth centuries B.C., the Calabaza was a clay gourd-shaped container in which foldings of their buried priests and medicine men were placed and wrapped with the mummy.

Calchas. In Homer's Iliad he is the prophet and diviner of the Greek army in Troy who divines the cause of the plague they suffered. He foresees the victory that will result from building the wooden horse; he is the diviner at the sacrifice of Iphigenia which launched the Trojan attack; and he prophesied subsequent actions that led to Troy's defeat. He was fated to die when he met a diviner superior to himself.

Caldwell, Charles Tayler. The first American phrenologist, who studied the subject with Johann Kaspar Spurzheim (q.v.) in Vienna in 1821. He practiced phrenology in Lexington and Louisville, Kentucky, lectured throughout the West, and became so popular and successful he was titled the "American Spurzheim."

Calmecac. In the Aztec culture this was an advanced school for religious leaders. The training, because of their highly developed mystery-magico-mathematical-astronomical knowledge, was a difficult and complicated course of study.

Calumet. The celebrated ritual peace pipe of the American Plains Indians which was lavishly painted with religious, mythological, and magical symbols. It was a uniquely important ritualistic object, having widespread use among the Plains tribes.

Cambridge Platonists. This body of 17th century English philosophers and clergymen embraced the wide range of Plato's philosophical conceptions; they were chiefly men at Cambridge University, notably Benjamin Whichcote, but also many were from Oxford. The latitude and humanistic tolerance of their philosophy attracted some of the most eminent figures in the nation (Henry More, Ralph Cudworth, John Locke, John Wesley, Milton, Coleridge, and Matthew Arnold). Some of this movement's leaders—Henry More and Joseph Cudworth, for example, who defended witchcraft, mysticism, and supernatural concepts—gave to the influence of the Cambridge Platonists a wide domain of insights.

Campanella, Tommaso (1568–1639). Italian philosopher, scholar and social utopian. He was a very important figure in Renaissance humanism. While he advocated the privacy of philosophy and religion in the world of thought and civic government, he also wrote significant works on magic and astrology. Several times arrested on suspicion of heresy, he managed to clear his record but had finally to flee to France for safety. His *The Messiah's Monarchy* and *The City of the Sun* (which contains a description of a utopian society with original notions on social, political, and educational reforms), along with his many other works on philosophy, medicine, theology, politics, magic, and astrology have assured his status as a notable thinker and occultist.

Camp Meetings. Meetings of mediums held in America regularly during the summer season. Lily Dale, New York, and Lake Pleasant,

Massachusetts are the largest. Many mediums travel from abroad to meet there.

Cancer (Astrology). Astrological sign (June 22nd–July 23rd); symbol—the Crab; ruling planet, the Moon; qualities—despite the fact that this is a water sign, they show unusual enduring love, are fond of tradition, travel, seascapes. They are sensitive, adaptable, introspective, shy, unusually patient, impressionable; but they are constant worriers; too often hermit-like because of the sensitivity, shyness, and introspective nature; and too changeable and restless for their own equanimity.

Candoblé. In various parts of Brazil this deeply-rooted religious movement flourishes. It includes elements of magic and sorcery. Originally the practitioners of candoble came from Africa. Women perform its major activities.

Cannibalism. This very ancient practice, which was used in many parts of the world, represents the eating of human flesh, very often for religious and magical purposes; the rituals were performed for many important reasons: purification, pacification of gods, ancestor worship, etc.

Cannibalism, Burial. In many areas of the world in ancient and even relatively recent times it was a very important practice, engaged in to obtain a part of the dead person's spirit. Either this was to gain the dead person's power or to ward off the evil in the dead soul whose body was eaten.

Canoe Magic. In a number of American Indian stories this magic canoe, like the famous Arabian flying carpet, has the power to move itself when given proper signals from its owner.

Capnomancy. Divination by reading smoke: of sacrifices; of jasmine or poppy seeds thrown upon burning coals; of the breathing the smoke of a sacrificial fire.

Capricorn (Astrology). Astrological sign (Dec. 23rd–Jan. 20th); symbol—the Goat; ruling planet, Saturn; qualities—the best astrologers assert this is a difficult sign to assess, for they show an enormous range of qualities from magnificent to abominable. But the highly developed Capricorn, like its symbol the Goat, is incredibly sure footed; also cautious, unsentimental, magnetic, industrious, logical, accurate, sky-high ambitious, born workers; but they tend to love only those who love them; are too practical; often despondent, melancholy; too often suspicious and very selfish.

Caqueox (Cacoox). Once a caste of rope-makers in Brittany, who because of rope's symbolizing slavery and death by hanging were held to be pariahs and considered sorcerers. Profiting from their ill repute, they did become sorcerers and magicians, selling talismans that made people proof against evil; and, like the sorcerers of Finland, they had a reputation for raising and selling winds and tempests.

Carbuncle. In ancient times this stone was deemed one ruled by the sun, and is both male and female; also, it possesses the virtue of eradicating poisonous air, and preserving the health of the body. Since it has a native light of its own, it ranked fifth after diamonds, emeralds, opals and pearls.

Cardano, Geronimo (Jerome Cardon) (1501-1576). This Italian physician, mathematician, astrologer, psychiatrist, and psychic researcher, who contributed valuable discoveries in all these disciplines, was the illegitimate son of a scholar, Fazio, friend of Leonardo daVinci. Because he scorned the deadening tradition of past medical authorities and depended on his own medical observations in every area of medicine—somatic, mental, and psychic—he made original descriptions of typhus fever, syphilis, infection, instruction of the deaf mute and blind, and the determination of character from facial traits. His extraordinary descriptions of his own mystical trances, his astral projections, his constant ESP and clairvoyant skills, and his capacity to dream beforehand of every important event in his life mark him as an unusual personality far ahead of his age.

Card Reading. Although it is possible to use any type of card and there are a large variety of methods, the Tarot pack is most generally the favorite. Usually the diviner shuffles the pack, then cuts it, and after requesting the client to make a wish or ask a question deals the cards out in patterns—such as the cross, the star, the pentagon, or others. While each card has a meaning, their positions in the pattern also influence their significance. It is now that the precognitive powers of the diviner determine the quality of the reading.

Carnelian. A red chalcedony (a variety of quartz) which was used for its magical properties, since it was believed to cure disease, give courage in war, protect against evil and injury. Muhammedans fashioned this stone into a form of an amulet, making it into a ring.

Carrel, Alexis (1873-1944). Nobel Laureate in medicine and physiology, surgeon, biologist, and sociologist, his probing research into the scientific foundations of man's biological nature led him to establish in France in 1941 the French Foundation for the Study of Human Problems. Here Dr. Carrel pursued his wide-ranging investigations of man's total dimensions. Out of this came the awareness that man was more than a material entity and was possessed with spiritual and supermaterial needs and powers. (See: *The Prayer, Journey to Lourdes,* and his world-famous *Man, the Unknown*)

Carrington, Dr. Hereward. Noted American psychic researcher and author of many books on psychic research. Was assistant to Professor Hyslop at the A.S.P.R. Made an important investigation of Eusapia Paladino's (q.v.) mediumship in Naples which convinced him of the existence of genuine phenomena, and led to his postulating the Spiritualist hypothesis as the only one to rationally explain all the facts.

This view of his was strengthened by his examination of Mrs. Eileen Garrett (q.v.) in 1933.

Castaneda, Carlos (1931–   ). Although he is a professional anthropologist, Castaneda has catapulted himself to a unique position of authority in the domain of occult experience with the publication of four books on the esoteric knowledge which he learned from a Yacqui Indian Brujo (a sorcerer). Born in Sao Paulo, Brazil, Castaneda gained a doctorate in anthropology at the University of California in 1970 on the basis of his five-year apprenticeship to his Yacqui teacher. This teacher he calls Don Juan in his first published book: *The Teachings of Don Juan: A Yacqui Way of Knowledge*. Having gone to Mexico, while still a student, to study medicinal plants, he was soon introduced by his guru into the startling universe of hallucinogenic drugs and initiated into the skills of achieving power over the demonic world. Beginning with his first book, Castaneda has continued in all his writing to explore and excitingly reveal the far-reaching uses of psychedelic drugs, the unexpected depths and forces of the unconscious, the great spiritual powers resident in man and the universe, the polar and illusory dimensions of man's psychic qualities, and the extraordinary esoteric knowledge and powers possessed by seemingly uncultured Yaqui sorcerers. No other modern teacher on the subjects of parapsychological, spiritual, and occult phenomena has so shaken the world of science or attracted the kind and extent of serious attention of scholars, scientists, writers and the public (all his books have been best sellers) as has Carlos Castaneda. (See: *Journey to Ixtlan, A Separate Reality, Tales of Power, The Second Ring of Power*)

Castle of the Interior Man. The mystical epithet given to the 7 stages of the soul's ascent towards Divinity: (1) Prayer to God; (2) Prayer for mystic insight; (3) The darkness of self-renunciation; (4) Prayer—surrender to God; (5) Union with God; (6) Ecstatic prayer where love enters the soul; (7) Ravishment—the mystic marriage—God and Heaven enter the interior man.

Catacomb. Place used by the ancient Israelites to bury their dead. Such a practice has primitive and Near Eastern roots with later religious belief intertwined, for the ancient Hebrews believed that upon the day of the Last Judgement and Eternal Life in the End of Days, the pious Jews would arise from their graves. Therefore, burial in subterranean chambers to protect the body against decay and defilement was essential. The early Christians, being recently members of the Hebrew religion, continued the practice in their various countries— the most notable of the catacombs built from the 2nd to the 4th centuries A.D., are now to be found in Rome. Since the Christians believed in the resurrection of the body on the Day of Judgement, the Roman practice of cremation was sacrilegious.

Catalepsy. A state of body rigidity during which the normal functions are suspended. The causes are unknown; it may last for several days. According to some authorities on astral projection, it is a temporary phase of projection while the astral body is within a few feet of the physical body, or within "cord range." Catalepsy, usually spontaneous, can be induced by hypnotic practices. Indian fakirs are said to use it sometimes when producing supernormal phenomena.

Catching, Soul. In many ancient cultures it was firmly believed that death could be prevented if the soul could be stopped from leaving the body, or, if it left, to catch it and return it to the dead person. In some cultures the shaman, sorcerer, witch doctor, or priest-magician performed this function; among the Jews this task was performed by the Chebrah Kadishah, the Holy Society or "Holy Brotherhood," a group of pious Jews who ringed the dying with their bodies to prevent Satan from using his naked sword to kill—but chiefly to help the dying in his titanic battle against Death.

Catheri. One of a number of sects that departed from the Roman Catholic Church during the Middle Ages, based in large measure on the dualistic philosophy of the Manichaeans. Believing that this world is under the domination of Satan, they taught that at death the soul (if it has united with Christ on this earth) receives the Beatific Vision and immortality in heaven. The Cathari lived with purity, but their priesthood lived austerely—with complete chastity, with a very limited diet (no meat, cheese, eggs, milk—since they were the result of sexual intercourse), and a rigid discipline. The Cathari were very important in the development (ironically) of the Black Mass (q.v.); but even more significantly, they played an instrumental part in the spread of mysticism in later Europe. (See: Ruysbroeck).

Catherine of Siena, Saint (1347–1380). Acclaimed as one of the greatest figures of the Middle Ages, an extraordinary mystic, diplomatic and charismatic personage, she was the daughter of a Sienese dyer; despite her inability to write, she dictated hundreds of letters to the great of her day and also one of the transcendent mystical works of Christianity, *The Dialogue of St. Catherine of Siena*. This book has been constantly popular throughout Christendom. Her life, in some respects similar to Joan of Arc's, reads like the epic of an omnipotent hero. For this uneducated, modest nun persuaded Pope Gregory XI to leave his exile in Avignon and return to Rome; as papal ambassador she established peace between Florence and the Holy See; she helped in establishing the office of a Pope; she created a spiritual revival in Siena; she was a pure, selfless, loving angel to the poor and sick; and she was the recipient of the stigmata. (See: *St. Catherine as seen in Her Letters*).

Catoptromancy or Enoptromancy. A method of divination by the use of a mirror, which touching water, revealed to the sick his prognosis. Also in Thessaly, it was a method of placing a mirror at the back of a boy's or girl's head with his eyes bandaged; then the reading appeared written in blood upon the moon. This art was acquired by the Thessalian sorceresses from Persia.

Cat's-Eye. A stone which has a line of light upon its crest. In China and many countries of the Far East this magical talisman was worn to protect the wearer against his enemies, the evil eye, and witches.

Catuari arya-satyani (Buddhism). The four noble truths: suffering exists; it has a cause; it may cease; there is a path that leads to its extinction.

Causal Body. Occult term for a permanent element of man said to reincarnate; composed of "higher mental matter" and having a sexless human form.

Caves, Sacred. Greek cave sites were used in the Pre-Hellenic period by many cults which worshipped primitive spirits and espoused oriental mystery religions. In Crete there was the cave, considered his birth place, where Zeus was worshipped; another famous cave was that of Trophonius, a hero cult at Rebadea. In Italy a renowned holy cave was the Lupercal on the Palatine. Mithraism from Persia had many cave worshippers. These caves and their cults played an important part in the development and content of subsequent religion, and magical and mystery sacred rituals.

Cayce, Edgar (1877–1945). American healer-medium, world famous for his cures, born on a farm in Kentucky, he had very little education. At the age of twenty-one he lost his voice, but regained it temporarily under hypnotic treatment. When speaking under hypnosis, he diagnosed his own trouble and cured himself by post-hypnotic suggestion. This was extended to diagnosis for others with astounding success; in trance, the ignorant Cayce spoke like a professional physician. The patient did not have to be present providing his name and address were given. Even "incurables" were cured. His first famous case was that of Aime Deitrich of Hoptonsville, Kentucky; considered a hopeless case, she was saved from a rare brain disease. Her father testified before a notary public on 8 October 1910.

Cazotte, Jacques (1720–1792). French author of two famous books of prophetic and occult reputation: *Prophetie de Cazotte,* and *Le Diable Amoreux* —the former prophesying the French Revolution and its actions and outcome, the latter a renowned novel depicting an occult romance.

Celestial. Heavenly, an adjective commonly used to denote the higher spheres in the Spirit world.

Celestial Magic. Asserts that the planets are controlled by spirits who have influence over man.

Cellini, Benvenuto (1500–1571). This famous sculptor, metalsmith, and writer was a true spirit of the Renaissance, a man of transcendent taste and skill, some of his works ranking next to Michelangelo's in greatness. His fame, however, rests on his *The Life of Benvenuto Cellini*, a book of surprising frankness and extraordinary authenticity. He records in this work several very hair-raising adventures with demons and adepts of the black art to which he was introduced by a Sicilian priest.

Celts. A group of ancient people who flourished from the 13th century B.C. to the 5th A.D. They lived in the lands of Europe north of the Mediterranean. Their religious rites were conducted by that extraordinary priest body the Druids (q.v.) whose religious, occult, magical, and learned body of knowledge were derived from the ancient past and from their schools in Britain. Italian, Greek, Scythian, German, and eastern elements also influenced their development. Their influence still lives in certain dialects of Ireland, Scotland, Wales and Brittany.

Census of Hallucinations. An inquiry conducted by a distinguished committee of the S.P.R. in 1889 to collect substantial data of apparitions. The report was published in 1894. Out of 17,000 people canvassed, 1,684 claimed to have seen apparitions.

Centers, Psychic. See Chakras.

Centurione Scotto, Marquis Carlo. Italian nobleman and medium. An M.P. for eleven years. Did much research work. At suggestion of American medium Valiantine, he developed direct voice mediumship very quickly. Other phenomena included levitation, transportation, apports, xenoglossy. The S.P.R. queried his phenomena, causing Sir A. Conan Doyle to resign from the S.P.R.; he considered it a slur on the reputation of Ernest Bozzano the original investigator.

Ceremonial Magic. Chiefly it is the art of dealing with spirits, a way of gaining from God the power to overcome evil spirits. Throughout the instructions of the Grimoires (q.v.) and *Keys of Black Magic*, the adept is constantly cautioned to center his hope on the benevolence of the great Adonai, for the Being whom it is desired to invoke is not Satan but the Jewish Jehovah and the Christian Trinity. Only purity in life and thought could achieve success; only by studying such books as *Key of Solomon the King*, and the *Book of Black Magic*, could the adept learn the best hours of the day, the astrological periods, the propitious planets, the occult objects needed (goat-skin, blood stones, incense, camphor, 4 nails from the coffin of a dead child, etc.), the Cabalist signs, and all the formulas essential to achieve success.

Ceremony, Morning Star. This star was considered a great god by the Pawnee Indians of America, and to show their intense reverence they would sacrifice to it a young maiden.

Ceromancy. Divination by inspecting melted wax that has fallen to the floor. Special meanings were deciphered from the shapes and sizes of the drops.

Chac. Among the Mayans, he was the important rain god.

Chacmool. In the Mayan occult ritual, this was a bench that utilized a human figure in its sculptured form. It is found in Mayan centers of influence in Yucatan.

Chakras. In Hinduism, literally wheels or lotuses in the body which are emotional or spiritual centers, providing psychic information and energy. According to Theosophy, these centers are within the astral model-body which permeates the physical body. Although there are ten chakras, it is advisable to use only seven: (1) at the top of the head, (2) between the eyebrows, (3) the throat, (4) the heart, (5) the spleen, (6) the solar plexus, (7) the base of the spine—the seat of the kundalini (q.v.). Mastery of the chakras is a lifelong task, guided by the supervision of a qualified teacher.

Chaldean Oracles. A famous poem written by Julianus "the Chaldean," who lived in Rome in the 2nd century A.D. This poem was highly esteemed by the Neo-Platonists. It portrays a rich combination of Platonism, Pythagoreanism, elements of various oriental cults, and the magico-religious practice of theurgy (q.v.). Important in the history of mysticism and the occult.

Chams. These people of Indo-Chinese origin who live in Cambodia and Southeastern Asia are considered sorcerers who can slay at a distance and, by the use of magic, guarantee ruin and disease upon enemies. Most of the Cham sorcerers are women; and so potent is their reputation for bringing evil, they are feared and hated by the indigenous populations.

Ch'an (Zen Buddhism). Through meditation and the method of the eightfold negation and the belief in the Buddha-nature in all things, one ascends to a direct intuition into the heart of the Buddha-nature. Developed in China, where it was also utilized by Taoists and Confucianists.

Changeling. A widespread ancient belief that it is the devilish work of gnomes, witches, or fairies when a child is born defective. Most ancient people believed that these supernatural entities had substituted a deformed baby for the normal offspring; further, it reflects the ancient notion that infants are extremely vulnerable until certain carefully observed rites are performed. Moreover, it was an accepted belief that a changeling can be made to disappear by making it laugh.

Ch'ang sheng (Taoism). Immortality which is the development of an internal alchemy and external alchemy. Developed by Taoist magician-priests.

Chaomancy. The art of divination through the careful perusal of atmospheric changes.

Charms. Universally used by man almost from the beginning of his history. They may be in the form of behavior, verbal formulas, or small objects—also spells and incantations. Almost every conceivable object has been used for charms, either to bring good fortune or to ward off evil.

Charon. In Greek mythology, the ferryman in Hades who carried the shades of the dead across the rivers of the underworld, being paid by the coin the Greeks placed into the mouth of the dead. The Etruscans, greatly influenced by Near Eastern mythology and the occult, had a demon hammer-god named *Charon*.

Chattas (Hinduism). Umbrellas of ceremonial importance that were carefully fixed into the central post of a memorial tomb.

Chatzozerah (Judaism). The wondrous, magical silver trumpet, fashioned by Moses under divine guidance, that was used by the Israelites in battle and ceremony.

Chela. Hindu and Yogic term for a pupil whose master is a Guru. This is a sacred relationship for the disciple, since he is learning to become his inmost being.

Chemical Phenomena. Have often been recorded in the seance room. Lights which are cold, ozone smells, phosphorescence, fire production seemingly in defiance of normal chemical means, are some of the phenomena recorded.

Chemicographs. Guillaume de Fontenay's term for supernormal photographs obtained without a camera.

Chen jen (Taoism). The supreme power which results in having transcended the self and the non-self, life and death, by attaining a state of mystical union with the universe.

Ch'i (Taoism). Represents the great breath, the life, the soul; in its deepest sense, the fundamental spirit of the living universe.

Chiao (Taoism). The belief and worship of Heaven, ancestors and the pantheon of benevolent spirits.

Ch'ien. In The *I Ching* (q.v.) the trigram of the male cosmic principle, yang, and the opposite of k'un. It represents Heaven, with the symbol [≡] in the Eight Trigrams.

Child Guides. Often encountered in a Spiritualistic inquiry. It seems that they retain the childish mannerisms of their last earth years, irrespective of the time they have spent in the spirit world. Their knowledge and intelligence however are usually adult in accordance with their growing to maturity in spirit life.

Chiliasm. The Jewish and Christian belief that when the Messiah (q.v.) appears at the end of time he will establish his heavenly Kingdom on earth for a thousand years.

Ch'i-lin. In ancient Chinese mythology this supernatural animal was held to be a very wise creature who heralds good fortune in the future. Accordingly, this animal, with a scaly antelope body, a bushy tail, and the head of dragon, was the most favored of mythical creatures in Chinese art.

Chin. In Chinese mythology and supernatural beliefs this was the observance in natural objects of clear signs of the extraordinary.

Ch'in. This symbolic ancient Chinese musical instrument contained five strings denoting the five known aspects of time, the upper part symbolizing heaven, and the flat bottom the earth.

Chindi. Among the Navaho Indians this was the dreaded evil spirit who lived in the bodies of the dead.

Ching shen (Taoism). The spirit and soul of man, which the magician priests call "the keeper of the life of man," endowed by Heaven. This is the polar aspect of the physical form formulated by the Earth.

Chin tan (Taoism). In the alchemical formula of Taoism this is the medicine of immortality. While this is designated external alchemy (to achieve through the magic nourishment of life, Tao and immortality), it also encompasses the arts of the transmutation of mercury into gold; the art of medicine; of charms; of magic; and methods by which to achieve bodily disappearance and bodily change of form.

Chiromancy. Palmistry. Divination by the lines and forms of the hand.

Choang Tze (Taoism). The Chinese philosopher, circa 400 B.C., whose great works, together with the Tao-Te-King, form the basic writings of philosophically and profoundly rich Taoism. The mystic insight he elaborates is seemingly simple, but in reality, subtle and constantly rewarding and revealing.

Chokata. The divinity who is the guardian of the calendar in the ancient mythology of Japan.

Cholula. An ancient and important religious center in Mexico. When the Toltecs defeated the original inhabitants of the area (north of Puebla), they changed the center with its many temples into one great shrine for the worship of Quetzalcoatl (q.v.). This tradition was carried on by the Aztecs when they overwhelmed the Toltecs, for Quetzalcoatl became one of the principal gods of their pantheon.

Chorten. A Tibetan monument in memory of a lama or saint, containing sacred relics. The five parts of a chorten represent the five cosmic elements: fire, water, air, earth, and ether.

Christ—the Meaning. Since Christ means "the Anointed One," also the "Master of Love," He is spiritual light, that supreme state of God Consciousness where all sense of self vanishes and one realizes his at-one-ment with God. The realization of "Christ in me" brings to a mystic, union with that one's divinity and Christ residing within. For the Hindu, the soul or spirit is within; for Buddha, the Light is also within. The Messianic or Christ spirit has inhabited many other supreme teachers of mankind outside the realms of Christianity.

Christian Science. Founded by Mary Baker Eddy in 1866, it asserts that as God and the mind are the only reality, the power of thought is sufficient to counteract all physical ailments and handicaps since they are "unreal." Basing her doctrine on the Bible, Mrs. Eddy held that Christian Science is the reinstatement of primitive Christianity—salvation from all evil, for God is good. He is spirit, infinite and omnipotent, and the only creator; man himself is made in the image and likeness of God. Finally, human consciousness is freed from fear and material limitations when the truth and perfection of God and all his creation is understood, which leads to better physical and mental health.

Christian Spiritualism. Spiritualists who believe, as orthodox Christians do, that Jesus was more than human, and recognize him as a divine spiritual leader.

Christology. The body of doctrines that asserts: Christ was Savior and Redeemer of man; the Messiah and fulfillment of that promise; the word made flesh; as God and Son of God on earth, he suffered birth, the passion, and the Resurrection; his record proves he was God, Son, and Holy Spirit, for his prophecies, miracles, and saintly life validate his own description of Godhead; He was both man and God; finally, he was also Father, Son, and Holy Ghost.

Chronicles of Japan. Written in 720 A.D., this book called *Nihongi* together with the *Kojiki* (q.v.) are the earliest sources of Japanese mythology. Using Chinese characters to depict the pre-or-semi-historic era, it gives a record of the creation myths and a history and evolution of the first gods along with many legends and supernatural stories.

Chuang Tzu (Chuang Chou, Chuang Chi-Yuan) (c. 399–295 B.C.). The greatest of the Taoist philosophers and profound mystic, (second only to Lao-Tzu q.v.), a follower of Lao-Tzu. He was born in Honan. An idealist who declined high office to maintain his freedom and peace; a rare thinker; a colorful writer; a superb stylist; a lover of nature. His book, *Chuang Tzu*, is one of China's most esteemed classics.

Church of Satan, The. Founded in 1966 by Dr. Anton Szandor LaVey, the Church of Satan is an organized religion that proclaims Satan a natural force which rules the world. Further, this force represents man and man's nature, adding that a Satanist knows that, like the gods of spiritual religions, he is his own god. Indulgence, vital existence, kindness only to the deserving and vengeance to enemies; responsibility only to the responsible; man is only an animal who because of his divine spiritual and intellectual development is the most vicious of all animals—these are basic beliefs. To be a Satanist means to follow one's natural instincts, to gratify every physical, mental, emotional, and sexual desire one has. Essentially, each Satanist lives according to his own set of rules—so long as no undeserving person is harmed by his actions. Finally, he is a realist who obeys society's rules, using his own sharpened ego in order to succeed; therefore, he is opposed to drugs and narcotics (except under a doctor's supervision) for these only achieve an escape from reality.

Churinga (tjurvnga). At native Australian totem centers, the Churinga (sacred flat pieces of stone or wood) are believed to contain some of a person's soul. At birth a churinga is made for each native; at death his family or relatives preserve it and use it in ceremonies.

Cinyras. Mythical King of Cyprus, founder of the cult of Aphrodite in his country, father of Adonis, the son and favorite of Apollo, a musician and seer and the symbol for riches and beauty.

Circe. Italian goddess, powerful in magic, living on the island of Aeaea, who changed the men of the Greek hero Odysseus (Homer, *Odyssey*) into pigs. But Odysseus possessed a proof armor given him by Hermes, the herb moly, so that her magic and spells failed against him and he forced Circe to restore his men. Further, after living with her a year and giving her two sons, Odysseus obtained from Circe the directions which enabled him to sail home. Circe's magic helped the Argonaut Jason and Medea by purifying them from the crime of murder.

Circle, Development (Spiritualism). A group of people who meet regularly for the purpose of developing any latent psychic abilities they may possess. Some circles sit for one particular type of phenomena, say clairvoyance or trance mediumship, but with most it is general. The time taken for individual development varies. Some people attain proficiency readily. Others may take five years of regular sitting or even longer. Physical phenomena usually take very much longer than mental phenomena and the conditions of their operation are much more exacting, perhaps explaining their comparative rarity.

Circle, Home. See Home Circle.

Circle, Magic. African magicians, Druids, medieval necromancers, Cabalists, and many sorcerers, shamans, and wizards since ancient times have used the circle drawn around themselves or others as a kind of supernatural defense against evil demons. Rings, bracelets, and similar circular talismans and charms (qq.v.) have served the same purpose. Materials with magic properties such as pebbles, thorns, fire, and water have served to draw or mark the circle.

Circle, Meditation. According to Eastern tradition, spiritual knowledge can be gained by the practice of meditation. By sitting quietly in a group and letting the mind play gently upon a given theme, an attunement with higher powers may be achieved.

Clairaudience. A faculty of extra sensory perception described as "hearing" by the medium. It is often blended with clairvoyance in demonstrations of clairvoyance. Mediums with this faculty well developed can often give evidential details of unusual names.

Clairsentience. Psychic perception by sensing conditions pertaining to communicating entities and auric emanations; a faculty often blended with clairvoyance and psychometry in mediumship.

Clairvoyance. The psychic ability to see things and events or gain information regarding them whatever the distance. However, this is an umbrella term which often refers to telepathy, spiritism, psychical research, second sight, and prophetic visions and dreams. But clairaudience and clairsentience are clairvoyant, for they refer to the ability to hear or feel information about events occurring at a distance. Clairvoyance may occur in a normal state, or, more generally, in a trance induced by various agencies, i.e., drugs, fasting, illness, hyperesthesia, or crystal gazing.

Clairvoyant Painting. Paintings inspired by the artist's own clairvoyant visions.

Clark, Vernon. A psychologist, formerly with the United States Veterans' Administration. He conducted a series of tests to prove the validity of astrologers' predictions. By measuring the predictions of nonprofessionals against a group of 20 astrologers—who were asked to determine the occupations of unknown persons merely from their birth charts—the answers of the latter group proved their superior predictability.

Cleromancy. An ancient form of divination in which pebble shapes are thrown on a flat surface, their movements providing readings.

Clown. The buffoon-jester is only one type of clown. Far older historically, more widespread, and of greater significance is the clown-magician with cosmic powers who acted as an intercessor between his people and the gods—also, to the souls of the dead. Most often they wore masks and costumes. They were an integral part of many North American tribes where they officiated in rituals and ceremonies.

Cocaine. This extraordinary drug is refined from the leaf of the coca plant which flourishes in the Andean highlands of Bolivia and Peru. The coca bush was worshipped by the ancient Incas, for they saw this divine plant as a gift of the lifegiving Sun God. The Inca rulers and the male aristocracy used it in their religious rituals to engender exalted states of divine transcendence. To this day most of the Indians in the high Andes chew coca leaves together with an alkali to produce the cocaine drug which gives them phenomenal powers of endurance. No less a figure than Sigmund Freud, who used cocaine for some years, thought he had discovered the magic elixir of great physical powers in the grains of this unusual drug. But its beneficent medical qualities are offset by its harmful effects when used injudiciously. In recent years, however, cocaine has supplanted narcotics and such hallucigens as LSD, and the amphetamines in popularity.

Cohen, Naphtali Rabbi. A famous German Cabalist of the late 17th and early 18th centuries. He was credited with making the sun shine in the middle of the night through his supreme powers as a Cabalist. So great was his reputation as a seer of the "Mystic Spheres of God," that he was accused of starting the Great Fire in 1711—which destroyed the Frankfort Ghetto—owing to his Cabalistic and esoteric experiments.

Coiled Serpent. See Kundalini.

Coincidence. The casual concurrence. This is held to be the result of chance. If, however, by calculation of probabilities, more than chance is required for explanation, psychic research may shed light on the problem. Many experiments in ESP are based on this.

Coleridge, Samuel Taylor (1772-1834). English poet, critic, philosopher, and mystic who along with Wordsworth (another mystic), changed the direction of English writing—especially poetry. His parents—observing that he was no ordinary child, that he consumed books and created a world of his own, and showed a pronounced feeling for mysticism by age nine—decided their child should become a clergyman. However, his mercurial spirit, extraordinary intellectual capacities and conversational talents made his Cambridge years difficult. At 22 he had his play published and two years later his first volume of verse. In 1797, he met Wordsworth; in 1798, they published their joint volume *Lyrical Ballads* which became a seminal book in English literature. Along with his friend Southey, he tried to establish a utopian society in America, to be called pantisocracy. His drug habit, which started when he was 24, stayed with him most of his life despite his efforts to eradicate it. Nonetheless, he continued to produce poems, publish papers, write philosophy, translate German literature and philosophy, give lectures, and write criticism, becoming one of the great figures of literature. The remarkable musical and supernatural qualities of his verse are best experienced in "The Rime of the Ancient Mariner."

Colet, John (1466-1519). English educator who was the leader of the

"Oxford Reformers." He brought to the English Renaissance from Italy the Florentine Platonism, an amalgam of Platonism and Neoplatonism, plus concepts of man, beauty, love and mystical union. Despite charges of heresy that were leveled at Colet by the English Church, he was so dazzling an orator and so logical an exponent of his doctrines that powerful friends helped quash the indictment. He won such illustrious converts as Sir Thomas More, Erasmus and King Henry VIII. Most lastingly, his beliefs stamped the whole of English literature, for they became the essential intellectual structure in the classic poems and writings of Spenser, Donne, and Milton.

College of Psychic Science. Formerly known as the London Spiritualist Alliance. Founded in 1881. Renamed as above in 1955. Not a religious organization, but non-sectarian. Membership of the association does not commit members to any definite belief. Objectives of the College are the investigation, study and classification of psychic phenomena, and coordination of scientific knowledge.

Colley, Thomas, Ven. Archdeacon of Natal and Rector of Stockton. English psychic investigator who once issued a £ 1,000 challenge to Maskelyne, the professional conjurer, to reproduce psychic phenomena. He promoted interest in Hope, the psychic photographer, and founded the famous Crewe circle. Died in 1912.

Colors. These have always had an important symbolic quality in psychic, mystic, and occult experience. Both Eastern and Western art, as utilized in supernatural representations, express these symbolic relationships. In the Roman Catholic Church in the West, white, gold, red, purple, green, and black represent special liturgical and religious significance. To Theosophists, color is nothing less than the substance of the soul, maintaining its existence through color. For Spiritualists, much significance is attached to colors perceived in the human aura. Colors are also used by spirit guides and controls, while color therapy is used by some healers.

Commonwealth of the S.A.G.B. A system of co-operation between the Spiritualist Association of Great Britain and various Spiritualist bodies and churches, by which interchange of services and facilities for members of all member bodies is secured.

Communication, Spirit (Spiritualism). Can be established in many ways. Human beings are the "instruments" employed, although many efforts have been made to construct mechanical apparatus to supplant the medium. Up to now the results are controversial. If they succeed, then spirit communication enters the domain of physics. Mental communication is effected by control of the vocal organs of the medium, by telepathy between spirits on different planes, by visual images, by auditory means or by sensing conditions. Automatism is common. Other means are communication by physical phenomena, when the medium's mind is not employed directly; rappings by code; direct voice; speech by a materialized form. We are told that the purpose of spirit communication is to uplift humanity from materialistic apathy to an awareness of each person's Divine participation, and responsibility for his inner intentions.

Communicator. A personality seeming to be that of a deceased person or other discarnate being.

Communigraph. The 'Ashkir-Jobson Communigraph,' a small table with a free pendulum beneath, which can make contact with a number of metal plates representing the alphabet. When contact is made, the appropriate letter appears illuminated on the table top. It was claimed that no medium was necessary for its operation.

Community of Sensation (Spiritualism). A relationship between hypnotizer and subject. The subject reacts to physical sensations experienced by the hypnotist. By this means taste, smell, vision and hearing are known to have been transferred. Mediums experience this when sensing conditions of past lives of their spirit contacts. Also the phenomena of psychometry (q.v.) are worth noting in this connection.

Compacts, Death (Spiritualism). An agreement between two people to endeavor to give evidence to each other of their continued existence after death. In *Phantasms of the Living* by Gurney, Myers and Podmore (qq.v.), twelve cases are recorded where an apparition was seen within twelve hours of death. In some cases much longer times are required, and of course the failures may be due to insufficient sensitivity on the part of the intended receiver. On occasions the apparition has been seen by a third party.

Compass Brothers. A magical, Cabalistic society which flourished in Lubeck, Germany from 1400 to 1790. Their emblem was a compass and sector hanging from a crowned "C"; they also had chains with these emblems joined by eagles' tails.

Conan Doyle, Sir Arthur (1858–1930). Doctor and famous author of Sherlock Holmes stories. One of Spiritualism's most earnest champions. He became president of many societies, notably the International Spiritualist Federation, the Marylebone Spiritualist Association (now the Spiritualist Association of Great Britain) and the London Spiritualist Alliance (now the College of Psychic Science). On several occasions since his passing he has given evidence of his continued existence. At a Reunion Service at the Albert Hall in 1930 he was seen clairvoyantly by medium Estelle Roberts, who gave a message to members of his family which was accepted as evidential by them. Another evidential communication was given to Harry Price (q.v.) through the mediumship of Eileen Garrett (q.v.).

Conant, Mrs. J.H. (1831–1875). American trance medium who, in col-

laboration with Luther Colby, editor of *Banner of Light*, gave free public seances in Boston for seventeen years. Her trance messages were
said to be perfectly in character with the communicator, and they
were published regularly. In trance she spoke in many tongues including Indian dialects of which normally she knew nothing.

Concentration. Meaning one-pointedness. To centralize our thoughts
on one focal point, it is necessary to have perfect control over the
mind. Both Hinduism and Buddhism have developed the best methods
by which to achieve this extremely difficult exercise, but once
mastered the benefits are extraordinary. It is no exaggeration to
assert that only the master of concentration can know the most profound psychic, mystic, and occult dimensions. Three elementary controls for the beginner are these: (1) your thoughts must be centered on
one thing at a time; (2) be conscious of what you are doing when you
are doing it; (3) do not let the mind wander. (See: Meditation)

Concord. A system of Spiritualist education for young people sponsored by the S.A.G.B.

Conditions (Spiritualism). Very frequently referred to among Spiritualists. Usually descriptive of the immediate environment of the medium and its psychic quality as affecting the ease or otherwise of
communication. Sometimes conditions are stipulated by the medium
before a seance. While these may seem whimsical or trivial to the
investigator, it is best to observe them as far as reasonably possible,
as experience has proved that the results are greatly affected by the
degree of cooperation accorded by the sitter.

Conjunction. Astronomically, the apparent meeting of two celestial
bodies; astrologically, this is held to be the most powerful "aspect,"
linking strongly the two principles associated with these bodies.

Conjureman or Woman. In the Southern United States this term refers
to one who engages in the arts of magic; it also refers to a witch. Since
the term has widespread use in the West Indies, where there are Con-
juremen and Women, that is most likely its origin.

Conjuring. The art of calling upon, summoning, charging, or constrain-
ing a devil or a spirit by invoking a spell or a sacred name. It also
refers to the practice of magic. Conjurers have also been called black
magicians, wizards, and sorcerers.

Conjuring Lodges. A hut or tent used by early North American Indians
for mediumistic purposes, probably as a primitive form of cabinet
(q.v.).

Conklin, J.B. American medium who specialized in billetreading.
President Lincoln was his patron and Conklin was often a guest at the
Presidential mansion.

Consciousness. Normal cognition. This appears to be a barrier to supernormal manifestation. By trance, meditation, or various drugs the subconscious can be freed. A stimulating discussion of this area is explored by Eileen Garrett (q.v.) in her book *Many Voices.*

Consciousness, planes of. Higher planes of consciousness can be achieved by meditation, awareness, knowledge, and understanding. These are as follows: (1) Mineral plane or elemental. (2) Vegetable or plant plane—lowest form of life. (3) Animal plane—instinctual. (4) Human plane—instinct and reason. (5) Super-consciousness—instinct, reason, and will. (6) Satvik plane—where instinct, reason, will, understanding, and intuition function in perfect harmony. Here is achieved complete wisdom and unlimited powers of understanding and knowledge. (7) Christ—or Cosmic plane, possessing God consciousness. This stage is achieved by the masters or adepts.

Constant, Alphonse Louis (c. 1810–1875). French occultist whose large body of works have been very influential ever since they were published. This "last of the magi," (one of his epithets), son of a shoemaker, apostate priest, and socialist propagandist, developed suddenly in 1855 as a major spokesman for magic, mythology, sorcery, and the transcendental mysteries. Some of his works, which he wrote under the well-known pseudonym of Eliphas Levi, are: *Doctrine of Transcendental Magic, History of Magic, The Key of the Grand Mysteries,* and *Fables and Symbols.*

Contact Healing (Spiritualism). Healing where bodily contact is made between the healer and the patient, either by "laying on of hands" or by rubbing and manipulation. Spirit healing where contact does not take place is known as "absent healing" (q.v.). There appears to be little difference in the effectiveness of either form of healing, proving that contact is not always necessary. Amazing results have been achieved by both.

Contemplation. A mental exercise whereby knowledge is gained by considering with continued attention a particular object. Often it is identification with the object, as in meditation of spiritual things; or a state of mystical awareness of God's being or presence—an ecstatic perception of God. Used by Eastern philosophers; important in Anthroposophy as a means to spiritual insight.

Control (Spiritualism). The state of possession of a medium by another personality. The spirit operator in charge of a medium or seance proceedings. They are often called "guides" when the personality is well known as a regular helper at a series of sittings, or is constantly associated with a particular medium. The control is usually the "expert" who directs the operation of communication, the medium being the instrument and often described as such by the controls. It should be mentioned that control by the living has been known, often without their knowledge. It may therefore be a function of the subconscious mind in these cases. Among controls, all nationalities are met, though for no clear reason North American Indians seem to preponderate. They make excellent guardians or doorkeepers, helpers for physical manifestations and circle development. Often strong healing powers accompany them. Many child controls are also known.

Cook, Miss Florence (1856–1904). Famous materialization medium of Sir William Crookes, responsible for the control "Katie King." These were the first materializations known to have been produced under test conditions in a good light. Some flashlight photographs were taken of her and Sir William arm in arm. Katie King could change the color of her skin and was different in stature and personality from the medium. Sir William Crookes published his report on her mediumship in 1874, bringing a storm of ridicule and sarcasm on his head.

Cooper, Mrs. Blanche. English direct voice medium who collaborated in a series of experiments with Dr. S. G. Soal, (q.v.) the eminent ESP researcher. One of these provided an instance of control by the living. Soal's friend, Gordon Davis, believed dead but subsequently discovered alive, unknowingly "communicated" through the direct voice phenomenon. All the mannerisms of his speech and voice were produced, and he described boyhood incidents known only to Soal.

Cord, Silver (Spiritualism). The link between the physical and etheric bodies, sustaining the physical body during earth life but severing at death. Often, but not always seen as a silver thread of indefinite extension by projectionists. Opinions differ as to its point of attachment, the majority saying the base of the skull, others the navel. According to Muldoon, when the bodies are within a few feet, the cord acts as a rigid arm which controls the relative movements at the beginning and end of projection, also the bringing together instantaneously should danger threaten the physical body.

Cordovero, Moses ben Jacob (1522–1570). He continued the evolutionary work on mysticism, the occult, and Cabalism which engaged so many Jewish scholars in this period of Jewish history. He was an important member of the group that had gathered in Safed in Upper Galilee.

Corpus Hermeticum. A body of eclectic knowledge that includes the whole spectrum of supernatural sciences dating from late classic times. It covers works of Hermes Trismegistus (q.v.) on through to the writings of the Middle Ages, the Renaissance, and those of the 17th century.

Cosmic Consciousness. This is one of a number of concepts which refer to a state of expanded awareness of the self's oneness with the universe. This state is often a level of psychic experience. Most frequently it is attained in a moment of ecstasy, coming unexpectedly, though strict meditation and contemplation can be an effective means.

Cottin, Angelique. One of the famous group of Electric Girls (q.v.) in the mid 1800's—so named because in their presence emanations of powerful forces occurred. Angelique Cottin, the most renowned of these women, was the daughter of a Normandy farmer in whose presence compasses spun wildly, metallic objects moved, and the mere touch of her clothing produced the same effects. Dr. Tanchon, the Frenchman who tested her powers, and other witnesses established her creditability. But like most psychics and mediums of unusual powers she was not always able to demonstrate her supernormal capacities.

Court de Gebelin, Antoine (1725–1784). Churchman, scholar, linguist, libertarian, this courageous French Protestant clergyman wrote a massive study of language and mythology which gave brilliant insights into the magic, mysteries, occult, and supernatural phenomena indigenous to the primitive world. Long before modern anthropologists understood the essential meaning and significance of these practices in the primitive history of mankind, Court de Gebelin laid the foundations for future explorations in this immensely important but difficult area of knowledge. He also studied "magnetism" among animals, his innovative observations stimulating Mesmer (q.v.) in his historic development of hypnotism.

Cousedon, Mlle. A noted medium in Paris in 1890's who manifested a great skill in the inducement of trances, at such times often becoming the Angel Gabriel. When possessed by the Angel Gabriel she spoke in language similar to Latin. The famed psychic investigator Professor Flammarion (q.v.) attests to the authenticity of this spirit possession.

Coutant, Millie. A psychic from Burnt Hills, upstate New York. She has had an extraordinary record of locating lost persons. For the past 20 years this bookkeeper has given her psychic service free to whoever required it. She has also been working with the Parapsychological Study and Investigation Society at Saratoga, New York, helping them in their research operations.

Coven. A regular gathering of witches, usually thirteen in number, including a high priest and six mixed couples.

Crandon, Margery. One of the most outstanding American mediums who helped to establish for all time the reality of physical phenomena. Under very strict control, excellent manifestations were obtained in the presence of many investigators. Harry Price's (q.v.) fraudproof table was levitated in white light twice to a height of eight inches. Chinese scripts were produced in red light when the medium's eyes were closed. Cross correspondence tests were successfully carried out with Dr. Henry Hardwicke of Niagara Falls, 450 miles from the seance in Boston. Hereward Carrington (q.v.) admitted himself baffled by the extraordinary powers of this medium.

Crawford, Dr. Painstaking investigator of the famous Goligher circle, vouched for by Sir William Barrett (q.v.), 1917–20. He formulated laws governing the production of telekinetic phenomena.

Cremation. Destroying a corpse by burning has been widely practiced in ancient times through the present, for it prevents the possible return of the dead; protects the body from wild beasts and evil spirits; secures warmth and comfort in the future world; and eliminates the possibility of transformation (q.v.).

Crisis Apparitions. In moments of crisis, apparitions would seem to be more likely to manifest than at other times. Many such cases are recorded in *Phantasms of the Living*, Gurney, Myers and Podmore (qq.v.).

Crithomancy. Divination using grain or particles of flour and observing the patterns formed. Most often it was a part of sacrificial rituals.

Crollius, Oswald. Disciple of Paracelsus and author of the *Book of Signatures* which presents a history of hermetic philosophy. Crollius asserted that since God and Nature have imprinted their names upon all their works it was only necessary to become an adept in the occult sciences to gain the skill by which to read the sympathies and antipathies of all things, the properties of substances, and the entire realm of the secrets of nature. Alphonse Constant (Eliphas Levi) (q.v.) considered him a major contributor to the master science of the universe that is yet to be discovered.

Crookes, Sir William (1832–1919). Great physicist of the last century. Upon entering his investigation of Spiritualism (1870), he made a public announcement that scientific methods would "relegate the worthless residuum of Spiritualism into the unknown limbo of magic and necromancy." He investigated D.D. Home (q.v.), assisted by his brother Walter, and Sir William Huggins, eminent physicist and astronomer and ex-president of the Royal Society, and Serjeant Cox, a well-known lawyer. His report was submitted in due course to the Royal Society but it was refused when it was found to support the truth of Spiritualistic phenomena. At that time his famous investigation of Florence Cook and "Katie King" (q.v.) seemed too fantastic to be credible to his contemporaries. In spite of the danger to his scientific standing, Crookes stood by his discoveries to the end.

Cross. In all likelihood the greatest magical, occult, and religious symbol ever developed by man. Not only is it one of the most ancient of supernatural artifact-symbols but it was used as such by all the major cultures of the ancients. The Chaldean-Babylonian people used an equilateral cross, symbol of their god Anu; the Ankh (q.v.) (handled cross) was the Egyptian version; among the Greeks Apollo's sceptre was carved like a cross; so, too, was Thor's hammer—the great thunder god of the Scandinavians; for India, their swastika and sauvastika is very ancient, the swastika often representing the male element, the sauvastika the female; and it was also used by the ancient Persians, Phoenicians, Etruscans, Romans, the Celtic people of Gaul and Britain, the Mexicans, the Peruvians and all through Central America.

Cross Correspondence (Spiritualism).Some of the most convincing evidence of survival of death has been obtained by this method, which rules out the possibility of telepathy or mind reading on the medium's part. By request, a spirit message is split up and the two parts delivered to different mediums simultaneously, but unknown to each other. When subsequently the parts of the message are assembled, the whole makes sense.

Crowley, Aleister (1875–1947). For close to fifty years, Crowley aggressively and insistently flaunted his Satanism and shocked a Victorian-Christian-Socialistic England with his blasphemous diabolism, and self-descriptions as "The Beast" and the "worst man in the world." His creed: "Do what thou wilt should be the whole of the law." Having begun the study of "magick" at Cambridge University, he then traveled extensively to enrich his knowledge of the subject. In Sicily, he set up a Gnostic temple for a period. On returning to England, he wrote his justly well-known book *Magick in Theory and Practice*. Although his writings and poetry were considered blasphemous and lacking authority, in actuality he acquired an extraordinary knowledge of the whole range of the occult, black magic, and mysticism; further, he was himself a mystic. Lastly, he was a courageous mountain climber. In the flesh, he was a man with a strikingly magnetic personality, who easily attracted many followers (society and governmental figures among them) to his various temples and lectures where he practiced a melange of Gnosticism, paganism, black magic, mysticism, and sexuality. Some of his books are *Libra, Diary of a Drug Fiend, The Blue Equinox, The God Eater, 777, The Moon Child* and *Equinox*.

Cryptesthesia. Coined by Dr. Charles Richet (q.v.) to describe a "sixth sense," perception by means of an unknown mechanism which produces cognition as an end result. It is activated by some mysterious external vibration which he termed "the vibrations of reality." It was offered as an alternative explanation to the spirit hypothesis to account for the phenomena of clairvoyance, premonitions, psychometry, dowsing and telepathy. The modern term would be extra sensory perception.

Cryptomnesia. Unconscious memory which may be drawn upon in special circumstances. In trance or under hypnosis, information may be given which at first sight seems foreign to the individual, but which may be traced to an early impression long since forgotten by the conscious mind.

Crystal Gazing or Scrying. A very old form of divination in which a clairvoyant state is induced by gazing at a crystal ball, at a pool of water, or a mirror. After an initial cloudiness, scenes and pictures appear to a sensitive. The developed clairvoyant is able to perceive persons or scenes, distant in time or space.

Culture Heroes. Historical personages whose teachings and adventures are propagated in the myths and legends of their people. They are usually raised by posterity to divine status, or considered to be incarnations of gods.

Cummins, Miss Geraldine. One of Ireland's most outstanding automatist mediums in the first decades of this century. Her extraordinary scripts, excellently constructed and written unconsciously at terrific speed, are worthy of close study by reason of the detailed information concerning little known periods of history, and certain Biblical and historical characters. Much of her detail has been verified by experts of these times. In collaboration with Dr. Connell of Ireland, she undertook a series of psychometrical experiments which succeeded in convincing the doctor that the origin of many patients' troubles was accessible by this means, and could be adduced as evidence for reincarnation and a form of "Karmic" law.

Curandera. In Mexico and in other parts of South America, a woman psychic who ministers to her clients in a variety of ways: as a psychologist, clairvoyant, medicine-dispenser (especially in the realm of sex), and psychic surgeon. Extraordinary feats of psychic surgery, attested to by journalists and doctors, have been performed by curanderas.

Curran, Joseph Mrs. One of the most remarkable cases of a medium whose control, Patience Worth (famous in psychic history), made her an outstanding phenomenon in American occult history. Mrs. Curran, a St. Louis housewife, of modest, almost colorless personality, in an experiment with a ouija board on July 8, 1913, suddenly discovered a "spirit" communicating with her—Patience Worth. This control dictated 3 novels, highly praised by the critics, and volumes of poems, dialogues, and poetic prayers. But only when she was possessed by her control did Mrs. Curran ever exhibit any wit or literary talent. Mrs. Curran became a national celebrity who was invited to the homes of scholars, poets, and eminent persons.

Curse. A form of attack which invokes a magical higher power to hurt an enemy, particularly so potent a formula as an appeal to a powerful demon or deity. A special priestly class, magicians, or those close to death possess unique skills in cursing. Contemporaneously, the curse can be delivered by Satanists, witches, sorcerers, etc. In the higher religions, historically, the curse was pronounced in public rituals and ceremonies.

Cursed Bread. Among the ancient Anglo-Saxons a form of divination. By casting a spell upon a piece of barley bread, then feeding it to a suspected individual, evidence of guilt was shown if he became ill or choked on it. But if there was no effect he was considered innocent.

Cybele. The great mother-goddess of Anatolia, Lydia, and Phrygia was primarily a goddess of fertility, but was also the protector of the total well-being of her worshippers, curing and sending disease, giving oracles and protectors in war, while her attendant lions declared her the goddess also of wild nature. She was associated with her youthful lover Attis. Her devotees engaged in actions which produced states of ecstasy, prophetic rapture and insensitivity to pain. She then conquered the Greco-Roman world, for by the 5th century B.C. she was worshipped in Greece, notably by the semi-demonic Corybantes, and was hailed in Rome in the years 205–204 B.C. where the spring rites in her honor ran for nearly two weeks. In her name the ritual of the *taurobolism* (q.v.) was performed. Still later, Attis became a solar god, and he and Cybele were regarded as astral and cosmic powers. Given official sanction, Cybele has constantly exercised a prominent position in the history and practices of magic and the occult. Psychiatrists refer to her as *Magna Mater*, Great Mother; and Jung used her name to designate one of the universal racial archetypes which is present in man's unconscious.

Dd

Daath (Judaism). Wisdom to the Jews,—"Chachmah"—was considered the "highest good," and it meant righteousness and "loving kindness." Daath, in mysticism and in the Cabala, describes wisdom in its dual sense: masculine and feminine. Chachmah represents the male aspect, Bihan (q.v.) the female.

Dactyls. A body of sorcerers and physicians originating in Phrygia who were also magicians, conjurers, soothsayers, and exorcists. They were considered very powerful magicians throughout the Mediterranean world. They were also credited with the discovery of minerals, musical notes, fire, musical instruments and with introducing them into Greece, Crete, and Italy. Hercules was said to be their chief.

Dad. Ancient Egyptian god who symbolized the human skeleton and perhaps the dead and dismembered Osiris. He had an influence on the restoration of the dead. (See: *Book of the Dead*.)

Daedalus. In Greek mythology, the most cunning artificer of mysterious work. Daedalus inherited this superhuman ability from his divine ancestors. He made the labyrinth for the minotaur in Crete, and the magical thread for Ariadne. He made figures with open eyes that walked and moved their arms. He is credited with making several pyramids in Egypt.

Daevaists (Zoroastrianism). Disciples of the Daevas (q.v.).

Daevas (Zoroastrianism). Evil spirits, also demons of the darkness. Although originally the same as "devas" in Hinduism, they became opposite in nature in Zoroastrianism.

Dagda. Among the ancient Celts and in Ireland the god of fertility.

Dagoba. A Buddhist shrine which contains relics of Buddha or a Buddhist saint. Found in Ceylon.

Dagon. The chief god of the Philistines, also worshipped by the Phoenicians, originally a fish god. There are many references to him in the Old Testament.

Daibutsu. In Japan the colossal images of Buddha. At Kamakura, near Yokohama, is the most famous, dated 1252; it is 50 feet high and 98 feet in circumference.

Daimon. Name of the famous supernormal guide who advised Socrates when in doubt. There are many modern parallels in clairaudient phenomena.

Daimonology. A body of information that spells out the rules for dealing with spirits, both how they are involved with human beings and the best methods of handling them.

Daityas (Hinduism). These titans together with the Danavas warred against the gods.

Daivers, Daivergoel. In Hindu mythology, genii dwelling in the Daiver–Logum, a locality all their own. Related to the Persian divs, the origin perhaps of the world "devil." Encompassing both material and spiritual bodies, they exhibit a number of human traits both good and evil.

Dalai Lama. The ruler of Lamaism on earth. His succession depends upon direct reincarnation; and although he is reputed to be an incarnation of a powerful Bodhisattva (q.v.), he is traditionally chosen by lamas from the common people's babies, who being born at an astrologically specified time must exhibit the necessary signs of wisdom. Once chosen, he is then carefully trained for his great responsibility.

Dance. An almost universal expression by man in all ages and nations, it is his most ancient expression of art, religion, magic, and mysticism.

Dance has been used to induce delirium and autointoxication by religious functionaries, while some groups, like the Bororos of South America, single out the ability to reach this kind of ecstasy as a criterion of priesthood. It has widespread use as sympathetic magic in funeral dances, the mimetic gestures being used as a means to influence the dead.

Dance, abdominal. A dance dating from possibly Neolithic times in which ritualized movements of the pelvic area are performed. Like numerous mythic developments, its origins may derive from fertility rites.

Dance, Astronomic. The oldest of the dances in ancient Egypt, in which the dancers' movements symbolized the movements of the heavenly bodies. In groups representing the signs of the zodiac, the dancers circled around the altar of the sun god Ra. The ancient Greeks performed this same dance around the burning altar of Zeus. Sometimes this dance was used in the worship of the sun, moon, or stars. Another name for this term is celestial dance (q.v.).

Dance Calumete. The American Indians of the Great Plains enacted this dance which was performed around a smoke offering to the Great Spirit. But many other Indian tribes also utilized this dance to the Great Spirit.

Dance, Celestial. An ancient Egyptian dance which symbolized the movements of the heavenly bodies. It was performed around the altar of the sun god Ra, in representation of the Zodiac. The Greeks performed the dance around the fiery altar of Zeus. Sometimes the dance is done to honor the stars, sun or moon. (See: Dance, Astronomic).

Dance of Siva (Hinduism). In metal or stone images as Nataraja, Siva is often depicted in a virile and energetic dance. The dance symbolizes his five activities of creation, maintenance, destruction of the world, embodiment of souls, and their eventual release from the life-cycle. The dance illustrates the cosmic process as it evolves in a succession of immensely long cycles in which change follows change.

Dancers. The mystic sect of Christians in France in the 14th century whose frenzied dancing in the streets brought forth ecstatic cries of seeing Heaven and Christ sitting with Mary. Disciples grew throughout Germany and the Netherlands and the sect flourished into the 17th century.

Daniel (Judaism). The prophet in Babylonian captivity whose awesome supernatural powers, wisdom, and skills in divination (interpreting the dreams of Nebuchodnezzar, and the handwriting on the wall for Belshazzar) won for him high office in the reigns of several Babylonian Kings. Daniel was also acknowledged to be the greatest diviner and seer of Babylon.

Dante, Alighieri (1265-1321). The Italian author of the *Divine Comedy*, statesman, and mystic, is one of the foremost figures in the history of literature. Not only is he the greatest of all Italian writers, but he set the style for all subsequent writing in Italy; his influence on writers in the Western World has been acknowledged in every generation up to the present. His knowledge of Medieval philosophy made him the interpreter of all Medieval Europe. Though he wrote a number of surpassing works in addition to the *Divine Comedy*, so tremendous are the literary qualities of that epic (its music, imagination, thought, and detail), and so overwhelming is the mystical revelation of the climax, that the work enjoys the status of a universal masterpiece.

Daphomancy. Divination in which the laurel is used. If it crackled when burning, the augury was benign, but if it failed to crackle it was an evil omen.

Dark-faces, Sons or Lords of The. These Asuras (q.v.), having incarnated in Atlantis (q.v.), raised a rebellion against the ruler of the famed mystery center—the City of the Golden Gates (q.v.).

Darshan (Hinduism). The blessing which is received upon viewing a saintly person. However, among the Jews it means a preacher who expounds Jewish law or scriptures.

Dasyus (Hinduism). These are evil spirits who prey equally on gods and on men.

Dava. Among the Tibetans, the astrological word for the moon.

Davenport Brothers (1841-1911). Ira Erastus and William Henry. American mediums of whom outstanding manifestations of physical phenomena were reported. Although they gave many public demonstrations in America, England, and France, they were never detected in fraud. No knots could hold them; mysterious hands played tricks with the investigators while the mediums were tied and immobile. In France they demonstrated before the Emperor and Empress Napoleon with a party of forty guests at the palace of St. Cloud. They also appeared before the Czar in St. Petersburg, and visited Australia.

Davis, Andrew Jackson. The Poughkeepsie Seer (1826-1910), famous medium and author of many Spiritualist books which had a great influence on the development of ideas about Spiritualism in his time. Born of uneducated parents in poor circumstances, Davis developed as a clairvoyant and clairaudient, but received no education until the age of sixteen, when he was apprenticed to a shoe-maker. After some experimenting with Mesmerism, he recounted a strange experience in 1844, during the course of which he said he met Galen and Swedenborg (q. v.) and received mental illumination. From that time he began to dictate many instructive books while in the trance state, and was able to answer difficult questions correctly. His Hebrew quotations were vouched for by Dr. George Busch, Professor of Hebrew at New York University. The publication of his great work: *The Principles of Nature, her Divine Revelations, and a Voice to Mankind,* was an overwhelming success; it ran to thirty-four editions in less than thirty years and made Davis famous. As head of a band of enthusiasts, he published a paper "Univercoelum." Late in life he retired to a small Boston bookshop where he sold books and herbal remedies.

Days of Creation. In most mythic creations it symbolizes vast epochs, not single days.

Dead Sea Scrolls. Ancient texts, written by a Jewish monastic order whose headquarters at Qumran dated from the end of second century B.C. to A.D. 70. Fragments of these scrolls have been found in caves since 1947. The community is generally identified with the Essenes, although this is not certain. The scrolls consist mostly of manuscripts and commentaries of Old Testament scriptures, and Rules for the Congregation of Qumran. Of special interest is matter relating to a certain "teacher of righteousness" antedating Jesus; this teacher was a member of the sect.

Deae Matres. Mother goddesses, usually three, belief in whom spread from Rome and Gaul throughout the Celtic regions of the Roman Empire and notably to the German Rhineland. The *Matronae,* as they are sometimes called, are generally shown in statues with fruit or viands.

Deane, Mrs. Ada Emma. English spirit photographer, who gave many sittings at the W.T. Stead Borderland Library. The A.S.P.R. in 1921 testified to a remarkable sitting with Dr. Allerton Cushman, Director of the National Laboratories of Washington, in which a startling likeness of his daughter appeared on the plate. Hereward Carrington (q.v.) tested this medium with success and reported the details in the Journal of A.S.P.R., May 1925.

Death. In the psychic, mystic, and occult, death is a fact of central importance; just as it is in most of the significant myths and religions. The great mystery of death has exercised man from his first days on earth until the present. Most cultures possess a concept of life after death. Unquestionably, in early societies, the fact of death was difficult to accept; often it was seen as the result of some malevolent person or influence—a concept still prevalent in many primitive communities. Many early societies regarded the corpse as dangerous; and in ancient Egypt and China, for example, elaborate ceremonies were utilized to protect the living against the soul of the dead. The return of the dead soul was universally feared. With Hinduism and concepts of reincarnation and karma (qq.v.), death was viewed as part of the cycle that leads to perfection and Moksha (q.v.); in Buddhism it leads to perfection through the attainment of Nirvana (q.v.). Spiritualism, Anthroposophy, and Theosophy see death as the casting off of the earthly garment—the physical body, and becoming the etheric body; and, following the notions of Hinduism and Buddhism, see man achieving his salvation after physical death through an evolution to higher planes of consciousness.

Death Dance. A widespread ritual engaged in to commune with the dead. Often it was performed to mollify a dead soul or to exorcise a demonic spirit.

Dee, John (1527–1608). One of the most remarkable figures in Elizabethan England, his cluster of eminent talents—as a mathematician, multi-sided scientist, clergyman, astrologer, and occultist-extraordinary made him much sought after. He was a favorite of Queen Elizabeth (for whom he used most of his talents), scientific advisor to Parliament, and highly favored by Emperor Rudolf II of Bohemia. He is best remembered, however, for his career as an occultist, having been accused of practicing sorcery against Queen Mary (though acquitted); his long interest in crystal gazing; and his explorations in astrology (cast the day for Queen Elizabeth's coronation), necromancy, alchemy, and demonology. All these made him famous in his own day throughout Europe. Unfortunately, owing to his trusting nature, he was duped by the unscrupulous Edward Kelley, an alchemist who claimed the skill of transmuting base metal into gold, bringing upon Dee a host of troubles. Dee wrote many works on mathematics, science, the occult, and was instrumental in preserving both England's colonial expansion and her scientific and cultural history.

DeFerriem, Madame. German medium and psychic whose phenomenal predictions astonished the world in the late 19th and early 20th centuries. She forecast, in 1896, a mining disaster that occurred in 1900 in Bohemia, her details so accurate many described it as an eyewitness description. In 1899, she predicted a devastating fire to occur on the New York waterfront, and again her descriptive details were eerily accurate. She predicted a volcanic eruption in the West Indies and the correct year of Alfred Dreyfus's prison release when his case seemed doomed.

Deiseal. A magical practice in Ireland of walking around certain sacred objects with the right hand pointing to them. Used as a ritual to obtain good luck, cure disease, gain protection.

Déja Vu. The feeling of having previously experienced an event that is being encountered for the first time. The phenomenon requires several theories to be adequately comprehended, for the possibilities include not only an imbalance in the physiology of perception, but also a memory from a previous incarnation and memory of a precognition of the future. Psychics also utilize this ability.

Deleuze, Jean Phillipe François (1753–1835). French scientist who advanced the work of animal magnetism and human rapport in mesmerism, and advocated the use of clairvoyants, mediums, etc. in the diagnosis of disease. He wrote a number of books illustrating his theories. (See: *Treatise on the Faculty of Prevision*)

Delphic Oracle. The most famous and most powerful oracle of ancient Greece situated at the foot of Mt. Parnassus. It was the shrine of Apollo and Dionysius. The priestess Pythia, seated on a golden tripod above a fissure through which came an intoxicating vapor, uttered her replies to questions in a frenzied trance. Her replies were interpreted by a priest. Since the answers were universally revered in Greece, they were enormously influential in the public, private, religious, political, and social life of the nation.

Deluge. Memories and experiences of floods throughout human history have been the source of many religious traditions and mythological beliefs and rituals. The Old Testament story of Noah and "the flood" is very similar to the Babylonian story of "the flood." Stories of "the flood" are to be found in Persia, China, India, etc.

Dematerialisation. The disintegration and disappearance of matter, or a materialized form which can occur at physical seances. Occasionally, small objects have also disappeared. If these reappear elsewhere, they are known as apports. (See: *Apports*)

Demiurge. The creator of the world in Greek mythology, and a skilled worker for the people. In Gnostic thought, an occult being who created the world in subordination to God.

Demogorgon. In the magical rites of the late Roman Empire, he was the most feared of the underworld gods, his powers so mysterious and terrible, that his mere name produced feelings of intense fright.

Demoniac. In the Roman Catholic Church, a person had first to be declared a "demoniac" (that is, one possessed by a demon, devil, or any evil spirit) before the rite of exorcism could be performed. Jesus had this magical power of "casting out" demons and devils.

Demonology. Systems of demonology have been developed by most peoples for dealing with demons—supernatural beings in rank below the gods who concern themselves with the affairs of men. Among the ancients there were an immense number of demons, having developed from a belief in the ghosts of the dead who wander the world as bodiless spirits; also from dreaming of strange beings while asleep. Originally considered neutral, in time good and bad demons became recognized. In religion, the good appear as guardian angels and patron saints, and in spiritualism as the "spirit guides" of the mediums, while the evil are seen as instruments of Satan. It is from the religion of Zoroastrianism that these classifications derive, passing on from Judaism to Christianity. Exorcists, a special order of the priesthood,

were responsible for expelling evil spirits from persons or from
places. The ogres of the nursery tales are possibly the oldest demons;
the Greeks had fauns, satyrs, naiads, and dryads; the Romans had
Lemures, spirits of the dead, who they worshipped as the Manes; to
the Scandinavians belonged the trolls, to the Celts and Teutons the
giants; among the Slavs there were blood-sucking vampires; among
the Muslems were the Jinn and Afrit; in India there were the Rakshas;
for the Japanese there were the Omi. Animal forms of demons were
prevalent in ancient Egypt and India; these were known as werewolves in medieval Europe; witches had their black cats; and in the
beginning, the serpent corrupted Eve in the Garden of Eden. The science of demonology has played an important part in the development
of black magic (q.v.).

Demonomancy. Using demons in divination—by their oracles or the
answers they provide to those who summon them.

Denis, Leon (1846–1927). Was successor to Allan Kardec. French
Spiritualist, medium, and author of many books.

Denk, Hans (d. 1527). German mystic, born in Nuremberg and rector
of the school of St. Sebald, he was a humanist, an Anabaptist, and an
important mystic of the Protestant Reformation. Steeped in German
mysticism and Christian Platonism, his many booklets were notably influential. Like thousands of Anabaptists of his time he had to flee from
town to town because of his views. He is also remembered for having
baptized Hans Hut, one of the very important Protestant reformers
who founded the Huterite Brethren.

Dermography. The appearance of writing on the skin, similar to stig-
matic writing except that it does not last for very long. Some mediums
have given answers to messages in this way. It is known that similar
marks can be produced in certain cases by hypnotic suggestion.

Dervish (Sufism). A member of an Islamic order particularly in the
Near East, which has developed from the Sufi movement (q.v.) dervishes are generally ascetics and mendicants. Of the many separate
orders of dervishes, the *Mevleviva,* founded by the memorable Sufi
mystic Jalaluddin Rudin (q.v.) about 1273 is known as the "whirling
dervishes" since they engage in a whirling dance that climaxes in a
trance or ecstasy.

Descartes, Rene (1596–1650). Famous French rationalist philosopher
who starting from the premise "I think, therefore I am," built up a demonstrable system of philosophy and founded the rationalist school
which believes that reason may attain knowledge, owing nothing to
sense experience (a prior knowledge). Mathematics and logic are good
instances of knowledge so gained.

Descendant (Astrology). That degree of the ecliptic which is setting.
Opposite the Ascendant.

Desmond, Shaw (1876–1960). Well-known Irish poet and Spiritualist speaker who wrote many psychic books. He was a firm believer in reincarnation, claiming remembrance of some of his former lives.

D'Esperance, Mme. Elizabeth (1855–1919). A non-professional medium who exhibited the whole range of mediumistic phenomena. Many attempts to discover fraud were unsuccessful but damaged the medium's health. In order that she herself might be seen at the same time as the materialized figures, she usually sat outside the cabinet. An interesting feature is her own account of the curious "community of sensation" she experienced with the materialized form. If, for instance, the form was embraced, she felt this in her own person. It was with this medium that Alex N. Aksakov (q.v.) witnessed the famous case of partial dematerialization of the medium from the waist downwards. Remarkable apport (q.v.) phenomena included the production of an exotic Indian plant (Ixoro Crocota), 22 in. high, with a stem filling the neck of a bottle containing the roots, and on another occasion, a great Golden Lily, seven feet high.

Deucalion. Son of Prometheus and in Greek mythology their Noah. When the earth was flooded by Zeus, Deucalion and his wife Pyrrha built an ark. At the culmination of the flood, Zeus advised them to throw their mother's bones over their shoulders which they understood to mean the stones of the earth. Those Deucalion threw became men, while those thrown by Pyrrha turned into women.

Deuce. In the mythology of ancient Britain she was the personification of evil, later equated with the devil.

Deva (Hinduism). A celestial being. Devas may be less than man, though there are gods higher than devas who yet are called devas. One class of devas is engaged in being builders, evolvers, and leaders of hierarchies; being their own innermost selves, they have passed the "Ring-Pass-Not" (q.v.), separating the spiritual from the divine.

Devachan (Hinduism, Lamaism). Describes an intermediate state between incarnations. Not to be confused with the spheres of Spiritualism. Among Tibetans the transcendental heaven—world to which the purified astral body ascends.

Devil. Lucifer or Satan (q.v.) who as one of the angels rebelled against God and was exiled from heaven into hell. Though chiefly considered to be the principle of evil, there have been groups like the Cathari (q.v.) and The Church of Satan (q.v.) which take other or opposing views.

Devil Worship. The worship of Satan or Lucifer along with other evil deities by nations or cultures has an ancient and continuing history. Satan worship or diabolism may stem from the Persian dual system in which Ormuzd and Ahriman (qq.v.) represent the good and bad prin-

ciples. The Sabbat rituals of witchcraft practiced the worship of
demons, in which the devil may be evoked to institute a pact. In the
church of Lucifer, there are those who adore the evil principle, and
those who claim the devil as the true God, since Adonai and Jehovah
are the true destroyers of man; therefore in the Black Mass (q.v.),
consecrated wafers taken from churches are destroyed as a ritual
act. Among primitive peoples, devils are their deities, this worship being widespread in South American and African tribes. For example,
the Uapes of Brazil worship Jurupari, a fiend-like deity, in the consecration of young men. Among the Chinese, throughout their history,
many practices have been used to placate devils; and similar practices obtain in Burma and Cambodia—though these practices must be
differentiated from worship.

Devil's Girdle. As a sign of devotion to the devil, witches in medieval
times were accused of wearing the *Devil's Girdle*. However, magical
girdles were a popular article among the people.

DeWohl, Louis. Novelist and astrologer, whose predictions to British
Intelligence of what Hitler's astrologers were telling him may have enabled England to strike against the Nazi war machine, in World War
II, with measurable effectiveness. DeWohl wrote a number of articles
in the *American Astrology* magazine describing this extraordinary
episode.

Dexter (Astrology). A term in astrology which means an aspect (q.v.),
this is computed backward against the order of the Signs (q.v.), and
has the aspected body elevated above the aspecting body. Most astrologers, utilizing modern astronomy, depart from Ptolmaic interpretations of Dexter and Sinister (q.v.) and assert that the desirability of
these aspects is to a degree weighted by the nature of the planets involved.

Dhama (Buddhism). This word has many meanings, each depending on
its usage in the passage. Some of its meanings are: system, law, form,
religion, virtue, cause, cosmic order.

Dharana (Hinduism). That level in Yoga meditation where the mind
learns to fix itself on one single object.

Dharma (Hinduism, Buddhism). This means right religion, right philosophy, right science, and the right union of these three— therefore,
they are the laws of religion, the laws of conduct. For example, the
Dharmasutras describe the regulations for the four forms of Brahman
life. It also refers to the body of cosmic principles by which all things
exist. In Buddhism, it is the ideal truth—the teaching of Buddhism,
and it is called *Dhamma*. Further, in Hinduism it signifies the judge of
the dead when Yama (q.v.) performs this function.

Dhyana (Hinduism, Buddhism, and Jainism). Meditation in the form of

an uninterrupted state of mental concentration upon a single object—
a religious object being one of the most important articles to use
toward gaining *Samadhi* (q.v.), the existence of utter tranquility.
Samadhi is that point of balance in the act of meditation which
achieves a mystic state of serene contemplation. In Chinese it is Ch'an;
also in Japanese Zen Buddhism (qq.v.).

Diablerie. Refers to sorcery, black magic (qq.v.) or devilish arts or
tricks, particularly those which are melodramatic and gaudy, weird
or uncanny. The scene of demon lore or haunts of the devil.

Diableros. Among the Sonoras, an American Indian tribe, the
Diableros are evil practitioners of Black Magic. They claim to possess
the power to transform themselves into animals, notably crows and
coyotes.

Diabolarch. The ruler of the devils.

Diabolepsy. In psychiatry and religion as also in the occult—being
possessed by a devil, or a delusion of such possession.

Diabolism. Belief in and worship of the devil. Also a ritual or act of
sorcery which may be initiated or done with the assistance of the
devil. (See: Satanism).

Diakka. The famous American psychic Andrew Jackson Davis (q.v.)
coined this term to apply to evil, ignorant, or undeveloped spirits.

Dialectical Society. Founded in 1867 "to investigate the phenomena
alleged to be Spiritual Manifestations, and to report thereon." The
published report in 1871, basing itself on the evidence obtained,
verified the existence of psychic phenomena. It is historically important as the first organized effort to study the subject scientifically.

Diamond. A very potent gem that offers many powers and protections
to its wearers. It has been credited with magical powers since ancient
times. Many Church fathers believed that the blood of the Cross, like
the diamond, softens the heart of man.

Diana. One of the earliest of the ancient Italian goddesses, worshipped throughout the peninsula, particularly at the grove near Aricia
where she symbolized the deity of the wood and the helper of women
in childbirth. Here the chief priest, named the "King of the Wood,"
who killed his predecessor with the aid of the magic "Golden Bough,"
ruled until he too was killed in the same fashion by his successor.
After Apollo and Artemis were brought to Rome, Diana was identified
with Artemis. In occult literature and practice she is significant as the
moon goddess. (See: J.G. Frazer's *The Golden Bough*).

Dicyanin Screens. Devices for making the human aura visible to normal sight, invented by Dr. Walter J. Kilner (1847–1920) of St.
Thomas's Hospital. They work by inducing eye fatigue in the short visi-

ble purple range thus making the eye temporarily more sensitive to waves beyond the normally visible. Two small dicyanin screens can be made into spectacles. They are then commonly referred to as "Kilner goggles."

Didyma. An oracle sanctuary of Apollo near Miletus. Controlled by a priestly class, it was, along with the oracle of Delphi, famous throughout antiquity. Egyptian Pharaohs and Lydian Kings honored the oracle. It was destroyed by the Persians. The rebuilt shrine is now one of the most magnificent ruins of the ancient world.

Dionysius the Areopogite, Saint. An Athenian Christian converted by Saint Paul and believed the first bishop of Athens. About 500 A.D. there appeared writings forged in his name (10 letters and 4 treatises) which later became a seminal influence in the Middle Ages, both on the development of scholasticism, and, more lastingly, on the development of Christian mysticism. They influenced such prominent thinkers as Albertus Magnus and St. Thomas Aquinas (qq.v.) and such eminent medieval mystics as Eckhart, Tauler, and Rolle (qq.v.). Central to his revelations is the description of the soul's ascent to God in ecstasy through a mystical union with God by way of "the darkness of unknowing," which is a process of suppressing the senses and all thought. Neo-Platonism and the theology of angels were transmitted to Western minds by way of these writings.

Dipper, Wise Men of the Great (Hinduism). In the ancient religion these were the 7 Holy Rishis who were embodied in 7 stars known as the constellation of Ursa Major.

Direct Drawing and Painting (Spiritualism). Psychic drawing and painting where the hand of the medium is not used, the materials combining directly to produce an artistic result. These are sometimes found to bear a striking resemblance to existing works of art.

Direct Voice (Spiritualism). The phenomenon of a voice proceeding from an artificial larynx, made from ectoplasmic material extracted from the medium and sitters.

Direct Writing. Psychography. Writing produced without visible contact with the medium, though synchronized movements of the hands have been known to accompany it (Eusapia Paladino (q.v.)). Partly materialized hands have also produced written messages. Writing has been obtained in a sealed metal box.

Dis or Dispater. Among the ancient Romans the god of the underworld, similar to the Greek Pluto.

Disassociation. Term used in psychic research for an independent activity of a part of the mind which behaves in some way like a separate individual.

Discarnate (Spiritualism). Not incarnate. Not possessing a body of flesh. Usually descriptive of a spirit person who has died in the earthly sense.

Divinas. Fortunetellers and diviners who are extremely popular throughout Latin America and famous for their ability to locate the missing property of their clients. They gaze into a glass, a jewel, or a bowl of water to achieve their psychic powers.

Divination. The method of gaining knowledge of the unknown, or foreseeing future events by use of omens, augury, or psychical talents of a diviner in which supernatural powers are implied as cooperating, has been universally practiced from the most ancient times. Almost everything has been used (stones, ashes, beans, cards, animal entrails, letters and words, chance meetings, etc.) in performing divination. But some of the most important are: astrology, oracular utterances, crystal gazing, haruspication, dreams, numerology, palmistry, cards, and the many forms of psychic revelations—by shamans, augurs, mediums, and psychics. All the great ancient cultures—China, Egypt, Babylonia, Persia, Greece, Rome, and Mexico—developed and utilized the important arts of divination.

Divine World. In Theosophy, the first or highest world, the world that was first created by the divine impulse to exert its creative power. This world is not attainable by man in his present state. Formerly known as the Adi plane.

Divining Rod. A V-shaped rod of various springy materials, traditionally a twig of hazel. When the dowser holds it in a state of tension the apex will move when a source of water or some specified hidden objective is traversed. According to J. Cecil Maby (*Physics of the Divining Rod*) there would appear to be a variation of muscle tone somehow influenced by the hidden sources, of which the twig becomes a sensitive indicator. But recent studies seem to indicate that chance or the diviner's sensitivity to visible clues (of which he is unaware) are the elements responsible for success.

Dixon, Jeane L. This world-famous Washington, D.C. psychic, writer, real estate broker, public-spirited citizen (founder of Children to Children, Inc; Chmn. of Christmas Seal Campaign, 1968) and first Anglo honorary Navajo princess, is probably best known for prophesying John F. Kennedy's death only a week before his assassination with her famous statement: "The President's going to be shot!" She has been consulted by many notable personalities, including Franklin D. Roosevelt. She has also predicted such well-documented events as Senator Ted Kennedy's injury in an aviation accident; the Alaska earthquake of 1964; Russia's creation of the Sputnik; the death of Pope John; the death of Dag Hammarskjold; and a long list of election results including Presidential contests. She has never charged for her consultations, believing this would mar her talent as a psychic. (See: *A Gift of Prophecy*, Ruth Montgomery)

Dixon Smith, Lt. Col. Spiritualist author who proposed a theoretical extension of known physics, based on the quantum theory, to account for the interpenetration of spirit spheres of existence with the earthly state.

Djemscheed, The Cup of. In ancient Persia, a famous divination cup which was filled with the elixir of immortality. Mirrored in this magical cup was the world, and it revealed all that was good and evil. It was the basis of many songs, poems, and myths, for no less than the prosperity of Persia resulted from the auguries emanating from this sacred cup.

Docetists. Early Gnostic-Christian sect who, considering matter to be totally inferior and impure, maintained that Christ had never taken the human body—it being a phantom—and that the Crucifixion, Resurrection, and Ascension were merely illusions.

Dogs. For many years ghost hunters in England have used dogs to determine the presence of ghosts since dogs with their extraordinary capacities of hearing and smell have frequently revealed signs of being terrified in the presence of ghosts.

Donnelly, Ignatius (1831–1901). Lawyer, publisher, author, political reformer, statesman, and visionary, he was an extraordinary figure on the American scene. He was the Republican lieutenant governor of Minnesota, a congressman for 6 years (1863–1869), editor of two influential newspapers, *Anti-Monopolist* and *Representative*, in which he wrote his radical views. He was founder of several third parties, and the leading theorist of the Populist movement. But he was also a visionary who in his books *Atlantis: the Antediluvian World, Ragnarok: the Age of Fire and Gravel, The Great Cryptogram*, and *Caesar's Column: a Story of the Twentieth Century*, was not only an immensely successful writer, but his prophetic insight has proven him a seer. His "Atlantis" has gone through more than 50 editions, and has been a phenomenal best-seller since 1882, the year it was published.

Door. In ancient times many tribal groups looked upon doors into buildings as possessing magic properties. They might be inhabited by guardian spirits, or be decorated with charms or amulets. But most particularly, death was seen as a door to another world.

Doorkeeper (Spiritualism). The personal spirit control of a medium, said to be responsible for the maintenance of the physical body during the production of mediumistic phenomena. North American Indians and Zulus are commonly met with in this capacity, presumably for their qualities of steadfastness and reliability. They work in close cooperation with a band of spirits who are combined for some specific purpose connected with phenomena.

Doppelganger. A person's double (q.v.) in ghost form who haunts him; usually visible only to himself.

Double (Spiritualism). Also known as etheric body. Interpenetrating counterpart of the physical body and linked to it by an extensible cord. Normally coincidental, but capable of detachment under certain conditions, spontaneous or induced. Photographic evidence for the existence of the double has been produced by Alex N. Aksakov (q.v.) and Julien Ochorowicz (q.v.).

Double Axe. In Minoan Crete, this sacred occult symbol made of gold and bronze had a double head with the two blades joined and ending in points at both ends.

D'Ourches, Comte. In the spiritualistic history of late 19th century France this magnetist and necromancer played a key role, for he associated himself with Baron de Guldenstubbe (q.v.) in making psychic phenomena respectable. He and Guldenstubbe were able to set up a number of spiritualistic circles which achieved such phenomenal results that both became famous.

Dowden, Hester (Mrs. Hester Travers-Smith, 1868–1949). Automatist from Dublin, Ireland, and psychic investigator. The medium operated blindfolded, with her hand on a heart-shaped pointer mounted on felt pads. With this device, words were spelt out at the rate of 2,000 per hour. Some automatic writing was also produced; among communications received were facsimiles of Oscar Wilde's script and signature, Ellen Terry's and Fanny Stirling's.

Dowsing. Water divining by rod, twig or pendulum. Also known as rhabdomancy, Radiesthesia. Nowadays dowsing techniques are applied to many fields: healing, the finding of missing objects or people, mineral prospecting, sexing of chicks, diagnosis by analysis of blood or sputum spots.

Dracontia. Since the Dragon (q.v.) was a widespread occult symbol, temples dedicated to his worship became popular. Two of the most noted were those in Karnak, Egypt, and Carnac in Brittany.

Dragon. In hermetic philosophy the dragon symbolizes the everlasting rebirth of things. The center of dragon mythology seems to have been of Babylonian origin, the dragon being a crocodile-like supernatural creature with some aspects of an eagle, hawk, or lion and most often exhibiting wings. It made fearful noises, breathed smoke or fire, and lived near water. In the early Hebrew tradition the dragon was regarded as the major source of evil in the world. In China, in Taoism, the dragon represented the vitality symbol. In Japan, the Dragon King was a beneficent patron to the great, magical hero Tawara Toda. In

Northern Europe, the dragon was the challenge to the hero who killed the beast on his road to spiritual enlightenment. In Christianity, Saint George was the slayer of the dragon, among his many heroic deeds. Western occultism, portraying the dragon biting his own tail, signifies him as the master of the future, since everything is destroyed or dies but is reborn, for nothing dies.

Drapery, Spirit (Spiritualism). Spirit robes. The simple flowing garments worn by spirit people in their own sphere are usually so described. If spirits wish to give evidence of survival they have to remember their former appearance, and somehow convey an image to the medium which can be recognized. This would have to include the appropriate dress. The drapery observed at materialization phenomena is ectoplasmic and is said to be drawn from the actual clothing of the medium.

Dream Body. See Astral body and Projection.

Dream Communications. These come usually as warnings to the individual, and are vivid enough in their impression to influence actions subsequently taken. This could well be a form of temporary clairvoyance or clairaudience on the part of the dreamer.

Dream Interpretation. Since the earliest times, divination by dreams was an important occult profession—in ancient Egypt, Babylonia, India, China, Greece, and Rome, for example. While no two diviners agree on the meaning of objects found in a dream, there is a basic residue common to them all. Nonetheless, that dreams go by contraries has become an important concept; that is, what the soul experienced in the dream was just the opposite of what should develop in the waking state. Visions which occur during sleep, known as the psychic dream in which future events are foreseen, are not related to dream interpretation.

Dream Prophecies. Are repetitive and often accompanied by sweating and trembling on awakening. They usually consist of some kind of prevision, quite detailed of some of imminent disaster. Many authenticated cases have been recorded.

Dream, Prophetic. Many dreams, those that have been historically reported with their interpretations (like those of Joseph to the Pharoah, Daniel to Nebuchadnezzar, etc.), those that are literally prophetic of future events, and those that psychiatrists describe as forecasting a wish that in the future comes true—are called dreams that are prophetically very significant.

Dream Telepathic. A rich history of dreams that are telepathic, revealing events that are occurring simultaneously with the dreamer's dream, has been reported throughout thousands of years. Many psychics have this gift in a highly developed form. But psychiatrists report dreams which are produced in the mind of the dreamer by transmission from other dreamers near him, especially in those of husbands and wives, and lovers.

Dreaming True. The possession of control and consciousness whilst in the dream state. This occasionally occurs spontaneously with some, but according to Dr. Hereward Carrington it can be acquired with practice.

Dreams. In the history of myth, religion, and the occult, dreams have played a dominant role. It is the dream that is responsible for the concepts such as the soul, life after death, supernatural entities, ghosts, tribal mythologies, psychic revelations, and continuity with astral realms. Among primitive cultures, for example, the dream often performed a primary function in medicine, magic, career selection, art, ceremonies, war, myths, and other activities. Contemporary scientific exploration of the dream has been impressed with the dimensions of its psychic relevance and the many unknown aspects that must still be explored. Spiritualists, Theosophists, and Anthroposophists maintain the possibility of visits by the double during the sleep state to the spirit spheres. Some spirit communicators have stated that they need to be in a dream state themselves in order to communicate.

Dreisch, Hans. Prominent German psychic investigator and Professor of Philosophy at University of Leipzig. President of S.P.R., 1926–27. Became convinced of the actuality of psychic phenomena. Author of several books on psychical research.

Druids. In ancient Gaul, Britain and Ireland, Druids were priests possessing great wisdom—being diviners, magicians, scientists, prophets, teachers, astronomers, physicians, and judges whose rank was just below the king's. With such an array of powers, Druids exercised absolute authority in a highly ritualistic religion, while their psychic talents enabled them to cause people to fall asleep, become ill, or die. Further, their knowledge of medicine and astronomy was very extensive. Unfortunately, their learning was not written down, and initiates, by verbal instruction, often spent 20 years learning the sacred, scientific, and occult lore. Worship of the sun was central to their religion. There was also a large pantheon of deities. They believed in the immortality of the soul, the doctrine of the transmigration of souls; and to them the mistletoe and oak were sacred. Once a year the confederation of Druids met in Gaul, probably on the site of Chartres. So powerful was their influence that the Romans tried to destroy them, but failed. Later, however, they succumbed to Christianity. Much has been conjectured and written about their relationship to Stonehenge, and prehistoric ruins in France, Scandinavia and elsewhere on the Continent (the menhirs of Carnac in Brittany, and many other stone circles and megalithic monuments). But the evidence, to date, remains debatable.

Druj (Zoroastrianism). A band of female demons.

Drujust (Zoroastrianism). Follower of the Druj (q.v.).

Druses. These Syrian people, who adhere to the faith developed by Hakim (a Fatimate caliph of Egypt) in 1029 A.D., believe the founder of their religion was an incarnation of the spirit of God. Their faith is a mixture of Muslem, Jewish, and Christian concepts suffused with Sufi mysticism.

Dualism (1). One of the fundamental philosophical concepts: that there exist two realities—a physical versus a spiritual; also, two opposing cosmic forces—one good, the other evil.

Dualism (2). An important basic notion of religious, hermetic, and occult writings and practices. The Manichaens, Zoroastrians, many mythologies, have held that the two principle powers of the world, forever opposed and warring with each other are: good and evil; God and Satan; God or the supreme spirit versus the world; spirit and matter; soul and body.

Dual Personality. Usually advanced by psychologists as an alternative to spirit control. There are many well-known pathological cases of dual personality, where the one body appears to be the battle-ground for conflicting personalities.

Dugpas (Lamaism). Much feared and known as the "Red Caps," they are malicious, evil sorcerers, and black magicians who in earlier times worshipped devils. They are the opposite of the Gelukpas (q.v.).

Duguid, David. A Scottish medium of the late 19th century who was famous for being able to paint when in a trance. These paintings, frequently copies of Dutch masters, and purportedly painted by them, were quite good. Amazingly, most of these paintings were done in complete darkness.

Dulia. Although in Roman Catholicism this is the worship offered to saints and angels, this was also an important part of the tradition of Hebrew mysticism, which later took a definite form in some aspects of alchemy and in the Cabala (q.v.).

Dunne, J.W. Originator of a philosophic conception of the nature of time, the universe, and the veridical nature of dreams. He wrote several books on his theory of serialism, in which he takes the view that man's consciousness follows a prescribed path through events; the "travelling now" he calls it. This accounts for possible pre-vision by a widening of the perceptive field of attention during sleep.

Dweller on the Threshold. An occult term for the "doorkeeper" (q.v.).

Dyaus (Hinduism). This masculine Vedic deity represents sky or heaven. The Greek term Zeus, and the Latin Deus and Jovis are related to this Hindu word.

Dybbuk. The Cabala describes the evil spirits or souls of the dead that enter the body of a living person and control him. In the ancient tradition of Hebrew mysticism under the name of "gilgul" this belief persisted and was resurrected by the Cabalists of Spain and Provence. The "wandering" soul of a sinner had to wander from one body to another (animal, inanimate object, or human being) until it had become pure and could return to the En Sof (q.v.).

Dynamistograph. A device which was created under spirit guidance by the Dutch physicists, Matla and Zaalberg Van Zelst, for direct communication without a medium.

Dzo. Some West African tribes use this immensely important term to mean "mana" (q.v.).

Dzyan, The Book of. H.P. Blavatsky (q.v.) credits this book as the generative "source" for her own famous work, *The Secret Doctrine.*

Ee

Ea. The powerful Sumerian god who was notable for his contradictory qualities. Primarily the god of waters beneath the earth, he was, too, the god of beneficence, but also of cunning and deceit; he was hailed as the wisest of the gods, but on occasion he could be extraordinarily foolish. Ea was also the oracle god and the patron of the exorcists. His holy waters were used in ceremonies of exorcism to cleanse all places, things, and persons inhabited by evil spirits. He was also the central figure in the deluge myth, who warned the Babylonian Noah (Utnapistim) of the future disaster.

Eagle. The mana (q.v.) of the eagle has been admired by man from the most ancient times; consequently the bird has been one of the most ancient symbols of the supernatural and the occult. In Egypt and Greece it was sacred to the Sun; it was also the venerated bird of Zeus. For the learned Druids it was transcendent, their foremost divinity. The Roman Legions adopted it as a consecrated mascot.

"Ear of Dionysius" Case. A notable cross correspondence of discarnate minds. (See: Balfour, Earl of)

Earthbound (Spiritualism). Spirits who are still operating close to earth conditions owing to old attachments, habits or ignorance of their state. Fixed habits are said to be the strongest factor in affecting the state of a person after death. Earthbound spirits are sometimes held to be responsible for hauntings. Unable to satisfy their earthly desires, they can exert a bad influence on earthlings of similar habits.

Earth Plane. All that pertains to the ordinary earth life, as distinct from the spirit world.

Easter. Fertility rites and nature's power of regeneration have made spring the magically potent time of year for mankind. It has been celebrated by every ancient tribe and nation in the symbolic ritual of the "death and rebirth" of their great gods. But the miracle of Christ's return from death and resurrection has given it a new meaning as the supreme sacrifice of love. The Norse Ostara, the semitic Astarte and Ishtar, and the Hebrew Esther (qq.v.) are sources of the name.

Ebisu. In Japanese mythology one of the gods of luck who is the particular benefactor of tradesmen and fishermen.

Eblis. The Satan of the Muslims, and originally one of the angels closest to God. He embodies the elements of fire. Eblis is also known as Haris. He is doomed to roam the world until the Day of Judgment.

Echidna. In Greek myth a monster, half woman and half serpent, who mothered a brood of monsters: Chimaera; Orthus (the many-headed dog); the hundred-headed dragon who guarded the apples of the Hesperides; the Colchian dragon; the Sphinx; Gorgon; the Nemean Lion; and the Eagle which consumed the liver of Prometheus.

Eckhart, Meister (Von Hocheim) (c.1260–c.1328). Among the eminent mystics, Eckhart takes his place with the class of great intellectuals. Acknowledged as Germany's greatest speculative mystic, he was a Dominican monk who rose to high office in the Church, being praised as a talented administrator and his nation's most popular preacher. For Eckhart, God is in every human being; nothing is apart from God; God himself is nothing (in the sense that nothing can be said about him); and the attainment of the oneness with God through seclusion is man's highest goal. The Church finally labeled him heretical.

Eclecticism. The creation of a unity from diverse notions. It was the famous Alexandrian School in Egypt (from the first to the fourth centuries A.D.) which combined the oriental and occidental thought and created a unity of occult and mystical concepts which has dominated all Western tradition in these disciplines.

Ecstasy. That state of emotional rapture, exhilaration, and mental exaltation, common to mystics and saints, during which a sort of trance prevails. Ecstasy embodies a oneness of consciousness, exclusion of the world of sense, passivity, intensity of joyous emotion, visions, and often an immediate divine experience. Supernormal feats have been achieved while in this state. It is engendered in the Yoga state of

"Samadhi" (q.v.) and in certain meditative practices. Many cultures from the earliest times have induced ecstasy by the use of drugs, fasting flagellation, and dancing. To some it comes suddenly, without effort, as witnessed by Plotinus, Eckhart, Pascal, Blake, etc. (qq.v.). While the results of the experience are often unique to each individual, there is a basic core common to the state of ecstasy.

Ectenic Force. A term for Psychic Force (q.v.) coined by Marc Thury.

Ectoplasm (Spiritualism). A subtle living matter present in the physical body primarily invisible but capable of assuming vaporous liquid or solid states and properties. It is extruded usually in the dark from the pores and the various orifices of the body, and is slightly luminous. This substance is held to be responsible for the production of all phenomena classed as "physical," and is the substance out of which materialized forms are built by the spirit operators. In addition they build elastic or rigid rods to produce movement in objects (telekinesis), raps and noises. The levitation of tables and heavy objects is accomplished by building extensible columns under them. Hands have materialized, dipped themselves into molten wax and then dissolved, leaving perfect molds behind that are impossible of duplication by ordinary means, (see Kluski). Ectoplasm has been photographed on many occasions and appears opaque white by infra-red flashlight which is the usual method employed.

Eddas. The Icelandic sagas which relate the history of the mythology and religious beliefs of the Northern European World. The Elder, or Poetic Edda, and the Younger, or Prose Edda, had a profound impact on the poets, bards, religion, government, and civic and social customs of these people.

Eddy, Mary Baker (1821-1910). American founder of the Christian Science movement in 1875. She elaborated her system after receiving healing from Dr. Quimby of "New Thought" movement. The two central doctrines of her famous book, *Science and Health with Key to the Scriptures* (1875), assert that mind controls matter, and that a steadfast belief in God can cure all illness.

Edinburgh Psychic College. Founded in 1932 by Mrs. Ethel Miller to investigate psychic phenomena and to assist in spreading knowledge concerning it.

Edmonds, John Worth ("Judge Edmonds" 1816-1874). Early American champion of Spiritualism who published his experiences in the *New York Courier* as early as 1853. Later he himself developed mediumship and exerted a great influence on the early growth of American Spiritualism.

Edwards, Harry. Famous Spiritualist healer of England. President of the National Federation of Spiritual Healers, he challenged the medical authorities on his test cases of healed "incurables."

Eel. Considered a fish with magical properties by the Egyptians, who worshipped it; but only the priests were permitted to eat it. Some people have believed that the eating of an eel's warm heart instills the spirit of prophecy. The making of magic eels out of flour and the juice of mutton was practiced in the 18th century in England.

Effigy. A representation made of a dead person to serve both as a memorial and a home for his spirit.

Egg, the Orphic. Symbol of unity in Orphism (q.v.); the original mystery of creation; the divine source of the one and the many; and the primal reality in the religious-esoteric teachings of the Orient, Egypt, Greece, Rome, and in the history of alchemistry.

Eglinton, William. English physical medium. Among his most startling feats was recorded that of his own transportation on 16 March 1878 through a ceiling to the floor above (*The Spiritualist,* 22 March 1878).

Ego. In Theosophy, the self-consciousness of the individual, that which says, "I am I;" the consciousness directed back upon itself, recognizing its own mayavi existence as a separate entity. (See: Anthroposophy).

Egregore. All the ancient hunting and agricultural societies engaged in the collective ritual of *egregore* to assure a plenitude of animals for the hunters or sufficient rain for the farmers. While a sorcerer or a witch was the chief figure in the ceremony, the collective community added their energy, the *egregore*—the magical mana (q.v.)—of the whole group, to the exertions of the sorcerer or witch. It is the universal practice of the fertility rites involved in rain making, the details of which have been long forgotten, that has produced the universal symbol of the witch with her phallic broom.

Egyptian Fremasonry. It was established by Cagliostro (q.v.) who utilized many occult disciplines, particularly the vast occult heritage of ancient Egypt. This organization played an important part in the late 18th and through the 19th centuries in disseminating a knowledge of occultism throughout Europe.

Egyptian Hypnotism. In the temples of ancient Egypt hypnotism was utilized by the priests in the treatment of the sick. Both a form of magnetic mesmerism and a sleep-producing technique were used in the temples of Isis, Osiris, and Serapis, These priests were also able to perform some of the most difficult of all operations, those on the brain, by hypnotic methods.

Egyptian Triangle. The Egyptian priests used as a symbol of universal nature a triangle with a base of 4, a perpendicular of 3, and a hypotenuse of 5—the base being Osiris (the male principle), the perpendicular, Isis (the female principle), and the hypotenuse, Horus, the product of the two elements. The mathematical concepts developed in this triangle were applied to the building of the pyramids.

Eidolism. The belief in the survival of souls or ghosts—called eidolon.

Eidolon. See Eidolism.

Eidos, The World of. The fourth sphere, level of consciousness, or the Plane of Color, as described in an alleged communication from F.W.H. Myers (q.v.) to a medium.

Eight Diagrams. The eight triplets of the *I Ching* (q.v.).

Eight, in Some of its Meanings. For the alchemists, salt—since it crystallized in cubes which have 8 vertices, symbolized density of matter and death. The 8th sign of the Zodiac, Scorpio, has been interpreted as symbolizing death, in the sense of the sacrifice of self for the universal, or the community. In ancient Egypt, it was a symbol of blessedness. Among the Hebrews, it was associated with purification. In the Cabala of Agrippa of Nettesheim (q.v.), it is associated with the birth of Dionysos who was an eight-months' child. Some Medieval writers on numbers assigned to 8 the number of immortality. With the ancient Chinese in the practice of divination, eight trigrams were used to determine good and evil fortune. *I Ching—The Book of Changes,* a Confucian classic now world famous, is based on these eight trigrams.

Eightfold Path (Buddhism). The central rule toward the development and achievement of Nirvana, of moral and intellectual maturity, which leads to enlightenment. These are: rightness of belief, resolve, speech, action, livelihood, effort, thought, and meditation. (See: Buddhism)

Ekagara (Hinduism). The base of this important word means "one," hence, a oneness of concentration.

Ekera. Among the East Africans and southern Ethiopians the belief in the survival of the souls of the dead.

Elan Vital. This term used by the French philosopher Henri Bergson (q.v.), and later utilized by other thinkers, indicates the mysterious power in the universe responsible for universal and human evolution.

Electional Astrology. In astrology this represents the most significant time to initiate an action, to start a project, to make an agreement or an appointment. By taking account of the presence of the various planets in the twelve Houses, astrologers are able to indicate what specific projects would meet with the best chance of success.

Electric Girls. A phenomenon usually ascribed to the presence of a poltergeist (q.v.) was attributed to certain girls from whom powerful emanations of electricity flowed. Beginning in France in the 1840's, these girls were able to make objects move, cold winds blow, magnetic needles waver, because of mysterious electrical currents they possessed. The most famous of these girls was Angelique Cottin (q.v.). Several of them were brought from France to America.

Electrical Phenomena (Spiritualism). These have been observed in the seance room. Dr. Ochorowicz discovered the fact that a medium could decrease considerably the electrical resistance of her body, confirming experiments by E.K. Muller of Zurich. Dr. Kilner found that the human aura completely dispersed under a negative charge. Some marks found on sealed photographic plates, after contact with a medium's fingers, suggest radioactivity. (See: Samadhi)

Elementals. Nature spirits who have great power in their natural element—fire, air, earth, and water. Salamanders live in fire; Sylphs in air; Gnomes in earth; Undines in water. These elementals were widely incorporated into many myths throughout early Europe, and later played a part in many literary and musical pieces.

Elementargedanken. A term coined by Adolf P.W. Bastian, a German physician, which means that there are certain elemental ideas common to all mankind because of man's psychic unity. This very interesting concept is related to C.G. Jung's famous notion of the archetypes of the collective unconscious, and to Noam Chomsky's revolutionary and widely accepted theory that there is a basic grammar common to all mankind.

Elementary. Occult term for an astral "shell" which is supposed to account for hauntings and poltergeist phenomena. The theory is that after death this shell gradually disintegrates, the 'wicked' ones lasting the longest.

Elements. Astrologers assign four elements to the twelve signs of the Zodiac: Fire (Aries, Leo, Sagittarius); Earth (Taurus, Virgo, Capricorn); Air (Gemini, Libra, Aquarius); and Water (Cancer, Scorpio, Pisces).

Eleusinian. The Eleusinian Mysteries, in ancient Greece, were associated with the worship of the goddess Demeter, her daughter Persephone, and Dionysus. The Mysteries symbolized the death and resurrection of the seed-corn, but much more importantly it celebrated the resurrection of the human soul, which profoundly affected the lives of the initiates. Eleusis in Attica, Greece, was the site of the sanctuary dedicated to Persephone and Demeter, and from which the mysteries take their name.

Elfstone. Offerings made to elves were placed on this stone.

Elliot, The Rev. G. Maurice. An English clergyman who in the early years of the 20th century campaigned to make the church hospitable to the significance of and to bring psychic phenomena to the notice of the church. He was Secretary to the Churches' Fellowship for Psychical Study and noted author of many works on theological, historical, and psychic subjects.

Elongation. A peculiar phenomenon associated with some physical mediums, in which the body of the medium is altered considerably in stature. D.D. Home (q.v.) exhibited this phenomena on several occasions, once to at least fifty people. His maximum "growth" was recorded as eleven inches. Home's own explanation was that the hip-bone and the short ribs separated to a greater than normal extent. Legs and arms are reported to have lengthened and shortened independently. Other mediums who produced this phenomena were: Florence Cook, Frank Herne, and Eusapia Paladino. Spanish musical prodigy Pepito Ariola at three and a half years could stretch only five notes, yet sounded full octaves during performances (q.v.).

Emanation. This occult concept, meaning the spirit flowing from the divine and passing through grades of angels and creative processes to man's mystic perception, has developed over many centuries. Among the Jews at Alexandria, the Neo-Platonists, Plotinus, and through the Arab thinkers—Avicenna and others, it passed into Christian Europe and to the Jewish Cabalists. To the latter, emanation being a process of creation out of nothing (this "nothing" being the fulness of mystical reality), it is the path to the Divine.

Emanations. Radiations of many kinds are now known to science. Those which are as yet unknown may be responsible for many of the problems of psychical research. In particular, the faculties of psychometry, dowsing and radiesthesia, may well be due to the interpretation of some emission from various objects and minerals. There have been positive tests demonstrating the radioactivity of living matter.

Emerald. In Poland and elsewhere this stone is associated with May, and with the belief that worn on Wednesdays it brings luck. The Bible mentions it as the New Jerusalem, and it was the material of the first Islamic heaven. Considered an important aid to healing, and used in divination.

En No Shokaku. Japanese Buddhist saint who lived in the 7th century A.D. His miracles were so astonishing he was condemned to death, but it is claimed that his mystic powers destroyed the swords of his executioners.

En Sof (Judaism). To the Cabalists God had created the universe, was of it, yet not in it. Having neither beginning nor end, they named him En Sof—"Without End." To avoid using the sacred name of God, this symbolic substitute was created by the Cabalist Azriel ben Menachem in the year 1240 when he wrote the Bahir (q.v.).

En-Gai. The supreme being to the Kenyans and Tangan-Yikans of Africa.

Engram. Term of scientology for a painful mental image, occasioned by suffering in a past incarnation.

Ennead. In the ancient religion or Egypt a group of cycle of nine gods. The most famous of these was the Ennead of Heliopolis.

Enoch. Author of the *Kabala* and *Book of the Tarot*, he was considered the Seventh Master of the world; moreover, he was identical to the Egyptian Toth (q.v.), the Phoenician Cadmus, and the Grecian Palamedes.

Enoichion. Leading to the way of seeing in the Greek Mysteries—"the inner eye" in the rites of initiation. Also, the gift of clairvoyance.

Entity. A discarnate personality. An individual.

Enumah Elish. The Babylonian creation epic in honor of the supreme divinity Marduk. This epic envisages the primordial state of the world as a vast watery chaos symbolized by the name Tiamat (q.v.) conjoined with Apsu who together became the progenitors of the gods. It was the Enumah Elish that served as the cosmogony for the Assyrians, except in their substitution of Ashur for Marduk; and it was this Enumah Elish that influenced certain aspects of the Hebrew creation literature.

Envoutement. A very widespread form of sympathetic magic (q.v.) practiced on a representation of a person to influence his actions or destiny, usually with evil intent. After the image of the person is made, often in wax or wood, some part of the victim's body (hair, etc.) is attached to it, which is then acted on in the same way as the magician wants to influence the victim.

Ephemeris. A publication which lists the positions that the Sun and the solar planets will occupy on each day of the year, noting their longitude, latitude, and declination. While the astrologer's ephemeris posts these positions in geocentric relationships, the astronomer's is guided by heliocentric considerations.

Epilepsy. Among many ancient people seizures of epilepsy gave proof of occult powers and oracular gifts, revealing in the epileptic a relationship to spirits of the dead or to divine spirits.

Epimenides. A noted poet, prophet, and seer of ancient Crete whose fame was so impressive that he was called by Athens in 596 B.C. to cleanse and purify the city of plague. He performed the task by utilizing his mysterious powers through rites and sacrifices.

Epiphany. The appearance of a deity in a particular place as God in the burning bush to Moses. It also signifies a moment of divine revelation. In Christianity, the feast of Epiphany commemorates the baptism of Jesus, the visit of the Wise Men to Bethlehem, and Jesus's miracle at Cana of turning water into wine.

Epoptes. In ancient Greece the "Epoptie" designated those who had reached the highest level of development in the Mysteries, and direct knowledge of the spiritual world.

Epworth Haunting. The appearance of a ghost or poltergeist in 1716 at the Epworth Parsonage, a home of John Wesley, founder of the Methodist Church, is celebrated in English ghost hauntings. For eight weeks the family was haunted by rappings, crashes, peculiar noises, which then disappeared but returned some time later. The case was well attested by John Wesley and five other members of the family.

Equinox. The point where the sun appears to cross the celestial equator; this occurs twice every year, when day and night are of equal length all the world over. The basis of our calendar measurement.

Ere. Among the Brazilian natives in their condoble cults (q.v.), and among the Trinidad Shango, a phenomenon where a childlike personality takes possession of those undergoing initiation ceremonies. It represents possession by the divine spirits.

Erh (Taoism). The fulfillment of Tao (q.v.) in the Yang and Yin (qq.v.) which fulfillment produces the infinite number of world things. It also means simply Yang and Yin.

Eromanty. Among the ancient Persians a use of air in divination. By wrapping their heads in a cloth and exposing a vase filled with water to the air, they uttered their desires into it and if bubbles developed, success was augured.

Eros. This Greek term is very important since it serves, in its basic meaning, as a measure and source of contrast. Basically it means the desire of sexual love. In Plato it is aesthetic, impersonal, and also erotic. By contrast there is: *Bhakti* (Hinduism), selfless devotion; *Metta* (Buddhism), disinterested benevelonce; *Jen* (Confucianism), humanity, charity and *Ai,* personal love and *Agape* (Christianity), sacrificial, protective, brotherly love.

Eryx. A mountain in the N.W. of Sicily which contained a famous temple to Aphrodite, built by the Phoenicians; from here it was introduced into Roman worship.

Eschatology. Ultimate concerns in religion that pertain to death, heaven, and hell.

Eskanye. The bread dance that brings food to the spirits, performed by the women of the Iroquois Indians.

Esoteric. That which is designed for and understood by the specially initiated alone, as doctrines or rites limited to a small circle of adepts and initiates. Also refers to the occult or secret.

Esoteric Buddhism. The occult schools of Buddhism.

Esoteric Christology. Refers to the occult knowledge of Christianity and the Christ-Being.

Esoteric Doctrine. Limited to a small circle—esoteric (q.v.). Theosophists consider this the essence behind every great religion or occult science, which, in sum, constitutes the universal esoteric doctrine. Early humanity was taught this doctrine by the Third Root Race of this Fourth Round of our globe, for it contains the relevant truths of the universe and the nature of our surrounding world.

Esoteric Language. Used to conceal the names of deities from the vulgar to prevent them from possessing magic powers over these deities. Further, it preserves occult secrets, the higher knowledge of the mysteries, and safeguards these from those not ready for them.

ESP. Extra Sensory Perception (q.v.).

Essenes. An early Jewish sect of high ideals, located in the Dead Sea region, contemporary with the time of Jesus, who it is thought by many may have belonged to the Essenes and imbibed their teachings. They may have originated from Buddhism, as they can be traced back from Judea to Egypt, then to Indian sources—especially as the life of Jesus forms a parallel in many respects to that of Gotama. In practice the Essenes were monastic, self-sacrificing and versed in the art of healing. With the finding of the Qumran Dead Sea Scrolls, much more knowledge of those times is coming to light. Some think it significant that Jesus, while rebuking Scribes and Pharisees, never criticized the Essenes. (See: Dead Sea Scrolls)

Estanatlehi. In American Indian mythology, notably among the Navaho Apaches, a female fertility goddess who possessed great power and such subtle magical skills that she was able "to recreate herself," which is the word's literal translation.

Ether. Hypothetical all-pervading, fluidic substance which fills the universe. This material of the spirit spheres permeates that of earth. It refers to those forces active in all life processes.

Etheric Body. A counterpart of the physical body which lives on after death. Also known as the spirit body, double or perispirit by Spiritualists. Although made of material substance it is considerably lighter than the visible body. It is purported to weigh about 2½ oz. based on results of experiments conducted in weighing dying persons. Normally invisible, it is occasionally seen by clairvoyants. During earth life it is linked to the physical body by a cord; when this is severed, death of the physical body takes place. Anthroposophists (q.v.) hold that the etheric (or life body) is responsible for the formative forces in the body; notably, they affect the glandular systems and the circulation of all the body fluids.

Etheric Double. See Etheric Body.

Etheric Plane, or Sphere (Spiritualism). That part of the spirit world adjacent to the earth. The landing place of all, in passing through the gates of death, and from which they gravitate to the various groups according to their spiritual development. This is the plane most often contacted for evidence of survival by mediums. The surroundings are said by its inhabitants to resemble the earth, but are more amenable by means of constructive thought acting directly upon them.

Etheric Senses (Spiritualism). These, so we learn by communication with the discarnate, correspond closely with our earthly senses, and function similarly. But there would appear to be important extensions of sense, difficult for us to comprehend, plus telepathy as a normal means of communication. Their senses, like ours, function only in their own sphere, the next higher remaining invisible.

Ethics. The greatest mystics, prophets of the occult, and psychic sensitives have all declared that an ethical foundation is absolutely essential to a true understanding of their revelations. Stripped to its core, ethics means love. Those who have been preeminent in any of the above areas have never used their supernatural insights for personal profit, but have always freely offered their knowledge as a gift of love to humanity. Ethics is the core of Theosophy and in the famous words of H.P. Blavatsky (q.v.), "Theosophist is who Theosophy does."

E.T.P. Extra Temporal Perception (q.v.).

Eucken, Rudolph (1846–1926). German writer, philosopher, and Nobel laureate whose spiritualistic-idealistic insights, his awareness that only spiritual strivings make human culture possible, and that there is an absolute need for each person to engage in the struggle to achieve these ends, has been an eminent influence. His work has influenced a wide audience and many notable thinkers.

Euhemerism. A view that divinities are merely deified men and women of eminence. It was advanced by Euhemerus (330–260 B.C.) in his *Sacred History.*

Eumenides. The Avenging Deities in Ancient Greek mythology and religion who were adopted by the Romans under the names of Furiae or Dirae. The fear of the Greek people of these goddesses (3 in number) was so great they dreaded to call them by their real name, Erinyes, and used the form Eumenides which means "the well-meaning" or "soothed goddesses." Dwelling in the realm of Tartarus (q.v.), they are represented as winged with serpents twined in their hair and blood dripping from their eyes.

Eumolpus. In Greek myth the son of Poseidon, who was considered the founder of the Elusinian mysteries (q.v.), the first priest of Demeter and Dionysus (qq.v.), and the progenitor of the Eumolpidae who were the hereditary priests of Demeter at Eleusis.

Euphemism. A name or designation which in seeking to placate or deceive refers to a deity, the devil, spirits, animals, or especially powerful persons with a substitute appellation. Yahweh, the Hebrew deity, was not mentioned by name, thus *Adonai* was substituted. Old Nick is used in England for the devil to prevent his actual appearance.

Euripides (c 485–406 B.C.). One of the greatest of the ancient Greek dramatists, the most modern in temper and insight and the one most frequently produced today. He was a poet with the spirit of a sophist, a rationalist, a pantheist, and a mystic. His *Bacchae, The Trojan Women, Electra* and *Medea* give an example of the spectrum of his art and mind. More than any Greek dramatist, he has influenced Western drama through his psychological and rhetorical genius.

Eva, C. Also known as Martha Beraud and Mme. Waespe, a French materialization medium who provided some of the best attested evidence of this phenomenon. She was tested by Charles Richet, then Baron Schrenck-Notzing (qq.v.), who employed detectives to check on her private life.

Everard, John (c1575–c1650). English mystic who was able to transform Christian faith into a new sect of Protestantism when Oliver Cromwell ruled England and permitted all Protestant religious belief to flourish. Everard's spiritualistic mysticism was a distillation of the insights of the great mystics of the past.

Evergreens. Among the Druidic nations evergreen decorated the homes in winter as a haven for the sylvan spirits until summer should produce natural shelter for them.

Everitt, Mrs. Thomas (1825–1915). The first non-professional British medium to produce the direct voice in England. Noted for the loudness of the voices, she also attained extraordinary speeds in direct writing.

Evidence, Criteria for. One of the thorniest problems in the domain of the supernormal is the establishment of criteria to validate evidence. Of course the same problem has always plagued philosophy and religion. And beginning with so famous a philosopher as David Hume—who pointed out in 1739 that the scientific concepts of "cause," and "necessity," and "certainty" are logically invalid—many philosophers and scientists have constantly asserted that induction cannot prove generalizations in science. With the advent of quantum physics and nuclear high energy reactions, the theoretical difficulties and the "uncertainty" of evidence has even more markedly increased. Most supernormal phenomena are by necessity singular events, as were the revelations of Moses, Buddha, Christ, Lao Tzu,

Muhammad; or Pythagoras, Socrates, Plotinus, Abu Yazid, Boehme, Swedenborg; or Rumi, Dante, Novalis, Blake, Coleridge, and Whitman (qq.v.); or any of the millions of unknown persons who, in the history of mankind, have experienced—and still do experience—periods of the supernormal. While empirical verification utilizing statistical and probability theories have been profitable solutions in the sciences, including parapsychology, in the validation of the supernormal these methods can only occasionally be employed—but, they are not the significant criteria. As an example of the former, recent studies by investigators at the University of Notre Dame have revealed that a large percentage of Americans have had mystical experiences, and this provides a kind of statistical evidence for the incidence of its occurrence here in the United States. Fundamentally, however, the test for genuine supernormal events must depend on a different type of investigation, for it rests on an immediate personal intuition (even in mass experiences of mystical feelings). This has been most clearly expressed by the philosophers Rudolph Otto, and Walter T. Stace; the former declaring that the "Idea of the holy," "mystery," and "feelings of truth" do not lend themselves to being conceptualized; and Stace in his important book *Mysticism and Philosophy* explaining that not only is the mystical experience a "fact" and "unique," but that science cannot ignore "the mystical experience simply because it is logically paradoxical." Further, it is noteworthy to recall that in the past such preeminent scientists as Newton and Kepler (qq.v.) believed in the supernormal. And that other surpassing figures such as Swedenborg, Wm. James, and Jung (qq.v.) insistently urged their fellow scientists to broaden their interests, determinedly asserting that their failure to do so robbed science of the necessary ingredients for the achieving of a fuller human existence. Therefore it is most promising that at the present time, and for the first time in human history, a large number of open-minded scientists are cooperating in many studies of supernormal experience and thereby trying to discover the most useful techniques for testing and validating such human events. Optimistically, then, such cooperation gives us a larger assurance than ever before that we can look forward to evidential criteria that will be more substantial than man has ever before had at his disposal. Nonetheless, this moment also demands a word of caution. In the last few years a number of books have proved that far too many individuals are indiscriminately and without any critical evidence "buying" all kinds of quick, shoddy, and often totally worthless panaceas in an effort to gain instant salvation, spiritual ecstasy, or a life-sustaining enlightenment. (See: *Powers of Mind*, Adam Smith; *Mindstyles/Lifestyles*, Nathaniel Lande; *The Mind Field*, Robert E. Ornstein. And, also, in this Dictionary: Martin Gardner, Samadhi, and Eileen Garrett)

Evil Eye. One of the most ancient and universally held beliefs. That the glance of certain individuals has the power to harm or destroy individuals or things was believed by all the ancients, East and West, and has continued to dominate the beliefs of vast numbers of persons in our own time. Throughout the world, numerous methods to ward off its effects have been developed: the ancient Egyptians wore amulets; the Chinese wore charms; the Romans and Greeks resorted to spitting. To safeguard animals from the evil eye, amulets are worn by them in the lands of the Arabs, Turks, Chinese and Ethiopians. Young children as well as young animals are considered especially vulnerable. While in the past it was women who were most feared as possessors of the evil eye, at present men more frequently are the malefactors. In recent years there was a fight manager in New York who used the evil eye (he could pop out his left eye terrifyingly) to scare opposing fighters of his own man. Though for a long time the world of science dismissed the phenomenon as a total superstition, science has now reversed itself, for experimental facts are now proving it to be a reality. Occultists have always known that each person gives off an aura, and that with some it is good, while with others it is evil.

Evil Spirits. One of the essential talents of Shamans, Medicine-Men, and Witch Doctors as well as specially trained priests—in most of the ancient world and much of the modern—has been the purgation of evil spirits from those possessed. Mainly these evil spirits are of three classifications: souls of the departed dead; evil supernatural spirits; and the spirits of enemies. In the Roman Catholic Church, for example, specially trained priests who exorcised the Devil used prescribed sacred formulae for this task. Among the Eskimos, many African tribes, and in many areas of South America, Medicine-Men under various names use elaborate procedures, such as incantations, fumes, emotion, and animal sacrifice to effect their cures. Scientists who have studied some of these medicine-men have attested to their often impressive achievements.

Evocation. By incantation, spells, and rituals the summoning of a spirit, or demon to aid in arcane activities such as necromancy, black magic, sorcery, etc. It also means the calling upon a benign deity for assistance.

Evolution, Theory of. The occult sciences, Hinduism, Theosophy, and Anthroposophy perceive evolution in a far more complex sense than is expressed in contemporary biology. To them it is cyclic, linear, and incomprehensible. Chiefly, it is through a long cycle of life-death-reincarnation that man achieves perfection, or, in the view of the Hindus, evolves finally to the state of Nirvana.

Exorcism. The driving out of harmful, evil, or malignant spirits by specialists in this skill is one of the most ancient and enduring practices in the history of man. It was an important occult profession in all the ancient civilizations—China, Japan, Egypt, for example, where the return of the spirits of the dead was constantly feared and to be prevented by every means—such as charms, rites, and especially exorcists. Also, the expulsion of devils or evil spirits from persons or places by special formulae was utilized not only by nearly all the ancient cultures, but the Christian Church adopted methods (by invocation of a holy name) to insure the same relief. Christ himself cast out devils, Today the practice is still found in many places in Asia, Africa, the West Indies, and South America. With the growth of witchcraft and occult practices in the West, exorcism has experienced a rebirth. The psychic perception of Spiritualist mediums is also utilized in exorcism. One of the most popular films of our time, *The Exorcist* portrays priests releasing a girl from demonic possession.

Exoteric. Not secret, opposite of esoteric.

Expiation. A widely held belief that to kill or punish a person who had committed a crime would appease the anger of the gods against some community.

Exteriorization of Motricity. Action of a medium's motor force outside the bounds of his body. Sympathetic movements of mediums which coincide with telekinetic phenomena. The modern view is that ectoplasm is the moving agent.

Exteriorization of Sensation, and Sensitivity. Sensory perception of the medium outside the bounds of his body, discovered by Dr. Paul Joire in 1892. Sensations exteriorized in the double were observed during studies of hypnology and psychical phenomena.

Exteriorization of Substance. See Ectoplasm, Emanations.

Externalized Impression. An impression perceived as though coming from without, but which has really originated from within the mind.

Extra. Descriptive of the supernormal appearance of a face or figure on sensitive photographic material.

Extra-Retinal Vision. The faculty which utilizes the skin to see instead of the customary method of using the eyes.

Extra Sensory Perception. Any information reporting an external event which is gained by means other than the generally known physical senses. Although this ability is as old as man (and there is evidence that it is also possessed by animals), in recent years science has explored some aspects of this phenomenon. Numerous experiments by many investigators—notably in the United States, in England, and in Russia—have repeatedly confirmed its existence. They have also discovered that extra sensory perception is an ability that fluctuates, showing peaks and valleys of performance in the same individual.

Extra Temporal Perception. (E.T.P.) ESP through time, as well as distance in space.

Eye-biters. Witches were accused of causing blindness in the cattle of Ireland in the age of Queen Elizabeth I. Many were executed for this crime of being *eye-biters*.

Eyeless Sight. A faculty for seeing from the skin, said to be a property of the etheric body.

Eye, the Third (Hinduism, Lamaism). In relation to the astral world, this notion in Hinduism represented the earliest vision, and was found in the center of the head. Through a process of evolution this "eye of siva" developed in the brain as the pineal gland. In Eastern occultism, particularly among Tibetans, training to "open" this "Third Eye" is practiced as a means of developing clairvoyance.

Ezra, Abraham Ibn (1093-1167). Jewish Neo-Platonic philosopher who was born in Spain. His wide travels enriched his thinking, and his mature work influenced both the Medieval Scholastics and the Cabalists. His work also reflects the teachings of Avicebron (q.v.).

Facsimile Writing. The reproduction of a dead person's writing, even his signatures, by mediums.

Fairy. A mythical creature in the folklore of many nations, represented as a tiny person, frequently garbed in green, whose abode is often in the woodland underground. Generally they are helpful to human beings, though occasionally mischievous and sometimes quite evil. On occasion, it is claimed, fairies marry human beings; but those who invade fairyland may be kept there for seven years before their release. Sir Arthur Conan Doyle and Wm. Butler Yeats (qq.v.) were among those in recent years who claimed to have had evidence of the existence of fairies.

Faith. In both the occult and religious sense—since it means absolute trust—it is the first step on the path of the initiate to higher development.

Faith Healing. Healing which is said to be effected by the patient's faith in Divine power. It is distinct from the term spiritual healing, in which the patient often has no faith. Sometimes an animal is treated and cured, which rules out faith as the necessary factor. The healing at Lourdes provides well attested cases of faith healing.

Fakir (Islam, Hinduism). The name for an Islamic mendicant dervish (q.v.); it is also a designation for certain Hindu holy men and wonder workers, and, too, for a certain group of showmen. The Islamic fakirs —ascetics dedicated to a lifelong search for God—belong to a number of religious orders, but nearly all share in common an adherence to Sufism (q.v.). Although the term "fakir" originated in the Arab world, it now more popularly is a reference to the Hindu fakir. Given the long history of Hinduism and its acute development of esoteric knowledge and disciplines, it is not surprising that most fakirs command an awesome range of powers. Many have utilized their powerful spiritual forces to become the spiritual and political leaders of numbers of India's villages. Others have concentrated on total asceticism with an occasional demonstration of their ability to perform miracles. But there is a large group of wandering fakirs who have devoted themselves to the art of producing amazing feats of magic—the type that most travelers see as they watch them charming their snakes on the street. Depending on the fakirs' creed, they were formerly known as *bawas, bhikshus, goswamis, sadhus,* etc.—the latter title, however, is still quite a common one. Almost all Hindu fakirs are able to exhibit an astounding capacity for biofeedback (q.v.). They are able to endure self-mortification; to be buried alive for periods of time; to control heart beats, blood pressure, brain waves, blood flow, body pain, and to speed the healing of wounds. But as mentioned above, there is a group of fakirs who are able to perform the most spectacular forms of magic and the most awesome demonstrations of psychic power: (making a baby fly out of the hands of its mother, ascend to the sky, and then return to the arms of its mother). (See *The Secret World of Witchcraft,* Ormond McGill). Only recently has the West discovered that these extraordinary feats are achieved by the street fakir only after long years of training, for this is the magic of illusion, and the illusion is made to seem totally real because the fakir has learned to plant into the minds of his audience whatever he wishes them to believe they are seeing. (See: Biofeedback, Samadhi, Justa Smith)

Familiar. A term much used in medieval witchcraft to denote a spirit attendant of a witch. Sometimes identified with the witch's cat. Socrates and Joan of Arc also claimed spirits which advised them in emergencies. This is another universal concept among mankind, for it describes a spirit or animal that is a subordinate and assistant to a wizard, sorcerer, or religious functionary; moreover, the familiar may be a double of its master.

Famous Returns. Many illustrious persons are alleged to have returned after death, but it is very difficult to prove these claims, the more so when we hear of the possibility of impersonation by spirits who possess histrionic powers and wish to shine in a little reflected glory. Oscar Wilde is alleged to have written through Hester Dowden (q.v.) and signed his name. It is easier perhaps for the average person to give evidence after death, as there are only a few who know very much about him, and there is little incentive for deception. (See: Facsimile Writing)

Fang Shih (Taoism). Priests and magicians in China, who were adepts in divination, magic, charms, alchemy, etc., skills which were used to achieve power, restore youth, superhuman ability, and immortality.

Fang Shu (Taoism). Divination and magic.

Fascination. A form of witchcraft by which certain possessors of this gift are able to bewitch, charm, or enchant by means of the eyes. This belief is prevalent among most of the world's peoples, though some nations have been regarded as having this gift beyond others. Varius in his *De Fascino*, 1589, describes this power in certain tribes. The Spanish physician Gutierrez in his *Opusculum de Fascino*, 1653, narrates accounts of persons possessing the gift against which the Spanish children of his time wore amulets. In more recent times it was believed by many that all Gypsies had the power to fascinate whomever they wished.

Fasting. Both an ancient and still-practiced method by which to communicate with supramundane powers. Chinese, Japanese, and Grecian oracles and diviners utilized this method, also some sects of the Ancient Jews, as well as Cabalists. The American Indian used it to gain a personal totem, some to achieve spiritual and prophetic gifts. It was widely practiced as a preparation for consulting oracles or a discipline for rituals.

Fatalism. Doctrine of complete determinism by divine power.

Fatal Look. A variant of the evil eye (q.v.), but much more dreadful, since instant death may be caused by looking at or being looked at by one possessing the fatal look. A common belief among certain people.

Faust. The hero of a number of great artistic works, he was a 16th century magician in Germany. Report credits him with having studied magic at Cracow, that he was a wandering magician and necromancer of great talents, that he blasphemed against the miracles of Christ, that he had wide knowledge of ancient mysteries, that he was killed by Satan.

Feminine Planets. In astrology: the Moon, Venus, and Neptune. (See: Masculine Planets)

Feminine Principle. Matter, wisdom and form, have been considered feminine by polytheistic religions. Occultists interpret these as passive, negative and receptive qualities of cosmic order.

Festival. Community observances which often are keyed to magical rituals. They sometimes alternate with a period of fasting (q.v.).

Fetch. In Irish legend and fold belief, this is the apparition of a living person, the wraith which resembles absolutely the person whose death it is supposed to foretell.

Fetishism. Objects or persons possessed by spirits which are not their own souls. Widely believed in the past. (See: *Dybbuk*)

Ficino, Marsilius (1433-1499). Few figures in the history of Western culture have made so enormous an impact on so broad a spectrum of its thinking as this Italian Renaissance humanist. Both during his own lifetime and for some three centuries following, the monumental scale and diversity of his translations, writing, and teaching dominated much of European thinking and writing in philosophy, religion, literature, the occult, mysticism, humanism, and ethics. For Ficino was a universal man—a physician, priest, philosopher, astrologer, occultist, mystic, teacher, and pre-eminent translator. He was the first in the West to translate from the original Greek all the works of Plato—a superb translation that was a major event in the intellectual life of Europe. Further, he produced excellent translations of all the works of Plotinus, Proclus, and Hermes Trismegistus (qq.v.), among others. He inaugurated the much-imitated Platonic Academy in Florence in 1462, and was the leading force in the spread and development of Neo- Platonism throughout all Europe. He further influenced the intellectual growth of Europe with his own writings; while his translation of the Hermetic writings, the Neo-Platonic thinkers, his own book on medicine and astrology—De Vita Libri Tres (1489)—his mystical doctrines, and his eclectic religious beliefs made him a gigantic stimulus in occult exploration. Philosophically, he saw the universe as a hierarchy of substances that descends from God to matter; the human soul being immortal, links the highest and lowest beings and acts as the central bond of the universe; the world is an animated being welded by a dynamic unity; the purpose of man is to make an inner ascent of the soul by way of increasing knowledge and love to a final contemplation and enjoyment of God. Ficino was also the creator of the famous concept of spiritual and Platonic love, a notion that shaped much of the thinking, poetry, and literature of the 16th century. His chief philosophic work, *Theologica Platonica de Immortalitate Animarum* ("Platonic Theology—On the Immortality of the Souls") (1482), plus his letters (1495), give an excellent insight into his philosophy. (See: Neo-Platonism, Plotinus, Proclus, Hermes Trismegistus, St. Augustine)

Figuier, Guillaume Louis (1819-1894). French physician, writer, and dramatist, whose eminence in science and as a writer made him a notable figure in his time. He also wrote a number of important works on the occult. These include, *A History of Modern Miracles*, and *Les Boneiuri D'outre Tombe.*

Findlay, J. Arthur. Perhaps the best known modern writer of spiritualist literature. Lecturer and researcher, founder of the Glasgow S.P.R. in 1920. Co-founder of Psychic Press Ltd., the proprietors of *Psychic News*. A prolific author, his best known work *On The Edge of the Etheric* ran to thirty printings in its first year. It has reached its fifty-ninth printing in the U.S., and has been translated into nineteen foreign languages.

Fire Immunity. There are many famous cases in history of those who it is claimed possessed the power to defy the ravages of fire; among them: St Francis of Paula, St Catherine of Siena, and St Francis of Assisi (qq.v.). Clovis, the Cansard leader in the rise of the Huguenots against Louis XIV, in the presence of 600 men is said to have stood in a pyre until it burnt out; he was unscathed. The Fire Ordeal of medieval times, though cruel, may have been the result of this phenomenon being connected with saintly persons.

Fire Perpetual. Fire has been associated with mythology, the occult, and religion from man's earliest period. Among the ancient Jews use was made of perpetual fire in synagogues; the Roman Vestal Virgins, consecrated to the goddess Vesta, maintained a perpetual fire upon her altar.

Fire Philosophers. Those occultists during the Middle Ages and the Renaissance who believed that fire was the symbol of God. They included: Hermeticists, Alchemists, and Rosicrucians (qq.v.).

Fire Signs. In astrology, these are termed the three inspirational signs—Aries, Leo, Saggittarius.

Fire Walking. Many ancient peoples used fire to test guilt or innocence, notably the Hindus, Japanese, Egyptians. (See: Fire Immunity). In India and Japan today many scientific studies and reporters' accounts have testified to the powers of fire-walkers. Contemporary opinion attributes the ability to absolute psychic concentration which is developed either through religious belief or mental-psychic training.

First Cause. Synonymous with Deity. And it also means, origin of the universe, and the beginning of all things.

First Fruits. To placate the gods, sacrificial offerings were made to them of the first food obtained—in hunting, fishing, or agriculture. Some ancient peoples even offered in sacrifice the first child born. Both the priests of Judah and the temples of Greece were supported by these first fruits.

Flagellation. Has been used to exorcise evil spirits, or as part of a magical ordeal; sometimes to gain illumination.

Flammarion, Camille (1842–1925). Famed French astronomer, past-president of S.P.R., who experimented with psychic phenomena and himself developed automatism. He readily accepted the independent existence of the soul from the body, also the existence of faculties unknown to science. "Telepathy exists just as much between the dead and the living, as between the living," he once asserted. He also believed that science had scarcely touched the surface of psychic phenomena. (See: Evidence, Criteria of).

Flower Clairsentience. (Spiritualism). This form of mediumship requires a flower from the sitter. By holding it, the medium can contact and interpret various personal psychic associations.

Fludd, Robert (1574–1637). Rosicrucian, alchemist, magnetist, Cabalist, and physician, he was one of the important English scientists and occultists of his time who also had a reputation on the continent. Although famous as a physician, his Rosicrucian and alchemical activities, his belief that men are controlled by demons which cause particular diseases, and his championship of the virtue of the magnet in medicine won him friends but also enemies. He wrote a number of enduringly influential books on Rosicrucianism, alchemistry, and medical subjects.

Fluid Motor. Invention of Count de Tromelin to demonstrate the power of emanations from the hands. A balanced paper cylinder would revolve by this power.

Flying Saucers. Technically described as U.F.O.'s, or unidentified flying objects. However, after thousands of sightings the world over, the famous saucer shape (once universally regarded as its only design) has now been discovered to be but one style among a number. Sound evidence for the prevalence of U.F.O's has been presented by some contemporary astronomers, and they have urged the scientific community seriously to study this epochal phenomenon. Unfortunately, there is much dubious literature on the subject which panders to the taste for sensationalism.

Fodor, Nandor. Psycho-analyst of Budapest, Research Officer of I.I.P.R., Hon. member Hungarian Metaphysical Society, Budapest, and S.P.R. assistant editor of *Light* 1933–35, lecturer and author of several books, including *Encyclopaedia of Psychic Science*.

Fohot. In Theosophy (q.v.) it refers to the power of the Logos.

Folklore. The mythology, supernatural belief, etc., of all peoples which is transmitted orally. While basically the same everywhere, there are different emphases in those stemming from the various continents, such as Africa, Europe, Asia, and South America.

Folk Soul. The spirit, between Angel and Archangel, which aids mankind during oracular dreams, and occurs in fables, myths, and folk-lore.

Fong Onhang. The Chinese claim these are magnificent and rare birds with the qualities of the immortal phoenix.

Food. Throughout the pre-history and history of man food has played a central part in his mythologies, rituals, religions, occult, and mystic conceptions and practices. Some of the many regulations once associated with food are: women and children were forbidden certain foods; the rituals that were performed for the "first fruits" (q.v.); prohibitions on eating particular foods to prevent acquiring their characteristics; elaborate ceremonies in presenting food to the gods, and also to the dead. One of the enduring practices has been the utilization of fasting (q.v.) to gain mystic or prophetic insight.

Ford, Arthur. One of the foremost mediums, spiritualists, and sensitives of our time, and an ordained clergyman. He has since 1929 (when he received a message from the dead Houdini confirmed by his widow) been a prominent figure in psychic demonstrations. It was he who made contact with the son of the late Bishop Pike. The events described in the Bishop's book *The Other Side,* and in Allen Spraggett's work *The Unexplained* give further testimony of Ford's psychic powers.

Fort, Charles. Author of a number of very significant books and articles in the early part of the century dedicated to proving that science was both blind and wrong in ignoring the psychic experiences and larger capacities of mankind.

Fortunes. In astrology Jupiter, the "Greater Fortune"; Venus, the "Lesser Fortune"; the Sun and Mercury, the Moon and Mercury, are benefic planets. Particularly is this so when the three latter bodies (Sun, Moon, Mercury) are well placed and aspected.

Fountain Spirits of Boehme. Jacob Boehme described seven principles active in nature—the *Fountain Spirits,* or "Mothers of Existence"—which he named: the astringent, sweet, bitter, fire, love, sound, and essential substance. Supreme unity occurred by their interaction, and they generate and are generated by each other. The seven golden candlesticks of the Apocalypse represent these seven principles.

Four-footed Signs. In astrology, the "animal Signs." When one has these in the ascendant (q.v.) it is believed that the individual expresses some of the qualities of these animals.

Four Noble Truths (Buddhism). The basic principles of Buddhism. These assert that all life is subject to suffering, that the desire to live is the cause of repeated existences, that only the elimination of desire can produce release, and that the way of escape is the elimination of selfishness by means of the Eightfold Path (q.v.).

Fourth Dimension. A mathematical welding of space and time, as a framework for all natural phenomena. It is now generally accepted by scientists as a working hypothesis; it grew from Einstein's relativity concept, and has now superseded the old idea of an all-pervading "ether" for which no demonstrable evidence could be found. It is interesting to note that some parapsychological experiments seem to deny the validity of ordinary "time" concepts.

Fox, George (1624-1690). Founder of the Society of Friends (Quakers). At the age of nineteen he received a divine command and forsook all family ties to preach against formalism in religion.

Fox Sisters. Kate, Margaret and Leah (the last named also known as Mrs. Fish, Mrs. Brown or Mrs. Underhill). They are usually acclaimed as the founders of modern Spiritualism. Leah Fox wrote a book *The Missing Link* which reported how in 1848 mysterious raps were heard in the home of the three sisters—an event that was to make them celebrities in the United States and Europe,. Margaret, however, eventually confessed that the three sisters were simply frauds.

Francis of Paola (c. 1436-1507). One of the surpassing clairvoyants of his age, this Italian monk founded the order called Minims. King Louis XI of France consulted Francis, valuing his clairvoyant and occult powers.

Franklin, Benjamin (1706-1790). This universal man who achieved greatness in all his undertakings, was also well-versed in the occult. When living in London and Paris, he imbibed the notions of eminent Freemasons, Alchemists, Hermeticists, and Cabalists. His study of magic squares, characteristically, led him to invent a notable one of his own.

Fravashis (Zoroastrianism). Spirits of the dead and the gods of the lower world. They are akin to similar Roman gods and beliefs, however, being the Fravashis, higher in spiritual elevation. Some believe they are embodied in human forms to aid Ahura Mazda's (q.v.) cause on earth.

Freud, Sigmund (1856-1939). Austrian physician who was the founder of psychoanalysis. His genius for creative perceptions and psychological discoveries continued till the end of his life. He investigated occult and psychic experiences as part of psychiatry. Despite his own deep-grained materialist bias, he had to admit that ESP was an actual fact. His sanction has stimulated research by such psychoanalysts as Nandor Fodor, Jules Eisenbud (qq.v.) and many others.

Freya or Freysa. The Venus of ancient Scandinavian mythology, goddess of love and night, whose chariot was sped by cats. Often identified with Frigga (q.v.).

Friends of God. A mystical society of Germany in the fourteenth century that catered to the poor; members belonged to every rank of society from knights to laborers, and their central doctrine was "Universal love."

Frigga. The mother of gods in the ancient Scandinavian mythology, who was queen of heaven and Odin's wife. But she was also the earth-goddess, and ruled over the marriage bed. Friday comes from her name.

Fruitful Signs. In astrology these are the Water Signs—Cancer, Scorpio, and Pisces. The ascendant, Moon, or Lord of the Ascendant (q.v.), in horary considerations, if strongly placed in any of these signs, signifies the bearing of children.

Frustration. In horary astrology (q.v.) the situation of three conflicting planets. This occurs when one planet, applying to an aspect of another, is interposed by a third, thereby frustrating the effect of the first two.

Fumigation in Exorcism. An essential rite during the exorcism of an evil spirit, which is a burning of a picture of the demon which has been fumigated.

Galactic Center. This is, in astrology, the gravitational center of the Sun's revolutions. The latest results of scientific measurements confirm the fact that astrology's calculations—at zero degrees of Capricorn—are exactly correct.

Galeotti, Martius (1442–1494). Italian astrologer who served the King of Hungary and later Louis XI as his state astrologer. His fame attracted the interest of Sir Walter Scott who portrayed him as an intimate of Louis XI.

Galgani, Gemma (1878–1903). This Italian visionary, who received the stigmata and also experienced a number of occult revelations, was venerated by those who knew her, owing to her spiritual elevation and saintliness.

Gall, Dr. Franz Joseph (1758–1828). The German anatomist, physiologist and physician who was the founder of phrenology. His extensive scientific background—he studied at three universities in Germany and Vienna—convinced him that man's talents, character, and personality are dependent upon the operations of the brain and that they may be deduced with exactitude from the external appearances of the skull. His lectures on phrenology in Vienna were so successful the Roman Catholic Church persuaded the government to ban his practice and lectures, whereupon he emigrated to Paris in 1805; there he continued his career as both physician and phrenologist, also writing a series of books that explained his theories.

Gandarvas (Buddhism). Vedic divinities of the atmosphere who served the gods by preparing the soma juice for them.

Ganga (Buddhism-Hinduism). A name for the sacred river, the Ganges.

Ganzfeld. A technique utilized in parapsychology using the phenonemon of altered states of consciousness to enable the occurrence of psi phenomena (q.v.), such as ESP, to take place more readily than in customary surroundings. It involves the production of a patternless visual and auditory input, and, as a reinforcing agent, the creation of an environment where the noise has been drastically curtailed.

Garatronicus. The Greek Achilles carried this red-colored stone into battle, for it made him invincible.

Garden of Delight. In the tradition of Judaic mysticism, it represents the occult arts. However, this tradition reports also that Akiba alone entered the Garden of Delight.

Gardner, Martin. One of a group of scientists who demand that parapsychologists, psychics, occultists, and all paranormal professionals adhere to strict facts and scientific rigor in their operations and reports. Among those joining him in this standard are Daniel Cohen, L. Jerome Stanton, and James Fadiman. Gardner, who is a noted science and mathematics analyst, points out that only the strictest adherence to rigor and discipline can safeguard paranormal developments from the hordes of pseudo-scientists and outright frauds who have long vitiated real progress in this important frontier of man's quest for a knowledge of the universe and man's highest psychic potential. (See: Evidence, Criteria of).

Garinet, Jules. The author of a *History of Magic in France*, written in 1818, which covers the evolution of magic, demonology, and the occult from ancient to modern times.

Garlic. The occult powers of this vegetable have made it, among the Greeks and Turks, a protection against vampires and the "evil eye." It is hung on boats and homes to ward off the envy of evil-doers.

Garrett, Eileen J. (1893–1970). Unquestionably the most unique trance medium ever known. Her powers of clairvoyance, telepathy, and prevision were outstanding, but she never took a penny in the exercise of her gifts. "I believe in the humanities and common decency," she once said, proving this as a socialist, editor, publisher, author, psychic researcher, and philanthropist. Intensely interested in a genuine knowledge of psychic phenomena, she exposed herself to the finest scientists and psychic societies for examination of her rich talents, and founded the famous Parapsychology Foundation in France for this purpose. Well-known as a publisher of excellent books, she was also editor-publisher (1941–1962) of the important magazine *Tomorrow*. She wrote: *The Sense and Nonsense of Prophecy, Awareness, Life is the Healer, Many Voices.*

Garuda (Buddhism-Hinduism). A half-bird, half-man, considered the king of the birds, upon which Vishnu rides.

Gassner, Herr. German priest and famous exorcist who lived in the latter part of the 18th century. Believing that all diseases were caused by evil spirits, he utilized hypnotism, stroking his patients, the Catholic liturgy of exorcism, plus a naked theatricality to obtain numerous cures.

Gastromancy. Divination that consults the belly, a method which was used by the Pythonesses, the priestesses of Apollo.

Gatekeepers (Judaism). These are the 50 gates which in Hebrew mysticism lead into reason.

Gatha (Buddhism-Hinduism-Zoroastrianism). The oldest songs in Zoroastrianism, believed to have been composed by Zoroaster (q.v.). These are the same as Sanskrit Gita.

Gayatri (Hinduism). One of the notable sacred verses of the Rig-Veda in worship of the sun. A name of Sata-rupa, Brahma's female half, daughter, and wife; also the wife of Siva in the Hari-vansa.

Gayomard (Zoroastrianism). The first of created men.

Geber (Abou Moussah Djafar al Sofi). This Arabian alchemist and physician, born in the 8th century, is one of the most famous writers on alchemy. The numerous works attributed to him had an immense influence on medieval alchemy, covering as they did every aspect of the art. As late as 1928 his work was still being translated into English.

Gehenna (Judaism). The place near Jerusalem where in ancient times the Israelites sacrificed their children to Moloch. It came to be considered an area of abomination, a place for deposit of garbage, the Hell of the New Testament, because Gehenna was a place of perpetual fire to prevent pestilence.

Geley, Dr. Gustave (1868–1924). Distinguished French psychic researcher, and Director of the Institut Metapsychique Internationale.

Many supernormal manifestations were produced in his fraud-proof laboratory. He suffered much opposition and prejudice from his former medical colleagues. Some of the best wax molds were produced under his direction, through the mediumship of Kluski. Geley was the author of several works of psychical research, including *From the Unconscious to the Conscious*, in which he accepted survival, reincarnation and communication with the dead as true.

Geller, Uri (1946–   ). This young Israeli, who first discovered his talents at the age of seven, has demonstrated surprising parapsychic powers—such as telepathy, psychokinesis, and precognition. A former nightclub magician, he asserts that outer-space intelligence directs his work—bending metal objects, breaking them in half, making objects disappear and reappear, running thermometers up and down, compelling watch hands to stop or to go backward, moving objects across rooms or from thousands of miles away—all by mind concentration. Researchers who have tested him, both in England (Cambridge University) and in the United States (the Stanford Research Institute in California), attest to the authenticity of his powers. But James Randi, a very popular magician, who is able to duplicate psychic feats with a magician's know-how and a dash of psychology, seemingly made Geller's powers vanish on a nighttime television show by instituting a set of controls during his demonstration.

Gelukpa (Lamaism). The chief and most conservative Buddhist sect who are referred to as "the yellow caps;" they are the opposite of the Dugpas (q,v,).

Gematria. The science of the dual interpretation of the Cabalistic alphabet utilized in conjunction with the *temurah*. The latter is the symbolic shorthand which is the complete science of the tarot (q.v.), and which reveals the application used to decipher all secrets. This method in Cabalism was utilized to deduce from the letters of words in Talmudic or Biblical writing their numerical value. Since each letter in the Hebrew alphabet represented a number, the combination of new letters made words of prophetic or magical import.

Gemini. Astrological sign (May 22–June 21); symbol—the Twins; ruling planet, Mercury. Sensitive to every aspect of their environments, they exhibit an incredibly mercurial personality; they are highly intellectual, versatile, tactful, diplomatic, and receptive to differing points of view. The danger of this sign is a lack of steadfast concentration, and a failure to express fully their talents in the kind of work and avocations to which they could give themselves fully. Being the arms and hands of the grand man of the universe in the Cabala, they symbolize the executive qualities.

Genethlialogy. In genethliac astrology the chart of the stars at one's birth upon which the astrologer bases his calculation of a person's character and the fundamental influences in his life. This term also refers to lineage of the gods.

Geomancy. Divination from inspection of the local geographic situation, or by the scattering of earth, or by marking in sand. A popular form of numerology in the Middle Ages through observation of the planets and stars.

Gerson, Jean Charlier de. Chancellor of the University of Paris who lived during the 14th and 15th centuries. His books, the *Examination of Spirits*, and *Astrology Reformed* were enormously successful.

Gertrude of Helfta (*c.* 1256–1302). A noted medieval mystic born in Saxony. A nun in the convent at Helfta, she experienced throughout her life numerous spiritual and mystical events which won her the epithet "The Great." The popularity of her writings was very high all during the Middle Ages.

G.E.S.P. General Extrasensory Perception. Parapsychologists distinguish this from ESP (q.v.).

Gestic Magic. Black magic in which assistance by evil spirits is said to be invoked.

Ghazali, al Abu Hamid (1058–1111). Although he was a brilliant philosopher, much more importantly he was the greatest theologian of Islam. Ghazali ranks next only to Muhammed in his influence on Islam, for it was Ghazali who definitively stamped it with both its mystical substance and its philosophical direction and content. So monumental has been his influence on religion and philosophy that he is known as the Thomas Aquinas of Islam. Two of his books have been particularly instrumental in shaping its character: *Tahafut al-Falasifa* "Destruction of the Philosophers" (a work that from then on obliterated the repute of philosophy in Muslim thinking), and his massive opus *Ihya Ulum ad-Din* "Revival of the Religious Sciences." In this latter study he asserts that it is the heart alone that gives certainty of knowledge by way of illumination from the Universal Soul, an experience that culminates in the only absolute certainty that man can achieve—the ecstacy of the mystical attainment of the soul's unity with God. Ghazali's radical formulations have been considered by some thinkers as more important than the philosophical critiques of Kant; but certainly Ghazali's demonstration that there is no such entity as "cause" predates by more than six hundred years the same enormously provocative concept of David Hume. When he was thirty-six, Ghazali underwent a crisis in his thinking and his beliefs which prompted him to resign his professorship and his post as rector of Nizamiya University of Baghdad. For the next ten years, wrapped only in the wool robe of the Sufi (q.v.) he completely devoted himself to a spiritual life and to solitary pilgrimages throughout the Muslim world. Thus, when he felt ready to write his "Revival of the Religious Sciences" he had tested himself existentially, he had tested and examined his ideas thoroughly, and he had tested and experienced for himelf the certainty of the attainment of mystic unity. It was Ghazali who made Sufism respectable in Islam by muting its pantheism and emphasizing its mystic insights in a way that made its total commitment to mysticism acceptable to the orthodoxy of Islam. (See: Sufism)

Ghost. Apparition or supernormal appearance of a deceased person to the living.

Ghost Club. Founded in London in 1862 for the investigation of current psychic phenomena. Many distinguished men were members when it was revived in 1881 by Sir William Barrett, F.R.S., and later in 1938 by Harry Price, when membership became open to both sexes. Its present object is to discuss and examine current psychic topics.

Ghost Dance. A religious and trance-creating dance of the North American Indians which brings the participants into contact with the unseen world and the spirits of dead friends. This is the chief ritual of the Paiute Indians created by the Indian Messiah, Wovoka, who taught the imminent coming of the millenium when the whole Indian race, the dead and living, would be regenerated in eternal happiness.

Ghost Who's Who, The. Published in England in 1977, and listing more than 500 ghosts that haunt the homes, the estates, the castles, and other places in England (the earth's most haunted island), this first such reference work was written by Jack Hallam, a retired newspaperman who is an acknowledged authority on ghosts. According to its author, ghosts are now an attractive feature to Englishmen buying or renting property, for the announcement of a ghost-in-residence increases the price of such real estate. This radical turn-about in attitude is the result of a changed viewpoint on ghosts: they are no longer looked upon as terrifying apparitions, but rather are considered quite harmless. It is the author's opinion that they are merely electrical energy imprints of once violent emotional activity, which continue to exist in the atmosphere. Further, he believes that given a person with sufficient perception or one possessing a talent for ESP (q.v.), they can make contact with these imprints, since he concludes that the murder of one in the prime of life, for example, releases a marked quantity of energy that survives through a definitely long time. Accepting present-day notions, Mr. Hallam holds that children and animals are particularly sensitive to these electrical imprints. It is not surprising that The Ghost Who's Who should have been published in England. Historically, at least 25,000 ghost manifestations have been reported (including the ghost of a Bronze Age man, the ghost of Henry VIII, as well as the ghost of an unknown gentleman who haunts one of the runways of London's Heathrow Airport). More significantly, perhaps some 20 percent of Englishmen believe in ghosts; a recent survey revealed that six million Englishmen assert they have seen some kind of apparition; and, too, in the last few years numerous books have been published on the history, the reality, and the mystery of ghosts. Not surprisingly, many Englishmen also believe that ghosts are sufficiently important to warrant a more sizeable scientific study than has so far been done on this subject. And once more reflecting the feelings of many Englishmen, Mr. Hallam claims that a natural acceptance of these apparitions will lead to an increase in our knowledge of this phenomenon. (See: Ghost Club)

Ghoul. In Hinduism and many Eastern nations an evil demon who robs graves and gorges himself on corpses.

Ghrana (Hinduism). The organ of smell, particularly in an occult sense.

Gibbes, Miss E., Writer of several articles on experimental psychic work.

Gikatila, Joseph (1248-1305). A disciple of Abulafia (q.v.). Born in Gerona, Spain, he wrote several Cabalistic works—*Ginnath Egoz*, "The Nut Garden," and the *Shaare Orah*, "The Gates of Light."

Gilgul, Gilgulim. See Dybbuk.

Gilles de Laval (1420-1440). Lord of Retzand and Marshal of France whose fame as a sorcerer, alchemist, voluptuary, and murderer, have made him an enduring figure of mystery and insured him the legendary reputation as the original "Blue Beard." His lust for wealth and sensual pleasures led him to pursue the demonic, the alchemical, the Black Arts and to make a pact with the Devil. Accused, finally, of the countless murders of women, boys and girls, he was sentenced to death in 1440.

Ginsberg, Allen (1926—). American poet who was one of the leaders of the Beat Generation. While still a student at Columbia University, he came under the influence of the English mystic William Blake; from then on he increased his knowledge of mysticism, Buddhism, and heightened states of psychic awareness, using drugs in the latter experiments. He has made several trips to India. His influence in poetry and his advocacy of new modes of insight have been a notable contribution in contemporary writing and psychic exploration. (See: *Howl and Other Poems*).

Gita (Hinduism). Song.

Giver of Life. Hyleg in astrology—that point in life, by consideration of the planets or parts of signs, that reveals life or death.

Glanyil, Joseph (1636-1680). English author of an influential work *Sorcerers and Sorcery*. Although primarily a philosopher, he maintained a belief in the occult. Charles II appointed him his chaplain. He asserted that God alone causes existence, and acknowledged his belief in witchcraft.

Glastonbury Scripts. A famous series of automatic communications covering the period 1918–27, which were published in nine booklets. In this case of cross correspondence, several widely separated mediums were involved at different times: John Alleyne, Hester Dowden, two American mediums, Bligh Bond, a lady from Winchester, and Margery Crandon. The communications were edited by Frederick Bligh Bond, and concerned unknown portions of Glastonbury Abbey and its history. Through the information obtained, the lost Edgar and Loretto chapels and the Norman wall of Herlewin's chapel were discovered by excavation.

Glossolalia. This is the psychic phenomena of speaking in tongues. Tests of many cases have seemed to prove that these are actual languages of ancient origin.

Glottologues. Mediums who are enabled to speak in unknown tongues. See Xenoglossy.

Gnani Yoga. The yoga path to the Absolute, by the attainment of wisdom.

Gnome. In Cabalism, a hunch-backed dwarf (who lives or swims through the earth) and is considered to be in the earth's exact center.

Gnosis. In the first Christian centuries the esoteric wisdom imparted by Jewish and Christian teachers. One of the principal concepts was the Logos doctrine, the knowledge of the Aeons. In particular it refers to the secret learning of the Gnostics (q.v.).

Gnostics. Members of an early Christian church sect, professing special knowledge of an Oriental esoteric nature, and claiming divinity for Jesus in opposition to the Arians, another sect, who did not.

Goat. In medieval folklore this animal, who is the Devil's invocation, symbolizes Judaism and the Hebraic God. The goat was also viewed as a symbol of the Jew's satanism. Since the Devil often took the body of a goat, being worshipped in this form by his followers, this animal was often used as a sacrifice to him. The Devil appears at the Sabat in many shapes, but as protector of witches and wizards he is embodied as a three-horned goat. While his middle horn is the torch of fire, his tail clothes his face-like buttock, which is kissed by his devotees.

Goblins. One of the elemental beings, such as the gnomes and elves (qq.v.), which can be evil, malicious, or playful to men and animals.

God. Power superior to man's, and one who controls the world in all its aspects. Ancient man believed it essential to appease and communicate with God-gods in order to thrive. There are numerous theories for the creation of God; fear, mysticism, nature's magnitude, fertility rites, etc. Gods have been categorized as nature powers, fertility gods, mediating gods, high gods, and supreme universal rulers. Every group and nation has developed its own theories on God-gods, and these reflect the evolutionary stage of the community. Modern man tends to shift God closer and closer to a relationship to man which reflects his well-being on earth and, further, his moral and mystical growth—seeing these as at least the basic essentials. Nonetheless, most religious thinkers believe it is the love of God and a constant existential integrity that are still the way by which man comes to his fullest relationship with God. And for most forms of mysticism this, again, is "the only way," since it is the pure love of God that ultimately makes possible the desired ecstatic climax of union with God.

Goethe, Johann Wolfgang von (1749–1832). One of the last universal men, who encompassed much of the learning of his time in addition to being one of the world's greatest poets and dramatists. His interest in science led him to make several discoveries, notably in botany, minerology, and color; conversely, his interest in alchemy and the occult was utilized in his masterpiece *Faust*.

Goetia. In occultism, the evil or malign—Black Magic (q.v.).

Gold. In the occult this metal represents the metal of the sun, of true knowledge, and of spiritual worth.

Golden Lane. A street in Prague, so named because it was a beehive of black magicians, alchemists, occultists, Cabalists, and their patrons. Such notable figures as Paracelsus, Nettesheim, and Trithemus (qq.v.) abided for some periods in Prague.

Golem. In Hebrew legend a lump of clay given life by the magical *Shem ha-Meforash* or Tetragammaton (q.v.). These artificial men, homunculi, androids, robots, were made by ancient sages—Raba, Chanina, Oshara. Eleazor of Worms in Germany also left such a magical formula, and during the Middle Ages a number of Golems were created. Elijah of Chelm, a Cabalist, used the Tetragammaton to create such an android in the 16th century. But the most famous was the Golem of Rabbi Judah Loew of Prague, the terrible monster who protected the Jews of that city.

Gorgon. In Greek mythology the three sisters with snaky hair and terrible eyes who turned all beholders to stone—notably Medusa.

Gotama. Gautama. (See: Buddha, Buddhism)

Gowdie, Isobel. One of the witches in the history of Scotland whose confessions in the year 1662 vividly pointed up the inner workings of witches and devils. In addition to revealing the existence of a cabal of thirteen witches organized in a coven (q.v.), she told of a meeting and a pact with the Devil in a church, of the Devil's mark implanted on her shoulder, and of having been rebaptized in her own blood by the Devil who had sucked it from her body.

Goya, Francisco Jose de (1746–1828). One of Spain's most eminent and most independent painters, who defied the genteel tradition in his vividly portrayed war scenes and his nude paintings of women. He is also noted for his etchings of forcefully dynamic and macabre satanic scenes.

Graham, James. Creator of a famous "sex-bed." He was an English disciple of Cagliostro (q.v.), but better known as the creator of a Temple of Health. His most famed innovation was an extraordinary bed which he characterized as his celestial, musico, magnetico, electrical bed, which sported a super-celestial dome and ethereal spices and odors, etc., with mirrors to enchant sexually engaged couples. He guaranteed to the occult clients of his bed that they would bear children who would be superior in every way.

Grand Grimoire. One of the most noted French books on black magic (q.v.). It is considered to have been written in the 18th century and has gone through a number of editions.

Graves, Robert Ranke (1895–   ). English poet, novelist, essayist, mythologist, and mystic. He is one of the most comprehensive and perceptive writers and thinkers on the contemporary scene, for he is a master of many genre and has always been an independent observer. *The White Goddess,* written in 1948, illustrates his insight into the mythic nature of man's highest existence. At the same time it expresses one of his persistent themes: it is the female in myth and in religion that is the great psychically civilizing, nurturing, and spiritual force in mankind's development—that the supplanting of the Great Mother goddesses of all nations by male divinity has retarded man's progress. He believes that the juice of the red-capped mushroom provided the *soma,* which produced the high spiritual ecstasy that inspired the Hindu Vedas, that wine drinking, on the other hand, has debased psychic growth. He has a deep interest in Sufism and has spent years learning from Sufi adepts. (See: *Difficult Questions, Easy Answers,* 1974.)

Great Beast, The. John Symonds' biography of Aleister Crowley (q.v.) which recounts the struggle of this English occultist and Black Magician to win the leadership of the Order of the Golden Dawn. Vividly it portrays the war of vampires, bloodhounds, evil emanations, Beelzebub and an army of demons.

Great Goddess. From the prehistoric fertility cults developed the grand notion of a great fertility goddess which in one form or another is found in all major mythologies and religions, and whose powers grew to be the generative force of the universe and of gods. The Minoans had such a Great Goddess. In the Celtic nations their Great Goddess was Diana. (See: Astarte, Isis, Cybele, Demeter.)

Greater World, The. Christian Spiritualist League that was founded in Britain in 1931; their first President was Alfred Morris. A worldwide organization, their teachings are based on those of "Zodiac," a control of Miss Winifred Moyes, trance medium and first editor of *Greater World.* The teachings claim to be purely Christian. "Zodiac" is said to have been the scribe mentioned in Mark XII, 28–35.

Greatrakes, Valentine. A well-known Irish hypnotist of the 17th century whose dream that he possessed the gift of curing the King's Evil led him to affect many cures merely by touching. Eminent persons in England testified to his psychic powers when he came to London where he practiced the art of "stroaking."

Great White Brotherhood. See White Brotherhood.

Great Year. In astrology, the year cut into twelve segments which correspond to the twelve zodiacal signs. It represents an era of 26,000 years.

Green. Green light perceived in the human aura is generally held to be indicative of intellectual activity.

Gregory Palamas (c. 1296–1359). The great mystic and proponent of Hesychasm (q.v.), a way of esoteric development. His technique of spiritual enlightenment has long been a recognized and widely practiced way of mysticism, particularly in Russian and Greek Orthodox monastic and lay circles.

Grimoires. Magician's Black Books often falsely attributed to great names: Solomon, Albertus Magnus, Popes, and ancient occultists. There were many such books, very popular during the Middle Ages, which described the arts of Black Magic, the occult, necromancy, and a host of arcane rituals and hermetic practices. Coming from many sources, some of the most popular were: *Oupekhat*, Hindu; *Shemophoras*, Hebrew; *Liber Spirituum*; *Grimorium Verum*, by Alibeck of Egypt; *The Constitution of Honorius*; *Tonalamatl*, Mexico; *Y-Kim*, China; *Hell's Coercion*, supposedly by Johannes Faust; *Lemegeton, or the Lesser Key of Solomon*; *The Key of Solomon* and *The Testament of Solomon*; *The Almadel.*

Gris-Gris. African tribesmen adorn themselves with these amulets believing they protect them against all evil forces.

Groote, Gerhard (1340–1384). Dutch Catholic reformer, one of the most learned men of his age, a master of philosophy, theology, law, and medicine, a professor at the University of Cologne, and a famous author and mystic. He retired from a worldly life to a Carthusian monastery under Ruysbroeck's (q.v.) urging, and became one of the most influential preachers of his age throughout the Netherlands. The founder of the Brothers of Common Life (q.v.), he is considered by many authorities to be the author of *The Imitation of Christ*, the most popular devotional book in the history of Christianity.

Grosseteste, Robert (1176–1253). Bishop of Lincoln, this English theologian, astronomer, mathematician, and occultist was considered one of the most learned men of his age. So eminent was his reputation also as a man of occult gifts and necromantic powers that it was believed he created a head of bronze that possessed the power of answering questions and foretelling the future.

Group Soul. An interesting and original explanation of soul relationship, by which many souls are linked by a group in a scale of spiritual evolution. In its complete outline (as purported to have come from F.W.H. Myers, in *Road to Immortality* by Geraldine Cummins), it involves the concept of reincarnation, each soul leaving an earth pattern or "karma" for a new soul of his group to be born into.

Guaita, Stanislas De (1861–1897). French Rosicrucian and Cabalist, narcotic addict and an adept of the occult, he founded a Rosicrucian Cabalistic Order in the latter part of the nineteenth century. His notorious "battle of bewitchment" with Abbe Boullan was a cause celebre.

Guardian. In the Eastern Orthodox Church the belief that in addition to a guardian angel each person has also a guardian devil.

Guardian Angel. A guiding spirit, control or guide, more particularly the personal control who is charged with the well-being of the medium, often known as the "doorkeeper."

Guide. Spiritualist term for a beneficent control who acts in a protective or instructive capacity. Distinct from discarnate friends and relatives, they are said to be advanced spirits who voluntarily return with a sense of a mission to fulfill. Many different nationalities seem to be represented, but North American Indians predominate. Some of these give typical Indian names by which they were known on earth, others say they are only mediums or mouthpieces for even higher entities. Their capabilities and temperaments vary widely, and discrimination must be used with regard to their teachings.

Guillaume De Postel (1510–1581). French mystic, Cabalist, astrologer, linguist, mathematician, and extraordinary genius. He came of poor peasants, yet was appointed Professor of Oriental Languages and mathematics. Having received a mystic vision from the stars, he accepted Gnostic beliefs, asserting he embodied male-female principles. He wrote *The Key of Things Kept Secret from the Foundation of the World*.

Guldenstubbe, Baron de. Leading occultist, mesmerist, necromancer, and spiritualist in France, who from the 1850's onwards was a seminal figure in the spread of his beliefs; he recruited numerous followers. He conjured up the spirits of many historical personages. His book, *Practical Experimental Pneumatology; or, the Reality of Spirits and the Marvellous Phenomena of their Direct Writing*, was, in its time, quite popular.

Guna-Guna. Indonesian Black Magic.

Guppy, Mrs. Samuel. British medium discovered by Dr. Alfred Russell Wallace in his sister's house. She had remarkable powers for telekinesis, and produced apports in large quantities, plants and flowers particularly. Her chief claim to fame was her alleged transportation from her home at Highbury to 61 Lambs Conduit Street, London, three miles away. She was never known to have made any financial gain from her mediumistic gifts.

Gurdjieff, Georges Izanovich (1866-1949) Trained in medicine and the priesthood in his native Russia, Gurdjieff exemplified in his life the meaning of the title "master." He was a master of religion (having studied some two hundred religions); a master of medicine, chemistry and mathematics; a master of psychology; a master of music and the dance; a master of gnostic wisdom; a master of ethics and moral behavior; and, certainly, a master teacher. The name of his famous school—Institute for the Harmonious Development of Man—which he conducted for many years at Fontainebleau near Paris, distils the purpose of his philosophy. The range, depth, and open-ended nature of his views together with the artistic quality of the physical techniques he used brought many students to his schools and lectures (in Russia, Turkey, France, England, the United States) who often studied with him for years. However, Gurdjieff stressed that the core of his teachings was quite simple. He explained that he taught nothing his students didn't already know, that he merely gave economy and order to their own knowledge. On the other hand—and this illustrates the polar nature of all his teaching—he also stressed that the student must work hard and work all his life if he desired to become a master of the Great Knowledge and a master of his own self. He also emphasized to his students the following germinative notions: the absolute adherence to the Socratic dictum "know thyself"; the necessity to learn the basic universal laws that govern all that exists in both the macrocosm and the microcosm (qq.v.) since the fundamental law of all Being is—"As above so below"; the constant pursuit of the Great Knowledge—unraveled from the knowledge of emanations proceeding from God—God the Father, God the Son, and God the Holy Ghost, the Law of Three; the understanding that everything in the Universe is material—even thought, for it is dependent on impressions; the faithful practice of the concept "Believe nothing, not even yourself" and therefore to obtain many verifications before making a claim of belief; analogously, the realization that one must work for guidance, not for belief; and, finally, the inner understanding that to create a human soul takes a lifetime of work. But still another challenging lesson of Gurdjieff's was his concept of magic: he taught that each person on his way to becoming a master of himself and the Great Knowledge does so by becoming a magician—that even Christ became a master through his skill as a magician. Most interestingly, this view of Christ as Magician was reinforced quite recently by professor Morton Smith's book *Clement of Alexandria and the Secret Gospel of Mark* (1973), which argues that Christ performed many of his "miracles" by using his ability as a consummate magician.

The four chief influences that molded Gurdjieff's philosophy were (1) his Greek ancestry (though he was born in the Russian Caucusus); (2) his study of medicine; (3) his journeys in the Far East; (4) his training in religion. His Greek ancestry led him to a careful study of Greek Philosophy; his medical background made him a lifelong scientist and taught him an acute knowledge of the mechanism of the human body; his training for the priesthood directed him to an intense investigation of the unitary fundamentals at the heart of nearly all religions and spiritual doctrines; and his travels in Tibet and the Far East did more than expose him to the world of Eastern wisdom: it brought him a sharp sense of what was useful in it and what was useless—and, in addition, taught him the true nature of the dance: its sacred roots and its curative powers. Gurdjieff's program of exercises and dance movements provides an excellent example of how extraordinarily meticulous, rich and creative was his approach to the achievement of inner harmony and self-mastery: his system was a colossal panorama of some 6,000 different movements. Among the well-known persons who studied with Gurdjieff was the mathematician-philosopher P.D.Ouspensky (q.v.), who utilized the former's doctrines in developing his own work. For the student of spiritual and psychic wisdom, it is most instructive to compare the philosophy of Gurdjieff with that of two other eminent figures who were in part his contemporaries: Helena Petrovna Blavatsky and Rudolf Steiner (qq.v.). Along with this comparison, the reader should also consult the following dictionary articles: Anthroposophy, Cabala, Ficino, Gnosticism, Magic, Plotinus, Proclus, Theosophy, Universals, Vedas, and Vedanta. A very important book on Gurdjieff is *Views from the Real World*, which is a collection of his early talks and lectures written down from memory by students who conversed with him privately or who attended his lectures. See the following posthumous books by Gurdjieff himself: *Meetings with Remarkable Men*(1963); *All and Everything: Beelzebub's Tales to His Grandson* (1964/73); and *Life Is Real Only, When "I Am"* (1975).

Gurney, Edmond (1847–1888). Outstanding English psychic researcher. First Hon. Secretary of the S.P.R., he was a classical scholar, musician and student of medicine. His interest in thought-transference and memory introduced him to a larger awareness of the range of psychic phenomena. He was the actual writer of the famous work *Phantasms of the Living* in collaboration with Myers and Podmore. After his death, Sir Oliver Lodge obtained remarkable evidence of survival from him through the mediumship of Mrs. Piper, (q.v.), an American medium.

Guru (Hinduism). The teacher whose spiritual knowledge and advice must be absolute in authority, and one the student must accept.

Guru Mantra. The sacred formula whispered by a guru into the ear of the disciple on initiation.

Guru-Parampara. This represents the tradition in ancient occultism of the unbroken continuity of teachers each of whom has received his mystical authority to head a school from his successor. In The Great Brotherhood of the sages and seers of the world we have an instance of Guru-paprampara. The Holy Association of the Masters of Wisdom and Compassion and Peace (the esoteric version of the former) is typified by the Theosophical Society, another example of Guru-parampara.

Gutenberg, Johann (c. 1397–1468). The German printer generally accepted as the European inventor of the printing press was in his time thought to be in league with the Devil and a practitioner of Black Magic and Witchcraft (qq.v.), owing to his "miraculous" ability to produce hundreds of books all alike. Up to his time books were hand-copied, and, consequently, each one was different in its mistakes, lettering, punctuation, page-content, number of pages, etc. Gutenberg's books, therefore, with their absolute page-by-page exactitude seemed to others to be proof absolute that his books were the work of the Devil. Fortunately, both his life and his invention were saved upon the discovery of his secret method of producing books.

Guya Vidya. The esoteric doctrine of mystic Mantras.

Gymnosophist. A sect of philosopher-mystics and naked mendicants that Alexander the Great discovered upon his conquest of India. These ascetics are reputed to possess eminent magical and mystical powers.

Gypsies. Originally from India,(their name is an abbreviation of Egyptian) they reached Europe about the 15th century and spread throughout the continent and Turkey. They have exhibited a wide range of talents, notably in music, dancing, fortunetelling (palmistry, crystalgazing) and prophecy. It is thought that every gypsy is a hypnotist, and can utilize "glamor" (q.v.) on people to create objects of illusion.

Gyromancy. Divination by continuing around a circle until exhaustion. The diviner notes the position of the fallen body in relation to the circle.

Gyud. This term refers to the ritual magic, in Tibetan mysticism, which is a stage in the growth of a mystic.

H. This eighth letter in the Hebrew alphabet, for Cabalists, has the magical property of imparting divinity to words to which it is added. Also, it refers to death and regeneration, the birth of a new spiritual life. To the Hebrews in its quality of eightness it was related to purification after uncleanness, since the temple was sanctified in 8 days. Agrippa of Nettesheim (q.v.) in his *The Cabbala* describes Dionysos as an eight-months' child.

Hacks, Charles. German physician of the 19th century, reputed author of *The Devil in the Nineteenth Century*, in which he describes his mysterious occult adventures with satanism.

Hades. The name is derived from the Greek where it refers to one of the sons of Kronos, Hades, the "grim-visaged," who was lord of the lower world. But during the classical Greek period, Hades never signified a place—it was always the name of a person. The elaborate mythology associated with Hades developed later. Nonetheless, the abodes of the dead assigned by the judges in the netherworld—to the terrible Tartarus, or the endless wandering on the Plains of Asphodel, or to the honorable world of Elysium, were not comparable to the Christian's Heaven, Hell, Purgatory, and Limbo. In Spiritualism it often refers to those insights developed by F.W.H. Myers (q.v.): there would appear to be intermediate states between each sphere or plane, where the soul reviews its past experiences and chooses to go either up or down the ladder of consciousness. There is no punishment except by the soul's own spiritual discomfort. Hades is classed as the Intermediate Plane, or the second level of consciousness.

Haggard, Sir Henry Rider (1856–1925). English novelist, whose popular romances with a South African background made him a bestseller. In his autobiography, *The Days of My Life,* he describes his lives in previous incarnations.

Hagith. One of the seven Olympian spirits in occultism. He is the master of Venus.

Hair. Considered the seat of the body's vital essence in esoteric doctrine; in Hebraic concepts; in ancient Egypt and among Buddhists, Hindus, Sikhs, Mongolians; in ancient Sparta; in Icelandic nations; among Eastern Christian priests, and the Knights Templar. Among Yogis, wearing the hair long is believed to preserve the years of life.

Ha-Levi, Judah (c. 1080–1140). Hebrew poet and philosopher whose book, *Kuzari*, is a refutation of philosophy's supremacy in favor of the primacy of the truths from revealed religion. It is the exaltation of the prophet's intuition, not philosophy which brings certainty in religion, and, therefore, assures that the prophet is the higher type of man than the philosopher.

Half Circle. In esoteric, mathematical mysticism this denotes the soul.

Hall, Manly Palmer. American Orientalist whose book *The Secret Teachings of All Ages: An Encyclopedic Outline of Masonic, Hermetic, Quabbalistic and Rosicrucian Symbolical Philosophy* is very highly regarded. Hall has also published many works on astrology.

Hall of Revelations (Taoism). The magicians and mediums of Taoism used this special building to induce spiritualistic revelations.

Halls of Learning (Spiritualism). Places for instruction in the spirit spheres. Sometimes said to be visited by earth people during sleep-state.

Hallucination. Perception which can be recognized as lacking any objective basis. Not to be confused with illusion. Hallucinations may be induced by suggestion in a hypnotized subject.

Halo. A circle of light often depicted around a saintly person's head. A nimbus. May have some connection with the aura as seen by clairvoyants.

Hamilton, Dr. Glen. American medical practitioner, and President of Winnipeg S.P.R. He had his own laboratory in which groups of stereoscopic cameras were trained on physical phenomena. His circle consisted of four medical men, a civil and an electrical engineer. He was responsible for many good photographs of levitation, telekinesis, and materializations. Dr. Hamilton's critical analysis of trance states is a valuable work for psychic researchers.

Hansa. The mystic bird in the occultism of the Asian nations.

Haoma (Zoroastrianism). A personified sacred plant the juice of which was used by the ancient Persians in their sacred rites. Authorities believe it was worshipped by the Indians also before they separated themselves from the Persians. (See: Soma)

Haptok-ring (Zoroastrianism). The star constellation that surrounds the doorway to Hell.

Hari (Buddhism, Hinduism). A name usually applied to Vishnu, but also to other gods.

Harmony, Pre-established. In Western thought this represents the perfect synchronization of soul and body as established by God. The soul and the body are in perfect harmony, in all their relationships, because of God's instrumentality in establishing this soul-body harmony.

Hasidism (Judaism). Founded in Poland by Baal Shem Tob (q.v.) about 1750, this Jewish religion stresses a livable relation to God in which song and dance, the lyrical, the wondrous, and the magical are close by. This was a radical departure from the formalistic, legalistic, Torah-Talmud theorizing, ritual-burdened, and dry-as-dust Judaism of the period. Hasidic Jews also became students of Cabalism (q.v.) and the arts of magic and demonology. Within 100 years of its founding about half of world Jewry had become members of the Hasidic movement. Millions of Hasidim were murdered by the Nazis, but Hasidism continues to flourish, particularly in Brooklyn, N.Y., where three Hasidic sects are currently centered.

Hatha Yoga (Hinduism). This form of Yoga (q.v.) is a training of the body in postures, breath-regulation, and related psycho-physical aspects, being the foundation of future spiritual development. Without the latter, the former lacks relevance.

Hauntings. Regular supernormal disturbances commonly attributed to spirits of the dead. The manifestations usually include: strange noises, objects moved, strange lights, chilliness, nasty smells and phantoms of various degrees of solidity. Little or no intelligence is displayed. One who suffers a violent death would appear to be the primary cause of haunting, not attributable to remorse, as it is the sufferer who haunts, never the murderer.

Hauser, Kaspar (1812?-1833). A mysterious German foundling who supposedly was reared in a dark prison. He appeared suddenly in Nuremberg in 1828, and quickly developed his mental powers. He had strange powers over animals. His autobiography made him a subject of wide interest, and he is the protagonist of *Caspar Hauser* by Jakob Wasserman.

Hayoth (Judaism). In the visions of the two prophets Ezekiel and Isaiah the "living creatures" which carry the Merkabah (q.v.). In Christian occultism they are the Evangelists: Matthew (Angel-Man, Aquarius), Mark (Lion, Leo), Luke (Bull, Taurus), John (Serpent-Eagle, Scorpio).

Hayz. In astrology, a sign of good fortune if the masculine diurnal planet and the feminine diurnal planet are in their proper signs.

Head. In the symbolism of Cabalism, notably in the Zohar (q.v.), the head—the peak of the Grand Man—represents in emblematic form the astral light.

Healing, Faith. See Faith Healing.

Healing, Magnetic. First named by Mesmer, who combined hypnotic passes with metallo-therapy (the "Baquet"). Mesmerism was superseded by Braid's exposition of the power of suggestion, or what is known today as hypnotism, used by doctors in medical treatment. Spiritualists believe that doctors passed to the realm of spirit are mainly responsible for healing through the channel of healing mediums. Yet contact healing may be due, at least in part, to some personal quality of the healer himself.

Healing, Spirit (Spiritualism). Healing by spiritualist healers is claimed to be primarily due to the power of doctors in the spirit world who are able to co-operate with them, following intercession for a particular patient. There are two main methods: contact healing, where physical contact takes place between healer and patient; and absent healing, in which case the patient may have been interceded for by a friend, and may be completely ignorant that he is being treated. The results of the latter method are surprisingly as good as the contact variety. Spiritualists are inclined to consider that healing by any means is helped by spirit doctors.

"Health" Aura. The first aura, the almost colorless lines radiating from the body. Moving straight out in health, in ill health they are said to droop and waver. Some occultists believe this aura emanates from the Etheric Double (q.v.).

Hearn, Lafcadio (1850–1904). American writer, born in Greece of Irish-Greek parentage; educated in Ireland, England, and France; American newspaperman; Japanese citizen. He was one of the first popularizers of Oriental occultism and Zen Buddhism. His early writing in a New Orleans newspaper won him attention, particularly his articles "Fantastics," and his book *Some Chinese Ghosts.* But from 1890 on till his death he lived in Japan, interpreting for the English-speaking world its culture and occult arts.

Heavenly Man. A Cabalistic and Hermetic designation for Adam Kadmon (q.v.); the son, in Christian esotericism.

Hebdomad. In Gnosticism (q.v.) the psychic, astral or soul-region, or body of man.

Hebrew Letters. Throughout the whole history of Judaic mysticism, most particularly in the Alexandrian period of Philo Judaeus (q.v.), the emphasis on the magical properties of the twenty-two letters of the Hebrew alphabet was extremely marked. The Cabalists developed this tradition to its highest point, laying special emphasis on the three maternal letters—Aleph (q,v,), Mem, and Schin. Being the first letter, Aleph symbolizes number one, the sign of fire, the heavens, summer, and the head. The seven double letters, and the twelve simple letters, are accorded particular meanings. (See: Golem, Tetragammaton, Gematria)

Hedonism. Philosophical doctrine that pleasure is the chief objective or good, in man. In this sense the devotes of black magic are Hedonists.

Hegel, George Wilhelm Friedrich (1770-1831). German idealist philosopher who attempted to represent reality as a development of Absolute Mind (*The Idea*), and vice versa; we could only really know ourselves by learning at many levels.

Heindel, Max. Author of many books of Rosicrucian philosophy and astrology. He conducted a healing clinic for thirty years that was based on astrological diagnosis and psychic treatment.

Hel, Hela. In Norse mythology, the Queen of the Land of the Dead. Originally the good earth-goddess, she evolved into the feared goddess of death. (See: Hell).

Helheim. In Norse mythology, the Kingdom of the Dead, the Land of Mist, a vestigial element of the Lost Atlantis. (See: Hell).

Helios, The World of, or The Plane of Flame. The fifth level of consciousness according to F.W.H. Myers's (q.v.) communication. He gave seven planes in all.

Hell Fire Club. An English pseudo-Satanic circle formed in the 18th century in England, headed by Sir Francis Dashwood, which was actually a hedonistic club for sexual pleasure.

Helper, Spirit. Term for a discarnate entity, not necessarily possessed of superior knowledge, but eager to assist a subject in a humble way. May be also an entity under the direction of a superior guiding spirit or band. Helpers are usually of more recent passing, sometimes deceased relatives and friends, as distinct from guides who have a greater experience and an understanding of spiritual matters garnered from higher spheres.

Henry III (1551-1589). This French king, considered a devotee of black masses (q.v.) at the Louvre, accused of sleeping with his familiar spirit, and of furnishing a prostitute for his favorite devil, was also one of the instigators of the infamous massacre of Saint Bartholomew's Day. Debauched and unscrupulous, he died by stabbing when barely thirty-eight.

Hepatoscopy. The use of the sheep's liver in divination, which reached a high state of skill among the Babylonians. Many nations used this form of divination.

Hephaestus. God of fire in Greek mythology and religion, he was originally an Asiatic deity of volcanic fire. He made many magical objects: Achilles' armor, Agamemnon's sceptre, Harmonia's necklace.

Heracleitus (c. 536–470 B.C.). The Greek philosopher, whom even Socrates considered a difficult thinker, was born in Ephesus in West Asia Minor. Since to Heracleitus all things are changing constantly, he considered the world to be an ever-living fire.

Herbal Exorcism. Abyssum in the four corners of a house exorcises evil spirits.

Hermanubis. A combining name of Anubis, one of the ancient Egyptian local gods of the dead, and the Greek god Hermes (q.v.). Under the name of Hermanubis in the celebration of the Greek Mysteries he was the revealer of the secrets of the lower world who carried the sacred Cross.

Hermes. Greek god of flocks, travellers and heavenly messengers; identified with Mercury by the Romans, and Hermanubis and Thoth by the Egyptians. Was once worshipped as the revealer of divine wisdom.

Hermes Unveiled. When it seemed that alchemy had lost its interest for occultists because of the vast shipments of gold from South America which cheapened the value of gold, Cyliani, writing in French, produced this interesting work on alchemy. It was maintained that his prescription for the transmutation of base metal to gold came to him by way of a woodland nymph.

Hermetic Axiom. This expresses the relationship of Macrocosm and Microcosm which is noted in the words "as above, so below."

Hermetic Philosophy. Properly, the writings of Hermes Trismegistus, supposed author of ancient sacred writings studied by the Egyptians, but often used today to describe occult teachings generally.

Hermit, Evemite. An ascetic who lives alone in his devotion to God. Contrasted with the Cenobite—one who lives in a community of fellow devotionists.

Hermod. The Scandinavian god, son of Odin, who when his brother Balder was killed tried to bring him back from the underworld to his home in Asgard.

Herrera, Abraham Cohen. Author of a unique Cabalistic concept,— an amalgamation of Neo-Platonism and the occult doctrines of Isaac Luria (q.v.). The only Cabalist who wrote his works in Spanish. He died in Amsterdam in 1639. His influential concepts came to be confused with those of Spinoza (q.v.), and his Lurianic Cabalism was equated with pantheism (q.v.).

Hesed. In the Cabala the masculine energy of justice, peace, and love, signified by the number 4 and the symbols of the sceptre, wand, and crook.

Hettinger, Dr. John. Writer on telepathy and ESP, who became convinced by his studies and experiments of the reality of survival.

Hex. The practice of witchcraft. Widely believed in Germany, where a Hegetisse, Hexse, Hexer was a wizard, it became popular throughout Europe and spread to many areas in the United States, notably in Pennsylvania. Here, many students of the art still continue the tradition. However, to hex a person, to inflict evil upon another by magic and witchery, is flourishing in many areas in the United States. The word has become a fixture in the American language.

Heydon, John. The 17th century English astrologer and Rosicrucian. After traveling in Spain, Turkey, and the Near East, he became a lawyer. But he made his reputation as an astrologer and explicator of Rosicrucianism. He wrote: *The New Method of Rosie-Crucian Physick, The Rosie-Cross Uncovered, A New Method of Astrology, Cabballa, or the Art by which Moses and Elijah did so many Miracles,* and many other works on the occult and Rosicrucianism.

Hibernian Mysteries. A reflection of the old Atlantean initiation. It depicted in an ancient manner the eventual union between two ways of spiritual knowledge—the "outer" and "inner," the "above" and the "below." In the Rose-Cross this Christian symbol pictured their union.

Hierarchy. In theosophy this term signifies the degrees, grades, and levels of evolving entities in the cosmos. In occult doctrine, the whole of the disparate parts of the universe are under the control of the "sacred governors"; that is, the spiritual world is reflected on earth in material form. St. Paul, Dionysus, Dante, and Thomas Aquinas (qq.v.) generally see these hierarchies as an infinite spectrum. Anthoposophy limits them to three groups, each with three entities.

Hierarchy of Spirit (Spiritualism). A term often used by controls of trance mediums. It is descriptive of the integration between the different spirit planes of existence; inspiration which is not passing direct, but by means of a system of delegation, a chain of communication through the spheres to the medium on the earth plane. The higher spheres are said to be conscious and observant of the lower adjacent sphere, where they are able to influence and impress; but knowledge of the higher can only be revealed through the mediumship of spirits at the lower level.

Hieroglyphs. In poltergeistic phenomena and in seances, the writing that is produced without a medium or any physical agent. It is called "direct" writing.

Hierogrammatists. Egyptian priests who wrote and read the sacred Hieroglyphs. They also governed the teaching of initiates into the Mysteries.

Hierophant. The chief priest of the Eleusinian mysteries, a hereditary honor of the family of the Eumolpides, who represented the Demiurge (q.v.)

Higher Self. An Eastern esoteric concept of a super-consciousness attainable by meditation practices. (See: Atman). It bears a similarity to the idea of cosmic consciousness.

Hildegard of Bingen (1098–1179). German Benedictine nun, visionary, mystic, sage and medical authority, she became one of the most notable personages of her age. She corresponded with four popes, two emperors, and many scholars. In the *Scivia* she set down the visions and voices that she had experienced since a child. She also wrote on medicine, the natural world, dogmatic theology, and the way of the Christian life. Her works have been compared with those of Dante and William Blake (qq.v.).

Hill, J. Arthur. Hon. Associate of S.P.R., well-known author of many books on religion, psychology, psychical research and Spiritualism.

Hillel of Verona (1220–1295). Jewish thinker, physician, and philosopher, whose views had an affect on Cabalism and Jewish mysticism. In his work the *Tagmule ha-Nefesh* he declares that the Universal Active Intellect acts upon the soul of each individual and aids it to develop its powers.

Himmler, Heinrich. Head of the Nazi SS Troops, and Director of the Jewish Elimination Program, was also the Master of Occult Projects under Hitler. He directed thousands of assistants and spent millions in research projects of Freemasonry, Rosicrucianism, Astrology, Runic explorations, mysticism, Eastern Occultism, and other magical lore. He also headed a "Circle of Friends," a group of rich men who contributed large sums to occult research. Hitler's horoscope was constantly being cast by astrologers, and Himmler sought out every astrologer who could cast a favorable reading for his Fuehrer. But like all else that was horrible, inhuman and irrational under Nazism, their desire to coerce the supernatural to achieve world supremacy produced nothing, only a holocaust.

Hinayana. The Southern Buddhist doctrine—an "inner" Buddhist creed supposed for the intelligent minority—also called "little system;" Mahayana, "great system" being the doctrine for the masses. Hinayana is mainly a technique for absorption into the Absolute, has no belief in Buddha as a continuant, and disclaims the notion of Buddhist saints or Bodhisattvas.

Hinduism. The main religion of India practiced by about 600 million people. The foundation of all existence is said to be Brahma (q.v.), the verbal image of the Deity who encompasses all things. There is also the doctrine of the Atman or Higher Self; a concept of a united self yet divided into many egos. This Great Self is later identified with Brahma. A fundamental notion asserts that it is necessary to discard the earthly experience as an unreal perception, as being worthy of only a misperceived "little self." Therefore meditation must center on the Great Self to conquer the little self. The sacred writings of the earliest periods are the Rig Veda, in ten books of 1,028 hymns dated 1500–1000 B.C., and later the Upanishads and the Bhagvad-Gita. The concepts of Bhaki, Karma, Moska development of the philosophy and teachings of Yoga (q.v.) (500–100 B.C.) also added to the profound wisdom of Hinduism.

Hiquet. In Egyptian religion the name of the frog goddess who symbolized immortality.

Hiranyagarbha (Hinduism). This is the name of the golden egg from which came the universe.

Historia Monachorum in Aegyto. Writings depicting the evil deeds of demons who lived in Egypt, which were the accounts of eremite monks. Their descriptions of the Devil and his demons as ugly and misshapen set the future pattern for literature and art.

Hitchcock, Ethan Allen (1798–1870). American general and literary historian. He was among the first in modern times to perceive the spiritualistic aspect of alchemy as a process of spiritual development engaged in by the alchemist which synthesizes mysticism and esoteric alchemy. He wrote *Remarks upon Alchemy and Alchemists*, and *Swedenborg, a Hermetic Philosopher*, both being significant works.

Hitlahavat (Judaism). God-intoxication which the Chassidim achieve through love of God's creations—nature, man, and God.

Ho (Confucianism). That harmony of the central self in all its expressions which is akin to the universal law and harmony found in the world. Similar to the concept of *Chung.*

Hod. In Cabalism the number eight signifying eternity.

Hodgson, Dr. Richard (1855–1905). One of the keenest and most critical investigators of the early days of the S.P.R. Australian born, he studied law at Cambridge. It was he who exposed Mme. Blavatsky when he was sent to India to investigate phenomena alleged to have occurred at the H.Q. of the *Theosophical Society* there. He was very sceptical of all psychic phenomena for the major part of his life, but changed gradually and completely after intensive investigation of Mrs. Piper's mediumship over the fifteen years that he served as Secretary of the A.S.P.R. During his last years he developed mediumship himself.

Hodur or Hod. The old Scandinavian god of night, son of Odin, who though enormously strong was blind. Loki (q.v.) tricked him into killing his twin-brother Balder (q.v.).

Holda. Originally a Teutonic goddess, Holda was one of the names of the Queen of the Night, the goddess of witchcraft.

Holy Grail, The. Much sought-for sacred vessel of innumerable symbolic myths and legends.

Holy of Holies. The most sacred room or area in the temples of the ancient world which were consecrated to the highest divinity, or some holy object associated with this God. Only the high priest had access to this area.

Hom (Zoroastrianism). Another name for Haoma (q.v.).

Home Circle (Spiritualism).The kernel of the Spiritualist movement. A dedicated group of about seven friends, meeting regularly but unobtrusively in a room of an ordinary home, rejecting all feelings of jealousy and animosity, united in their belief that spirit helpers are ready to uplift them and stimulate their efforts to serve humanity or to develop their psychic powers for the same ends. No formal ceremonies, "mysteries," creeds or hymns are required. There is usually, but not always, a developed medium present, who can sense the appropriate conditions generated, besides forming a mouthpiece for the control. One member is nominated "leader," somebody of experience who is in charge of the proceedings. The subsequent course of action for the circle is given by the chief control or guide who issues instructions and teaching from time to time. Some home circles, already developed, sit for specific purposes: absent healing, individual psychic development, direct voice, or the gaining of inner wisdom by meditation.

Home, Daniel Dunglas (1833–1886). Scottish physical medium, perhaps the most outstanding in history. Confronted with his startling powers, many eminent hardheaded critics melted overnight. He appeared before W.M. Thackeray, Robert Browning, Lord Lytton, Mr. and Mrs. Trollope, and a number of kings and queens and emperors of Europe. His phenomena included levitation, fire immunity to an astounding degree, strange music from nowhere, and elongation of the body.

Homunculus. A term used in Jewish mysticism to refer to the creation of androids. (See: Golem). Its core meaning is little man, dwarf. Alchemists asserted that making the homunculus was possible and could be achieved without sexual intercourse.

Honey. In ancient times, in the Mediterranean World, honey was considered a heavenly gift with religious qualities. It was believed that it dripped from trees in the Golden Age; that being heavenly it had mystic virtues and was therefore used in drinking to the dead. It was believed that the Greek god Zeus, who was also called Melissaios (honey-nurtured), achieved his supremacy owing to having fed on honey as an infant.

Honochenokeh. Spirits of Good-will among the Iroquois Indians. They are the elemental beings of nature, the invisible helpers.

Hoodoo. In Voodoo any entity, person or place that is considered bad luck. Also an evil spell.

Hope, William (1863-1933). A carpenter of Crewe who became famous as a spirit photographer medium. The center of much controversy and accused of fraud, he was nevertheless able to convince many of the leading investigators that he possessed genuine powers. It is in his favor that he never commercialized his gift.

Hopkins, Matthew. The notorious 17th century Englishman who called himself the "witchfinder." He impressed the natives of Suffolk with his uncanny ability to nose out witches. Hopkins and the noted clergyman Dr. Calamy were relentless witch enemies: the former rounding them up, the latter painting their horrors. Hopkins asserted he had the list of all the witches in England, and between 1645 and 1646, in some 14 months, he sent to their death more witches than all the other witch-hunters in England. Finally, the people killed him as a witch.

Horary Astrology. This branch of astrology deals with the problems or questions asked by a querent (q.v.), and the interpretation of the chart set up for the time of the "birth of the question." Generally, the first house of Ascendent is deemed to represent the querent at the moment of the question and the houses at this time, and then the questioner's birth planets are fixed into these houses.

Horned Hand. An occult sign which renders the Devil powerless, made by depressing the middle fingers and the thumb while raising both the index and little fingers.

Horoscope. A symbolic map of the heavens at a particular moment, drawn by an astrologer from astronomical data, for the purpose of interpreting correlations between the positions of the celestial bodies and earthly tendencies at that time. The chart is based upon the circle of the ecliptic and the zodiac signs, upon which are inserted the planets, sun and moon, the whole being quartered by the horizon and meridian of the observer. A further hypothetical division into twelve segments shows the "houses." Each house has as its "lord" one of the heavenly bodies, and the one in the "ascendant" is the one of greatest significance to the inquirer, giving him his personality and good and bad fortune. Many early astronomers, Johannes Kepler for example, were skilled astrologers and drew horoscopes as part of their careers.

Hotoru. The wind god of the Pawnee Plains Indians. Certain medicine men kept the wind in leather bags and had the power to release it to patrons.

Houdini, Harry (1874–1926). An American magician whose escape feats (locked in chains, strait-jackets, submerged in chains and boxes under water) made him world famous and a household word in his time. But like many great magicians he resented what he considered misrepresentation, and he campaigned against psychics and those who claimed supernatural talents. He wrote: *Miracle Mongers and Their Methods*, and *A Magician Among the Spirits*. Nonetheless, he made a pact with his wife that the first to die was to try to communicate with the survivor. This spiritualistic experiment had a mysterious ending, for in 1929, three years after Houdini's death, Mrs. Houdini declared that the medium Arthur Ford (q.v.) had received a message from Houdini; a few years later she reversed herself and declared she had received nothing.

House. In astrology, this term is distinguished from the term sign (which refers to the spatial division of the Zodiac), for house is based on the time element. The houses are divisions referring to the time involved in the earth's daily rotation on its axis as it moves around the sun, and they cover a two-hour segment of a twenty-four hour period. House also refers to the fact that each planet in astrology possesses two houses, one of the day, the second of the night.

House of Life. In astrology these are all the influences, good and bad, that concur to affect the life of each person.

Household of The Upper World (Judaism). After the Jews had been exposed to the Babylonians during their Babylonian Captivity they assimilated many notions from the Assyrian-Babylonian religions. This concept refers, in Hebrew mysticism, to the highest rank of angels.

Hrishikesha (Hinduism). An appellation for Krishna or Vishnu. Literally it means "with erect hair."

Hsiao yao yu (Taoism). The ultimate happiness achieved through following nature beyond matter, into the infinite and into a state of transcendent bliss.

Hsi ch'ang (Taoism). A method of practicing the Eternal by noting the small, preserving one's weakness, utilizing the light, and using wisdom "to avoid disaster to life."

Hsin (Taoism). The original or intuitive mind of man; also the pure and distilled part of the vital force, "chi," the spiritual faculty or consciousness of man; and the mind conceived as identical with reason and intuition.

Hsin Chai (Confucianism). Mencius (q.v.) developing Confucius' (q.v.)

thoughts used this term to mean "fasting of the mind." This is a condition of pure experience with no intellectual content, for it is immediate knowing—and the attainment of a mystical state of unity.

Hsing (Confucianism). That which is beyond mere corporeality—the Great Ultimate.

Hsu (Taoism). The important concept of emptiness, non-existence, that complete peace and purity which allows the mind to receive all thoughts with total equanimity.

Hsuan (Taoism). This term central to Taoism means the "mystery of mysteries, the gate to all existence," that which is mysterious, the Supremely Profound Principle.

Hsuan te (Taoism). Profound virtue achieved through total natural being, the cultivation of one's original nature, and returning to the quality of Tao—the "way." This is the "way" of identification with the "beginning," to attain emptiness and vastness, and to enter into mystic union with the universe.

Hsuan tsung (Taoism). One of the names for Taoism, meaning the Religion of Mystery.

Huebner, Louise. American witch who is considered the "official witch" of Los Angeles. Her "spellcasts" which bring huge crowds to the Hollywood Bowl are witchcraft festivals designed, she has said, "to increase sexual vitality."

Hugin and Munin. In Norse mythology the two Ravens who sat on the shoulders of the blind Odin and guided him. The names mean memory and thought.

Hugel, Baron Friedrich Von (1852–1925). Though born in Italy, this Austrian nobleman and philosopher spent most of his life in England. He became a leading Roman Catholic philosopher, developing concepts of mysticism. For him the Infinite played a signal part in man's development since it was spiritual in nature. He wrote: *The Mystical Element of Religion as Studied in St. Catherine of Genoa and Her Friends.*

Hugo, Victor (1802–1885). The great novelist was convinced of the truth of Spiritualism. He wrote of French Spiritualists: "To avoid phenomena, to make them bankrupt of the attention to which they have a right, is to make bankrupt truth itself." When he died he left an unpublished manuscript on Spiritualism to Paul Meurice.

Hugo of St. Victor (1096–1141). One of the first notable encyclopedists in the Middle Ages of philosophical Christianity in the Roman Catholic Church (which included such figures as Peter Abelard, Peter Lombard, St. Thomas Aquinas). His works consisted of many diverse religious opinions, particularly of the great Church fathers, in order to reconcile their views. Hugo of St. Victor's summa is important, for he was among the eminent mystics whose work was extremely influential in the subsequent history of Catholic and Christian mysticism.

Huitzilopochtli. Among the Aztecs the divine hero to whom blood-sacrifices were offered to maintain his strength. In the meaning of "Humming-bird wizard," his name was a combination of astrality and black magic. When the great pyramid temple was dedicated to this god in Mexico in 1486 over 20,000 people were sacrificed in the ceremony.

Human Personality. Occultism by revealing man's enormous potentialities as a part of universal nature increases the complexity of human personality. It would appear that the earthly individual is only part of a larger entity—the Group Soul—which he will join at a later date, having formed by his reactions an earthly pattern for a new successor of the group to follow. The exact relationships of all these "facets" of a large human personality are fraught with interest. We can see that the human senses are not confined to the physical body. It is conceivable that at a later stage of development, they may all be incorporated in some greater being, where all these facets of experience which we call "persons," may be united for the benefit of the whole. Theosophists make a distinction between personality and individuality—the former being the psychical, astral, and physical impulses, while the latter lead to the spiritual and higher qualities.

Hungan. Among the Voodoo cults the Hungan is the priest.

Hunting Magic. Since prehistoric times man has used many magical rituals to insure success in the hunt. Some of these are: drawing pictures of animals (which we see in many cave paintings); the worship of the tribal totem; the use of the tribal egregore (q.v.); and the great multi-notional concept of mana (q.v.). Some Eskimos use a form of magic in their hunting, the Iglukik still utilizing drawings as did their prehistoric ancestors.

Hurrian Hymn. The world's oldest song to the gods and goddesses which dates from about 2000 B.C. and belongs to a lost early Assyro-Babylonian civilization. The Hurrian was deciphered in 1972 by Dr. Anne D. Kilmer, professor of Assyriology at the University of California. Found in the ancient city of Ugarit, now Syria, it is written in a diatonic seven-note scale, proving that the Hurrian people, not the Greeks, invented the basis of Western music. This ode to the Hurrian Pantheon of divinities, the only and oldest one now in existence from the Near East, gives proof of the communal-mystery-religious-cults practiced in this region.

Huysmans, Joris Karl (1848–1907). French novelist of Dutch extraction, who converted to Catholicism. His most noted work is *Against the Grain*; but his novel on Satanism, *La-Bas*, reveals his deepest feelings and his intense pessimism. In it he declares that darkness and light struggle to conquer the soul, but that the "God of light is in the eclipse," since evil has conquered the world.

Hydesville Phenomena. Hydesville, said to be the birth-place of modern Spiritualism, is a small hamlet in New York State, where the Fox sisters (q.v.) in 1848 first discovered and demonstrated their mediumship.

Hyle. Meaning "first principle" or primordial substance of the material universe. Paracelsus (q.v.) equated the word with Azoth. For the alchemists it was the basic state of matter, the initial point of their process. In the work of Boehme (q.v.) it meant the "substance" of the Edenic Garden.

Hylozoism. A doctrine that life is a property of matter, all things being alive.

Hypatia. Greek scholar, daughter of a mathematician, she was noted in Alexandria (c. A.D. 400) as a teacher of Neo-Platonism. A mob of Christians, incited by their bishop, tore Hypatia to pieces in the year 415.

Hyperaesthesia. Extreme acuteness of the normal senses, often noticed with hysterics and hypnotized subjects. Hallucinogens and psychedelics create an intensified sensory perception that may be expansive or distorted with strong feelings of euphoria or despair.

Hyperamnesia. Extension of the memory powers, a quickening of the mind's sensitivity. Has been noticed in hypnotized subjects.

Hyperborean. See Root Race.

Hyperouraniol. In Neo-Platonism these are the twelve super-celestial divinities.

Hypnotic Regression. Hypnotic technique whereby the subject is able to recall evidential details of events far back in his personal history. Its interest for psychic research lies in the apparent success of some hypnotists who claim to have regressed the memory to events before birth. The substantiation of these events is advanced as evidence for the theory of reincarnation.

Hypnotism. The modern development of Mesmerism. An artificially induced kind of sleep state, the peculiarity of which is the "rapport" which can exist between the hypnotist and the subject. A suggestion by the hypnotist to the subject may be obeyed to a supernormal degree; it may even be delayed to the normal waking state before it takes effect quite independently of the subject's own consciousness. The hypnotic trance can be self-induced in order to attain greater self-confidence or mastery over pain. The mediumistic trance seems to be self-induced, though it may be due to spirit hypnotists. The main difference is the absence of suggestibility in the medium; the person longed for does not always communicate in accordance with the "suggestion" of the sitter.

Hyslop, James Hervey (1854–1920). Distinguished American psychic researcher, Professor of Logic and Ethics at Columbia University, New York. He became convinced of personal survival through the mediumship of Mrs. Piper, and regarded survival as scientifically proved. Also, he made an intensive study of multiple personality and supported the view that it was due to spirit possession. Hyslop founded an institute for the treatment of such cases by mediums.

I. Represented often as a hand with bent fore-finger in occult writings, it is the 9th letter of the English and the tenth of the Hebrew alphabet, signifying one in both, and ten in Hebrew.

Ialdabaoth. In Gnosticism the evil demon who gave birth to the Lower World. It is part of the liberation of alchemical transmutation, representing the demiurge in the darkness of matter which now shines forth in its pristine state.

Iamblichus, also Jamblichus (270–330 A.D.). An important Syrian Neo-Platonist who by his commentaries made Plotinus (q.v.) more widely known. Further, Iamblichus enriched the work of Plotinus; thus his own philosophy became an important source for scholastic and Cabalistic thought.

Iao. The name is synonymous with IHJH of the Hebrew Mysteries among the Gnostics (q.v.); the mystic symbol of the Supreme Divine World among the ancient Chaldeans and Phoenicians; the name which is not to be spoken because of its sacredness. Also, the polar male and female generative symbol which this mystic name represents was worn by the initiates of the mysteries of Serapis—an Egyptian-Grecian-Roman deity.

Iblis (Islam). The Devil, the former archangel, whose domain is now the earth and its souls and whose cult is the Devil-worshipers.

Ibn Ezra, Abraham ben Meir (Judaism) (1093–1167). Occultist and well-known Spanish Hebrew poet.

I.C (Astrology). Imum Coeli, an astrological "angle" of importance, corresponding to the point where the meridian of the observer, at any given time, cuts the lowest point of the ecliptic.

I-Ching. The Chinese Book of Changes, the experimental basis of classical Chinese philosophy, in which a grasp of the total situation at any given moment is said to be obtained. It deals with the interplay of dual cosmic principles, the Yin and the Yang. The psychic and physical worlds are held to be the dual expression of a living reality. The method consists of dividing forty-nine yarrow stalks into two random heaps, and counting them by threes and fives, or in throwing three coins six times, each line of a hexagram being determined by the value of heads and tails. Thus each of sixty-four mutations is held to correspond to a psychic situation. There is a similar Western method known as Ars Geomantica or Art of Punctation. Increasingly in recent years the techniques of *I Ching* have been utilized in various scientific disciplines, particularly in game plan theory.

Ichthus. Greek for a fish. These letters form the Greek phrase "Iesous Christos Theou Vios Soter," in early Christian times ascribed to Jesus Christ, Son of God, Saviour. Early Christians were also called "fish" and drawings of fish were found in the Catacombs.

Icthyomancy. Divination by a study of the entrails of fishes. This was one important means of divination practiced by many nations in the ancient Near East. *Icthys,* Greek for fish, was used by the early Christians as a symbol for Christ.

Icu. In Cuba this West African god is the god of death. Certain practices are engaged in to thwart Icu when someone is dying.

Identity Proof (Spiritualism). Before evidence of survival can be accepted, the communicator has to prove his identity to the satisfaction of the inquirer. This may not be successful at the first sitting, but this is not surprising if one considers the difficulties from the communicator's point of view. He has to remember something specific of his earthly life, yet not commonly known, by which he may be recognized. He may be successful in transmitting his evidence through the medium, but the sitter may not know of the matter mentioned, or its verification may not be possible.

Ideomorphs. Molds obtained supernormally.

Ideoplasm. A term for ectoplasm with the additional implication that it is capable of being molded into any desired shape.

Idisi. Demonic female spirits in Germanic mythology.

Idol. The sculptured object which embodies the divine entity, becoming, thus, the focus of worship and ritual. The creation of idols is a universal phenomenon in the history of man. Sometimes, as in Egypt, a combination human-animal figure, such as the Sphinx, serves as an idol. In many ancient nations, notably Greece, the idols supposedly contained the divine spirits within themselves; accordingly, they could move their eyes, turn their heads, or raise their arms. Judaism forbids the worship of idols.

Idolatry. The worship of idols (q.v.).

Idra Rabba (Judaism). In the section of the *Zohar* (q.v.) under the title of "The Greater Holy Assembly" are to be found the teachings and meditations of an important group of students of the Cabala.

Idra Suta (Judaism). In the section of the *Zohar* (q.v.) under the title of "The Lesser Holy Assembly" are to be found the teachings of this esoteric group of students of Cabala.

Ieu. The Gnostic term for the *Pistis-Sophia*—the archetypal or first man, corresponding to Adam Kadmon (q.v.).

Igaluk. Among the Indians of Alaska, the name for the moon.

Ignatius of Loyola (c. 1491–1556). A man of profound esoteric life and spiritual insight; founder and leader of The Society of Jesus (Jesuits). His book *Spiritual Exercises*, originally published in 1548, includes a comprehensive system of mystical training, and has had a broad influence among students of the spiritual life both in and out of the Roman Catholic faith.

Igneous Demons. Those malevolent spirits who never permit sorcerers on earth to use them as familiars, remaining in their own domain.

Ignis Fatuus. Peculiar lights which appear in cemeteries or marshy places. Although generally ascribed to natural causes, some sensitives claim to see lights where sudden death has occurred.

Ikyom The Moon goddess among the Maya Quiche Indians of Guatemala, patroness of birth.

Illa. Amulets, charms and magical pieces worn by the Incas. (q.v.).

Illapa-Katoylla. Among the Incas he was the god of the souls in the underworld.

Illuminati. The brotherhood of the enlightened adepts in the occult arts which flourished in Spain and France throughout the latter part of the 15th century and the 16th. The Rosicrucians also called themselves by this name. Adam Weishaupt also founded the Illuminati in Germany in 1776. His was a republican, revolutionary organization. He wedded it to mysticism and the occult and the Free Masons to disguise his real intentions. But in 1785 the Church and the state of Bavaria, learning of its real import, destroyed the organization.

Illusion. Perception with an objective base, but which is falsely interpreted. The work of expert conjurors could be correctly described as illusory. (See: Hallucination).

Illusion, Plane of (Spiritualism). According to an alleged communication of F.W.H. Myers (q.v.), the third level of the seven planes of human consciousness. Also called by him "the immediate world after death." Here, the mind's creative powers are sufficient to formulate appropriate environs according to the habit of thought of each individual spirit. Thus they are enabled to follow an objective life similar to that of earth, only on a more ambitious scale, as the struggle and effort of earthly life are absent. The care of the body—the greatest limiting earthly factor—is no longer the primary consideration, as it is said to be nourished directly from cosmic sources.

Ilmatur. The virgin who falls from heaven into the sea before creation; the daughter of the air, mother of seven sons (seven nature forces). In Finnish mythology, her story is told in *The Kalevalla* (q.v.).

Imbele. The consecration of the sacred mistletoe cut by the Druid priests with the golden sickle during the Celtic festival at the beginning of February. It is the time when the sickle stands in the constellation of Leo at midnight.

Imhotep (c. 2680 B.C.). Egyptian god of learning, of builders, and of physicians. Although Imhotep was a historical figure, so illustrious were his abilities as a statesman, sage, architect, priest, physician, and magician that he was deified at his death—an honor accorded to only one other person in Egypt's long history. There is good evidence for the claim that he was the designer of the great Step pyramid at Saqqorah. Imhotep's many temples were enormously popular with those seeking medical cures. The Greeks identified him with Asclepius (q.v.).

Immanence. In theology, the indwelling of Deity within the world. (Equivalent to pantheism).

Immortality. Historically, in the relationship of man to divinity, man's soul has been considered divine, a view which has led to many concepts of the soul's immortality. This was central to the religions and myths of most nations in ancient times, and has continued to be central in most contemporary religions. Spiritualism, theosophy, anthroposophy, (qq.v.) etc., see immortality as an evolution, in which the soul or astral body undergoes a spiritual growth in successive planes, or, in the case of the latter two, in successive births. This concept reflects Vedic and Buddhist (qq.v.) influences.

Immunity from Fire. See Fire Immunity.

"Imperator." Chief control of the Rev. Stainton Moses, who came with a spirit band, as missionaries, in an endeavor to uplift humanity. This control once admitted to being Malachias the prophet. His communications did not come directly, but through the agency of another spirit named "Rector." Many instances are known where this same "Imperator" is alleged to have communicated through later mediums, notably Mrs. Piper, Mrs. Minnie M. Soule (Mrs. Chenoweth), and Dr. Hodgson.

Impersonation (Spiritualism). The imitation by one spirit of another's person and character. This can happen in mediumship, and is due to the fact that discarnates were once incarnate and sometimes retain a liking for mischievous pranks. Controls should be treated as rational human beings, and extravagant claims should be well tested before credence is given to them.

Impression. (Spiritualism). Descriptive of the process by which entities can influence the mind of a mediumistic person. The actual method may be telepathic or hypnotic; the impression may be visual, tactual, or perhaps a sudden urge to a certain course of action. An intensification of impression would amount to control.

Imprints, Psychic. See Molds.

Imum Coeli. See I.C.

Inca. The name for the Indian people of ancient Peru and the name given to the creative gods and later to the ruler of the country, "Son of the Sun." Owing to their very highly developed civilization it was said that after the destruction of Atlantis (q.v.), there were seven Incas who then repopulated the earth.

Incantation. The expression of special formulae to achieve a certain magical effect through some supernatural power. This may result in the bewitching of someone, or the exorcising of a demon.

Incantatrix. A witch in the Middle Ages.

Incarnate. Clothed in flesh, a spirit animating an earthly body. The individual earthly state of being.

Incarnation. The embodiment of the Godhead in a human or animal body. In Christianity, Jesus (q.v.) is God born as a man. The notion of incarnation is prevalent in all religions. In Persia, the kings possessed the "divine light." In Egypt, Pharoahs were carriers of the sun god Re (q.v.). In Greece, Zeus, Poseidon, and Apollo (q.v.) were incarnated in many forms. In Hinduism, Vishnu (q.v.) has appeared in numerous avatars (q.v.). In Mahayana Buddhism (q.v.), the bodhisattvas (q.v.) become incarnated to aid desperate humanity. In Tibet, both the Dalai Lama and the Tashi Lama are considered incarnations. In Islam, the Imams and the Madhi are incarnations of the Divine Being.

Incarnation of Satan. It is believed that certain Satanic figures on earth are incarnations of Satan; for example, such personages as Nero, Attila, Napoleon, Hitler and Stalin.

Incense. Used in worship, and since its fragrance delights the gods, it is believed to possesses supernatural qualities. That it was able to dispel odors may have symbolized its ability to banish demons. Incense in modern ritual possesses the virtue of intensifying psychic concentration during spiritual involvement, collectively or for one's self.

Incommunicable Axiom. The catalytic knowledge in the occult which has been considered the magic code. Once this is solved, the occultist has deemed himself omnipotent. Many have believed that the four letters of the Tetragram, the Cabalistic words Azoth and Inri (qq.v.), for example, contain this divine code, once the adept arranges their letters properly.

Incubation. In the early centuries of the Eastern Orthodox Church, an ill person followed an esoteric practice of sleeping in a church dedicated to Cosmos and Damian, two martyrs. The hope was to be favored with a dream leading to a physical cure.

Incubus. An evil spirit, a vampire type related to the Succuba (q.v.) and considered more dangerous than an ordinary nightmare. It descended upon sleeping persons, especially to have sexual intercourse with women at night. In esotericism they are considered elemental soulless beings without sense or form. In Hinduism they are known as Pischas who are considered responsible for many terrible happenings.

Independent Voice. A term for physical voice phenomena, independent of apparatus. A form of direct voice (q.v.), but produced without a trumpet or megaphone.

Indra (Hinduism). In early Vedic times a god of the first rank, the god of the sky, the sovereign of the world, the life-giver, the bestower of benefits, the creator of fertility, the sender of rain, and the hurler of thunderbolts. Nearly one third of the hymns of the Veda (q.v.) are addressed to Indra. Although in the later Hindu mythology he is inferior to the Triad (Brahma-Vishnu-Siva), (q.v.) he remains a powerful divinity. Indra is pictured as riding on an elephant as a human being with a thousand eyes, which is sometimes said to represent the stars in the sky.

Ineffable Name. Traditionally, a name for God which must not be spoken.

Infant Prodigies. See Prodigies.

Infichiuma. An Australian magical ceremony to increase the supply of the totemic animal which is hunted for food.

Infinite. Boundless, without end or limit. "The Infinite," God, Deity, or the Great Spirit.

Influence (Spiritualism). Mediums often refer to spirit influences, usually meaning impression or clairsentience. The term has been applied to objects belonging to the sitter, which seem to assist the medium to contact the ideas of communicators. This process is often confused with psychometry.

Influenced Writing. Writing, the substance of which is affected by remote suggestion from another mind.

Ingram, M.V. He published a book on the Bell Witch of Tennessee, which was one of the most famous of American haunted houses. The haunting lasted from 1817 to 1820; the house was visited by neighbors from miles around and travelers from many parts of the country. It also attracted the attention of clergymen and doctors. But nothing stopped the ghost from killing the father of the Bell family in 1820, and from compelling the daughter, Betsy Bell, into breaking off her marriage to her suitor, an action demanded by the ghost. Dr. Nandor Fodor (q.v.) called it America's greatest ghost story. Ingram's grandiosely titled book, published in 1891, was called *An Authenticated History of the Famous Bell Witch. The Wonder of the 19th Century, and Unexplained Phenomena of the Christian Era. The Mysterious Talking Goblin that Terrorized the West End of Robertson County, Tennessee, Tormenting John Bell to his Death. The Story of Betsy Bell, Her Lover and the Haunting Sphynx, Clarksville, Tenn.*

Initiate. One admitted to knowledge of occult mysteries by systematic psychic development.

Inner Light. Term used by the Society of Friends that describes the human capacity for spiritual experience of God.

Innocent VIII, Pope. He issued a Papal Bull in 1488 against Devil worship and witches. The Pope asserted that sexual intercourse with infernal fiends and the defilement of holy symbols (wearing a crucifix upside down) were rampant. He also declared that witches blighted the corn in the fields, the vineyard's grapes, and the tree's fruits and herbs.

Insanity. It has been said that mediumship is a threat to sanity. However, there is at present no definitive data on this subject. The famous medium Eileen Garrett (q.v.), for example, who was troubled by this problem, on her own initiative subjected herself to a number of tests by psychiatrists. A survey made many years ago by Dr. Egen Crowell did come to a negative conclusion, but the subject has not really been investigated.

Inspirational Speaking. Impromptu addresses by mediums in various degrees of trance, the contents of which frequently surpass their own capabilities. Many good mediums of this kind are known.

Inspirational Writing and Drawing. Akin to automatism, but without the hand itself being controlled. The writer or artist consciously records a series of mental impressions supernormally received.

Institut General Psychologique. Founded in Paris 1904 for psychical research. It did conduct a memorable investigation of the phenomena of Eusapia Paladino 1905–08, but has now ceased to function.

Institut Metapsychique International. Founded 1918 in Paris by Jean Meyer. First directed by Dr. Gustave Geley, whose committee contained among other distinguished people: Professor Richet, Camille Flammarion, Sir Oliver Lodge and Ernest Bozzano (qq.v.).

Instrument (Spiritualism). A term often used by a control when referring to the medium. Although this would suppose a completely mechanical transmission, this is not so, as the medium's mind and vocabulary have to be employed by the spirit operators. Therefore the habitual mental associations of the medium are apt to present themselves in addition to the transmitted material.

Insufflation. Eliphas Levi (q.v.) deemed this one of the most important aspects of occult medicine, being a perfect sign of the transmission of life. Insufflation means to blow or breathe upon; and an alternation of cold and warm blowings, being a replica of the body's polar vitality, is one of the most potent methods to utilize. Either cold or warm are useful (the former being negative, the latter positive), for each has its own virtues in illness.

Interlocked Rings Experiment. A famous case in which two rings of different woods were prepared by Sir Oliver Lodge (q.v.), and, at his request, were interlocked by the mediumship of Margery Crandon (q.v.). Photographs of them were taken and the rings placed in a museum; but at some subsequent date, they were found parted again.

International Spiritualist Federation, The. Founded in 1923, revived in London 1948. It aims to strengthen Spiritualism as a world movement, and to foster international relationships by affiliating properly constituted bodies with a spiritualistic or psychic basis which accept (a) personal survival, and (b) communication with the spirit world. Also it aims to co-operate in the study of psychic phenomena from scientific, philosophical, moral and religious aspects. Its membership is open to approved societies, groups and individuals.

Interpenetration of Matter. See Matter through Matter.

Introspection. Observation of one's own mental processes.

Intuition. Instant knowledge obtained without reasoning. How far impression may be responsible, it is difficult to say. The basis of all knowledge in science and the occult is intuition.

Intuitional World. In theosophy this is the sixth world, the one from which intuitions are received. The Buddhic Plane.

Invocation of a Demon. Many formulae have been prescribed to invoke the aid of demons, one of the most notable being the utterance of

the nine Hebrew names anciently identified with mystic powers—
Eheieh, Iod, Tetragammaton Elohim, El, Elohim Gibor, Eloah Va-Daath,
El Adonai Tzabaoth, Elohim Tzabaoth, Shaddai. In Cabalism, how-
ever, an amulet with the name of Shaddai (one of the mystic names of
God) and a special formula which began "In the name of Shaddai. . ."
were especially potent against demons who inflicted illness.

Iron. In Roman times this metal in the form of an iron nail taken from
the coffin was considered a charm against demons that haunt the
house at night. In parts of Scotland and Ireland an iron poker laid
across a cradle protects an infant from malevolent fairies until the
babe is baptized.

Isaac of Holland. While little is known of this alchemist, most authorities place him in the fifteenth century. He and his son were the first to
develop alchemy in Holland, to give it there a solid foundation. Both
Paracelsus (q.v.) and the eminent English chemist Robert Boyle valued
his work.

Isaac of Stella (c. 1100–1169). English priest who studied in France,
where he became Abbot L'etoile. He was the greatest exponent of
Neo-Platonism and the pseudo-Dionysius of his age. His writings, widely accepted, made him also the most influential teacher of the doctrine
that the Roman Catholic Church is Christ's mystical body.

Issac The Blind (fl. 1190–1200). Working in the tradition of Judaic
mysticism, he popularized the central concepts and mystical developments of the ancient rabbis. Isaac, a French Jew, was especially interested in God's emanations in the physical world, the creation of
matter, and man's mystical involvement with God.

I.S.F. The International Spiritualist Federation (q.v.).

Islam. One of the world's great religions, founded in A.D. 622 by Muhammad. Soon after the age of forty he became a prophet through
hearing voices urging him to proclaim the name of the Lord. Islam is
the worship of Allah the Deity, not of Muhammad the prophet. Their
sacred writing is the Koran (Qur'an), which contains the utterances of
Muhammad in 114 Surahs (the chapters or divisions of the Koran).
The declaration of belief by Islamites is the *Shahada*: "There is but
one God (Allah), and Muhammad is the Apostle of God." Every Muslim
is commanded to proclaim this credo aloud at least once in a lifetime
with the deepest conviction. In Islam, the Koran is held to be the definitive word of a sequence of God-given scriptures that have been revealed to a line of prophets, the greatest of whom were: Abraham,
Moses, Jesus, and Muhammad. One of the highly important beliefs of
Muslims is the doctrine that at death the soul remains in the body during the first night, and at this time it is questioned by two angels who
judge the soul's quality of faith to determine who will rest in peace
and who will be admitted to heaven (after the Resurrection) and who

will suffer punishment during "the Interval." However, the souls of martyrs immediately enter heaven, with no waiting, as a proof of God's love.

Ithyphallic. The male sexual organs carried during the festival of Dionysius in ancient Greece. All phallic religions displayed exaggerated sexual organs. These were symbolic of the generative power in nature.

Iynx. A Chaldean symbol of universal power, its emblem is a winged globe. By the power of the mind numerous Iynexes of potency were produced. Some consider the Hebrew Yod a corresponding Iynx, since all letters are formed out of this one.

Jackson, Shirley. American novelist who died in 1965. She was a brilliant creator of multiple personalities and stories of the eerie and the mysterious. *The Haunting of Hill House,* an intensely gripping novel, and a book of short stories, *Come Along With Me* illustrate her psychological sensitivity and psychic perceptions of human beings.

Jacob's Ladder. In Cabalism this represents a symbolic vision of the powers of alchemy in visible nature. In Jacob's dream the "ladder" symbolized a "rainbow," or prismatic staircase between heaven and earth; moreover, red and blue were the two original colors—the first depicting "spirit," the second "matter"—and from them came orange, yellow, (through mixture with the light of the sun), green, and violet. For the sun is alchemic gold, the moon alchemic silver, and from these two mystic rulers of the world, astrologically understood, all things on earth were produced.

Jada (Hinduism). That which is unconscious, being in this sense inert and inanimate, lacking heat.

Jagad-guru (Hinduism). Signifies Brahma, Vishnu, or Shiva (qq.v.); therefore, its meaning is the Teacher of the World.

Jagd, Jagat (Hinduism). Indicating the principle of movement; in essence, therefore, the world, the Universe, and also a world-period.

Jagd-atman (Hinduism). A concept indicating the soul of the world. It corresponds to a very popular term in Western occultism—*Anima Mundi.*

Jagrat (Hinduism). The state of consciousness when one is awake.

Jail, In A Dream. According to old dream interpretation, dreams of being in a jail, indicate that honors or dignities will be conferred upon the dreamer. As with many dreams, the content goes contrariwise to what occurs in reality. It was supposed to be especially fortunate for politicians and appointed officials.

Jainism. The religion of Jina "the victor," the great Indian prophet. Arising in the 6th century B.C. as a protest against the complicated ritualism and impersonality of Hinduism, Jainism asserts that everything in the universe is eternal; spirits know their identity through successive incarnations; a belief in Karma (q.v.); after nine incarnations, the attainment of Nirvana; salvation by way of the three gems—right faith, right cognition, and right conduct. Yatis (ascetics) attain Nirvana with the five vows: to injure no creature, to speak truth, to abstain from stealing, to renounce all worldly goods, to practice sexual continence, and to gain self-mastery. Many of the Hindu gods are worshipped by Jainists, along with their two great prophets, Mahavira and Jina. Jainists believe that a succession of 24 Tirthankaras (saints) originated their religion, Mahavira the great hero and Jina, actual historical figures, being the last of such saints.

Jakin and Boas. The two symbolical pillars of Solomon's Cabalistic temple, one white the other black (good and evil), which explained all mysteries; for "two" is the key to cohesion and stability in the world.

Jalalu 'D-Din Rumi (1207-1272). Persian poet, mystic, Sufi devotee who is considered the most famous of Sufis. His poems, which are replete with the most delicately conceived symbols, express the highest reaches of mysticism. Many consider him the greatest of all the brilliant school of Sufi Masters whose poems are the glory of Persia. (See: Sufism)

James, William (1842-1910). Professor of Psychology and later of philosophy at Harvard University. James had the rather unique distinction of being both an internationally famous psychologist and an internationally famous philosopher; in the latter role he was one of the creators of the philosophic concept known as pragmatism. He was also a founder member of the A.S.P.R. (q.v.) and the president of the S.P.R. (q.v.) during 1894-95. He was responsible for the introduction of Mrs. Piper (q.v.) to the S.P.R., and had contact with her mediumship for many years. Not only was James a firm believer in the reality of psychic phenomena, but he played an instrumental part in making psychic phenomena a part of psychology.

James IV of Scotland (1473–1513). A devotee of alchemy and the occult who aided the practitioners of these arts during his reign of twenty-five years.

Janaloka (Hinduism). This is the portion of the universe in which Brahma's sons Sanaka, Sananda, and Sanat-Kumara live.

Janardana (Hinduism). A name of Krishna, meaning "the adored of mankind."

Janis, Byron. Prominent American concert pianist who was a child prodigy and a student of Vladimir Horowitz. He has toured much of Europe and South America, and is also a noted psychic. His ESP is of such a pronounced intensity that on several occasions he has directed a search for lost Chopin works: in Paris, in 1967, his psychic knowledge led to a discovery of two lost Chopin waltzes, and later, to the finding of additional lost manuscripts of Chopin. He has experienced being out-of-body during concerts, watching himself play; and knows intimate facts about the lives of strangers. Mrs. Janis, a painter, is herself a student of psychic healing.

Japanese Exorcism. Out of the complex of their religions, based on Shinto and various forms of Buddhism, they developed a form of exorcism utilizing lights and an incantation which is recited one hundred times.

Japanese New Year. Celebrated by casting peas and beans from the home, an act which eradicates evil. In addition, the mystical digits—3, 5, 7 are also utilized for this purpose.

Jars, Canopic. In ancient Egypt the set of four jars, containing the organs of the dead, which accompanied the body on the journey to the next world.

Jataka (Buddhism). The book which depicts the former lives of Buddha.

Jati-smara (Hinduism). That state of psychic growth which enables one to remember one's life in a past incarnation.

Jayas (Hinduism). These represent the 12 Emanations of Brahma. They are the operation of the creation from the beginning of the Kalpa (q.v.), and represent the 12 Creative Hierarchies of Hinduism.

Jeans, Dr. Norman. Experimented on himself with various anaesthetics and discovered that under the influence of nitrous oxide (laughing gas), he was able to witness events at distant places.

Jebal Djudi. In old Arabian mythology this was the "Deluge Mountain," reflecting the widespread legends of great floods, such as Ararat in the Hebrew Noah story, and that in the Babylonian story of Xisuthrus who settled, after the great flood, on Mount Mizir.

Jelly, In A Dream. In old dream interpretation, dreams of receiving pots of jelly or of eating jelly, signify good fortune and long life.

Jesus of Nazareth. The opinion of most reputable scholars could be summed up as follows: Jesus was an outstanding Jewish prophet born about 4 B.C. of Jewish parents. He probably studied the principles of the Essenes in addition to the Old Testament at some time during the early years of his life although little is known for certain. As a healer, a preacher, and mystic he gained a great following; but his outspoken criticisms of the narrow ways of orthodox creeds angered the authorities, who saw in his popularity a threat to their power; so they had him arrested and put him to death. It is possible that he materialized soon after to some of his followers. Jesus was a Jew throughout his life, and so far as we know, never claimed to have founded a religion. Although the New Testament teachings are one of the world's superlative religious statements, they are not in any sense original documents. The words used are not translations of the actual words that Jesus used: these were never recorded. Therefore Jesus was a great teacher from whom we can learn; inspired as he was, by a supreme moral, ethical, and spiritual sensitivity in union with and illuminated by a transcendent religious genius. Revelation continues today as it has always done—through prophets and mystics.

Jettatura. In Italy the term for the spell which is cast by a person with the evil eye (q.v.).

Jetzirah. Among the works of Cabalism the *Sepher Jetzirah* is acknowledged to be the most profoundly occult. Basing itself on the twenty-two letters of the Hebrew alphabet, it develops a system of correspondences and numbers. It asserts that God created the universe by way of thirty-two paths of secret wisdom, using ten additional fundamental numbers (those out of which the whole universe evolved). The twenty-two letters follow these categories: three Mothers, seven double consonants, and twelve single consonants.

Jinn (Islam). The invisible spirits which are lower than the angels and able to appear in any shape, mostly animal and human forms however. They are capable of influencing man for good and evil. One of the Jinn is Satan. They quickly punish violators of their many rules.

Jinx. Derived from the Greek term *iynx*, which meant a bird used in witchcraft. Denoting that which is able to cast a spell, it still contains its original sense in modern usage. A jinx in modern terminology is a person, thing, or influence which brings bad luck. To "jinx" anything is to cast bad luck upon it.

Jiva (Hinduism). "The Spark of life." Refers to the principle of life that is within us.

Jivanmukti (Hinduism). The achievement, through yoga devotions of liberation while within the body, of never lacking consciousness of the atma or true self.

Jnana, Jnanam (Hinduism). The vision of clairvoyance; occult insight; spiritual perception.

Joan of Arc (c. 1412–1431). The country maid who rallied France to defeat the "invincible" English invaders. She was steeled to her heroic achievement by visions and mystic experiences. Although the Church at first accused her of witchcraft, this charge was withdrawn, and she was burnt at the stake as a heretic. Joan of Arc stands as an inscrutable example of the powers of mysticism and visionary belief in the achievement of superhuman endeavors.

John Climacus (d. 649). While little is known of the life of this Christian monk and abbot of the monastery at Mount Sinai, his important book *The Ladder of Divine Ascent* reveals him to have been an eminent mystic. Already in his own time he was revered throughout Palestine and Arabia as a possessor of profound mystical wisdom, of spiritual insight, and as a man of saintly character.

John of the Cross (1542–1591). One of the most fascinating and influential of Christian mystics, this Carmelite Spanish monk has had a profound influence on mysticism—both Christian and non-Christian. His writings possess an extraordinary intensity and symbolic depth, while the beauty of their insights has made them enduring reading. His important books are: *The Dark Night of the Soul*, *The Spiritual Canticle*, and *The Ascent of Mount Carmel*.

Johnson, Alice. Secretary of the Society for Psychical Research, who discovered a remarkable example of cross correspondence (q.v.) between the messages of three mediums, two American and one English. Mrs. Verrall, Mrs. Piper (q.v.), and Mrs. Holland (from England, and the sister of Rudyard Kipling) were all found to have utilized the Myers Control (Frederick W. H. Myers, q.v.) in the recording of their messages. None of the mediums was aware of the others' work or messages.

Johnson, Margaret. Accused of fornicating with the Devil, who had metamorphosed himself into a cat, this 17th century woman was indicted for being a witch.

Jolivet-Castelot. One of the leaders of the French Rosicrucians, whose alchemical knowledge and achievements gave an impetus to the latter science that brought its return to favor.

Joris, David (1501–1556). Dutch poet, artist, and mystic who asserted that God saves man by way of seeding the Word in his heart. The leader of a pacifist group in Delft (where he was born), he preached his radical mystical ideas to his followers, explaining that true faith forbids the persecution of others and that the church demonstrates Christian faith by being meek, gentle, and lowly. He had finally to flee to Switzerland to save his life, keeping his identity there secret until he died. His very interesting opus, *Book of Wonders* (1542) is a unique mystical doctrine that only an artist-painter could experience and portray.

Joshua Ben Levi (c. 200 A.D.). A legendary Rabbi in Palestine, of whom it is related that he robbed an angel of his sword and through this heroic feat ascended to Paradise alive.

Joy, In A Dream. Since dreams often operate contrariwise, to dream of feeling joy, according to old dream interpretation, is a sign of pain, trouble, and future unhappiness.

Joys. Astrologers describe the planets as being in their joys during the periods when they are harmoniously located. They then inhabit their strongest and most influential houses, and, accordingly, have some dignity. Illustrations are Mars in Scorpio, the Sun in Leo, and Jupiter in Libra.

Jubilee (Judaism). An ancient ritual of the Mosaic doctrine according to which in the year of Jubilee (since all things in the world belonged to God alone), all slaves were freed, all debts were cancelled, all prisoners were to be restored to their families, and each man was to have returned to him his possessions. In the Year of Jubilee, which occurred every fifty years, God's love was to prevail.

Judah Chasid (d. 1217). The most eminent Rabbi and mystic during the Middle Ages, his prodigious reputation and popularity for wonder-working and performing miracles made him a household name to Jews all through Central and Eastern Europe. Judah Chasid was also the writer of the "Songs of Unity" and the "Song of Glory" which still remain prominent in the present religious services of world Jewry. His book, *Sefer Chasidim* (Book of the Pious) was for many years a famous volume found in the home of almost every Jew.

Judo Buddhism (Japanese Buddhism). One of the sects of Japanese Buddhism, founded in the 13th century by Honen who believed that only Amida Buddha could bring deliverance from evil. Good deeds and the chanting of the words "Nanu Amido Bertsu" (Homage to Amida Buddha) bring salvation and rebirth into Amida's Pure Land of Perfect Bliss. (See: Nichiren)

Juggler's Lodge. Among certain American Indians living near the Great Lakes region, the Lodge of the Shaman (q.v.) which often shivered; this was caused by the spirit the Shaman kept under his subjugation.

JuJu. In West Africa, an object with supernatural potency.

Jul, Yul, Yule. In ancient Scandinavia, a term for the disc or wheel of the sun. This was the period of the year which, being sacred to Freyer or Fro, the Sun-god, celebrated his powers as the ripener of fields and fruits, and harbinger of the harvest.

Julian The Apostate (332–363 A.D.). The Roman Emperor who almost destroyed Christianity. Having become a pagan and experiencing mystical transcendence, he returned to the worship of the Persian cult of Mithra and the Sun-God. During his residence in Mesopotamia and Ephesus, before becoming Emperor, he had been initiated into these former Roman practices. He was a genuine mystic who responded to the ineffable and cosmic universality.

Julianus. Ancient Roman occultist, necromancer, and sorcerer, he is said to have utilized occult powers to rid Rome of the plague.

Jung, Professor C.G. One of the leading pioneers of psychology, who has made a special study of symbolism and methods of divination, particularly the I Ching and astrology, in connection with his theory of synchronicity. This theory challenges the causal principle, and he tries to correlate "meaningful coincidences," unusual occurrences with a discernible acausal connecting principle as a special class of natural events. These form another category with space, time and causality. He recognized the importance of alchemy in the history of man's evolution.

Justin Martyr. Church father in Palestine in the second century, he was author of the theory that Satan tempted Eve. By this nefarious action Satan became damned, doomed forever to remain the Devil.

Jyotis (Hinduism). That light from the sun which is both physical and spiritual—being the light of fire, of lightning, and also the light of intelligence.

Ka. Ancient Egyptian equivalent for the double or etheric body. Represented in drawings as a birdlike duplicate of the deceased. It was supposed to have lived in the tomb, its life depending on the buried provisions, and it presumably haunted any neglectful relatives. The soul, which left both bodies at death, was called the "Ba."

Kabbala. See Cabala.

Kahuna. The name for sorcerer in Hawaii.

Kai. King Arthur's seneschal in the *Morte d'Arthur*, a hero of indefatigable powers. Originally a rain-and-thunder god, he metamorphosed into a human here in the King Arthur legend.

Kairos. The god of opportunity in Ancient Greece. Its devotees belonged to an ancient cult which worshipped at the altars in Olympia. There they also worshipped Ion who personified opportunity, the divinity who was the youngest son of Zeus.

Kakatyche. In ancient Greece, bad luck; in Greek astrology it indicated the Sixth House.

Kala (Hinduism). Time as the source of all. A name of Yama (q.v.), and also a form of Vishnu (q.v.).

Kali-Yuga (Hinduism). The fourth and present age of the world which had its beginning in 3102 B.C. The Kali-Yuga is to endure for 432,000 years, and this period will be a time ravaged by the evils of violence, bloodshed, and wars. It is the briefest of the four Yugas. The first was Krita; second, Treta; third, Dvapara.

Kalki Avatar (Hinduism, Buddhism, Zoroastrianism). The tenth avatar of Vishnu, his last incarnation, the "White Horse Avatar," during which he will demolish the wicked and bring back purity. Some Buddhists see this as the Maitreya Buddha. Zoroastrians conceive this as the incarnation of Sosiosh.

Kallofalling. Among the Eskimos an evil spirit which cruelly pulled courageous hunters down to the depths in water.

Kalpa (Hinduism, Buddhism). A day and night of Brahma, which equals 4,320,000,000 years.

Kalu. Among the Melanesian Fijis, South Pacific islanders, Kalu represents anything that is marvelous or that pertains to the deity.

Kama Rupa. (Hinduism). Hindu term for an "astral shell" or eidolon, said to persist after the death of the physical body, but gradually disintegrating unless its existence is prolonged by feeding on the vitality of those on earth who would wish to preserve it.

Kami. A term in the ancient religion of Japan which means spirit (also ancestral spirit), divinity, and God. It also means that the sun is supreme. Although it pre-dates Confucian and Buddhist religions in Japan, it still commands Japanese devotion.

Kammatthana (Buddhism). The spot of mental activity which is the object of meditation and a spiritual exercise.

Kamrusepa. The Hittite goddess who was the great practitioner of witchcraft.

Kant, Immanuel (1724–1804). Renowned German philosopher who advanced on the Empiricist-Rationalist dilemma, and was responsible for a new objective theory of ethics. In this, he allowed determinism in man to a large extent, but drew attention to the conflict between what a man desires and what he feels is his duty. To Kant, the sense of "ought" or duty came from a world of reality outside of the nature perceived by our senses—the unknowable world, yet it was realized by what Kant called the "practical reason" (almost synonymous with intuition). The "theoretical reason" was governed entirely by the world we build for ourselves.

Kapparah (Judaism). The "scapegoat" whose annual sacrifice for the guilt of the people appeased the wrath of the gods and ensured the group's protection (in many ancient cultures this annual sacrifice was a human being) was among the Israelites an actual goat. But upon the Destruction of the Temple in 70 A.D., a chicken was substituted for the goat, and each person after a *Kapparah* ritual, had the chicken ritually slaughtered. The shed blood of the fowl atones for the sins committed throughout the year. A mystical formula and Cabalistic number—three—is used during the rite of *Kapparah*. This practice is still observed by very Orthodox Jews.

Kardec, Allen (1804–1869). (Hippolyte Leon Denizard Rivail). His famous *Book of the Spirits* (*Le Livre des Esprits*) has become a classic among French and South American Spiritualists. The book emphasizes a doctrine of reincarnation which is not accepted by all Spiritualists. Kardec and his original followers used the term "Spiritist" to describe themselves. It was Professor Pierart who used the word "Spiritualist" to indicate his rejection of the dogmatic assumption of reincarnation theory.

Karma (Hinduism). This is the law of behavior in an individual's life, the aspect of cause and effect which governs a person's conduct. For an individual's future incarnations are directly dependent upon his ethical behavior during his life. A person's human condition in any of his incarnations is a reflection and result of his behavior in his previous existences. In essence, a person's life and his Karma are thus one and the same.

Karma Sannyasin (Hinduism). Those who live a life of seclusion to follow the way of Karma (q.v.).

Karma Yoga (Hinduism). Yoga pathway of consecrated unselfish action.

Karra-Kalf. Contemporary magic in Iceland, in which an initiate, to achieve powers, licks the Devil in the form of a newborn calf.

Karshipta (Zoroastrianism). The sacred Bird of Heaven, which symbolizes both man's soul and his higher ego.

Kasios. An Oriental or Semitic god with cults at Antioch and Pelusium who was most likely a mountain- or weather-god.

Katchina. A mask, statuette, or similar object used by the American Hopi and Pueblo Indians. The Katchinas confer upon the men who wear or carry them a symbolic nature, for they represent supernatural persons, often identified with the dead mythical ancestors who are believed to visit the earth in the winter after having resided in the spirit world the other half of the year. The Katchinas bring fruitfulness to the earth. The masks were given to men so that they could accomplish good deeds through impersonation.

Kathemotheism. This term describes the monotheism of the Vedanta, according to which the sequence of the supreme gods is so ordered that each reigns in turn, but each supreme god is always being replaced by another without denying that the other gods exist.

Katherine of Genoa (1447–1510). Italian mystic whose singular devotion to the Christian ideal, whose spiritual wisdom, and enduring care of the sick, won her immense adoration and respect. The book, *Spiritual Dialogue,* bearing her name, but most certainly written by another, narrates the beauty and the profound depth of her spirituality and mysticism.

Kau. In Tibet it is an article of absolute faith that he who possesses a *Kau,* a very potent talisman, is impervious to bullets or any weapon. In fact, in the 1940's there was a famous bandit who marauded from Lhasa to China immune for years against bullets and attack, owing to the magic Kau he wore. Only the recital by a lama of a miraculous formula in the bandit's presence ended his criminal career.

Kaufman, George A. Modern mathematician, lecturer and writer on Spiritual Science who wrote "The Pyramids and Mysteries of Time and Number."

Kaustubha-Jewel (Hinduism). A famous jewel created by the churning ocean and decorating the breast of Krishna or Vishnu (qq.v.).

Kephalomancy. A form of divination in which various signs were made on the baked head of an ass. In ancient practice, lighted carbon was placed on the ass's head, and the names of criminals recited. If crackling occurred, this revealed the guilty.

Keres. In ancient Greece, these were the malignant spirits who brought every kind of evil: pollution, blindness, many diseases, old age, death, and spiritual blindness. Also considered to be the souls of the dead.

Kerheb. In ancient Egypt these were the priestly class who compiled the books of necromantic works and were known as "the scribes of the divine writing." So important were they that the sons of the Pharoahs were members of this priestly organization.

Kerner, Justinus (1786–1862). German occultist, poet, physician, and philosopher who was the author of a number of books on the supernatural. So popular and striking were his insights and the revelations in his books that a new philosophy was developed based on his work.

Keshara (Hinduism). A yogin who can enter his astral form. The term means "sky-walker."

Kether. In Hindu astrology, the first Sephira of the Tree of Life, which is the Crown located in the realm of Atziluth. Considered to be the highest point in a figure of the heavens.

Kether Elyon (Cabalism). The first of the Ten Sephiroth (q.v.) with the meaning "the Supreme Crown."

Key. The magical properties of keys have a very ancient history. In many religions a key represented a method of ascending to heaven, so much so that many deities were considered to carry keys. Further, keys, since they possess magical and medicinal qualities, were often worn as charms.

Key of Solomon, The. This is the most notable of all grimoires (q.v.) or handbooks of magic. Though accredited to King Solomon, it is of relatively recent origin; that is, belonging to the twelfth, fourteenth, or fifteenth centuries. Suffused with Jewish occult knowledge, and the art of summoning evil spirits, its chief directions relate to the magic of discovering treasure, and the domination of the will of others. *The Key of Solomon* was translated into many languages. In the main, those in French or Latin were done in the eighteenth century. Aleister Crowley (q.v.) has translated it into English. The *Legmegeton,* or *Lesser Key of Solomon,* which goes back to the seventeenth century, and is considered by some to be superior to the first, is divided into four parts—*Goetia, Theurgia Goetia, Pauline Art,* and *Almadel.* These four parts enable the adept to control all the spirits and demons. *Pauline Art* concerns itself especially with the angels of the hours of the day and night, and the signs of the Zodiac.

Keys of the Tarot. Twenty-two cards (major arcana) of the Tarot pack.

Key Words. In astrology, one of the lists of designations which give the essential quality of each of the twelve signs of the Zodiac. One of the most accepted is the following:

Aries — Aspiration	Libra — Equilibruim
Taurus — Integration	Scorpio — Creativity
Gemini — Vivification	Sagittarius — Administration
Cancer — Expansion	Capricorn — Discrimination
Leo — Assurance	Aquarius — Loyalty
Virgo — Assimilation	Pisces — Appreciation

Khaba. For the ancient Egyptians this term signified man's astral body (q.v.).

Khado (Lamaism). The name in popular mythology in Tibet of the evil female demons.

Khaib. In ancient Egypt, the shadow which left the body at death and continued its own existence. It was symbolized in the form of a sunshade.

Khepra. In ancient Egypt the god of rebirth, symbolized by either a scarab or a human being with the head of a scarab.

Khu. The ancient Egyptian concept for the immortal spirit in man. Meaning "clear" or "luminous," it was symbolized by a plume of fire.

Khunrath, Henry (c. 1560–1601). German occultist, alcnemist, mystic, and physician. He wrote a famous book, which though unfinished at his death, describes the seven steps that lead to universal knowledge by a process of magic and mysticism. It is titled *Anphitheatrum Sapientioe Aeternoe Solius Veroe, Christiano Kabbalisticum Divinio Magicum (Christian-Kabbalistic, Divine-Magical Ampitheatre of the Eternal)*.

Ki. The term for the human aura of mesmeric and potent emanation. Its powers have been studied by parapsychologists.

Kilner, Dr. Walter J. (1847–1920). Of St. Thomas's Hospital, London. Noted for his experimental work on the human aura. By means of dicyanin dye screens (q.v.), he was the first to demonstrate objectively the existence of the aura. The eyes are first sensitized by looking through the screen; then, by gazing at a naked figure in a dim light against a black backcloth, three distinct bands of radiation become visible to some people not otherwise sensitive. He found that illness affected the size and colors of the radiations, and that the aura shrivels at the approach of death and ultimately vanishes.

Kilnerscreen-goggles. Popular name given to screens made in the form of spectacles, based on Dr. Kilner's discovery.

Kinandi. In Africa, the "devil's harp," a musical instrument remarkably similar to the ancient Greek lyre. Occasionally, tin pans with camel skins stretched across them are used as crude Kinandas. Many tribes use the Kinandi for occult and supernatural purposes since it is believed to possess magical power.

"King, John." A well-known spirit control who has manifested through many physical mediums. He claimed to be Henry Owen Morgan, a buccaneer who was knighted by Charles II, and was appointed Governor of Jamaica from 1673–80. His first recorded appearance was with the Davenport brothers in 1850. Other mediums who claimed his influence were: Mrs. Guppy, Mme. Blavatsky, and Eusapia Paladino (qq.v.)

"King, Katie". Beautiful spirit control of Miss Florence Cook, who claimed to be the daughter of "John King" (see above). She appeared many times in Sir William Crookes' investigations, during which he photographed her forty times. Crookes was completely sure of her independence of the medium, and risked his scientific reputation by making known his findings.

Kircher, Athanasius (1602–1680). German Jesuit mathematician, physicist, philosopher, and linguist who wrote many books on the occult significance of numbers. He asserted that much of Egyptian philosophy and religion was founded almost entirely on mathematics, and that nature was also interpreted on this principle. For him the knowledge of the occult was derived from the profound wisdom of numbers.

Kirchweger, Anton Joseph. German alchemist of the 18th century who wrote what is probably the most important alchemical book of his century, *Aurea Catena Homeri*. Kirchweger saw that there was a universality of natural laws which operated in similar ways in macrocosm and microcosm.

Kirlian Photography. Pictures which show the auras of living things or "energy flows," or the "energy body" around the plant, animal, or the human part which has been photographed. The Russians Semyon Kirlian and his wife Valentina developed the method. In recent years it has been widely used in paranormal experiments, one of its leading experimenters being Thelma Moss, University of California psychologist, who has taken numerous photographs displaying this phenomenon. Many psychics believe paranormal powers are directly dependent upon these auras or energy flows captured by the Kirlian photographs. More recently, however, biologists who have studied Kirilian auras have discounted their existence.

Kirubi. In ancient Assyrian religion, the guardian spirits of the entrance of temples.

Kischuph (Cabalism). The higher magical influence, which encompasses the elementary and the spiritual, and includes exorcism. Sorcerers and witches, it is claimed, could change into animals, and the women could make pacts with demons and consort with them. Material *Kischuph* deals with the art of using various substances to control the natural elements.

Kiss of Shame. During the Sabbat (q.v.) this followed the assertion of allegiance to Satan, in which the participants kissed the buttocks of the Devil.

Kittel (Judaism). Since ancient times male adult Jews have at certain religious ceremonies worn this loose white robe. Some consider it to symbolize purity; others, like Maimonides, assert that it symbolizes the great insight that death approaches, and serves to remind them to abandon their follies, and follow the way of God.

Kleshas. The five causes of human trouble in yoga mysticism: ignorance, self-personality, desire, aversion, possessiveness.

Kluski, Franek. Polish poet, writer and physical medium through whose powers plaster casts of spirit hands and feet, it is claimed, were obtained in the fraudproof laboratory of Dr. Gustave Geley.

Knorr von Rosenroth, Christian (1631–1689). German alchemist, hermeticist, and mystic. The *Kabbala Denudata* (q.v.) (*Kabbala Unveiled*) which he edited and translated, represented the first occasion when these writings appeared in another language outside the original.

Knot Tying Experiments. See Matter Through Matter.

Koan (Zen Buddhism). A paradox or insoluble problem suitable for meditating upon in the practice of Zen Buddhism. It works on the principle that a sudden impasse or jolt to the intellect can bring insight.

Kobolds. Elemental beings considered in some respects as evil "house spirits;" also, in Medieval occultism they were pictured as familiars (q.v.) of the magicians.

Koji-Ki. Oldest known Japanese historical document covering the period from the time of creation to A.D. 628 (compiled A.D. 712).

Kol (Judaism). Meaning a Voice, the Voice of the divine world.

Kolotl. The name among the Aztecs for their dog-faced god.

Konx-Om-Pax. Mystical "words of power" (q.v.) which were uttered during the Eleusinian Mysteries in ancient Greece; considered taken from the Isis cult of Egypt.

Koons' Spirit Room. Jonathan Koons, American spiritualist, who built a huge log seance room on his farm in 1852, was inspired by a prophecy that he and all eight of his children would become mediums. The room was famous for the most rambunctious scenes in the history of spiritualism, numerous musical instruments, for example, (fiddles, guitars, banjos, harps, drums, accordions, etc.) accompanied the voices of famous phantoms, ghosts, and spirits. The movement and hurling of furniture for great distances drew mammoth audiences.

Kosa (Hinduism). One of the coverings of pure consciousness, which conceals the soul or self. In the Vedanta there are three: the coverings of pleasure, intellect, and food.

Koskinomancy. Divination by peering through a sieve, which in ancient times was held lightly in the hand and revolved; as the name of a suspected criminal was uttered, his guilt or innocence could be determined by this operation.

Kosmon Bible, "Oahspe." An astounding work of automatic typewriting, produced by J.B. Newbrough (q.v.).

Kra. Among the African tribes of the Gold Coast, the Kra is a ghost like a second self.

Kraft, Dean Ira. The young Brooklyn, New York psychic whose phenomenal healing and psychokinetic talents have been certified by a number of scientific agencies and physicians. The latter have attested to more than 200 patients whom he has markedly helped or completely cured. Extraordinarily generous and ethical, he takes no payments for his healings. Further, he accepts only those patients who believe in medical science, and who are either under a physician's care or who have truly exhausted medicine's resources. During 1972-1973 a rare series of spiritual messages (witnessed by two other friends) revealed to Kraft that these messages were coming to him directly from God. He was told that he was the archetypal Adam with many reincarnations, and that he was a gifted healer who must use his powers carefully. Having exhibited his incredible psychic powers to the most prestigious scientific testing institute in the United States, and having performed feats no other psychic has achieved, he is being sponsored by a team of physicians and an important United States Governmental agency—both to utilize his talents and to study the mechanics and sources of psychic power. Kraft's personal ambitions are twofold: to cure as many people as he can, and to help establish the credibility of psychic healing.

Kramer, Heinrich (c. 1430–1505). This Dominican prior wrote, with Jacob Sprenger, the treatise *Malleus Maleficarum*, a famous book on witchcraft which was the origin of all later books on this subject.

Krishna (Hinduism). The most popular of all the Hindu divinities—the 8th avatar or incarnation of Vishnu. His story is related most fully in the *Bhagavad-Gita* and *Bhagavata Purana*. His father, warned by the cruel deaths of his first six sons, saved the eighth, Krishna (meaning "black"), by having him raised by a poor herdsman. In manhood, as the charioteer of Arjuna, he persuades Arjuna of the rightfulness of fighting his kinsmen to win a kingdom. His "*Song of the Adorable One*" is one of the great philosophical poems. Certain parallels between Krishna's birth and infancy, and Christ's, link these two significant figures.

Kronos. In ancient Greek mythology, the youngest son of Heaven and Earth. Having castrated his father, he and his fellow Titans ruled the earth. Kronos married his sister, and fathered Hestia, Demeter, Hera, Hades, Poseidon and Zeus. Seeking to vitiate a prophesy that one of his sons would kill him, he swallowed them at birth; but Rhea, his wife, tricked him, and he vomited up his male offspring. They finally overcame him after a mighty struggle. Kronos has been pictured in some legends as King of the Golden Age or of a distant wonderland, and through his identification with Saturnus as civilizer of Italy. But mainly, Kronos was considered a forbidding divinity.

Ksanika-vada (Buddhism). The concept which asserts that everything exists but momentarily (Ksanika), and therefore is undergoing perpetual change.

Kuei. In ancient China man's spirit following death; also considered to be earthly spirits (shen) who co-existed with the heavenly spirits. The yin aspect of the soul (passive, negative), in contrast to yang (active, positive) which is designated hun.

Kukulcan. Among the Mayans their name for the Aztec Quetzalcoatl (a god the former had inherited from the Toltecs) whose name means the "Plumed Serpent."

Kulagina, Ninel. Modern Russian sensitive whose ability in psychokinesis (q.v.), causing objects to float in mid-air, has given her a large audience in Russia. Though she has been apprehended in some fraudulent behavior, many in her country, scientists among them, consider her talents genuine, and that she possesses paranormal ability.

Kuleshova, Rosa. Russian psychic who has demonstrated an amazing ability to "read" with her fingertips while wholly blindfolded. Parapsychologists in Russia have made many tests proving her psychic capacities.

Kumbha, Kumbhaha (Hinduism). The shutting off of the breath by closing nostrils and mouth. The phase occurring between intake and exhalation of air.

Kum-bum, The (Lamaism). One of the most famous temples in Tibet, and most fascinatingly the word means "The Hundred Thousand Pictures." Symbolically, it is a reasoned and systematic synthesis of the Buddhist universe, a complete cosmography, for it is a guide to the Buddhist heavens and beyond that the infinite heavens. The foundation of the Kum-bum is called the Lunar Lotus because Dorechang, the Absolute, rests upon it. Each story of this mysterious temple has five faces, each one boasting the symbol of one of the five Dhyani Buddhas (q.v.).

K'un. In the *I Ching.* (q.v.) these are two elements: the first is the trigam of the element earth of the eight trigrams (pa kua); the second is the trigram of the female principle of the universe.

Kundalini. According to Yoga teaching, a hidden psychic force which lies coiled at the base of the spine (the semen), dormant until roused by the various Yoga disciplines and techniques. As it rises to the psychic centres or chakras, it activates them and brings into operation psychic powers appropriate to the centers affected. Often referred to in occult works as the "coiled serpent."

Kuo Hsiang (Taoism) (c. 312 A.D.). Considered the foremost authority on Taoism in medieval China. He wrote the classic explication on the great book *Chang Tzu*, which was mostly written by the great master Chang Tzu (q.v.).

Kurdaitja. Among the Arunta aborigines of Australia a name for sorcerer; often he is also an executioner.

Kutower, Abraham (d. c. 1762) (Cabalism). A prominent follower of the Lurianic Version of the Cabala, this Polish rabbi helped to disseminate the faith in the Cabala at a time when the Jews of Poland were in desperate need of help against oppression.

Kuvera (Hinduism, Buddhism). In the Vedas he is the chief of all evil spirits. He is also the Hindu god of wealth.

Ll

Laburum (Cabalism). This Cabalistic sign is centered in the Great Magical Monogram—the seventh and most important pentacle of the Euchiridion (q.v.).

Ladder of Life. A very inclusive term utilized by many occult schools and religions. In a profound sense it is interchangeable with the terms "The Hermetic Chain," (q.v.) or "The Golden Chain." Mainly, it refers to the ascending grades or stages of the universe's development and also of the spiritual, mystical, and occult ascent of the adept. In Hinduism, we have the Ladder of the Brahmins; in Cabalism, the Ladder to the En Sof; in Judaism, Jacob's dream of the Ladder; the Ladder in Mithraism; and John of the Ladder—the Christian ascetic. For the Alchemists, the Rosicrucians and Theosophists it was a key symbol.

Lady-bird. Divination by this fly in which the captured insect was bidden to fly "north, south, east, or west," the resulting direction of flight revealing the area of the future husband of the young lady who conducted the divinatory trial.

Laing, Ronald D. (1927–   ). The Scottish psychiatrist, psychoanalyst and mystic whose radical investigations of mental illness have altered long-held views and practice in the approach and treatment of what is often incorrectly designated insanity. After intense research in hospitals, clinics, and actual home settings, and the use of psychedelics (q.v.) as part of real social situations, Laing has concluded that madness is the condition of society, not the so-called mentally ill. Mental illness is frequently the only normal sanity. For it is an effort to return to the true inner self, and to the self's exploration of the cosmic universe, by way of a mystical experience, the only experience that can provide human sanity. This mystical revelation and the necessary return of the egoic self into the social world is the only means to create the sanity and humaneness for man's health and survival. (See: *The Politics of Experience, The Divided Self*)

Lakshmi. The beautiful wife of Vishnu, who is also known as Maha Sakshnii. She emerged with her golden skin from an ocean of milk and is worshipped as the goddess of love, beauty, and good fortune. She is represented with a lotus in her hand. Some of the many names she bears are: Sri, Padma, the Lotus, and Padmalaya.

Lalita-Vistara (Buddhism). The story in prose and verse which recounts the life of Buddha from the moment when he elected to be born, up to the time of his first sermon. Largely Mahayanistic in doctrine, and believed written in the 5th century A.D., it is the prime version of Buddha's life.

Lama. Tibetan or Mongolian priest of esoteric Buddhism, favoring elaborate ritual, and worship by formal and repetitive prayers.

Lamaism. In Tibet, Lamaism represents the body of religious doctrine and institutions which was derived from Mahayana Buddhism (q.v.) and which was introduced in the 7th century. This Buddhism was wedded to the native Shamaistic Bon religion and to Tantric elements. The original Bon was a religion of magic and exorcist practices, which has given to Lamaism its dependence on Mantras, elaborate ritual, and the worship of guardian deities and living incarnations of the Buddha. The double incarnation of the Bodhisattva (q.v.) is represented by the institutions of the Dalai-Lama (the political power) and the Tashi-Lama (the spiritual power). The two repositories of Lamaism are the Kan-jur with 108 books, and the Tan-jur containing 225 volumes.

Lamb of God. An epithet referring to Jesus Christ.

Lamennais, R. (1782-1854). French Catholic priest who introduced a Platonic-Christian movement in the Church and advocated the notion of humanity as best summarized in the phrase "inspired mankind."

Lamia. A child-stealing demon popular since Grecian times in European folk mythology. Her demoniacal character is reputedly the result of the destruction of her own children by Hera, Zeus' wife, because Lamia was his mistress. She is pictured with the head and breasts of a woman and the body of a snake.

Lang, Andrew (1843-1912). Philosopher, poet, scholar, president of S.P.R. in 1911. Author of many books on anthropology, mythology, ghosts, and history. Also a student of dowsing and crystal gazing. Once he made a study of Joan of Arc from the point of view of psychical research.

Lankavatera Sutra (Buddhism). Represents one of the most important texts of Mahayana Buddhism. It is an exposition of the basic principles which are the source of Zen Buddhism, and the most seminal force in Japanese Zen development.

Lanoo. A term which was used in ancient Asiatic mystical training-schools, meaning "disciple." (See: Chela).

Lao Tzu (c. 604-?). The reputed founder of Taoism (q.v.), he was believed to have been a priest-teacher who advocated the supreme doctrine of "in-action" or "letting alone." Considered to have been the keeper of the royal archives at Chow, in old age he made a pilgrimage to the lands in the West. As he was departing his province of Honan, the warden of the gate begged him to leave a work of his wisdom, which Lao Tzu honored by elaborating his beliefs on Tao—"the way and virtue" in his book the *Tao Te Ching*. The legend holds that he was a contemporary of Confucius, that they met in 517, and that Lao Tzu criticized his worldly ambitions. The *Tao Te Ching* is a work of profound mystic insights and many illuminating perceptions.

Lares. In ancient Rome these were the familiar household gods, guardians of the home. They were believed to be ghosts of the dead. Their powers spread and they were also deities of the farmland, the guardians of all crossways, and the guardians of travellers. The Penates (q.v.) were linked with the Lares.

Law of Evidence. See Evidence.

Law, William (1686–1761). English Methodist Clergyman who was an unexcelled writer on the spiritual, ethical, and mystical dimensions of Protestantism. Ordained in 1711 and elected a fellow of Cambridge, he refused to take an oath of allegiance upon the accession of George I. As a consequence, he was dismissed from the university and lost all chance of advancement in the Church. His book *A Serious Call to a Devout and Holy Life* is considered an eminent work in practical religion. Moreover, as a mystic and an enthusiastic admirer of Jakob Boehme (q.v.), his *The Way to Divine Knowledge*, *The Spirit of Prayer*, and *The Spirit of Love* reveal a mysticism that proclaims the need for a union between man and God. His work influenced many writers and religious thinkers in his own time and the future development of Methodism and English mysticism.

Laya-Center (Hinduism). The mystical point where a thing disappears in one plane as it passes to another. At the point where it reappears, it becomes the center of active life. It is the point where concentration occurs.

Laya Yoga. Yoga pathway of divine union through the etheric plane.

Laying on of Hands. Healing practice, performed by Jesus and once very common, now gradually regaining favor in some churches. Equivalent to the Spiritualist's "contact healing" (q.v.).

Lead or Leade, Jane (1623–1704). English mystic and visionary, disciple of Jakob Boehme (q.v.), her works brought many converts to her revelations. Having experienced mystic awareness as a girl, her continuing insights flowered into several books: *A Fountain of Gardens Watered by the Rivers of Divine Pleasure*, *The Heavenly Cloud Now Breaking*, and *The Revelation of Revelations*. Her daughter and son-in-law, Dr. Francis Lee, a physician, formed a Theosophical sect, the Philadelphians, which had many members in England and Europe.

Leader, Circle. (Spiritualism). It is usually advisable to nominate a leader for a circle, apart from the medium. This person should be experienced in Spiritualism, levelheaded and trusted by the other members. The leader is responsible for the conducting of the circle procedure and for arrangements generally, and should be competent to deal with any emergency.

Leading Houses. According to astrology, these are the Cardinal Signs—the first, fourth, seventh, and tenth.

Leaf, Horace. English clairvoyant, psychometrist, healer, lecturer and author. His interest in Spiritualism and psychical research was informed and scholarly.He also became a very widely travelled Spiritualist missionary. Horace Leaf lectured on mediumship at several learned institutions, including the State Hospital at Copenhagen, Johns Hopkins University, Dartmouth College, Swarthmore College, Oxford and Cambridge Universities.

Lecanomancy. Divination by tossing an object into a full container of water then making an interpretation on the basis of the formed image or the sound of its striking the water.

Lee, Mother Ann. The founder and prophetess in 1766 of a cult of Shakers—the United Society of Believers in Christ's Second Coming—who lived communistically and asexually in Watervliet, New York. But it was in 1837, when a barrage of mysterious rappings startled this quiet, industrious community, that these wide-eyed Shakers decided that Mother Ann was now reaching out from heaven to make communication with them. Throughout the next seven years these ghostly rappings from Mother Ann, which were publicized in the area, occurred frequently, thus setting the stage for the beginnings of spiritualism in America. It was some ten years later, in 1848, that in this New York area spiritualism actually had its beginnings—at the Fox household, Hydesville, New York. (See: Katie Fox)

Lees. Robert James. English clairvoyant medium and author. He was received by Queen Victoria several times. Lees was also a medium for spirit healing, with an amazing ability for diagnosis; some remarkable instantaneous cures were achieved.

Left-hand Path. Many esoteric occult and mystical teachings throughout the whole world refer to this path as "The Path of Darkness" or "of Shadows," in contradistinction to the opposite "The Right-hand Path" (q.v.). In Hinduism, the Left-hand Path is known as "Brothers of the Shadow." In ancient Greece, devotees of this path were deemed depraved lovers of matter and embodiments of spiritual obscuration. Modern Satanism refutes these views and considers them mistaken. (See: Satanism).

Legba. Among the Dahomey tribes on the French Gold Coast of Africa this god is the messenger to the gods. He propitiates them in favor of men; moreover, he brings messages from the gods to diviners, enabling the latter to predict the future.

Leibnitz, Gottfried Wilhelm (1646–1716). Famous German philosopher who believed in restoring balance and the conciliation of extremes. Of particular interest is his "Monad" system: a dynamic conception of reality which replaced the older "substance" theories. A monad (q.v.) was a non-physical "centre of force," a living "atom" in the structure of reality. An infinite number of monads existed in hierarchies extending to God. They all possessed potentialities of perception and movement which became self-consciousness and will. The goal of man was therefore the intellectual love of God.

Lemuria (I.) In ancient Rome on the fateful days of May 9, 11, 13, kinless and hungry ghosts, *lemures*, were believed to prowl through houses and could be appeased only by a prescribed ritual of feeding. By throwing black beans in what was believed their direction, it was thought the Lemures would snatch them up and do no harm to the living.

Lemuria (II). (Theosophy). This lost continent which preceded Atlantis (q.v.) was considered to have existed over a large area from India to South America. (See: Root Race)

Le Normand, Marie (1771–1843). One of the most successful and acclaimed occultists and diviners of her age, she was hailed as "The Sybil of the Fauburg Saint Germain." She predicted the careers of the famous French revolutionists Marat, St. Just, and Robespierre; read the horoscope of Napoleon to him; gave Tarot card readings to many of France's aristocracy; and after the fall of Napoleon, Russian, German, and English officers flocked to her for readings, even Emperor Alexander and the Belgian Prince of Orange.

Leo. Astrological sign (July 24–August 23); Element—Fire; Symbol—the Lion; Ruling Planet—the Sun. Qualities—possess great charm and personality, endurance and loyalty; mysterious supernatural powers; ambitious, impulsive, talented in many directions; able to inspire love, trust, and loyalty; but they can be ruinously restless, hot-headed, impetuous, tricky, overly stubborn and opinionated.

Leonard, Gladys Osborne. Well-known British trance medium who sat with Hewat Mackenzie, founder of the British College for Psychic Science; he was responsible for arranging her first sittings with Sir Oliver Lodge. It was through Mrs. Leonard's mediumship that Raymond Lodge, Sir Oliver's son, first communicated after his death. She received these messages at about the same time as two other mediums—who did not know each other—also received them. (See: the famous Piper-Verrall-Leonard Cross-Correspondence.)

Leprechaun. In Irish folklore a wrinkled old elf, shoemaker to the fairies, a prankster, but one who knows the place of buried treasures. Originally called "Cluricaune" in Ireland, but modernized as Leprechaun.

Levi, Eliphas (1810-1875). Born Alphonse Louis Constant, he was a priest who was defrocked; a prophet of socialism which he deserted; a French Mason from which order he was expelled; and also an important Cabalist and Occultist, whose books made a very strong impression on the readers of his time. Many of his works have been translated into English, including: *Doctrine of Transcendal Magic, History of Magic,* and *The Key of the Grand Mysteries.*

Levita, Elias or Elijah (1469-1549). One of the greatest Jewish grammarians of the Hebrew language who wrote a myriad of works on this subject and other Hebrew studies. He was also a profound student of the Cabala. In fact, it was his knowledge of the Cabala which enabled him to gain the Roman Cardinal Egidio Diviterbo as a patron; the latter sustained him in Rome in his scholarly works during some 14 years, in exchange for Levita's instruction in Cabalism.

Levitation. A surprising amount of historical evidence from early days exists concerning the supernormal rising of chairs, tables, human bodies and heavy objects into the air. The saints are reputed to have risen often when praying, or in a state of meditation or rapture, usually at the altar. Levitation was once considered to be a sign of possession, and liable to be followed by charges of witchcraft. In the 19th century we have several accounts of mediums' levitation: Henry C. Gordon in 1851 and 1852 at Dr. Gray's house in New York. Then the famous D.D. Home (q.v.), of whom levitation was reported on good authority over one hundred times. The most famous eyewitness account was that of Home's levitation on 13 December 1868, at Ashley House, Victoria Street, London. Before Lord Adare and Charles Wynne, Home floated from a third-story window and returned through a window of another room. Other well-known mediums reported to have levitated are: Stainton Moses, Mrs. Guppy, Herne, and Eusapia Paladino (qq.v.). Explanation ot this feat is speculative. Yogis claim that suitable breathing techniques practiced over long periods can reduce the body weight sufficiently to float in air. Ecclesiastics believe the rapture state to be necessary. Parapsychologists have produced evidence of psychokinesis (q.v.) which is a somewhat related phenomenon.

Lewis, Matthew Gregory (1775-1818). Better known as "Monk" Lewis, English politician and author. His books and plays on the occult were very popular. His play *Castle Spectre* (1798) had a long run at Drury Lane, while his *Tales of Terror,* and *Tales of Wonder* were likewise well received.

Libation. Pouring a liquid on a symbolic figure of a deity, or on the ground. The ancient Romans poured libations upon their *lares* and *penates* (qq.v.).

Libra. Astrological sign (September 24-October 23); Element—Air; Symbol—the Scales; Ruling Planet—Venus. Qualities—exceptionally well-balanced, generous, sociable, esthetic, intuitive, also very logical, perceptive, adaptable, humane, critical; but Librans exhibit a tendency to drift, to be materialistic, careless of necessary details, easily hurt, and impatient.

Lichtenberger, Johannes (1445–1503). One of Europe's noted astrologers, hailed "the Ptolemy of his time" he was also deeply versed in occult learning.

Life. In astrology this refers to the Hyleg (q.v.), the Giver of Life, and to the Apheta (q.v.) which influences the life and death of the subject.

Life Waves (Theosophy). These life waves are disseminated through the instrumentality of the Logos. The first Life Wave creates all matter; the second Life Wave creates life from matter; and the third Life Wave creates man. Will, Wisdom, and Activity are the three aspects of these Life Waves.

Light (Spiritualism).Those mediums who produce physical phenomena usually require a very dim light or complete darkness to manifest satisfactorily. Experience has shown that sudden light admitted during a physical seance can cause severe shock to the medium's body— bruises, weals, and hemorrhages have been known to occur as the result of careless treatment in this way. Some experiments suggest that the shock is caused more by the light falling upon the medium than on the ectoplasmic formations. It was found that if the medium was shielded from the light the emanations could be photographed by flashlight. Moonlight has been found to be ideal. It should be noted that a few mediums on occasion have demonstrated good physical phenomena in bright daylight.

Lights. This term in astrology refers to the two most important planets, the Sun and Moon: the light of the day and light of the night.

Lights, Spirit or Psychic. See Luminous Phenomena.

Like Attracts Like (Spiritualism). An important "law" of spirit contact. It would seem to depend upon the respective qualities of individual auras. The outer auric fields of the human body are generated by the mind and the emotions. If two persons incarnate or discarnate have similar tastes and desires, their auras, it is said will blend, and they will be able to approach or even mingle their rays, resulting in a degree of mental rapport. If violently dissimilar, there is automatic repulsion. Between a medium and his control, there is a very close blend of personalities, developed over many years, which enables the control to enter the auric field sufficiently to gain control of the medium's faculties through manipulation of the subconscious mind. This can also explain possession or obsession by undesirable entities.

Lillith. Demonologists describe Lillith as being either the prince or princess who ruled the succubi (q.v.). The demons who served Lillith were engaged in destroying newborn infants. Ancient Jewish legend holds her to have been the wife of Adam who was superseded by Eve. Her origins are in Assyrian demonology. But in *Isaiah* her name means "night monster," and in former years Jews wrote a formula on the corners of a birth bedroom aimed at forbidding the presence of Lillith.

Lilly, William. English astrologer who predicted the death of Charles I and the Great Fire of London in 1666. Arrested for the acute accuracy of his latter prognostication—on suspicion of arson—he was, fortunately, determined to be innocent. He wrote a number of books on astrology.

Lily Dale Assembly Camp. Located in northern New York, it is one of the oldest meeting sites in the United States devoted to spiritualist demonstrations and meetings.

Lingam (Hinduism). The stone male sexual organ which since ancient times has represented the god Siva (q.v.), and is the most prevalent object of worship. It has been used to deflorate girls before marriage to assure fertility. Often associated with the Yoni (q.v.). Over the Millenia the Lingam has become stylized, evolving from an exact phallic representation to its present columnar shape, either in stone or plastic mud. The pouring of Ganges water or milk over the Lingam are rituals of worship.

Lingayats. One of the Siva sects in Hinduism. Siva is their god; they are puritan, ascetic, caste-less; and men and women are equal. Brahmans are not considered the elite; sacrifices and rites are rejected; and the dead are buried, not cremated.

Litanies of the Sabbath (Witchcraft). It is recounted that during the late Middle Ages on Wednesdays and Saturdays, it was the practice to sing at the Witches' Sabbath the list of great spirits, angels, seraphim, cherubim, etc., and the demons, and princes of hell, asking that they have "pity on us."

Lo. In China a gong used for many purposes. But it is also sounded during funeral processions to frighten off any evil spirits pursuing the dead.

Loa. In the Voodoo (q.v.) religion, these gods are appeased by the offerings of their worshippers.

Lodge, Sir Oliver, (1851–1940). The great British physicist, who thoroughly investigated the phenomena of spiritualism, and became a fearless champion of survival in the teeth of much scientific opposition. The return after death of his son Raymond (q.v.), first delivered through Mrs. Piper (q.v.) in 1915, then by cross correspondence (q.v.) through several mediums including Mrs. Osborne Leonard (q.v.) and Alfred Vout Peters, constitutes one of the best attested cases of proved spirit identity. Sir Oliver wrote several books on psychical research. He was deeply interested in reconciling science and religion and the investigation of psychic phenomena.

Logos. The Divine Word, as representative of the Deity incarnate. In Greek and Hebrew metaphysics it links God and man. To the Stoics the Logos meant God.

Loka (Hinduism). Place or locality, that is—Rupa-lokas (material worlds) and Arupa-lokas (spiritual spheres).

Lokayatas (Hinduism). A materialistic sect of Hinduism (also called Charuakas) who believe that happiness is the highest level of existence, that one must indulge his senses to the full, and that the body creates the life of the mind. Though they deny all the beliefs of Hindu theology, they are counted within Hinduism.

Loki or Lopt. The Scandinavian god of evil, who had formerly assisted Odin (q.v.) in the creation of the world. He fathered Hel, goddess of Death and Hades; the colossal serpent Jormungader; the Fenris-Wolf; the Midgard Snake; and Augurburda, the messenger of sorrow. Loki, obsessed with evil, wrought havoc on earth, devised the death of Balder (q.v.), and continued to flourish after the coming of Christianity as the instigator of sensuality, under the name of Satan.

Lombroso, Cesar (1836–1909). Italian psychiatrist and criminal anthropologist. He sat with Eusapia Paladino on many occasions, and gradually became convinced, not only of survival, but of the truth of the spirit hypothesis. His open declarations carried great weight among his scientific contemporaries, and induced some of them to investigate psychic phenomena.

London Dialectical Society. See Dialectical Society.

London Spiritualist Alliance. A Spiritualist society first formed from the British National Association of Spiritualists in 1884. It was incorporated in 1896. The London headquarters are now known as the College of Psychic Science.

Lord. In astrology this includes the ruler of a sign and the lord of a house. A planet is lord of a house either because it is in the house, or if there is no planet, because it is the ruler of the sign appearing upon its cusp. There is the lord of the geniture (q.v.), and the lord of the hour, referring to the planet that governed at the hour of the casting of the figure (q.v.). The lord of the year refers to the planet with the most dignities in a solar revolution figure or in an ingress figure which is interpreted by mundane astrology (q.v.).

Lord, Professor. The American Columbia University Professor who in 1910 set a trap for Eusapia Palladino (q.v.) and caught her cheating during her last American seance. But the Professor is but another minor foot-note in the history of psychic exploration. Those who knew the phenomenal Eusapia were unimpressed with Lord's discovery.

They knew the great Eusapia cheated on occasion (as have many other notable psychics) when things were not working, but this in no way tarnished or diminished her incomparable feats over many years of truly extraordinary psychic demonstrations.

Lord of the Flies. This name of Satan, an extraordinarily apt epithet, is the literal translation of the ancient Hebrew symbol of pollution and the evil Baalzebub.

Lossky, Nicholas Onufriyevich (1875–1965). One of Russia's most important modern philosophers and eminent mystics. He was exiled from Russia, where he had been Professor of Philosophy at the University of St. Petersburg. When he left his native land in 1922 he taught in Prague; in 1946 he emigrated to the United States where he continued his teaching. In the *Intuitive Basis of Knowledge,* Lossky reveals his central insight—that man's ultimate destiny is to experience complete being through an intuition of the Absolute which is the living God.

Lost Word Of Cabalism. The Cabalists and the Masons believe this *word,* now lost, will in the future reappear and reveal the enigma of Creation.

Lotus (Hinduism). The most prominent flower in this religion, it symbolizes the earth. Representations of the lotus are frequent in depictions of the gods, and the creator of the world reclines on a lotus. In Egypt, the lotus is both the national emblem and a sacred flower from the remotest times. The latter flower is blue and white; the Indian lotus has large pink flowers.

Lotus Seat. The crosslegged meditation posture of Yoga, designed to still the body and assist the psychic "circulation" or the rising of the Kundalini (q.v.) to the various chakras (q.v.) or psychic centers.

Lotus Sutra. A classical Buddhist document, a prominent feature of Northern Buddhism (Mahayana). It is famous in the Far East where a transcendant Gotama preaches on a mountain peak to a gathering of disciples the doctrine of a Cosmic Buddha "in which all things consist," accompanied by various miraculous signs and wonders. (This is reminiscent of the cosmic Christ which is revealed in the Epistle to the Ephesians.) This teaching put forward the idea of repeated saintly incarnations of Gotama (Bodhisattva) as a Buddha-spirit, Dharmakaya, or Vairocana. Nirvana (q.v.) in this scheme is represented as a celestial home of social pleasures.

Loudun, Nuns of. In the year 1633 one of the most famous outbreaks of diabolical possession broke out in the Ursuline Convent in Loudun, France. Most of the nuns began to speak with tongues and to behave hysterically. The outbreak soon spread, enveloping the residents of the neighboring town, and drawing the attention of Cardinal Richelieu to the phenomenon . Richelieu appointed an investigatory commission. The possessed were put through several rituals of exorcism without success. Finally, Father Urbain Grandier, Confessor of the Convent, was accused of sorcery and yoking the nuns to the Devil. Although he was tried and found guilty, and burned at the stake in 1634, the diabolical possession continued for many years. Strangely, the three exorcists who accused Grandier all suffered evil consequences—insanity in two cases, and diabolical possession in the other. See: Aldous Huxley's *The Devils of Loudun*.

Lourdes. French resort, famed for its miraculous cures. In 1858 the Virgin Mary was supposed to have appeared in a grotto to Bernadette Soubiros, an invalid child. There is no supporting evidence for the apparition, but some cures are certainly reported on good authority.

Love in Dreams. In old dream interpretation, a dream that one is in love indicated the individual would make a fool of himself, the dream operating by the contrary. Moreover, if the dreamer was a young girl with a dream of falling in love, it meant she would shortly be laughed at and ridiculed because of an act of folly.

Lower Astral. Common term for that part of the spirit sphere nearest earth. The level of ghosts, apparitions and poltergeist activities.

Loyola, Saint Ignatius (1491–1556). Born Inigo Lopez de Loyola of an ancient noble Basque family. his ambition to become a great soldier spurred him to enter military life. But a severe wound in a battle forced his return home where during a long convalescence his reading of a life of Christ and a book of saints converted him to the path of God and Christ's way of holiness. In the course of a year of hermitlike living in 1522 he experienced a number of ecstatic visions, and from this period till his death he followed an unflagging determination to bring and teach the way of Christ to the world. Toward this end he spent the years 1524 to 1535 studying at four great universities, and making two trips to the Holy Land. In 1534 he formed the Society of Jesus—the famous order of the Jesuits; became a leader in the Catholic reform movement; and wrote his enormously important *Spiritual Exercises*. This work emphasizes the multi-faceted personality and program of Loyola; that is, to become a "soldier of Christ" one must have an iron will, follow Chirst completely, experience both contemplative and active Christian discipline, and bring one's life in a series of four steps to the perfect life of mystical union with God. Saint Ignatius Loyola is in many respects one of the most unusual of the great Christian mystics.

L.S.A. See London Spiritualist Alliance.

Lucidity. A collective term for the faculties by means of which supernormal knowledge may be acquired. It includes the phenomena of clairvoyance, clairaudience, psychometry and premonitions.

Luciferians. In Medieval times sects of occultists who debased and damaged Eucharistic wafers in the presence of a figure of Lucifer.

They were considered Satanists, worshippers of the Devil as the omnipotent god of the universe.

Luck in Dreams. In old dream interpretation, to dream of being the recipient of luck was a sure sign of coming misfortune.

Lugnasad. An important Druidic ritual, the sun-festival, occurring at the beginning of August, when the Druid priests led their Celtic worshippers in prayer to Llwy or Lug for a fruitful harvest.

Lull, Raimon or Lully (c. 1235–1315). Spanish poet, monk, Arabian scholar, philosopher, Cabalist, alchemist, and mystic, who was one of the most learned men of his time. After teaching at several colleges, he devoted his life to writing his mystical and occult works, to philosophy, and in journeys to North Africa to convert Muslims to Christianity. A man of universal knowledge, he has been praised for his *The Ars Magna* or *Genealis*, one of the first great systems of universal logic from which all knowledge—scientific, philosophic, religious, and logical—could be deduced. Alchemists and occultists have attributed many works to him, and his writings have had a profound influence on mysticism, the occult, philosophy, and science. See: *Thoughts of Blessed Ramon Lull for Everyday*, also, *Alchimia Magic Naturalis*, *De Secretis Medicina Magna*, and *Opera Alchima*.

Lumbini Grove (Buddhism). Where Gotama Buddha was born. It is in Lumbini Park near Kapilavatthu.

Luminous Body. Pythagoras' term for the astral body.

Luminous Phenomena (Spiritualism). Associated with physical mediumship. It would appear to have a chemical origin, the substances used being derived from the organism of the medium. These lights vary in brilliance and size, sometimes colored. They appear as semisolid objects which float about the room. Slight smells of phosphorus have been recorded as accompanying the phenomena. It is also interesting to note the many accounts of lights appearing at religious revivals and about the persons of saints in ecstasy.

Lunation. Astrologers deem the New Moon a mediator that connects or binds together the Sun and the Moon.

Luria, Isaac (1534–1572) (Cabalism). Cabalist and mystic, born in Jerusalem. He lived and studied in Egypt and was part of a group devoted to the study of the mystical aspects of Hebraic religion. A follower of the Zohar, he developed a body of doctrines which initiated the modern esoteric development of Cabalism. His work took root in Eastern Europe, and profoundly influenced the Hasidic cult (q.v.). His work was organized by the Hasidim into aspects combining the speculative and the ineffable sense of the mystic.

Lycanthropy. In many folklores the fear of human beings becoming wolves. There have been many tales of werewolves, notably in Central Europe and Russia.

Lyons, Arthur Jr. Has written a popular book on Satanism (q.v.), *The Second Coming* (1970), which gives a detailed account of Satanism in the United States. It also provides information on the tenets of modern Satanism not generally understood.

Maa Kheru. In ancient Egyptian religion this expression when uttered, enabled the soul of the dead to proceed to the underworld and win the powers of the gods.

Mabinogion, The. This Welsh volume of ancient Celtic legends recounts the mystery-wisdom of Druids and the Druid priests.

Macarius the Elder (*c.* 300–*c.* 390). A Christian monk, one of the Desert Fathers, who was a noted mystic and is recorded to have borne the stigmata (q.v.).

Macrocosm. This term frequently used in the occult, in alchemy, necromancy, and magic represents the omnipotence of great supernatural powers, of the universe of God. Sometimes it signifies God or the universe contrasted with man. (See: Microcosm)

Madhva (1197–1276). The Hindu philosopher and theologian who in his departure from the Monistic and Karmic doctrines of much Hindu thought, asserted a doctrine of dualism and that there are three kinds of entities in the universe. His tripartite system asserts that there are: life monads (q.v.) or souls, nonintelligent substances, and God. He also distinguished between the material cause of the cosmos—nature and its constantly-changing world,and the absolute changelessness of God who is able to transform, create, sustain, and destroy the cosmos. For Madhva the difference in the destinies of individuals is the result of innate differences peculiar to each individual, and that it is God who imposes on each life monad its complete destiny. For some individuals God has decreed that they will suffer everlasting punishment in hell, for others that they will transmigrate forever without release. In these theories of predestination, Madhva opposes the common notions of Karma (q.v.) and the causes of the soul's round of rebirths.

Maga. The general name for witch, but particularly a hedonistic witch.

Magen David. The "Star of David" or the "Jewish Star"—a hexagram formed by two interwoven triangles. It became a universal symbol of Judaism only relatively late in Judaic practice. Its actual widespread acceptance as the Hebrew symbol was the work of the practical Cabalists who in the Middle Ages introduced it as a mystic-magic amulet serving to protect the wearer against a host of evils. As such, the "Star of David" amulet became hugely popular.

Magi. A learned class of the ancient Medes and Persians who studied and practiced magic. "The Magi," the three "wise men" of one of the scripture stories concerning the birth of Jesus. The Magians were priests of religious settlements from Mesopotamia and its surrounds, and existed up to the Christian epoch. They believed in an old nature religion of Iran, which preceded Zoroastrianism.

Magia Naturalis. This phrase described the operation of nature's forces—magnetism, electricity, etc., and was used by the natural philosophers or "scientists" of the 15th through the 17th centuries. Their wonderful experiments and achievements were contrasted with the use of magic, which was efficacious through "purely spiritual" agencies.

Magic. Since the most ancient times magic has been utilized by mankind in numerous ways. In actual fact, it was man's first science; for the techniques of magic were frequently efficacious. But chiefly, since magical success often meant food or starvation, tribulation or survival, the magicians (whose necks depended on producing results) became increasingly more sharp-eyed, professional, learned, skilled. The ancient Chaldean astrologers, the Chinese magicians, the Egyptian priests, the Greek oracles, the Celtic Druids, and a myriad of Shamans, Medicine-Men, and witchdoctors, worldwide, attest to this process and development. Public magic (diviners, astrologers, oracle-priests); Black Magic (q.v.); White Magic (q.v.); and Popular Magic (group ritual performed for survival needs—agriculture, hunting, human fertility) are some modalities of magic. In sympathetic magic—an article is identified with a person, and treated as such. It should be noted that psychic phenomena are supernormal; i.e., they work in accordance with natural laws and therefore should not be classed as supernatural.

Magicians. Professional modern illusionists who employ legerdemain and expensive stage settings for their tricks.

Magic Squares. A square divided into parts, each labeled with numbers or letters, containing the magical property that, read up, down, or diagonally, it forms the same sum or word. In ancient times, notably in China, India, and Arabia, such squares were often used in the occult, in magic, and astrology. They were also worn as amulets. In more recent years, some of the world's greatest mathematicians have discovered extraordinary mathematical properties in magic squares, notably the more complicated and larger examples. One of the early magic squares is the following:

4	9	2
3	5	7
8	1	6

Magisterium. In alchemy, a term describing the "process" that led to the knowledge of the Philosopher's Stone (q.v.). Sometimes it may mean particular substances, for example, antimony, gold, mercury, etc.

Magnetic Healing. See Healing.

Magnetic Phenomena. Known in mediumship and in some psychics. Henry Slade and Mlle. Tomczyk, for example, were mediums who could influence compass needles. More recently, the well-known psychic Uri Geller (q.v.), along with a number of others has performed many varied types of magnetic phenomena.

Magnetometer. Instrument of Abbe Fortin. A paper indicator suspended by a silk thread in a glass cylinder was deflected by the presence of a hand, over a dial of 360 degrees. A similar instrument has been used for study of terrestrial magnetism and dowsing.

Maha-bharata (Hinduism). One of the world's great epic poems, written between 200 B.C. and 200 A.D., and containing some 220,000 lines, it is probably the longest poem ever written. Fundamentally, it recounts the dynastic struggles of the Pandavas, and their three cousins the treacherous Kauravas. In the climactic final battle, in which the saga of the *Bhagavad-Gita* (q.v.) occurs, the Pandavas are triumphant. Yudhisthira, the leader, becomes king. But depressed by the empty glory of existence, he relinquishes his throne, follows the path to heaven, and is rewarded by eternal bliss. The *Maha-bharata* also tells the story of the 8th incarnation of Vishnu.

Maha-guru (Hinduism). The great teacher.

Mahakalpa (Hinduism). A standard measurement of time, a cosmic era.

Mahamaya (Buddhism). The name of Gotama Buddha's Mother. For the Hindus, it is the name of their sacred city, Gaya.

Maharishi Mahesh Yogi. Founder of the Spiritual Regeneration Movement and apostle of the system named Transcendental Meditation (q.v.). He was born in India and for thirteen years was a disciple of the renowned spiritual teacher His Divinity Swami Brahmananda Saraswati. From his teacher, Maharishi learned the method of Transcendental Meditation. In 1958 when Maharishi founded the Spiritual Regeneration Movement in Madras his purpose was to spiritually regenerate every man in the world. Since then he has established the headquarters of the Academy of Meditation at Rishikesh, a pilgrimage town at the foot of the Himalayas. Here during three months of the year (giving the remaining part of the year to other centers) Maharishi trains his corps of students from around the world to become teachers of Transcendental Meditation. (See: Transcendental Meditation).

Mahat (Hinduism). Meaning in the ancient Sanskrit "great," "mighty," it represents the first great principle created by *prakriti* (q.v.), which is the universal cohesive power of spirit, idea, or ideation.

Mahatma or Mahatman (Hinduism). Few Westerners in early years realized that Mahatma Gandhi was not the great Indian's name, but that the epithet "Mahatma" meant a person of great prestige, worthy of reverence, imbued with wisdom and selflessness. It also means one who has achieved Nirvana (q.v.) but remains in his body in order to help mankind progress. For Theosophists, a Mahatman is an Indian or Tibetan sage of superior knowledge and power.

Mahayana (Buddhism). Meaning the Great Vehicle or Carriage of Salvation, it is this version of Buddhism that predominates in China, Mongolia, Japan, Korea, and Tibet. Contrasted with the Hinayana (q.v.), the Little Vehicle, it glorifies the Bodhisvattva's ideal of the renunciation of Nirvana and his decision to help struggling humanity. Basically, its central teachings are a belief of Bodhisattvas and man's power to become such; an ethical ideal that all must do good in the interest of all; that accrued virtue must be donated to the less fortunate; and a belief in a myriad of supernatural beings known as Buddhas.

Mahdi. A future Messiah of Islam.

Maimonides Medical Center. In the Division of Parapsychology and Psychophysics at this New York Medical Center experiments have proved that "images" in the thoughts of waking subjects have been successfully transferred, through ESP, into the brains of sleeping subjects closeted in another room. Dr. Montague Ullman, Chief of the Center, which was formerly called the "Dream Laboratory," is now engaged with his co-workers in a variety of experiments such as those involving altered states of consciousness, and sensory deprivation. His results through the years have convinced him that given sufficient financial assistance, within the next ten years they should witness a major breakthrough.

Maitreya (Buddhism). The compassionate Buddha who is to come in the future, after 5,670,000,000 years, and save mankind. Represented as fat and laughing, with a rosary in one hand and a bag of benefits for man in the other. In Japan he is addressed as Miroku. In Hinduism he has the name of a Rishi (q.v.).

Malefica. A witch who inflicts injury both mental and physical, and who has been tutored in her evil by a demon.

Malkuth. In Cabalism the tenth sefirut, called the Crown, for it embodies the power of the nine others which have emanated from the supreme En Sof (q.v.).

Mallet. In Japanese mythology, Daikoku, the god of wealth and one of the seven gods of good fortune or luck, is often represented as bearing this fortune-favored artifact.

Malleus Maleficarium. This was the huge, famous, definitive book which identified with unerring certainty the witch and the practices of heresy and witchcraft. Published in Germany in 1486; written by Jacob Sprenger and Henricus Institoris (Kramer), inquisitors; titled *Malleus Maleficarium* "the Witches' Hammer"; translated everywhere in Europe (in English—1928, 1951); hailed as the definitive exposition on all aspects of witches and witchcraft; it declared that carnal lust was the origin of witchcraft; proposed torture, life imprisonment, and death for the unrepentant witch; and asserted that loss of reason proved demonic possession. For nearly 400 years it reigned as the sovereign authority on the subject for both Catholic and Protestant.

Mambo. In the Voodoo religion she is a priestess.

Mamitu. The Mesopotamian goddess of fate.

Mana. A Polynesian term for supernatural forces of nature or magical powers. This magical power may inhere in objects or persons.

Mandala (Buddhism-Hinduism). In Sanskrit Mandala means a "Circle." It is mystic symbol of an immensely concentrated quality, for its geometrical design (a circle enclosing a square) is an intricate composition of symbols of divinities. During meditation, one first perceives it as a map of the world; secondly, as one's self; thirdly, as a mediator that connects the identification of one's self with the cosmos; and, finally, all these stages culminating in the attainment of Samadhi (q.v.).

Mandara (Hinduism). This is the great mountain used by the gods when they churn the ocean.

Manas (Buddhism-Hinduism). A term describing mind. In its broadest meaning, it is the seat of intellectual operations and emotions.

Mandrake. A plant of the potato family, famous in ancient times as a love philtre and "the plant of Circe," who reputedly used it in her witch-brews. Because it often grows in the shape of human limbs, it has earned with the years an evil reputation years as a demonic plant. Nonetheless, it is also claimed to have the power of prophecy, and the alchemical potency of producing gold.

Manes. In early Roman religion this was the name given to the collective souls of the dead, who were deemed "good" and worshipped as gods, particularly at the three important festivals—the Feralia, Parentalia, and Lemuria. The deities of the underworld, Dis, Orcu, and Persephone also bore this name. In later times, Manes was used for the souls of the individual dead and their names added to grave inscriptions.

Manetho. The Egyptian priest of Serapis, who in the 3rd century B.C. wrote a notable book on the religion and history of Egypt. Though now lost, it was the source for others of much important data on the Egyptian occult.

Manichaeism. A Gnostic religion which flourished in A.D. 400, founded by Mani, a Persian, in an attempt to combine traditional eastern asceticism and Zoroastrian principles with Christianity.

Manjursi (Lamaism). Here in this major Bodhisattva (q.v.) of Mahayana Buddhism (q.v.) is incorporated a cluster of qualities that is a particularly revealing insight into the complex structure of Tibetan religion. Although Manjursi means "wonderful and auspicious," he also represents the divine substance of wisdom. The five curls on his forehead symbolize the cosmic five-fold wisdom of Buddha, but from his hand there also extends a sword. He is considered Buddha's chief disciple, sometimes his son; and always he is worshipped as a magnificent prince of the Bodhisattvas. But he also carries a sword. And in this martial aspect (Dorje-chi-che—"Terrifying Lightning") he is the supreme monster of Lamaism. He is startlingly represented with 16 legs, 34 arms, and 9 heads; and while crushing animals with his feet, he is also engaged in sexual intercourse with a *shakti* (q.v.) who holds a blood-filled skull-cup in her left hand. Decorating his body are a mass of liturgical objects, necklaces, skulls, legs, animals, jewels, sexual organs, and the skins of wild beasts. Centered in his jungle of arms is a grotesquely monstrous bull's head, with flames for hair, yet carrying a third eye—the third eye of mystic wisdom. Moreover, above this monstrous maelstrom, above the bull's head, is the small beatific head of the angelic Manjursi, enraptured by mystic meditation, floating in a halo of small white clouds and brilliant rainbows.

Mansions of the Moon. In astrology the 28 divisions of the moon's journey through one complete circuit of 360 degrees—representing one day's average movement of the moon.

Manson, Charles. Leader of the Manson "family," who was variously acclaimed "God," "Jesus," and "Satan." His "visions" and his practices of witchcraft, and reputed magical powers ended, finally, when he commanded his followers to commit a series of ritualistic murders (See: Tate, Sharon). In 1971 he and three members of his "family" were convicted of murder.

Mantic. The art or science of magic, particularly divination (q.v.).

Mantis. Among the Bushmen of South Africa, he is an insect-god symbolizing the power of good.

Mantra (Hinduism). That segment of the Vedic literature made up of hymns. A mantra, being a hymn of praise, by the power of its cosmic radiations, when it is used in incantation, creates positive changes in the cosmic self. *Om Mani Padmi Om,* the name of the Supreme Deity of the Golden Lotus of Wisdom, is a popular and powerful mantra. But the most famous and most powerful mantra is the following: *Om! Bhur Bhuva Swah. Tat savitur varenyam bhargo devasya dhimahi. dhiyo yo na prachodayat.* Translated: O All-Life! All-Holiness. All-Joy! the Lord of upper, lower, and happy regions, our Maker, the Supreme Being, we meditate upon Thy adorable form of spiritual light, which dispels the darkness of sin from the mind. May Ye illuminate our intellects. The use of mantras is now widespread in contemporary meditation.

Mantrika Sakti (Hinduism). Numbers, sounds, and letters in the Vedic Mantras (q.v.) were considered to possess an additional factor of occult power, being intelligible essences of the Atman (q.v.).

Manu (Hinduism). The creator of the "laws" or "code" of Manu—the latter meaning "the man." This name is given to each of the fourteen forefathers of the human race. The first, Swayam-Bhuva, wrote the Ordinances of Manu. The seventh is the hero of the flood epic—the Hindu Noah—the forefather of the human race.

Many Mansions. The many spheres of spirit existence.

Mara (Buddhism). The personification of the power of evil, who is killer, murderer, and death himself.

Marduk or Asaru. In ancient Chaldea the god of happiness for man; similar to Jupiter. Among the Babylonians, the god of magicians.

Mare. This Germanic demon, a hideous hag, equivalent with the demon Incubus (q.v.), sits on the chest of her victims, relentlessly smothering and suffocating them by squeezing out their breath.

Margery Mediumship. See Crandon.

Marryat, Florence (1837–1899). English authoress, daughter of the noted English novelist, Captain Marryat. She knew most of the famous mediums of 1870–80 in England and America, and eventually wrote several books on Spiritualism since she possessed mediumistic gifts herself.

Mary The Jewess. Famous in ancient times as one of the most accomplished of sorceresses. She has been described as the sister of Moses and said to have derived her awesome powers from the hand of God Himself. Many occult writers have attributed to her a number of works.

Marylebone Spiritualist Association. See Spiritualist Association of Great Britain.

Mascal. In southern France, in former times, the name for a witch.

Maschalismo. In the ancient Near East a practice of murderers where the hands and feet of the corpse were severed and tied under the armpits—to prevent the ghost of the murdered from walking or being able to take revenge on them.

Masculine Planets. In astrology: the Sun, Mars, Jupiter, Saturn, and Uranus. (See: Feminine Planets)

Maskim. The seven maleficent devils, in ancient Babylonian religion who, remarkably, bore close resemblances to the planet deities.

Masleh (Judaism). In the mystical writings of the ancient Hebrews, the angel who ruled the Zodiac, and whose influence enabled the Messiah to transfer his power and influence to the realm of the Zodiac.

Mass Hypnosis. A theory often advanced to explain extraordinary feats by fakirs—their achievements being the result of hypnotizing the entire audience.

Mastema (Judaism). In the Book of Jubilees, the King of the evil spirits, half human, half fallen angel, whose legions of satanic angels aided Satan on earth. Playing the Devil's tempter, he urged God to test Abraham; later, he tried to destroy Moses in Egypt by lending his powers to the magicians contending against him.

Master. An Adept; occult title for an "Initiate" who has reached the highest degree of occult attainment possible in this world. These people are supposed to have conquered human limitations and are said to be responsible for spiritual administration in the world. It is claimed that they inhabit remote fastnesses and control the world's progress by deep meditation and influence over their distant pupils.

Matambala. In the West Pacific Solomon Islands, this is a secret society (q.v.), especially on Florida Island.

Material. Pertaining to matter, as distinct from "spiritual." Mediums often refer to this as "material conditions," meaning the ordinary circumstances of earthly life.

Materialism. A philosophy which refers all known phenomena to a material origin, and is completely exclusive of spiritual interests.

Materialization (Spiritualism). A form of physical mediumship whereby the visible production of temporary ectoplasmic forms, in various stages of solidity and completeness, may be observed. The ectoplasm is a substance, normally invisible which flows from a physical medium, augmented to some extent by the sitters. It is first seen as a slightly luminous vapor or fluid which apparently organizes itself into some recognizable form. According to spiritualist belief, experienced discarnate operators can mold this living material to their own former likeness, or utilize it to produce lever-like structures for telekinetic phenomena, levitation of tables, raps, etc. Although it may appear incredible to the layman, these phenomena have been thoroughly investigated many times under laboratory conditions and some reputable investigators have vouched for the genuineness of the phenomena. A warning is necessary here, for the benefit of inexperienced would-be researchers: this form of mediumship is rare, and unless encountered under strictly controlled conditions by a competent body of experienced workers, is always suspect by reason of the conditions of darkness usually laid down by private physical circles. For the purpose of gaining evidence of survival, mental mediumship provides the safest and surest path for the ordinary investigator.

Matha. Famous Serbian psychic of the 19th century whose list of uncannily accurate predictions were so phenomenal they came to be known all over Europe, and were titled the Black Prophecy of the peasant Matha.

Mathers, Samuel Liddell. The English founder of the Cabalistic and Occult Order of the Golden Dawn discovered the principles of his society when he and his wife deciphered a mysterious manuscript in 1884. Mrs. Mathers was a French clairvoyant. The manuscript, which he titled *Kabbalah Unveiled*, contained writings of the Cabala and Tarot. According to Mathers, he discovered there the means by which man may relate to God and "the Divine Man latent in himself." Mathers also edited and translated the *Key of Solomon* (q.v.) and *The Sacred Magic of Abramelin the Mage*. After Aleister Crowley (q.v.) became a member of the Order, their personalities warred against each other, and some believe that Mather's death in 1918 was directly caused by Crowley's use of Black Magic (q.v.) against him.

Mathra (Zoroastrianism). The holy word. A point in the holy scriptures.

Matter. An aspect of the energy in the universe detectable by the physical senses. The phenomena of materialization may show the amenability of matter to an organizing impetus from unknown sources. At the same time physicists have discovered that the ultimate particles continue to decrease both in mass and lifetime. Although the fundamental electron possesses continuous movement, the principle of uncertainty makes it impossible to locate this essential particle in both space and time at the same moment. Many great philosophers have realized the futility of apprehending matter directly; its so-called attributes are our own interpretations of our sense data, true perhaps by analogy only, to the "real" world. When one hears from spirit communicators of similar environs in the spirit world, but not subject to the senses as on earth, one wonders if perhaps they do not indeed inhabit the "real" world.

Matter Through Matter. These curious phenomena have been produced in the seance room on several occasions. Knots have appeared in endless cords (Professor Zollner); sewn-up clothing has been removed from mediums and replaced intact. Two rings of dissimilar woods, prepared by Sir Oliver Lodge himself, were linked together. The production of apports, the removal or introduction of a variety of objects from sealed or locked containers, was successfully achieved in most carefully conducted experiments with Margery Crandon of Boston, 1932, reported by William H. Dutton in *Journal of A.S.P.R.* August–September, 1932.

Matutine. In astrology, the appearance in the morning of the Moon, Mercury, or Venus, that have arisen before the Sun. Such a star or planet remains matutine until it achieves its first station (q.v.) where it enters the phase called retrograde (q.v.).

Maya (Hinduism). In the *Upanishads* this term, meaning "illusion, deception, the demoniac power" which are embodied in ultimate reality, are not real at all, but only ignorance. The female divinity, *Maya-deui* or Durga, personifies this deception, responsible for deluding mankind. Only those who rise above Maya are now free to achieve *Moksha* (q.v.), salvation.

Maxpe. Among the American Crow Indians a visionary who received his power and luck from supernatural spirits.

Maxwell, Dr. Joseph. Psychical investigator, Attorney General at Bordeaux Court of Appeal. Author of several books on divination. To equip himself for an analytical study of mediumship, he undertook a six years course of study for a medical degree, after which he was fortunate enough to contact a medium, M. Meurice, who produced telekinetic phenomena in good light, and also Mme. Aguilana. He was with Col. Rochas in the study of Eusapia Paladino's mediumship. One of his interesting discoveries was that mediums possessed the common physical characteristics of spots in the irises of the eyes. His conclusions were, that phenomena were genuine, but attributed the intelligence to the forming of a collective intelligence of the sitters.

Maya. The entire phenomena of the physical world, considered to be illusory by orthodox Hindus. Its influence can be traced to the interpretation of the *Upanishads* known as the Mayavada Vedanta by Sankara.

Mazda (Zorastrianism). The name of the one, supreme god, Ahura.

Mazdayasnian. In Buddhism, reference to a worshipper of Ahura Mazda (q.v.).

M.C. Medium Coeli (q.v.).

Mc Dougall, William (1871–1938). British-born psychologist and physician who in 1920 became a Professor of Psychology at Harvard, and, in 1927, until his death, taught at Duke University. Like William James and Gardner Murphy (qq.v.), he lent his high prestige in psychology to furthering the scientific status of psychical research, while others were engaged in limiting psychology to "pure" science. More than that, he was the first eminent psychologist who sponsored the ESP investigations of J.B. Rhine (q.v.) as far back as the 1920's. See: *The Energies of Men,* 1932.

Mdoki. In the African Congo, an evil spirit.

Mead. The offering of fermented honey and water drunk by the Teutonic people in worship of their gods whose own thirst-quencher was also mead. This drink of the gods was provided by Odin's (q.v.) goat.

Measure of Stature (Judaism). In ancient Judaic mysticism a tractate which elaborates the mystical relation of numbers and their symbolic nature.

Medea. Fabled witch, sorcerer, and goddess, she helped the Greek Argonaut Jason by tricking her father and enabled Jason to perform an impossible feat, and, finally, to win the treasured Golden Fleece. When she escaped to Greece with Jason, as his wife, she again exhibited her remarkable occult powers by making Jason's old father young again. After Jason deserted Medea for another woman, Medea used her magical talents to murder her, then murdered the two children she had with Jason, and fled to Athens. Worshipped by some cults as a goddess, she was universally acclaimed a witch of rare cunning.

Medical Astrology. That aspect of Astrology devoted to reading the planetary causes of disease.

Medicine Man. A general term describing the Shaman (q.v.) or magician among many primitive and modern tribes, notably the American Indians. Wielding many powers as doctor, magician, spirit-mediator, priest—his training was and is arduous and his vocation generally inherited.

Medieval Astrology. In the 14th century it was not considered merely an occult diversion; rather, it was taught by official sanction. So much so, that Charles V (1337–81) of France, after collecting and having translated all the books he could find on astrology decided to build a college of astrology to add to the University of Paris. After donating to the University his immense collection of astrological lore, he also provided a fund for the teaching of astrology to two students entitled "King's Scholars." The astrological interpretation of the symbolism of medieval cathedrals reveals significant information. At the prestigious University of Padua in Italy, geomancy (divination by markings of/ or on earth) was part of the curriculum. Almost all royal personages had their official astrologers.

Meditation. A mental discipline whereby the mind dwells upon a single notion, mental object, or mantra which is generally employed for the purpose of gaining insight into the inner nature and meaning of the universe. In the past it was a discipline almost exclusively utilized by eastern ascetics, Yogis, monks and spiritualist development circles. However, more recently, and largely owing to the immense popularity of Transcendental Meditation (q.v.), Zen Buddhism (q.v.), and a host of other teachings, the use of meditation to achieve cosmic and spiritual insight or merely effective relaxation has become a widespread practice in the West. (See: Samadhi)

Medium. A subject who, under certain conditions, can be the means of relaying information from deceased persons to the living. The physical state of mediumship is not pathological, as it leads to an expansion and development of original powers, and is distinct from hysterical states or epilepsy, which degenerate the mentality.

Medium Coeli. Astrological term for the intersection of the observer's meridian with the ecliptic, an angle considered to be of prime importance in the horoscope. Also known as the "Midheaven."

Mediumistic Development. See Circle, Development.

Medusa's Head. In ancient Grecian mythology, Medusa, one of the three Gorgons, was punished by Minerva (for using one of her temples to sleep with Neptune) by turning her hair into hissing snakes. But her dread fame was owing to the fact that those who looked at her were frozen into stone.

Memory. That faculty of the mind which can retain and recall ideas and impressions. Under hypnosis, this faculty may exhibit supernormal powers, to the extent of recalling minute details from early childhood. There are even claims of memory extending to previous incarnations on earth (see Hypnotic Regression). Certain Yoga practices are said to similarly extend the conscious memory. On passing to the spirit world, we are told that our memories become complete, but if attempts at communication are made, by entering earth conditions the memory again becomes impaired.

Memory, Cosmic. An idea similar to that of the Akashic records (q.v.), a "pool of memory" which may be tapped by individuals during certain trance states. (See: Cosmic Consciousness).

Memphite Drama. The oldest metaphysical treatise known, showing the existence of a mature mode of thought in Egypt, already ancient by 2500 B.C. In it, the world of nature is held to be the product of divine intelligence. The copy is incised on a black stone, and may be seen in the British Museum.

Mental Body. Occult term for that part of a human personality which is composed of "mental matter." It is concerned with thought processes, abstract in a higher mental body, and concrete in a lower. Said to possess a life and consciousness of its own.

Mental Healing. (Spiritualism). Spirit healing has been known to give easement for every kind of illness. Mental troubles may be treated with success either with or without the actual presence of the healer. Absent healing can be just as effective, by the guides and spirit doctors restoring the mental balance of the patient through the spirit body.

Mental Radio. A term for telepathy, used by Upton Sinclair in his experiments.

Mentiferous. Conveying or transferring mind or thought: telepathic.

Mercury. The Roman deity (counterpart of the Grecian Hermes); however, it was not the *Caduceus*, but a sacred branch that was his emblem of peace. His festival was celebrated near a sacred well of magic powers, and he was believed the inventor of incantations for use in the occult. In Alchemy, the name of Quicksilver. Theosophists ascribe to Mercury the 2nd stage of the Earth Epoch.

Merlin. In ancient Britain an enchanter and sorcerer at the Court of King Arthur, believed to have been born of Satan, but he may have been an early Celtic god.

Meru (Hinduism). The mountain abode of the Hindu deities, located in the center of the earth.

Mescalin. A drug prepared from a Mexican cactus plant, used by local tribes to induce trance and clairvoyant states. According to Aldous Huxley, who was one of the first prominent Westerners to experiment upon himself, the sense of time recedes, and a heightened awareness of color and form is experienced under mescalin's influence.

Mesmerism. Early form of hypnotism, discovered and used by the German physician Mesmer in 1815. His method employed hand passes which were thought to convey a vital essence or fluid, and were used to dominate the patient's will. It was also called "animal magnetism." Mesmer had success in his healing methods, but antagonized the orthodox medical opinion of his day and was branded as an imposter. Hypnotism is now used by the medical profession.

Mesoptamian Celestial Omina. These were collections of celestial omens. The Baru, who was the official prognosticator, interpreted these omens, and when ill fortune was promised advised the king on how to avoid them. The collections of celestial omens, the work of the royal astrologers, gave weather or disease information that might affect agriculture, animal life, and man; further, they warned on military affairs and the fortunes of the king and his family.

Messages, Spirit. See Communications.

Messiah. In the Hebrew this word means the "anointed," he who is to be God's messenger, the "redeemer," greatest of all prophets, he who is to establish God's Kingdom on earth. There have been numerous "Messiahs" in Jewish History (see: Sabbatai Zvi); however, none thus far has proved to be God's genuine messenger. But the notion of the Messiah is as old as man's civilizations, for the Egyptians, Babylonians, Persians, Greeks and Romans all proclaimed a diversity of concepts about the coming of a "Redeemer." In Hinduism he is Krishna. Indeed, many American Indian tribes have also maintained such apocalyptic beliefs. Since the Jews described the advent of Messiah as one who would be a member of the house of David, born in Bethlehem (Micah 5.2), Jesus Christ announced himself as the Messiah—and Christianity is based on this prophetic announcement—pointing out that He, Christ, is foreshadowed in the whole of the Old Testament. The very name Christ is a Greek word which means Messiah. For the Jews, the Messiah promised God's Kingdom on earth where the former would reign in glory; Christians, however, see earthly life as a preparation for heaven, and only the second coming of Jesus reflects the Hebrew tradition.

Metagnome. A word for "medium" coined by Emil Boirac (q.v.) for psychical research, and defined: "a person from whom supernormal phenomena originate, or in express relation to whom these phenomena occur; he is thus essential for psychic research." The reason for its adoption was to eliminate the spiritualistic associations of the word "medium."

Metagraphology. Psychometry from handwriting.

Metaphysics. That branch of philosophy which seeks to determine the nature of things which exist—the true nature of that which underlies the familiar world.

Metapsychics. A term proposed by Charles Richet for a science dealing with mechanical or psychological phenomena due to forces which seem to be intelligent, or to unknown powers latent in human intelligence. It was divided into two classes: objective and subjective. The word "parapsychic" (Boirac), was adopted in Germany and has proved the more popular term today.

Metapsychic Institute. See Institut Metapsychique.

Metempsychosis. The belief that the soul at death can reside in a succession of bodies, human or animal. In the Greek world it originated with Pythagoras, but the word designating this doctrine was coined in the Christian era. Fundamental to Hinduism, Buddhism, and Theosophy (qq.v.). Most occultists would limit metempsychosis as human to human only.

Metetherial. Term coined by F.W.H. Myers, (q.v.) meaning beyond the ether, the transcendental spiritual world.

Methodists. Protestant church body, founded in England by John and Charles Wesley; administered on Presbyterian and Congregational lines.

Mettraton (Judaism). In ancient Israel, the legend was that he was the great angel who helped God in his work. Having the pure essence of God, he infused this into all life.

Meyer, Jean. Founder of Maison des Spirites, Paris, which aimed to promote the works of Allan Kardec (q.v.). Also founder of Metapsychique Internationale for psychic research, which was recognized by the French government in 1919.

Miao (Taoism). That unknowable, omnipotent, creative Power (Shen) in the infinite number of things which is the mystery of all existence.

Microcosm and Macrocosm. The concept of man as a small universe, a replica of the macrocosm—the great universe.

Midheaven. See Medium Coeli.

Midiwiwin. Objibway Indian society of Shamans and magicians. They must undergo a series of tests with the aid of the snake-spirits before becoming masters.

Millesimo Castle. Situated in the Italian province of Savona. It was the setting for many important psychic investigations from 1927 onwards. (See: Centurione)

Mimpathy. A sharing of feeling, but not necessarily sympathy. A community of sensation.

Mind. The thinking faculty, in earlier periods often termed the soul, spirit or ego; the stream of consciousness that makes personality. But in less than 100 years, modern explorations of the mind have revolutionized our understanding of this supremely important human organ.

Beginning with the foundation of the Society For Psychical Research (q.v.) in England in 1882, the epochal work of Sigmund Freud in psychoanalysis in the 1890s and the signal experiments of J.B. Rhine in parapsychology in the 1920s, there has been a remarkable coalescence of these three streams of research since about the 1930s. Many eminent researchers in these disciplines have contributed to the creation of an impressive new awareness of the structure, mechanics, and behavior dynamics of the mind. Among the most noteworthy advances are: the discovery of certain brain waves (alpha, beta, theta, etc.) and their significance; the utilization of biofeedback (q.v.); the meaning and dynamics of the right and left hemispheres of the brain; the range of paranormal abilities (telepathy, clairvoyance, precognition—ESP manifestations; and psychokinesis); the use and effect of mind-altering drugs (mescalin, LSD, peyote, etc.). Finally, a number of eminent investigators in all these disciplines have suggested that the mind can only be completed—that is, function at its highest level when it is committed to an infinite orientation—spiritual or religious. This latter position has been held by, among others C.D. Broad, Otto Rank, Gregory Zilboorg, Carl Jung, and Ernest Becker.

Mind Cure. First developed by Phineas Quimby, an American (1802–1866), and a mesmerist who believed that all disease was a delusion of the mind. One of his patients was Mary Baker Eddy (q.v.), the founder of Christian Science, who afterwards elaborated his teachings.

Mind Reading (Spiritualism). Often casually advanced as an explanation of clairvoyance. If mind reading was a recognized ability, there might be some grounds for truth in this, providing we include "reading" of the memory and the subconscious as well. Often, however, information given is not in the mind of the sitter, but has to be verified later. The only recognized form of thought transference that has been proved in any sense is telepathy or Extra Sensory Perception. Note that the results of zener card (q.v.) experiments are quite different from the detailed clairvoyant message, one symbol only from a possible five being transferred by a sender to a recipient; the results are only significant by statistics proving a degree of accuracy above chance level over many thousands of guesses. The medium does not reciprocate the thoughts, wishes or desires of the sitter; the communicator (q.v.) is often someone quite unexpected.

Minor Arcana. The fifty-six suit cards of the Tarot.

Mirabelli, Carlo (b. 1889). South American medium of Italian parents of whom most extraordinary stories have been reported. Most of his phenomena were reputed to have taken place in daylight. His powers were first observed by psychiatrists who had him under observation.

Mirablis Liber. Latin, meaning *Book of Wonders*. A 15th century book of prophecies, which among other predictions of national events forecast the French Revolution.

Miracles. Effects or events which are supernatural. Spritualists do not believe in the supernatural, but have ample evidence of the supernormal which does not contravene natural laws.

Mirrors. In Japanese folklore, mirrors reveal the soul of the onlooker; hence, they are often found in sacred places. One of the important Japanese proverbs runs: "When the mirror is dim, the soul is unclean."

Miru. A monster female spirit, in the Cook Islands of the South Pacific, who gorges herself by devouring souls.

Mirza Ali Mohammed. Persian mystic who in 1844 announced himself as the twelfth Imam—the prophet of Him who was to come. While he wrote several books, and won many followers, when he was condemned to death by hanging and the rope suddenly broke, he could not avoid death by the executioner's bullets.

Mishnah (Judaism). The earliest division of the Talmud, composed of traditions touching the close of the Old Testament until the end of the 2nd century A.D. In its some 63 tractates are descriptions of Hebrew ritual, and many Judaic laws. Simeon B. Johai, one of the most noted authorities on the Mishnah, is the reputed author of the *Zohar* (q.v.).

Mistletoe. The white-berried evergreen steeped in mystery and occult qualities, which was the sacred plant of the Druids (q.v.) who saw in it a cosmic fertility principle. The Roman Aeneas through the power of the mistletoe, The Golden Bough, journeyed to the underworld. Throughout the world's folk-legend the mistletoe has been believed to cure disease, heighten fertility, bring the desired lover. It is so mysterious it must never be cut. Its widespread use at Christmas time exhibits its continuing popularity as a unique plant.

Mitchell, Edgar. Ex-Astronaut who during his Apollo 14 moon mission engaged in telepathy experiments with persons on earth, and who also experienced an altered state of consciousness in outer space, is convinced of the authenticity of paranormal phenomena. Toward the aim of investigating occurrences that escape the methods of rational science, he has established the Institute of Neotic Sciences in Palo Alto, California. He has worked at his Institute with psychic investigations that might establish, among other parapsychological phenomena, powers existing in outer space such as the computers named SPECTRA described by Dr. Andrija Puharich in his book on Uri Geller (q.v.).

Mithra (Zoroastrianism). The Invincible Sun-God, born in human form who, as the chosen servant of God, kills a sacred bull, the blood of which fertilizes the earth. After performing other miracles, he ascends to heaven. Worship of Mithra took place in caves, Mithraeums, owing to the legend that such was his birthplace. In the Vedas (q.v.), Mithra is the god of heavenly light, but in the *Avesta* he is described

as a warrior god, fighting with Ormuzd (q.v.) to bring men righteousness and light.

Mithraism. A religious cult of fertility which originated in Persia (now
Iran) about 400 B.C. Later it became very popular with the Roman
legions who carried it with their conquests as far as Britain. The Mithraic cult centered around a savior sun-god, Mithras (q.v.), who lived
and died for the sins of the world. They had no priests as a professional class, although a man could pass through many grades in its
service. They believed that the world's events represented a chain of
divine action. The official adoption of Christianity by Rome absorbed
the cult, along with much of its ritual and doctrine.

Moha (Hinduism). This term describes the sense of bewilderment
which drives mankind to accept the false reality of the world.

Moksa (Hinduism). Salvation from Maya (q.v.), and liberation from the
effects of *Karma* (q.v.), by identification of the self with the ultimate
reality, the eternal and changeless Brahma or Atman.

Momus. In Greek mythology, the god who is the son of night and the
symbol of the sharp-tongued fault-finder. Momus was the sanctioned
grumbler who constantly directed his grumbling at the gods in whose
activities he discovered nothing but faults.

Monad. One of the key universal concepts in Western culture which
has fundamentally influenced such diverse disciplines as mathematics, philosophy, religion, mysticism, Neo-Platonism, occultism, alchemy, spiritualism, pantheism, and Theosophy. Indeed, Monad together with God, soul, Logos, and spirit make up the West's supreme
pantheon. In its original Greek sense, Monad means "one," "unit,"
but as its usage developed it became the master unitary concept opposing the materialism of the unitary doctrine of "atom." Pythagoras
(q.v.) first used it in an expanding sense to mean the "one" of mathematics, the generative number from which the complete number system evolved, and, therefore—since all was number—that system from
which the whole universe is derived. Pythagoras' monadic doctrine influenced Plato in his central notions of "ideas" and "forms."
Pythagoras' doctrine was also adopted by the religious cult of Orphism (q.v.). From Pythagoras, Orphism, and Plato, it passed on to
Aristotle, the mathematician Euclid, to the Stoics, the major Neo-
Platonists (notably Plotinus (q.v.), to Boethius, St. Augustine, St.
Bonaventure, Lull, Eckhart, Cusanus, Bruno, the school of Christian
Platonists (notably Henry More), the pantheists, the alchemists, the
occultists, the Theosophists; and to such eminent modern philosophers
as Descartes, Liebniz, Kant, Whitehead, Husserl, etc.

Obviously, the theory of monads has been an illuminating, vital,
complex, and fecundating conception. The essential meaning of monad, including its early and later proliferations, is that of a divine

essence of God embodied in a simple indivisible unit which is psychic and spatial, corporeal and spiritual, yet having neither extension nor shape, possessing its own vital force (the cause of all its changes) that is totally self-contained and yet related to all other monads, and, besides, is imperishable. Furthermore, the universe is comprised of an infinite number of Monads, these being the source of cosmic harmony. Moreover, the monad is the microcosm which is an exact duplicate of the macrocosm (qq.v.); further, it is the mirror of God, and God is the highest in the hierarchy of monads. It is easy to trace all these notions in the range of disciplines listed above, for the doctrine of monads became the central, or a fundamental, or an important aspect of all of them. Finally, it is noteworthy that through the experiences and writings of the great mystics, who perceived in the doctrine of monads a means of individual union with God (Augustine, Boethius, Bonaventura, Eckhart, Cusanus, etc.), Luther was influenced to inaugurate the Protestant revolution which has changed the cultural and spiritual structure of Christianity. Monadic concepts have also importantly influenced Hindu religion, notably in the work of the Hindu philosopher and theologian Madhva (q.v.). (See: Alchemy, Cabalism, Logos, Lull, Mysticism, Neo-Platonism, Pantheism, Paracelsus, Plotinus, Theosophy)

Mondrian, Piet (1872–1944). Dutch painter, Theosophist, co-founder of the de Stijlart movement and creator of a pure geometric genre of painting that has profoundly influenced modern art, architecture, furniture design, advertising art, and typography. Although most art historians trace Mondrian's development to the impact of other painters and styles of painting (impressionism, *art nouveau*, fauvism, cubism, etc.) this is only one aspect of his unique development. To begin with, both his father and his uncle guided him in his early painting while the stimulating heritage of centuries of great Dutch painting excited his interest and developed his early naturalistic painting. He also studied at the Academy of Fine Arts in Amsterdam. But Mondrian was a mystic, and in 1909 he joined the Dutch Theosophical Society. Following years of painting and intense inner growth, Mondrian founded in 1915, with another painter, the famous de Stijl movement, dedicated to purity of style. This showed itself in Mondrian's work by 1920 when he reduced his painting to the abstract purity of line, plane, and pure color in which he utilized just vertical and horizontal lines and black, white, gray, plus the three primary colors—red, yellow, and blue. His revolutionary creation, as he explained in his essay *Le Neoplasticisme* (1920), was the evocation of his theosophical insights, for to him art was the direct expression of the universal within man: the microcosm that duplicates the macrocosm. (See: Microcosm-Macrocosm)

Monism. Philosophical systems which uphold the fundamental unity of the universe, as opposed to dualism.

Monition. A supernormal warning: the revelation of some past or present event, by other than the normal senses (Richet).

Monotheism. Belief in a single universal God, Creator of the cosmos. Particular to the Hebrew people. In ancient Egypt, Pharoah Ikhnaton believed in monotheism.

Moreau, Gustave (1826–1898). French painter whose erotic, religious, symbolist, and mysterious paintings won notable acclaim and many honors and prizes. When he was appointed to the prestigious professorship at the Ecole des Beaux-Arts he was a favorite with the students, teaching, among many others who later won renown, Roualt and Matisse. The secret, however, of his deeply-felt religious paintings and the strangely powerful, mysterious quality of his work was Moreau's life-long awareness of his mystic oneness with the universe.

Morin, Jean-Baptiste (1585–1656). Astrologer, astronomer, and adviser to both Cardinals Richelieu and Mazarin. He is believed to have been one of the last great astrologers. His important treatise *Astrologica Gallica* has not yet been completely translated, but has been judged as superior to many contemporary works on the subject.

Mormonism (Church of Jesus Christ of Latterday Saints). A religion of modern times, founded by Joseph Smith in 1830 after he had received a revelation concerning a portion of the lost ten Jewish tribes. This revelation explained that after fighting among themselves this fragment of Judaism had supposedly landed in America. The name was taken from an alleged fifth century A.D. scripture, telling of a prophet, Mormon, and his son Moroni, who hid the records which were engraved on gold plates. Smith formed a self-supporting community at Salt Lake City, Utah, with its own laws and regulations. Polygamy was instituted in an effort to stimulate their numbers at first, but has now been discontinued.

Morris Pratt Institute, of Wisconsin. An institution of learning established under the auspices of Spiritualism. Founded by Morris Pratt, an American Spiritualist who made a great fortune from the finding of valuable mineral deposits disclosed to him by his Red Indian guide. The building and land were deeded to seven well-known Spiritualists as trustees.

Morse, J.J. (1848–1919). Outstanding British trance medium. Morse had very little education, yet when in trance he was able to converse with eminent philosophers on abstruse subjects. He also possessed powers of physical mediumship, demonstrating the fire-immunity and elongation phenomena.

Morselli, Enrico (1852–1929). Professor of Psychiatry at Genoa, formerly at Turin. He was a complete skeptic of psychic phenomena until he sat with Eusapia Paladino, (q.v.) an experience which convinced him of its truth. Later, he propounded an important psycho- dynamic theory of materialization phenomena.

Mortuary Magic. In ancient Egypt the art of magic rituals for the dead insured the safety and happiness of the soul in the next world. This practice was widely used in the ancient world.

Moses ben Shemtou de Leon (*c.* 1250–1305). Spanish Cabalist whose works on this occult subject made him prominent among Hebrew scholars in Castile. He had a part in the creation of the great Cabalistic work, the *Zohar* (q.v.).

Moses, the Rev. Stainton (1839–1892). A very important name in Spiritualism. He was a minister of the Church of England, an author, and later the editor of *Light*. His psychic powers were amazing, powerful, and varied for he was able to produce: levitation, telekinesis, automatic writing, apports, psychic lights, musical sounds, scents, and many other manifestations. He never worked for money and his habitual sitters were few. The identity of his controls were kept secret for many years. They comprised a band of forty-nine spirits whose missionary effort was directed to the upliftment of the human race. From 1884 until his passing Moses was the president of the London Spiritualist Alliance in London, now changed to the College of Psychic Science. Under the pen-name of M.A. Oxon he wrote *Spirit Teachings,* often referred to as the "Bible" of Spiritualism.

Mother Bridget's Dream Book and Oracle of Fate. One of the all-time best-sellers. For fifty years—between 1800 and 1850—it was reissued annually in both England and the United States. Besides interpreting dreams, it also foretold events according to the days on which they occurred. This book is an excellent repository of yesterday's history of dream interpretation.

Motor Automatism (Spiritualism). Phenomena classified by F.W.H. Myers (q.v.) as "active" (similar to the "muscular automatism" of Maxwell), meaning movement of the medium's head, tongue or limbs by an inner motor impulse beyond the conscious will. He listed these as:
1. Strong impulse to action without reason.
2. Table tilting, ouija, planchette.
3. Supernormal musical and histrionic execution, contagious dancing.
4. Automatic drawing and painting.
5. Automatic writing.
6. Automatic speech.
7. Telekinetic movements. (See: Phenomena of Spiritualism)

Motricity, Exteriorized. See Exteriorization of Motricity.

Motzu. (c. 500–396 B. C.). Soldier, statesman, philosopher, and prophet, he is considered to have been the only creator of religion in ancient China.

Moving. In old dream interpretation, a dream of moving from your residence or place of business is a positive sign of future poverty.

Moyes, Miss Winifred. Her control, "Zodiac," was responsible for the teachings upon which the Greater World Christian Spiritualist League was founded. Zodiac claimed to have been a teacher in the time of Jesus. The Movement has a small network of churches over England. Their acceptance of Jesus as sole leader separates them from the larger proportion of Spiritualists.

Mrityu (Hinduism). An epithet of Yama (q.v.) which means "Death."

M.S.A. The Marylebone Spiritualist Association, now known as the Spiritualist Association of Great Britain.

Muhammad. The founder and the prophet of Islam (q.v.).

Mukti. Same as Moksa (q.v.)

Multiple Personality. See Personality.

Mummification. An unusual form of mediumship, by which a perishable object may be preserved by passes or contact with the medium's hands. Bacteria of various types have been destroyed by this method. Dr. L. Clarac and Dr. B. Llaguet of Bordeaux conducted a seven-year investigation with Mme X, and published a report in 1912 proving the existence of a fluid emanation which prevented decomposition of plants and animals. Similar phenomena were produced by Joanny Gaillard of Lyons in 1928. Heinrich Nusslein, a German medium, also had this power, and could preserve cut flowers for many days. Contemporary scientific experiments seem to indicate that many people possess this power and its manifestation is due to an unusual quantity and quality of both physical and psychic energy.

Mundane Aspects. In astrology these are signified by the planets' occupying cusps. The nature of the planets involved and their relationships to other planets are of critical importance. Further, mundane aspects can be calculated only on a chart erected for a birth moment.

Mundane Astrology. That aspect of astrology which is devoted to prognosticating the future of a country and national activities rather than those of individuals.

Mundus Intelligibibilis. The divine pattern from which all imperfect things on earth originate. Plato's *Ideas*, and St. Augustine's *Eternal Realities* which embody this notion influenced much occult development.

Muni (Hinduism). A title of Rishis, meaning holy, pious, a learned sage.

Murphy, Gardner (1895–   ). American psychologist and past president of the American Psychology Association. He belongs in the tradition of such eminent psychologists as William James and William McDougall who championed and furthered the development of psychic studies and research. Gardner Murphy's numerous honors and prestigious teaching posts (Menninger Foundation, Columbia University, George Washington University, Consultant to Ministry of Education, New Delhi, India, etc.) have never interfered with his determined effort to install psychic research in the world of science. See: *Challenge of Psychical Research*, 1961; *William James on Psychical Research*, 1960; *Encounter with Reality*, 1968.

Murray, Professor Gilbert (1886–1958). Regius Professor of Greek, Oxford University, President S.P.R. 1915-16. He was a psychical researcher who was famous for his work on thought transference, a faculty which he possessed to a marked degree. Murray was in agreement with William James on the concept of consciousness as a stream with a "bright center and dim edges" which they both considered a useful hypothesis for the working of telepathy and clairvoyance.

Muscular Automatism. Classification by Maxwell, similar to "Motor Automatism" of F.W.H. Myers (q.v.).
  1. Simple. Typtology, alphabetic systems.
  2. Graphic. Automatic writing, drawing, painting.
  3. Phonetic. Trance speaking.
  4. Mixed. Incarnations.

Music. There are many instances in history of strange music heard by people during religious revivals. We hear of it again at deathbeds (see Phantasms of the Living). With mediums it is rare without instruments, the exceptions being D. D. Home, Stainton Moses (qq.v.), and Mary Jobsen. Cases are known where instruments of various kinds have been played supernormally during seances.

Music of the Spheres. Pythagoras' purely speculative mathematical relationship between the frequencies of the diatonic scale intervals, and the orbital distances of the planets (then unknown).

Myers, Frederick William Henry (1843–1901). A pioneer of psychical research, he held the post of Inspector of Schools for thirty years at Cambridge. Philosopher, scholar, and poet, Myers was a fellow founder of S.P.R. in 1882, and was president in 1900. His main work was *Human Personality and its Survival of Bodily Death*, an exhaustive study of the human mind and its powers. He drew in detail a vast picture of the subliminal self, which he affirmed was the real ego, of which the ordinary consciousness was only a small part. The book covers almost all of the field of psychic phenomena, and relates it in an orderly system. The Reverend Stainton Moses (q.v.) was his friend, and he was also a guest of Charles Richet, Sir Oliver Lodge and Julien Ochorowitz (qq.v.), in the famous experiments with Eusapia Paladino (q.v.). After his death, proofs of his continued identity were communicated through Mrs. Piper (q.v.) by cross correspondence. Sir Oliver Lodge (q.v.) received independent evidence through Mrs. Gladys Leonard (q.v.) from Myers which asserted that he was communicating through Miss Geraldine Cummins the automatist.

Mylitta Temple. In ancient Babylonia, the custom that every woman once in her life must give herself to a stranger inside the temple. Believed to have been linked to the fertility goddesses Aphrodite and Ishtar (qq.v.). The awaited stranger was considered a god in disguise.

Myomancy. Divination by watching the actions of rats and mice.

Mystagogue. He who initiates or interprets for novices the lore of mysteries (such as the Eleusinian in ancient Greece), or who is a teacher or prophet of mystical doctrines.

Mysticism. An overwhelming feeling of being in direct contact with the Deity or Cosmos. Though it is most often linked to religion, some notable mystics like Baruch Spinoza, and Bernard Bosanquet (qq.v.) were mystics without a formal religion or institutional affiliation. The greatest mystics, contrary to popular notions, have generally been individuals of enormous practical capacity, such as Dante, St. Augustine, St. Francis, Groote, Joan of Arc, Fox, Swedenborg, and Schweitzer (qq.v.). Fundamentally, mystics believe that on sudden occasions man can transcend himself and become one with God or can do so through a sequence of stages; or, that God is immanent and can be discovered by an inward movement which returns one to the innermost core of one's own being. Some of the world's great religions —Judaism, Christianity, and Islam—maintain that God is both a transcendent manifestation and an indwelling spirit. Among Christian mystics the journey of the soul to the engulfing light of God is generally described in the symbolic language of love. In Hindu, Buddhist, or Taoist mysticism the feeling of union with God or Nature most frequently results in an inward ecstasy that expresses itself in a quietly benign and assured integration. However, there are Hindu and Buddhist sects which renounce the total bliss of Nirvana (q.v.) in order to help mankind in its struggle to salvation. In Judaism, the long history of mystics and the mystical tradition has culminated in the doctrines of the Cabala and the Hasidic sect (qq.v.). In Islam, mysticism in the Sufi sect (q.v.) stresses the immediate union of one's self and soul with God. Mysticism, then, is the source of all religion, for it is a direct, immediate awareness of God, or the Ultimate Reality, or Brahman, or Atman. The word is derived from the Mystery Religions of ancient Greece, (to initiate into religious rites) for the initiate who imparted the "secret" was called a *mystes*. It was Dionysius the Areopagite (q.v.) who introduced the word into the Western World, meaning the "unknowing knowing." In the occult and psychic it denotes an additional domain of esoteric knowledge and paranormal communication.

Myth. A metaphorical or symbolical truth that tells the legends of cosmology, history, and the origin of traditions, with divinities as the heroes. The great elements of the universe—the sun, the stars, the planets, the sky, and the soul's life after death are major sources of myth.

Na Chia (Taoism). The combination and union of the Ten Celestial stems with the Eight Elements. This results in the First Stem (the active or male cosmic force) and the Second Stem (the seat of the passive or female force) gathering themselves into the center and apex of the universe.

Naga (Hinduism, Buddhism). The legendary, semi-divine cobra snake with a human face, and the tail of a serpent, which was widely worshipped among the pre-Aryan aboriginal people of India. It also refers to a race of people believed descended from the Naga.

Nagual. Among Central American tribes the Nagual, which is generally an animal, the guardian spirit of the individual that becomes one's spirit at birth. Since the Nagual, half spirit, half body, and the individual possess the same soul, injury or death to the Nagual brings the same to the individual.

Nail Fetishism. A frequent practice in the Congo area of Africa as well as parts of South America, involving wooden fetishes. Devotees drive nails into these fetishes so that the fetish is assured they are praying to it.

Nakshatras (Hinduism). These 28 daughters of the moon by Daksha were worshipped as lunar deities.

Nal Jorpa (Lamaism). Psychic-mystic-medium among the Tibetans, who in a trance-like state becomes privy to events at a distance; through his dream-knowledge he knows the future.

Name. Throughout human history names and naming have been of tremendous importance in religion, mythology, magic, the occult, and psychic phenomena. At one time names were themselves objects, independent of the objects they identified, which to know gave one power over the person or object named. In primitive times, names were often secret, to prevent their use by enemies. In some religions, the god's names were concealed. To this day among the Jews Yahweh's real name can be pronounced but once a year by the Rabbi in the Synagogue or Temple and only in the place designated the Holy of Holies. Some modern psychics have been able to influence others, for good or evil, by concentrating on them and their names.

Names in Dreams. In old dream interpretation, to be insulted in a dream by malicious names foreshadowed the receiving of an honor.

Nana-dassana (Buddhism). Represents that vision which is derived from recognition.

"Nancy." Among the West Indian and Africans the stories about the mystical spider—"anansi." But among the American Creoles this became any myth, fairy tale, or legend.

Nandana (Buddhism, Hinduism). The grove of Indra.

Nangara. A medicine man among the aborigines of central Australia, the Arunta.

Naos. In ancient Egyptian religion this was a small wooden or stone shrine in which the spirit of a divinity was ever-present.

Napiwa. To the American Blackfoot Indians, Napiwa was a white god in human form.

Nara (Hinduism). "Man" as universal, that is, the original eternal man.

Narada (Hinduism). A number of hymns of the Rig-Veda are considered Narada's, who is one of the seven great Rishis (q.v.).

Naraka (Hinduism). The Hindu hell where an onslaught of numerous punishments ultimately cleanses the souls of those who have lived evil lives on earth. However, before the depraved ones descend to the nether region of Naraka, they must first endure the awful crossing of Vaitarini, the swift-running river that leads to the infernal world, a river that is filled with blood, excrement, and stinking masses of filth. Naraka itself is a world of eternal darkness: here the wicked are assailed by fire, serpents, venomous insects, frightful birds of prey, the noxious fumes of gases, burning oil and a host of other loathsome torments. But this relentless punishment eventually ends when the evil souls have expiated in some measure for their crimes; then they are released to make their painful ascent up the stairway of lives.

Narayana (Hinduism). He is the son of Nara (q.v.). He is also described as Brahma, the Creator, and as Vishnu.

Narjol (Lamaism). In Tibet, holy men and yogins who are considered persons possessing occult powers.

Natal Astrology. The art which is concerned with nativities; that is, the influence which planets and signs exert upon the life, history, and personality of the individual.

National Federation of Spiritual Healers. A federation of healers founded in England in 1954 by an amalgamation of county and regional healers associations. The purpose of the Federation is to serve the public good through the practice and teaching of healing and to speak for healers on a national level on matters relating to healing. It is a non-sectarian organization.

National Horoscope. A map which is used in astrology to read the future of a nation. While such maps are difficult to erect, since few nations have a moment of birth, there are clues (declarations, congresses, coronations, signing of proclamations) which astrologers use to chart national horoscopes.

National Laboratory of Psychical Research. Established by Harry Price in London 1925, to investigate every phase of psychic phenomena. Many works have been published of their findings.

National Spiritualist Association of Churches. Chief American Spiritualist organization which claims that Spiritualism, as represented by the N.S.A.C., is to teach and proclaim three aspects: the science, philosophy and religion of modern Spiritualism, expressed in the "Declaration of Principles" and in the adopted "Definitions" as well as in the objects of organization. "Science" because it investigates, analyzes and classifies facts and manifestations demonstrated from the spirit side of life. "Philosophy" because it studies the laws of nature both on the seen and unseen side of life and bases conclusions upon present observed facts. It accepts statements of observed facts of past ages and conclusions drawn from there when sustained by reason, and by results observed from facts of the present day. "Religion" because it strives to understand and to comply with physical and spiritual laws of Nature—which are the laws of God.

Nativity. In astrology, this is the birth moment; also referred to as the geniture, the birth map, or the horoscope.

Nats. (Hinduism, Buddhism). Those celestial spirits who are superior to human beings, but of a lower order than gods.

Naturalist Theory of Ethics. Philosophical term for the assumption that the "natural world" including our minds and emotions is the only order of reality, thus reducing ethics to psychology. Moral judgements, by this view, would be due to concealed fears or mental complexes.

Nature Spirits. Non-human spirits rarely mentioned by spirit communicators. A few psychic people claim to have seen them, and even photographs are shown as evidence of the "little folk." They are generally supposed to be helpfully disposed towards humanity. Primitive peoples and occultists believe in powerful "elemental" spirits, said to control natural forces.

Na Vilavilairevu. In the Fiji Islands, in the South Pacific, this term means "fire walking."

Nebo. In ancient Chaldea the god of wisdom and learning, whose votaries were widely famous for their skill in astrology.

Nebuchadnezzar, Temple of. Upon excavation, it was discovered to symbolize in an astrological chart, by way of a structure of seven stages, the then known six planets and the sun: Saturn, Jupiter, Mars, the Sun, Venus, Mercury, and the Moon.

Necromancy. One of the most widespread forms of magic which has persisted from earliest times, and that utilizes the conjuring up of the ghosts of the dead. Since these ghosts are considered to have godly omniscience, to obtain from them their knowledge imparts to the necromancer immense magical powers and prophetic capacities. Although necromancy has been used to mean almost any kind of magic (being termed "nicromancie" in earlier English—black divination, or Black Magic (q.v.)), its essential meaning and operation applies to the "dead"—that is, divination by means of the dead.

Nectaneous. Acclaimed magician and Egyptian Pharoah of the fourth century B.C. whose skills in divination and formulation of philtres were legendary. It was said of him that he was able to divine through magical figures the state of his armies on the field of battle.

Nefer. In ancient Egypt a necklace or pendant worn by both the living and the dead; it was decorated with beads of gold, porcelain, silver, lapis lazuli, or emerald bearing pictures of the gods. These pendants were thought to possess magical powers designed to protect the owner whether in life or in death.

Negative and Positive. These polar terms have had an enduring universality, for they have evolved and have been a basic concept in every one of the great and near-great human cultures. They are an instrumental element in every sphere of man's preoccupations: the occult, religion, art, philosophy, science, mysticism, and the paranormal. The existence of these concepts as a polar underpinning in all the forms of man's expression certainly gives to these disciplines at least one common bond and one unseverable relationship. And this relationship may explain, in part, the modern coalescence of what for many centuries were so many antagonistically disparate fields and systems of study. (See: Samadhi; Yin/Yang; Ormuzd/Ahriman; Tao; J. Boehme)

Negative ESP. Parapsychologists utilize this term to describe experimental situations where the number of correct responses drops below the average.

Negative Hallucination. This is an effect which occurs in hypnosis or in suggestion when the individual fails to perceive an object which in actual fact is present to the senses.

Nelson, Robert. Director of the Central Premonitions Registry. This agency, located in Connecticut, has set itself the ambitious task of verifying the reliability of the prophecies indicated in the dreams and visions that they receive from all over the United States.

Nemesis. This ancient Greek divinity was one of the most puzzling of the Greek goddesses, being identified with various qualities at different periods; that is, with Artemis, as a fertility goddess, but at other times in her role as a war-goddess. Nonetheless, in the main, she represents retribution, or indignation by the gods at human arrogance. Nemesis is the inescapable power before which all must bow.

Neophyte. A candidate for initiation.

Neo-Platonism. A philosophic doctrine which has exerted an enormous influence on European and Arabian philosophy, on Western religion, on Western literature, and on many occult doctrines. It was first formulated by Plotinus (q.v.) in Rome in the third century B.C., drawing essentially from Plato's theory of innate memory. To this were added influences from Hebrew mysticism and the Vedanta (q.v.).

Neo-Pythagoreanism. Philosophical-religious system developed in Alexandria, Egypt, in the first century B.C. Building upon the tenets of Pythagoras, it also incorporated elements of Platonism, Aristotelianism, Stoicism, plus mystical and theosophical influences derived from Eastern thought. Neo-Pythagoreanism became more popular than Neo-Platonism for many years, and continued for centuries to enrich the views of alchemists and mystics in Western thought, since it stressed numbers, miracles, transmigration of souls, and the oneness of all in God.

Nephehs (Cabalism). That which, being the lowest state of human existence, knows and dwells only in the physical world.

Nephelomancy. Divination by reading the portent of the clouds.

Nero (37 A.D.–68 A.D.). The Roman emperor whose ambivalent nature—inhuman monster and lover of the arts—caused him to murder his mother, his first wife, and his famous tutor, Seneca, plus a host of others. He considered himself the greatest of poets, horsemen, and masters of magic and the occult. He came by the last interest somewhat naturally, for his mother had widely publicized the story that Nero had had a miraculous childhood. Yet however much Nero

desired to obtain supremacy over the powers of gods and other familiar spirits, and however much he was instructed by the great magician and occultist Tyndates, King of Armenia, he failed in this ambition as in all else, for the hatred of his people forced him to commit
suicide at thirty-one.

Nerve Aura. Term coined by Dr J. Rhodes Buchanan, 1814–99,
discoverer of the psychometric faculty, to describe the emanation of
the human body which could be perceived by sensitives.

Neshamah (Cabalism). The achievement of the topmost arc of being
which enables the adept to perceive the divine world, and the soul's
union with the divine soul.

Netchilik Shamanism. The Shaman of the Netchilirimint Eskimos,
whose control of the supernatural spirit, the *tunraqs*, is dependent on
the success of this spirit. However, if the *tunraqs* fails to accomplish a
mission, it feels it has lost face and in revenge it turns remorselessly
on its master, the Shaman.

Netzah (Cabalism). The seventh of the Ten Sephiroth (q.v.) which
signifies the "lasting endurance" of God.

Neumann, Therese (b. 1898). A Bavarian peasant, whose stigmata
and visions aroused world-wide notice. In 1922 owing to a throat
abscess she abstained from solid food. Her stigmata were situated on
the left side, hands and legs, and bled profusely on Fridays. Linguists
have vouched her speech in Aramaic was authentic. She seems to
have experienced in her own body the whole drama of the crucifixion.

Neurypnology. Term first used by Braid for what is now called hypnotism.

Newbrough, Dr. John Ballou (1828–1891). New York medium for clairvoyance, automatic writing and painting. His main work was the astounding production of "Oahspe, the Kosmon Bible in the words of Jehovah and his angel ambassadors" (q.v.). This was the result of man-
ual automatism on a typewriter. It took fifty weeks, working half an
hour before sunrise every morning according to his own account.

New Motor. A visionary venture by J.M. Spear (1804–87), American
Spiritualist preacher. He built at Lynn, Mass., a motor intended to be
self-generative, at the grand sum in those days of 2,000 dollars. But as
with all perpetual motion machines, it was doomed aborning; and after it failed to work it was removed to Randolph, Mass., where it was
destroyed by superstitious villagers.

Newspaper Tests. Experiments devised by spirit communicators to
eliminate the possibility of telepathy. Their method was to give names
and dates to be published in certain columns of a newspaper yet to be

printed. This information was at once posted to S.P.R. Astonishing results were obtained in this way through the mediumship of Mrs. Osborne Leonard.

Newton, Sir Isaac (1642-1727). One of humanity's greatest scientists, whose formulation of the laws of gravitation and the laws of motion, and his work in mathematics (discoverer of calculus), in light, and in physics, set him entirely apart. He studied astronomy in order to better understand astrology, and is said to have studied alchemy and the philosophy of Jacob Boehme (q.v.).

N.F.S.H. The National Federation of Spiritual Healers (q.v.).

Nichiren (Zenshobo Rencho) (1222-1282) (Japanese Buddhism). Japanese religious saint and prophet, he founded the important Nichiren sect of Japanese Buddhism. Following years of ascetism and intense study, he announced in 1253 that the essence of Buddha's teaching was to be found in the Lotus Sutra (q.v.). Not understanding, but belief in the sutra leads to enlightenment, was Nichiren's doctrine, and he advocated *shodai* or constant repetition of the name of the sutra "Namu Myoho Rengekyo"—"Adoration to the Lotus Sutra of Perfect Truth."

Nicholas Von Flue (1417-1487). Swiss mystic and patriot, leading member of "The Friends of God," an influential Swiss mystical group. He combined his skills in the occult with practical affairs by helping to maintain Swiss unity through his "Compromise of Stans" in 1481.

Nichols, Miss Agnes. See Mrs. Guppy.

Nichusch (Cabalism). Stems from the belief that all events are interlocked and interact. Any entity, or any event, or any person may emerge as a prophetic sign, becoming at such a time a Nichusch.

Nicodemnus of the Holy Mountain (c. 1748-1809). Monk and mystic at Mt. Athos, whose compendium of selections from the Eastern Church Fathers he called *Philokalia*. It had a marked influence on Russian readers, and has continued to reward students of contemporary transcendental meditation (q.v.).

Nictalopes. Persons possessing the rare faculty of being able to see in the dark.

Night Houses. In astrology, the six houses below the horizon, in the darkness of the night. They constitute: the first, second, third, fourth, fifth and sixth houses.

Night Spell. The recitation of sacred words, psalms, and special prayers to safeguard the sleeper against the evil devices of Satan. In 1686, Guazzo's book *Compendium Maleficarum* listed formulae for Night Spells.

Nihongi. All Japanese mythology depends on two basic books, the *Nihongi*, written in 737 A.D., and the earlier book, the *Kojiki*, written in 712 A.D. These two volumes hold the prehistoric tales of ancient Japanese mythology.

Nimbus. That aura which some parapsychologists believe surrounds all living organisms. (See: Kirlian photography). This has become stylized into the form of a halo of divine light which is believed to be glowing around the head of Christ, the Virgin Mary, or the saints. However, this knowledge of the aura was understood by the ancient Hindus, the Egyptians, the Greeks, and Romans, for it is also seen in their symbolic representations. (See: Halo)

Nine. In ancient esoteric mystery, mystic numerology, folklore, and mythology, nine was considered the number of aspiration and wisdom and the "harmony of harmony" since three times three equals nine. It was considered "unbounded," containing in itself all numbers. For Pythagoras (q.v.) it was the emblem of matter. In ancient Greece, initiation into the Eleusinian Mysteries (q.v.) took nine days. Nine was the number of the Greek Muses. The Romans held nine in such reverence that they proclaimed a feast every nine years to honor it—the *Novennalia*. In Northern European folklore and mythology, the cat had nine tails—a symbol of practical wisdom; Merlin (q.v.) had nine bards; King Arthur battled with an enchanted pig nine days. In the Cabala (q.v.) there are nine degrees, all emanating from God.

Nine Mystic Names. The mystic list of names to conjure demons— Eheieh, Iod, Tetragammaton Elohim, El, Elohim Gibor, Eloah Va-Daath, El Adonai Tzabaoth, Elohim Tzabaoth, Shaddai.

Nio (Japanese religion). Guardian kings whose images are erected at temple gates to frighten off demons. One Nio symbolized Indra, the other Brahma (qq.v.).

Nirvana (Buddhism) The supreme attainment, the final goal of the Buddhist. For the achievement of Nirvana is the godly state which breaks the wheel of Karma (q.v.) and releases the individual from the confinements and limitations of existence. It destroys the possibility of metempsychosis (q.v.), the need to be born again, freeing one forever from the bonds of material being.

Nix or Nixie. In Germanic myth, evil water sprites who had the power to assume such diverse shapes as horses, humans, and half human-half fish. The females are the Nixies, of which the Lorelei and the Rhine Maidens are examples.

Niyama (Hinduism). Second stage of Yoga. Withdrawal from the world, purification of the mind and the attainment of contentment.

Nodes. In astrology, rays or lines of force which mainly come from the action of the moon, though planets also have such nodes. These are points where the moon crosses the ecliptic, from the south latitude to the north, or the north to the south. The North Node is called the Dragon's Head, the South Node is called the Dragon's Tail. The North Node is considered beneficial, the South Node malefic, to the signs and houses in which they appear.

Normal. The usual clairvoyant demonstration is an example of a medium functioning "in the normal," i.e., not in a state of trance. The messages so received could be described as "normal communications."

Norns. In Scandinavian and Germanic mythology the semi-divine goddesses who seal the fate of men. In time the three Norns came to represent all time—past, present and future.

Northern Signs. In astrology, the sequence of signs which runs from Aries to Virgo.

Nostradamus, Michael de (1503-1566). Famous French physician and astrologer. Counselor to Kings Henry II and Charles IX. In 1555 he published ten "centuries" of a hundred verses or "quatrains," all coded in a medley of languages, but crowded with amazing predictions, still in the process of fulfillment.

Notarikon (Cabalism). The mystic method of using the words of the Bible to interpret this Book. Notarikon utilizes the procedure of devising new words from combinations of the first or last letters of special words. Two other methods using different devices to gain similar enlightenment are Gematria and Temurah (qq.v.).

Nous. A term derived from the Greek philosophers, meaning reason. Also, the ability to know the eternal aspects of things, most particularly the essence of the divine godhead which, finally, is the truly divine and eternal. These latter concepts played a signal role in the evolution of all Western occult and mystical exploration.

Novalis (1772-1801). The pseudonym of George Friedrich Philipp Von Hardenberg, German mystic, poet, novelist, and mining engineer whose early death deprived Germany of one of its most prominent literary geniuses. His extraordinary sensitivity to every aspect of thought (he studied under the greatest philosophers), feeling, religion, and art is best expressed in his superb novel *Heinrich von Ofterdingen*, in his poetry in *Devotional Songs*; his mysticism is most clearly expressed in *Hymns and Thoughts on Religion*. He was one of the seminal figures in the revolutionary literary movement, romanticism, which swept all of Europe, influencing every phase of thought and all the arts.

N.S.A.C. National Spiritualist Association of Churches (q.v.).

N'toro. Among the Ashanti, an African people who are now living in Ghana, the N'toro is one's spirit, which is inherited from the male line of one's family.

Numbers. Throughout human history numbers have signified magical, mystical, and supra-mundane powers. Pythagoras (q.v.) considered numbers the secret of the universe. Egyptian, Babylonian, Chinese, Hindu, Hebrew, Greek, and Mayan cultures built their societies, their religions and their occult practices in marked measure on numbers. Most peoples considered odd numbers masculine, even numbers feminine. In the Chinese *I Ching* (q.v.) there are eight Trigrams, and four forms. For the Greeks, three, the essence of a triangle; four, the essence of a square; five, the essence of a pentagon represented mystic universal, and cosmological qualities. The Golden Number in Christian mysticism is 19—the number of the year of the Lunar Cycle. The number 666, in *Revelation* 13.18, is "the number of the beast," the antichrist, the symbol of evil. For the Cabalists one, two, and nine have unique properties. Seven has always been the magic number par excellence, and among the ancient Celts five and seven, giving twelve, incorporated the essence of practical, spiritual, and mystical wisdom. Many moderns believe thirteen unlucky; astrologers do not. (See: Nine; Numbers in Astrology)

Numbers in Astrology. First, there are the 12 houses. The aspects are counted by numbers or degrees; likewise, ages and epochs. Trines are designated either 5 or 9; squares—4, 7, or 10; sextiles—3 or 11.

Number 13. Astrologers call this the earth's number, since it is the center of the 12 houses. Contrary to popular belief, it is not unlucky, representing, instead, virile determination and strenuous work, and success is often designated as one who is obviously a lucky thirteen.

Numinous. Referring to the feeling of the mysterious, awe-inspiring, the holy and sacred, which is beyond all reason. Man being born with this perception is enabled by it to become aware of the Divine. The concept was developed by the German theologian and philosopher Rudolph Otto in the 1920's, and is explained in his famous book *The Idea of the Holy*, translated in 1958.

Nzambi. Among the Congo people, one of the sky gods.

"Oahspe." Kosmon Bible, automatically typed by J. B. Newbrough (q.v.).

Oak. A tree of magic which has been widely associated with spiritual powers. It has been associated with lightning, death, fire, and has been worshipped as representing a host of gods. (See: Mistletoe)

Oak Apples. Once used as a divinatory test to determine whether a child was bewitched.

Oath. A statement which implicates the maker in dire evil if he is lying, for an oath is often a sacred promise or relation of absolute truth. Since for many people words are magically potent, to utter the words of an oath bound one to a supernatural or spiritual judgment.

Obeah. In the West Indies the Obeah Man or Woman, being master of sorcery and magic ritual, is able to control that most dreaded of evil gods—Obi. So widespread is the worship and fear of Obi among the West Indians, that the Obeah Man or Woman is constantly consulted to use their wide repertory of skills to cast spells, find missing objects, exorcise evil spirits, prevent theft, inflict harm on enemies, and influence court cases.

Obelisk. In ancient Egypt, a long tapering pillar of stone, as high as a 100 feet and more, often square, always made in pairs, and frequently gracing either side of a temple's main entrance. At the top they usually bore representations of offerings to the gods, while the main body boasted a pharoah's achievements. Obelisks symbolized many facets of Egyptian religion, and have been called a ray of light, a god's finger, sun god memorials and fertility symbols in their phallic aspect.

Objective Phenomena. That phenomena which has external reality, and which may be perceived by others present in the same way (as distinguished from subjective phenomena).

Obsession. That state of being in which the mind, emotions and spirit are besieged by the Devil or another malevolent demon, and which compels one to act in ways inconsistent with one's usual behavior. One may also have as an obsession a supernatural entity, such as a ghost; which, can compel one, sometimes, to bizarre behavior. Spiritualists believe it is an invasion of the living by a discarnate spirit or spirits, tending to complete possession for the purpose of selfish gratification. Trance mediums utilize this situation to effect a cooperative relationship, while the medium's normal self is only in temporary abeyance during the period of control. Some mediums, specializing in this work, have been able to help possessed individuals. Jesus had the power of "casting out" evil spirits—devils or demons. In the sense that the "Dybbuk," (q.v.) among the Jews, represented an "evil" soul that took possession of another human being (first mentioned by the Cabalists in 1571; and also in a legend about the great Cabalist Luria) (qq.v.), this too represented obsession.

Occidental. In astrology, this represents the Western side of the figure. The Oriental houses of the horoscope occupy the Eastern side of the map. A planet is Oriental of the sun if it rises or sets before the sun; Occidental if it does the reverse. Planets are stronger if Oriental of the sun, Occidental of the moon.

Occult Hierarchy. See White Brotherhood.

Occultation. Since in astrology "occult" means "hidden," occultation refers to the situation when a planet is hidden as the Moon crosses its face, or when one planet passes and hides another.

Occultism. That which is covered or hidden. In many languages the word "Hell," since it refers to the place of the dead, also means the occult or that which is hidden. The occult in its widest sense applies to the whole universe of the supernatural, and man's ability through trained or gifted individuals to utilize a large number of arts to divine this universe and use it to obtain certain ends—basically, White Magic or Black Magic (qq.v.). The vast range of divinatory practices, of alchemy, magic, necromancy, astrology, sorcery, palmistry, witchcraft, esoteric and mystic cults and practices, are all aspects of occultism. No culture has ever existed which has not been influenced and molded by its occult knowledge. Occultists generally maintain that essential wisdom was known to a greater extent among the ancient civilizations of the East than it is today, and many of them study old writings in the attempt to find hidden indications of this knowledge.

Ochorowitz, Dr. Julien (1850–1918). Eminent psychical researcher, lecturer in psychology at the University of Lemberg, and Co-director of the Institut General Psychologique of Paris from 1907. Of the genuineness of psychic phenomena he was convinced; he attributed it to the action of a fluidic double working independently of the body. It was he who discovered Mlle. Tomczyk, a physical medium who produced phenomena in daylight. For his photographs of this phenomena he gained an award of 1,000 francs from the Comite d'Etude de Photographie Transcendental. One notable example of his work was the photograph of an etheric hand imprinted on a rolled film enclosed in a bottle.

Others included pictures of objects suspended in air, as if attached to the medium's fingers by invisible threads.

Oculus. In ancient times, since the bow of a vessel was the sanctuary of a patron deity, the oculus (a round hole in the bow) was an "eye" which supposedly enabled the vessel to find its path through the sea. Interestingly, this notion of the eye (now used as religious symbolism) is to be found in many European churches where the oculus, a round window, is located at the top of the west side of these churches.

Od.—Odic Force. An all-penetrating force which was reputedly discovered by Baron Reichenbach (q.v.). According to his findings the mouth, hands, forehead and occiput emitted the strongest emanations. They diminished with hunger and at sunset, and increased after a meal. He claimed that this peculiar force also exists in the rays of the sun and moon, and can be conducted to great distances by all solid or liquid substances, bodies being charged and discharged by contact or proximity. (See: Emanations)

Od (Lamaism). Meaning light, radiance which is the result of increasing esoteric wisdom.

Odilia (d. c. 720). The mystic whose shrine in Arlesheim, Switzerland, is a holy place for those suffering eye maladies or blindness. Foundress of the nunnery at Hohenberg, she was born blind, and after becoming miraculously healed devoted her life to God.

Odin. The chief Norse deity, who was called Woden by the Germans and English, and deemed the all-wise ruler of Asgard and Valhalla, and patron of poetry. Odin had but one eye, having given the other to obtain his wisdom.

Ogdoad. In ancient Egyptian religion, a sequence or cycle of eight gods and goddesses.

Oils, Seven Holy. In ancient Egyptian funerary rites, these were the seven magical oils given to the mummy to protect it on its voyage into the lower world. The oils bore the names: *nam, beknu, sefth, seth-heh, ha-ash, tuaut,* and *tet-ent-theb-enu.*

Oken, Lorenz (1779–1855). In his own time this German physician, philosopher, and mystic was considered one of the most brilliant thinkers by many Americans, particularly by the New England transcendentalists. To Oken, God desires to exhibit himself in nature; and when God comes to man he meets himself, for man is a god created by God. He was much influenced by Pythagorean mysticism; he also declared himself a pantheist (q.v.).

Olcott, Col. Henry Steel with Mme. Blavatsky. Joint founders of the Theosophical Society. On behalf of an American newspaper, Olcott made several investigations of physical mediumship, notably the Eddy brothers, Holmes, and Mrs. Elizabeth Compton, which established him as a psychic researcher. He met Mme. Blavatsky at Chittenden during his investigations. Olcott showed amazing energy in lecturing and organizing; finally, he established a headquarters for Theosophy at Adyar in India.

Old Hat. A popular method in former times of raising the Devil, in which a hat was placed in a circle and the Lord's Prayer was intoned backwards.

Old Soul. Term for a soul who has incarnated many times on this earth, and has presumably gained much wisdom in the process. (See: Reincarnation)

Om, Aum (Hinduism). The mystic, holy word which being symbolic of the three major Vedas (Aum—the union of Vishnu, Siva, and Brahma) precedes all prayers. Also, when meditated upon "Om" has the effect of creating mystic power.

Om Mani Padme Hum (Lamaism). Well-known mantra of Lamaism, a prayer said to be particularly efficacious by its repetition.

Omen. A magical, supernatural, or divinely inspired clue to the future. Omens may also result from divination (q.v.), or they may occur spontaneously at any time or place.

Omete cutli. Among the Aztecs one of their supreme deities.

Ometeotl. The supreme God of the Aztecs, in whom all the powers of their pantheon of gods was reflected, Ometeotl combined within himself both male and female, good and evil, light and darkness, the positive and the negative; and all of these qualities were forever engaged in an eternal struggle, since change dominated the world, where peace and stability were impossible.

Omnipotent. The Almighty. All-powerful, as applied to Deity.

Omniscient. Knowing all, as applied to Deity.

Omniverse. In astrology, the whole of space, as distinguished from the universe which includes our Solar System and the whole Milky Way Galaxy, of which our Solar System is but a part.

One. Mystics have always transcended existence by experiencing the "One" of the universe, although it has been explained by many different means. In Hinduism and Buddhism the "One" is beneath all, the real ultimate reality, the World-Soul. For the Greeks, the "One" was the Nous. In Christianity, the "One" was God. In the philosophy of mysticism, beginning with Plato where the "One" was the Supreme Idea, it became with Plotinus and later mystics the Absolute First Principle.

Onion. To the ancient Egyptians a symbol of the universe; also, hung in rooms to ward off illness.

Ontology (Aristotle). Science dealing with the fundamental essence of things. Metaphysics.

Onychomancy. Divination by studying the reflection of the sun on a boy's fingernails and prophecying the future from the shape of the figures thus formed.

Open Circle. See Circle, Open.

Ophanim (Cabalism). The angels of the spheres.

Opposition. Astronomically, when one celestial body is exactly on the opposite side of the ecliptic circle to another. Astrologically, when two planets are in opposition, or 180° apart; this represents either a favorable or an unfavorable aspect (q.v.): since it is the nature of the planets which is the determining factor. The two principles would be in a state of high tension.

Orb of Influence. In astrology, this refers to that area of continuing influence which extends beyond an aspected (q.v.) planet of some 10 degrees, or 5 degrees on either side. In contrast to the planets the Sun and Moon have twice this number of degrees when aspected or aspecting.

Orchis Root. The root of the Satyrios Orchis was formerly considered a certain charm against bewitchment.

Ordeal. In many past cultures and into the late Middle Ages, a trial in which the accused was forced to prove his innocence by enduring a dangerous experience, such as holding hot coals. If he was honest, the gods or the supernatural spirits would protect him against harm.

Orenda. Among the American Indian Iroquois this represented a supernatural power which objects, animals, humans or even the voice of a magician could possess, the possession of which gave to the owner remarkable powers, both of good and evil. This notion seems to have been held quite widely, and under different names to have been believed by: the Melanesian Islanders (*Mana*); the Polynesians (*Mana*); the American Algonquin Indians (*Manitou*); the Sioux Indians (*Wakan*). In Madagascar it is called (*Hasina*); in Morrocco (*Baraka*); and among the Australian Kabi (*Manngur*).

Origen (c. 185–c. 254). One of the greatest of Christian teachers, he was an eminent scholar, philosopher and mystic. He was born in Egypt, where he became famous for his Christian and Greek erudition, his preaching, and his saintly purity—having castrated himself in his zeal for godly devotion. His school at Caesavea was a renowned center. Reputed author of some 800 works, his *Hexapla*, a juxtaposition of the versions of the Bible (Hebrew and Greek) in six volumes was enormously influential in Christian scholarship. His philosophy was Neo-Platonic, and incorporated Orphism (q.v.), Gnosticism (q.v.), and Stoicism. It was these so-called pagan elements which led to his condemnation as a heretic by many influential churchmen.

Ornstein, Robert E. One of the important new figures in contemporary psychology. He is focusing his research interests on the "intuitive" component of man's consciousness. Believing that the intellectual component has for too long dominated psychology's interests, Ornstein is concentrating on that half of consciousness, the right side of the brain, which explores meditation, mysticism, non-ordinary reality, and the influence of "the body" on "the mind." For investigators like Ornstein, Zen meditation, Sufism, mysticism, bimodal consciousness, psychosynthesis, physiological feedback, the paranormal, and psi processes are aspects of consciousness that can yield rewarding new insights into man's mental and psychic capacities. Robert Ornstein is a psychiatrist at the University of California Medical Center, a research psychologist at the Langley Porter Neuropsychiatric Institute, a former consultant to the magazine *Psychology Today*, one of the co-founders of the new magazine *Human Nature*, and the author of: *On the Experience of Time*, *On the Psychology of Meditation* (with Claudio Naranjo), *The Psychology of Consciousness*, *and The Mind Field*.

Orphic Literature. Orphism (q.v.) stimulated a number of Greek poets, but the most important of all works attributed to Orpheus or Orphic writers was the work *Rhapsodic Theogony*. This work has been quoted numerous times by many Neo-Platonic writers and has been important in the history of mysticism, alchemy, and the occult. (See: Orphism)

Orphism. The Greek philosophic religious cult which was enormously important in Greek culture, in later Western mysticism and in occultism. Beginning in the 6th century B.C. and attributed to the mythical Orpheus, it celebrated the concepts of reincarnation; a Greek version of Karma (q.v.); a history of the universe founded by Chronos who formed an egg and created the first king of the gods— whom Zeus supplanted and who then fathered Dionysus—the divine child. Orphism held that the body was a prison of the soul; animals were not to be killed or eaten; the good were rewarded, and the evil punished in the Nether World; and, finally, self-denial and seriousness in religious matters. Additionally, Apollo, who was considered a kindred god, demanded purification and righteousness. Plato and Pindar understood the great thoughts of Orphism, and alchemy and mysticism drew deeply from its wisdom.

Orthos. A term descriptive of the spirit world, coined by the spirit of Betty Buck in a complete spirit philosophy which was communicated in trance.

Osiris. The chief god of the ancient Egyptians, who symbolized the awesome, for he represented the sun, fire, was ruler of day and night, and arbiter of the soul's destiny in the worlds of the living and the dead.

Ossowiecki, Stephan. An outstanding Polish medium who could read sealed envelopes, see auras, and move objects without contact. At the International Psychic Congress, Warsaw 1923, he read successfully the contents of a note sent by the S.P.R. (q.v.), wrapped in several colored folds of paper and sealed by Eric John Dingwall in an envelope. For this he was acclaimed by the Congress.

Osty, Eugen. French physician, Director of Institut Metapsychique Internationale, successor to Gustave Geley (q.v.). He was the first to employ infra-red and ultra-violet techniques in the study of Rudi Schneider's (q.v.) mediumship. He wrote several very important books on psychical research.

Ouija Board (French "oui" and German "ja"). A small wooden board with a pointer, placed under the medium's hand, and resting on a polished surface which shows letters of the alphabet. Under control, messages are spelt out by the hand's movements. A similar appliance is known to have been used in Pythagoras' (q.v.) time.

Oupnekhat, The. A Persian text on mysticism which reveals the method to become one with the Brahma-Atma—the divine spirit.

Ouroborus. The mystical-magical figure of a snake biting its own tail, an occult symbol of the Hermetic Mysteries—meaning everything changes but nothing dies. A very popular symbol in alchemical and mystical writings.

Ouspensky, P. D. (1878–1947). Russian mathematical student who became Gurdjieff's (q.v.) most important and most influential disciple and interpreter. However, Ouspensky was also an original thinker, and owing to his mathematical and scientific training he developed an extraordinarily profound viewpoint of his own. Although much of his work is often difficult to comprehend, his fourth dimensional philosophy distils the essential aspects of Western rationalism and joins them to Eastern mysticism. The richness of his insights continues to attract an ever-increasing audience. (See: *Fourth Way, Tertium Organum, New Model of the Universe,* and *The Psychology of Man's Possible Evolution.*)

Overself. The Great Self. Atman. The ancient Hindu conceived of the Great Self as differentiated into individual lesser selves in a state of Maya or illusion. Hence the search for the Higher Self which knows the reality of the eternal state of being, by means of ascetic practices, borrowed and elaborated in recent times by some Western philosophers and writers.

Overshadowing (Spiritualism). The controlling of a medium by a discarnate spirit. More often used when the control amounts to only a slight impression. Also used to describe rudimentary transfiguration.

Oversoul. A term very loosely applied to concepts of Brahma, the Absolute, group-soul, higher self, etc. Not definitive.

Owen, Robert (1771–1858). Famous English Socialist and humanitarian. He became a Spiritualist when he was eighty-three after a sitting with the American medium Mrs. Hayden.

P. For the Cabalists the letter P symbolized the Messiah, the "Redeemer," whose name was Podeh.

Pacifist. Non-aggressive. One who practices non-violence.

Paigoels, The In India and in Hindustan these are devils. The Hindustans believe the Paigoels were either created or driven from heaven. Being denizens of the earth, they tempt men to sin or enter their bodies and possess them. Hindus assert that the souls of wicked men become Paigoels.

Painting, Psychic. See: Automatic Painting, Clairvoyant Painting. Direct Painting.

Pairikas (Zoroastrianism). Evil female beings whose entrancing beauty seduces men and drives them to commit degrading deeds. Eventually, Pairikas evolved into beautiful fairies.

Palengenesis. This ancient Greek term means "becoming again" as the seed of the oak tree recreates its parental oak. This identic life in cyclical recurring phases is the essential essence of this term, being the continuous transmission of the same life-stream.

Palladino, Eusapia (1854–1918). Famous Italian physical medium discovered by Signor Damiani through the agency of a control "John King" (q.v.), who claimed Eusapia as his reincarnated daughter, and gave precise directions by which Damiani found her. Eusapia's phenomena were powerful and diverse: heavy objects moved at her glance and gesture, or floated in the air according to her wish. Facial imprints were made in clay; her body was levitated. Telekinetic movements were accomplished by extra "limbs" extruded from her body while she was held down. So many famous scientists were convinced of her phenomena, that there is no doubt of her powers. Yet she attempted to cheat in a childish fashion when given the chance. As a person she was illiterate, ignorant, but shrewd. Yet all tests proved her a great medium.

Palladium, Order of. Masonic-diabolic order founded in Paris in 1737. Also known as the Sovereign-Council of Wisdom. Women adepts bore the appelation Penelope.

Palmistry, or Chiromancy. Divination by means of the lines and configurations of the hands.

Pancha (Hinduism). Meaning "five," a number that represents destiny.

Panentheism. Awareness of the nature of God that sees all things within God, but understands God as much more than the total of actual things. This view of God asserts both His immanence and His transcendence.

Pantheism. The feeling that God is all and all is God. That God is immanent in all things is one of the oldest intuitions of man. But pantheism has never been a body of doctrine. It has always tended to color the thoughts and feelings of poets, philosophers, mystics, and highly spiritual persons. We find it in Brahmanism—the oldest existing religion, in the Vedas, as far back as 1000 B.C.; in Egyptian religion where Ra, Isis, and Osiris were identified with all that exists. The great Greek philosopher Parmenides is considered by many philosophy scholars to have been a pantheist, as were Plotinus, Erigen, and Spinoza. Notable pantheistic poets were Goethe, Coleridge, Wordsworth, and Emerson. It is also part of the world-view of many modern poets.

ParaBrahm (Hinduism). The source of all creation, being God without form—that which is beyond Brahman. It also relates to the two indestructible laws responsible for all creation: ParaBrahm is the illimitable which interacts with Mulaprokriti (the undifferentiated primordial substance) to form the Universal Life. One of the four creation principles of Cabalism (q.v.).

Paracelsus (Philippus Aureolus Theophrastus Bombastus von Hohenheim (1493–1541). This dazzling name, crowned by its owner with Paracelsus, belonged to one commonly known as a Swiss physician and alchemist; but he was, in reality, one of the brilliant and boldest giants of the Renaissance. He made lasting contributions in chemistry, pharmacology, psychotherapy, and medicine; he had a profound insight into the mystic, spiritual, and occult relationships of man; and his scientific researches anticipated modern views in many ways. But he was in key respects far ahead of most scientists today, especially doctors.

Having hungrily studied at all the best medical schools of Europe and having enriched this vast theoretical knowledge with an enormous practical experience, his extraordinary competence and absolute honesty made him bitterly aware of how much fraud was dispensed under the name of medicine. He constantly exposed all charlatans, paying for it with hatred and slander. In his practice he used astrology, alchemy, mysticism, magic, the Cabala, religion, philosophy, psychotherapy, and his own advanced pharmacology. For Paracelsus was that rarest of human beings—the master-physician—who treated the total man—and then even more: the man who also lived within a mysterious universe.

Paraclete. A name referring to the Holy Ghost, or Holy Spirit who is a consoler.

Paraesthesia. Abnormal prickling or tingling sensations. Mediums are often able to identify a particular control by such physical sensations, which appear to be signals of the entity's presence.

Paraffin Moulds. See Moulds.

Parakinesis. The movement of objects where the observed contact is insufficient to explain the motion observed.

Paramechanics. One of the newest of the scientific disciplines in parapsychology. It is a study of paranormal psychical phenomena.

Paramesthin (Hinduism). One who stands in the highest place—a title of gods and great men.

Paramita (Buddhism). The six stages by which to attain spiritual perfection and by which the Bodhisattva attains Buddhahood.

Paramnesia. Confusion of the memory; especially a false sensation of a previous experience when, in fact, it is being experienced for the first time.

Paranoia. Chronic mental derangement, characterized by hallucinations.

Paranormal. Supernormal. Those psychic or mental phenomena formerly believed by science to be outside the range of the scientific knowledge of human behavior or the known action of physical energies.

Parapsychology. The branch of psychology which investigates psychic phenomena that were formerly considered by science to be outside the range of physical energies. Parapsychology studies the following important types of psychic capabilities: telepathy, clairvoyance, precognition, and psychokinesis (qq.v.). After many years of research, parapsychologists have developed the necessary devices of experimental control that make it possible for them to repeat their experimental results. A further increase in the scientific rigor of the discipline has been the creation of a systematic scientific-philosophic body of interpretative concepts; this growth in knowledge and skills now enables parapsychologists to achieve greater predictability and richer insights into the psychic phenomena they study. (See: Freud, James, Jung, McDougall, Rhine)

Parapsychology in U. S. Colleges. The importance of this branch of psychology, which interested many of the early great psychologists like James, Freud, and Jung (qq.v.), has enormously increased. Where there were no such courses in the early 1920's there are now more than 100.

Paraskeva, Saint. Famous in pre-communist Russia for his powers as an exorcist. This saint, on whose feast days thousands of pilgrims came to St. Petersburg, congregating at the Church of St. Paraskeva to witness devils being cast out and epileptics cured, was a powerful figure in maintaining the peoples' belief in demonological obsession.

Parinirvana (Buddhism). The bodily death which culminates in complete Nirvana (q.v.).

Pari-Vrag. Also known as Pari-Vrajaka, it signifies a Brahman in the fourth and final stage of his spiritual life; a chela (q.v.), who having completed his first initiation, has now entered on the Path

Paroptic Sense. A faculty of seeing with the etheric body, without use of the eyes.

Parousia. In Christianity, a term referring to the second coming of Christ.

Parsis. One of Persian descent who follows the religion of Zoroaster in India.

Pasqually, Martinez de (1715?-1779). Theosophist, Cabalist, and mystic whose national and racial antecedents are uncertain though he is by most believed to have been French and of Portugese-Jewish descent. What is certain, however, is his Cabalistic knowledge and his ability to inspire followers who called themselves *Cohens,* his influence on many French Masonic lodges, his Theosophic, Cabalistic, and mystical knowledge, and his eminent disciple Louis Claude de St. Martin (q.v.).

Passing (Spiritualism). Synonymous with "dying" in Spiritualist terminology. For Spiritualists death is not cessation but a passing from one state of existence to another; accordingly, Spiritualists dissociate themselves from the traditional gloomy trappings of funeral lamentations, which are said to distress the departed friend, and observe a simple service for such occasions.

Patanjali Yoga System (Hinduism). An adjunct of one of the most ancient of India's philosophical systems. The Yoga, which was an outgrowth of this philosophy, was founded by Patanjali, and is based on the two active principles Prakriti and Purusha (qq.v.).

Path, The. Theosophical teaching which refers both to the probationary learning and this learning which lifts one onto the Path. The Path means the spiritual purity and wisdom which enables one to reach the highest: service to God and service to his fellow human beings.

"Patience Worth." Woman who apparently lived in seventeenth century England and claimed that she was later killed by Indians in America. In 1913 she began lengthy communications via the ouija board with Mrs. John Curran of St. Louis. Through her control, Patience Worth, Mrs. Curran wrote in Anglo-Saxon English (which was considered authentic by some authorities) three notable novels, a flood of poetry, and other literary works which critics adjudged decidedly superior. Many psychic investigators regard this a classic case of automatic writing.

Pearls. The occult, medicinal qualities of pearls have been heralded since ancient times. The oneirocritics, interpreters of dreams, used pearls to implement their interpretations. Pearls were believed to portend a flood of tears, and it is recorded that the Queen of Henry IX of France dreamed of pearls a few days before his assassination. Paracelsus (q.v.) lauded the medicinal qualities of this gem; Dr. Schroder, the "chymist," wrote in 1669 of their marvelous medicinal characteristics. Pearls were thought to strengthen the balsam of life, resist poison, pestilence, to cure the Quartan Ague, putrid ulcers, pestilential fevers, fluxes of the blood. They were so used throughout China, Egypt, Greece, Rome, and Europe.

Penates. In ancient Roman religion the household divinities; their worship was centered in the hearth where a permanent fire honored them. They were closely linked to vesta and the Lares (qq.v.). Castor and Pollux were the chief Penates.

Pendulum. An instrument used by dowsers and radiesthetists, consisting of a bob suspended by a short cord held in the fingers. According to the amplitude and direction of its gyrations, various deductions are made suitable to the matter in hand. The results are possibly due to psychic powers of the operator, the pendulum acting merely as a focus of attention.

Pentacle. A magic symbol used in the occult and Black Magic (q.v.), which is a five-pointed figure that serves as a talisman. Originally it was a five-pointed star.

Pentagram. The five-pointed star, which is formed from the diagonals of a regular pentagon and deleting the sides. In the occult this five-pointed star represents the highest power of spirituality on earth.

Pentecost. The "miracles" recorded of Pentecost, have their modern counterparts: "tongues of fire"—psychic lights, "speaking in tongues"—xenoglossis, "sound of the wind"—psychic breezes and draughts.

Percipient. The receiver in telepathic communications.

Percussion. A common feature of the physical seance, usually known as raps, for which a coded communication is possible. It is believed that the noise is produced by flexible ectoplasmic rods striking various objects in the room.

Peregrine. In astrology, this means foreign and alien, and thus describes a planet in a sign where it has no essential dignity. In horary astrology it is generally weighed as detrimentral.

Perfectio. For the Medieval alchemists this was 6th step on the meditative journey. In the doctrine of Boehme (q.v.) it is the stage of "Tone, Speech, and Song" the aural world.

Perfumes, Psychic. See Smells.

Periapt. A charm worn as a protection against evil.

Personality. The sum total of that which constitutes an individual. The characteristics which distinguish one person from another, incorporated in a stream of consciousness. The establishment of the continuance of this stream of consciousness after death is considered a proof of survival of personality. Secondary personalities intrude when a complete loss of consciousness occurs; cases of this are well known to psychiatrists. Multiple personalities of one person have been frequently documented . In mediumship, the control is a different person, a separate entity; and the evidence of this is in the manner of cooperation between medium and spirit, as well as in the higher level of intelligence manifested. Eileen Garrett (q.v.) was especially interested in this aspect of the medium's powers.

Personation. See Impersonation.

Peter of Apono. Italian philosopher, mathematician, astrologer, and physician born in 1250, whose practice in Paris brought him wealth. But his skills in the occult arts were equally famous, and his talent for acquiring wealth so notable that he created enemies who accused him of sorcery and of being in league with the Devil, which led to his being condemned to death by the Inquisition.

Petro. In the Voodoo cult possessor of supernatural powers.

Phallic Cults in Japan. In the ancient Shinto religion, Inari, the Rice god-goddess (symbolized in both sexes), belongs to one of the mountain cults—mountains being a phallic representation. The gods of the roads are also connected with phallic worship. Izanagi was the god who used a staff to save himself from enemies, for sticks are the *shintai* (a form of body) of phallicism since a shintai can be possessed by an invisible deity in order to approach his devotees.

Phallic Food. Food has always been associated with the potency of the sexual organs, notably fish, cake, and certain plants. Moreover, because of their supernatural-fertility relationships, food has been eaten for religious, ritual, and ceremonial purposes.

Phallism. Religious, magical, and occult veneration of the male sex organs was one of the most widely observed practices from the most ancient times, since they served as a symbol of the fertility and the generative principle in nature. While many early religious cults contained phallic worship, it was also an important aspect of Hindu, Japanese and Greek religions. (See: Lingam, Dionysius)

Phantasm. A fanciful image possessing no reality. The substance of hallucination.

Phantasmata. Occult term for "thought forms" capable of communication.

Phantom. An apparition or ghostly figure.

Phases. In astrology, this term chiefly applies to the Moon, but also to Mercury and Venus. The phases of the Moon are crescent, half-moon, gibbous, and full moon. Some astrologers have asserted that as the Moon grows to fullness things swell with moisture. Farmers in the past responded to this astrological concept in their planting.

Phenomena (I). Astrologers apply this term to those supplementary data in the ephemeris (q.v.) showing the precise times of eclipses; of the passing of the nodes (q.v.) and other points in the orbit; of conjunctions; and such similar occurrences.

Phenomena (II). Things perceived by observation or experiment.

Phenomena of Spiritualism. There have been several attempts to classify these: the categories most generally used today are three: "Mental," "Physical," and "Healing." By mental phenomena is meant those phenomena where the spirit operators use the medium's mind as their instrument of communication. In physical phenomena, the operators use ectoplasm—physical material of the medium to form a communicating instrument. Healing may partake of either or both, varying greatly with individual cases. Mental phenomena again may be divided into two classes: (a) where the medium works in the "normal" by sensory automatism, i.e. clairvoyance, clairaudience, clairsentience, psychometry (qq.v.), and (b) where the medium works in trance by muscular automatism, i.e. automatic speaking, writing, painting, oui-ja, planchette (qq.v.). Physical phenomena are: materialization, trans-figuration, levitation, telekinesis, direct and independent voice, ap-ports, lights, raps, psychic photography (qq.v.).

Phenomenalism. A philosophy which holds that phenomena only may be apprehended, not the underlying cause.

Phenomenon. In the occult, this refers to a universal element or psych-ical projection exhibited by those who are sensitive to nature's subtle powers.

Philadelphians. A pantheistic religious body that flourished in the 17th century, whose believers deemed themselves inspired by the Holy Spirit.

Philalethes, Eirenaeus. This alchemist who flourished about 1660 was a pseudonymous Englishman, friend of the noted chemist Robert Boyle, and believed in actual life to have been one of several well-known Englishmen. But nothing is certain here. He emigrated to Amer-ica, and though he is credited with having written many books, only three books on alchemy actually carry his name. He was, however, in-fluential in stimulating alchemical knowledge in his adopted country.

Philo of Alexandria (30 B.C.-50 A.D.). The most famous Hebrew philosopher and mystic of the Alexandrian School in Egypt, he was also an eminent theologian. Believing that Greek thought utilized Mosaic teachings, he, in turn, borrowed from Greek philosophy for his spiritual interpretations. For Philo, the achievement of union with God, by way of self-renunciation and the divine Logos, is the supreme blessedness. He had an enormous influence on the history of mysti-cism and the Cabala (q.v.).

Philosopher's Stone. Believed to be the chemical that turned base metal into silver or gold, it was often termed the Powder of Projection. Zosimus in the 5th century was the first to mention it. Eventually, the Philosopher's Stone took on a wider range of powers, being considered not only the secret of life and health, but also possessing a spiritual significance. The transcendent school, first elaborated the latter no-tion in the 13th century contained a program that led the alchemist through strict devotion to exact ritual and to purification. Further, the Philosopher's Stone signified the force behind the evolution of life and that universal binding power that unites minds and souls in a human oneness. Finally, it represented the purity and sanctity of the highest realm of pure thought and altruistic existence.

Philosophy. A comprehensive study of all mental and material phe-nomena. Any particular system of philosophic thought.

Philosophus. A term coined by Aleister Crowley (q.v.) designating the adept who undergoes the Cabalistic progress through sephira 7, to possess the occult power of God, which becomes immanent in himself. Thus he concludes his moral discipline before the ultimate test of the Order.

Phoenix. The legendary bird found in Egyptian mythology that reputedly lived in the Arabian desert to the fabulous age of some 600 years; then, after setting itself afire, was born anew with youthful freshness out of its own ashes. Since this bird was regarded as a symbol of immortality and reincarnation, it was a very popular illustration for the alchemists.

Phone-Voyance. Clairvoyant faculty akin to "psychic television" over the public telephone system. It was discovered in himself by Vincent N. Turvey in 1905. He was often able to describe accurately conditions at the other end of the line, and give additional information unknown to the listener there.

Photography. See Psychic Photography.

Phrenology. A once popular system and study of the shape and contours of the human head. Phrenology champions the theory that there is a correlation between these shapes and contours and the mental faculties and potentialities. (See: F.J. Gall)

Phrygian Cap. The classic cap used in the Persian Mithraic religion (q.v.) by the priests in the ritual of sacrifice. This ancient cap of occult significance was utilized by many cults and religions. It was the official headdress of the ancient Jewish high priest. It was worn by the women of ancient Greece and Rome, but in reverse as seen on the sculptures of Pallas-Athene and Minerva. It is the source of the miter (from Mithros q.v.) which is worn by abbots, bishops and Popes. The gnostics used it; and it adorned the ancient Mexican diety Cinteotl.

Physical Medium (Spiritualism). One whose ability to produce ectoplasm of suitable substance and quantity, is able to specialize in the production of physical phenomena. Such mediums are usually very sensitive to actinic light, and need to be shielded from it during a seance. Failure to do this may result in serious physical injury to the medium, due to the sudden elastic recoil of the ectoplasm.

Physical Phenomena. As distinct from mental phenomena, involves the production of ectoplasm in order that various structures may be used for materialization, telekinesis, etc.

Pico Della Mirandola, Giovani, Conte (1463-94). Italian scholar, renowned for his vast learning; a brilliant humanist whose mysticism made him a heretic in the eyes of the Church. His book condemning astrology was never completed, but the study of magic he praised as the noblest part of the natural sciences, and he wrote *Strige*, a work on witchcraft.

Pilgrim. In many religions, one who makes a journey to a religious place or a shrine for the purposes of devotion, of becoming familiar with it, or of fulfilling a sacred vow, petitioning for a special favor, or doing penance.

Pink. As an auric color, it is associated with affection.

Piper, Mrs. Leonore E. of Boston. One of the most outstanding trance mediums in the history of psychical research, she was responsible for the conversion of such persons as Sir Oliver Lodge, R. Hodgson, J. Hyslop, William James (qq.v.), and many others, to the spirit hypothesis and the certainty of human survival. Her daily life for twenty years was continuously under the direct supervision of the A.S.P.R. and S.P.R. without once giving cause for suspicion by her actions. As an experiment, she was transferred from America to London to see if her mediumship would be affected by new surroundings. Living in Sir Oliver's own household, where she was tested by independent observers, her extraordinary powers continued unabated.

Pisces. Astrological sign (February 20–March 21); Element-Water; Symbol—two Fishes; ruling planets—Jupiter and Neptune. Qualities—being the last of the 12 signs, the union of the head and feet, these people have lofty ideals, an attractive personality, psychic and occult gifts, and are artistic. But they can go in two directions at once, can be drifters, completely impractical, and famous worriers. Some astrologers, however, have seen this as a mean, petty, vindictive sign, but by far the larger number decidedly agree with the qualities here described.

Pitakas (Buddhism). "The three baskets," which are divisions of the Buddhist Pali scriptures.

Pivot Stone (Japanese Buddhism). At the Kita-ura Lagoon, named Kashima, is an ancient temple at which hard by stands a chunk of worn stone, considered a pillar. Its foundation is believed to be the center of the world.

P.K. Psychokinesis (q.v.)

Plaat, Frau Lotte (Mme. von Strahl). Dutch psychometrist whose psychic talents were regularly employed by the German police for tracing criminals. Important experiments were conducted with her at the Laboratory for Psychical Research in London.

Planchette. A small handrest of castors, in which a pencil is fixed. The planchette was invented in France in 1853. If a suitable medium places his hand on the apparatus, it may write or draw. Some authorities believe that this faculty should only be developed in a properly conducted circle.

Planetary Ages of Man. In ancient astrology, the planets determined the powers influencing each age of man. For example, the Moon, governing growth, dominated the first four years; Mercury governing education—the period from five to fourteen; Venus, emotion, fifteen to twenty-two; the Sun, virility, twenty-three to forty-two; Mars ambition, forty-three to fifty-seven; Jupiter, reflection, fifty-eight to sixty-nine; Saturn, resignation, seventy to ninety-nine.

Planetary Information. There have been several alleged communications regarding life on other planets, and descriptions from "astral travels," all of which must remain speculative. Swedenborg was the first who claimed knowledge of the planet Mars.

Plastics. See Moulds.

Plato (429–348 B.C.). Perhaps the most important of all philosophers, Plato was born in Athens, and for eight years was a pupil of Socrates (q.v.) and for twenty years was the teacher of Aristotle (q.v.). The creator of an idealist philosophy and the first Utopia, his writings formed the first systematic body of philosophic thought. Plato considered the human soul immortal. And since for him the controlling realities were such notions as "beauty," "truth," "justice," and "goodness," which being universals, exist as "Ideas" in a divine world, the knowledge of Good, the supreme Idea, should be man's highest ambition. So immense has been his influence in the whole structure of Western culture that it marks directly or indirectly every period of its history: Particularly, he was a powerful influence in Arabic, Jewish, Christian and Western mysticism and religion.

Pleroma. A name formerly used for the totality of the heavenly gods.

Plotinus (205–270). One of the most famous mystics of ancient Greek and Latin philosophy whose Eastern and Hebrew influences greatly enriched his system of thought. To him all that is real consists of a series of emanations from God, the first being *Nous* (Mind) and the second *Psyche* (soul). Man must regard his soul as part of the World-Soul, and the union with God is the ultimate goal. Not only did his work influence a host of philosophers, but many Christian thinkers (St. Augustine, Erigena, Dionysius the Pseudo-Areopagite etc. (qq.v.) incorporated his ideas into Christianity.

Plutarch (c.46–c.120 A..D.). Greek writer, priest of the temple of Delphi, and the author of the famous *The Parallel Lives* of Greek and Roman men of eminence, which has remained a widely read book for nearly two thousand years. Five of Shakespeare's plays utilize Plutarch's "Lives" for their plot and story. His interesting essay "On the face of the moon's disk" asserted the advanced notion that the moon is a second earth; but also, that it is inhabited by demons who on occasion visit the earth; that the "demon" of Socrates and the "oracle" at the Oracle of Delphi, for example, were demons who came from the moon.

Another very important body of his writing are Plutarch's essays—some 60 in number, which are collectively known as *Ethica* or *Moralia*; these range over a wide variety of topics (ethics, religion, science, politics and literature), and they, too, have had a significant influence on many writers and thinkers.

Pluto. In astrology, this last of the planets to be discovered represents man's urge to develop and make flourish his culture and its institutions. Plutonian doctrines impregnate the words of talented artists, investing them with the highest insight.

Pneumatographers. Mediums for the production of direct writing.

Podmore, Frank (1856–1910). Well-known British psychic researcher who first accepted Spiritualism, then rejected it, and was exhaustive in his attempts to provide alternative explanations of its phenomena. He was the author of many works, including the collaboration with Myers and Gurney for the well-known *Phantasms of the Living*.

Point of Love. In astrology, Venus' position in a solar chart which is always in the 1st, 2nd, 11th or 12th House.

Polarian. See Root Race.

Poltergeist. A mischievous agency or entity who makes inexplicable noises, moves and throws objects about, causes fires and breaks dishes, glassware, and such items. These phenomena are spontaneous and usually occur in the immediate vicinity of some young person around the age of puberty. It is as if this person is haunted or persecuted by some spirit. The presence of others may aggravate the phenomena or cause it to cease. The throwing of small stones is very characteristic of this phenomena all over the world. Peculiarly, the flight of these stones does not follow a normal trajectory and they are frequently reported as hot to the touch.

Polyglot Invocation. In demonology, a potent spell that calls upon Hebrew, Greek, and Syrian gods, in order to compel the spirit invoked to be ruled by the summoner.

Polyglot Mediumship. See Xenoglossy.

Polytheism. The worship of many gods.

Pontica. A stone with lurid blood markings which the possessor uses to force demons to reply to his questions.

Popol Vuh. The name of "Bible" among Maya-Quiche Indians of Guatemala, a member of the tribal group of the once dominant Mayans of Central America. The *Popol Vuh* records their cosmological, spiritual, mystical, and occult beliefs.

Porphory (c. 232–305 A.D.). Disciple of Plotinus (q.v.) whose works on logic dominated medieval training. He was a student of demonology, believing that the evil demons could only be controlled by esoteric rites and formulas, and was author of a mystical work titled *On the Return of the Soul.*

Positive. See Negative.

Positivism. A materialistic philosophy which denies metaphysics. The positive philosophy founded by Comte, 1798–1857, conceived science to be an end in itself, evolving through three stages: 1. theological or mythical; 2. metaphysical or abstract; 3. positive or concrete.

Possession. Temporary surrender of a person's body and personality to the control of another spirit, usually discarnate, though possession by the living is also well known. The discernible difference between possession and subconscious personation is whether new knowledge has been given. An endurance of possession against the subject's will would be called obsession.

Post-Cognitive Telepathy. Term used in parapsychology (q.v.). An extra sensory correspondence between a present mental pattern of A and a mental pattern of B—of which B was conscious in the past, but of which he is not contemporaneously conscious.

Post-hypnotic Suggestion. Actions carried out by a subject in a later time which have been given to him by the hypnotist while under hypnosis.

Post Mortem Messages. Instances where a deceased person communicates the contents of a sealed letter written prior to his death for the express purpose of proving survival.

Postel, Guillaume (1510–1581). French Cabalist and visionary. He translated the *Sepher Yetzirah* (q.v.) into Latin, and parts of the *Zohar.* Postel believed that God had ordered him to establish the union of all men under one law.

Poughkeepsie Seer The. See Davis, A.J.

Powder of Projection. See Philosopher's Stone.

Powell, Evan J. (1881–1958). This English Justice of the Peace was a non-professional trance and physical medium. He was always tied to a chair by his own wish, before the drawn curtains of the cabinet. His chief control was an American Indian named Black Hawk. Powell gave many sittings to the British College of Psychic Science.

Power, Psychic. A general term descriptive of the various forces employed in the exercise of psychic or mediumistic faculties. Although in recent years much important experimentation has been done in this area, the various theories have not yet achieved a comprehensive definition. In our present state of knowledge it is difficult to differentiate between the various power sources. Some phenomena seem to be entirely mental, while others are due to physical emanations, with many combinations of the two classes. (See: Emanations).

Prajna (Buddhism). Transcendental wisdom, the divine intuition, and the achievement of the six paramitas (q.v.).

Prana. (Hinduism). A subtle form of energy permeating the universe, but manifesting in a special form in the human organism. This force is capable of being transmitted from one organism to another, and is the energizing power by which many forms of occult and magic phenomena can be produced (Swami Bhakta Vishita). Yogis believe it can be inspired with the breath.

Pranasophie. A recreation of the old German adherence to Teutonic superiority, but in its modern development it represented a new Teutonic myth infused with occult theosophy and the esoteric mystical theosophy of Odinism. The followers gathered in secret graillike sects and held spiritual seances seated on bearskins. Altogether, in final form, Pranasophie also contained aspects of the Iranian doctrine of Genesis, the Logos (q.v.) of the Christian Gospel, the Paracelsian *Spiritus Vitae*, the "Water of Life" of Omar Khayyam, and the *elan vital* of modern vitalism. The favored symbols of this movement in Germany have been the Aryan Sun Savior and the Edda plus the magical power of the Swastika (q.v.).

Pranayama (Hinduism). The fourth stage of Yoga. The science of breathing, particularly the regulation of the breath.

Pratya Hara (Hinduism). The fifth stage of Yoga. Withdrawal of attention from objects.

Pratyekabuddha (Buddhist). The Buddha who attains Nirvana (q.v.) without then devoting himself to the delivery of other human beings, as the Sammasambuddha (q.v.) does.

Prayer. A mental attitude of reaching out to absorb a greater awareness of spirituality (see Awareness). A communication mental or vocal addressed to a good or a higher or spiritual intelligence.

Prayer Flag (Lamaism). Tibetans run flags across the entrance gates to their cities, believing that these fluttering pennants carry prayers into the skies to Buddha.

Prayer Wheel (Lamaism). An instrumental religious object of Tibetan Buddhists, being a revolving metal case or drum containing written prayers.

Preanimism. That first feeling of fear, of awe, of wonder instigated by supernatural events. Also the earliest of beliefs that all objects are alive with life, energy, or spirits.

Precession. See Aquarian Age.

Precious Stones. The occult qualities of precious stones, beginning with ancient times to the present, stress their direct power on the owner and wearer. Each precious stone embodies a certain benignant and malefic force, which are in harmony or disharmony with each individual, though some stones like diamonds and emeralds have a wider range of benevolent power than, for example, pearls and rubies. Astrology assigns to each birth sign its own stone. Plato believed the origin of precious stones to be the vivifying spirit abiding in the stars. In India, Chaldea, and Greece, precious stones were related to man's essential nature. The medicinal value of precious stones has been heralded by many ancient priests, occultists, physicians, and alchemists. (See: Pearls).

Precognition. Prediction in which the percipient is correctly positive that a particular event is going to happen.

Precognitive Clairvoyance. Term in parapsychology. An extra sensory correspondence between a present mental pattern of A and a future object or event in the physical world (Soal and Bateman).

Predestination. In the strict Christian sense, God's election of certain people to eternal heavenly grace in his foreknowing they will live a wholly Godly life, or His choice of certain individuals and instilling them with the saintliness to be rewarded with eternal salvation. Some Christian groups, Calvinists for example, believe God both elects and condemns, fating the soul by his foreknowledge.

Prediction. The foretelling of any kind of future event. There is ample factual evidence of this occurring. When it involves the fate of nations or large units, it is termed prophecy.

Predictions in Astrology. The finest astrologers all agree that the stars may impel, but they do not compel. And they concur that by knowing the conditions of one's astrological situation, an individual can act intelligently and utilize his conscious control to best effect.

Pre-existence. The belief that we have had a previous life before our earthly birth or that our souls have had a separate existence before human birth is both an ancient and a modern doctrine. The ancient Egyptians and Pythagorean Greeks accepted this theory and it is a basic tenet of Hinduism and Buddhism. Plato (q.v.) held that this principle accounted for the individual's remembrance of Universals. Theosophists and Anthroposophists (qq.v.) assert that both reincarnation (q.v.) and earthly preexistence is an essential part of their systems. Among Spiritualists there is a divergence of opinion: some spirits say they remember former lives while others do not.

Premonition. Prediction where details are not precisely outlined. The lowest degree of prophecy. To be a true premonition it cannot be attributed to chance or sagacity. Premonitions may be received in normal, trance, hypnotic or dream states.

Presbyterianism. A form of church government by a body of elders, ruling along with a group of ministers of equal rank the churches of a particular district.

Presentiment. The prediction of vague future events of a personal nature only. Vague non-personal events are premonitions.

Pretas. In the mythological works of the Hindus, these are malevolent ghosts.

Prevision. Presentiment in a visual form.

Price, Harry. British ghost-hunter and student of psychic and occult phenomena, he was the founder and Director of the National Laboratory for Psychical Research, a former Research Officer of A.S.P.R. (q.v.) and Hon. Vice-President of the Magician's Club of London. He was also the author of many works on psychic research. He reported before his death in 1948 that in England there were many persons of good family and high education who worshipped Satan. (See: Aleister Crowley).

Priest. Though a clergyman in modern times, in the past he was a specialist in magic, the occult, and numerous other supernormal powers. Essentially he was an intermediary between the spirits and men, or the gods and men. It is believed that priests evolved from the witch doctor, the shrine guardian, the medicine man, or the shaman (q.v.). Among the Egyptians and the Druids (q.v.) the priests were the most learned men of their time. Among the American Objibway Indians some deformed persons were made priests in the belief they possessed special gifts.

Primum Mobile. This is the ancient notion of the first mover, the outermost sphere,—the tenth, which carried all the fixed stars in its daily motion. It was based on the notion that the heavens revolved about the earth. Strangely, though the theory is invalid, yet because of the Earth's motion and the seeming movement of the stars around it, this theory is still applicable in astrology.

Prince, Walter Franklin. Ex-clergyman of the Episcopal Church, he was the Research Officer of the Boston S.P.R. and A.S.P.R., and President of S.P.R. in 1931-32. Extremely skeptical, he was remarkable for his studies of the "Patience Worth" case, the Antigonish Ghost, and his curing of Doris Fischer in a case of multiple personality. Dr. Prince was the author of many books.

Principles of Man. According to long occult tradition, the seven principles of man constitute the seven principles of the cosmos, being but the one reality of the universe merely differentiated. There are seven qualities of all entities. In man they are composed of the following: divine, spiritual, psychic, egoic, astral, etheric, and physical.

Priscillians. A Christian sect in Spain that flourished in the 4th-5th century, and followed a system of beliefs that combined Gnostic and Manichaean ideas (qq.v.).

Private Sitting. One person only, sitting with a medium. Authorities believe that in these situations evidence can never be guaranteed.

Prize. In dream interpretation in former times, to dream of winning in a lottery was a certain sign of poverty and misery. If your lottery ticket, however, contained a majority of odd numbers, those might come in, but even numbers never.

Probationary Path (Theosophy). The initial act of turning away from earthly desires that leads one to the path of highest spiritual living. Theosophy here follows the Eastern concepts of distinguishing between real and unreal; indifference to the external world; control of thought, body, sensual desires; plus endurance, forebearance, faith, balance, and, finally, desire for liberation.

Proclus (c.410–485). The last of the great Greek philosophers and a profound mystic, his mastery of Platonism enabled him to become one of the most influential figures in the development and history of Neo-Platonism (q.v.). Living as a semiascetic, a vegetarian, and devoted to the practice of meditation, he was also an inspired teacher and thinker. For Proclus, the "One" unifies and incorporates all that is divine— in which he includes not only God and the gods, but also the Sun and the Moon, and the Good. Proclus, moreover, incorporated Orphic-Pythagorean and Egyptian and Near Eastern beliefs into his Neo-Platonism. Thus, in this richly elaborated philosophical-religious- mystical system, reality is mental; life's goal is a renunciation of the senses in all their aspects in order to reach the transcendent One through "faith," which is the highest "kind of intuition." His book *The Platonic Theology* is the best introduction to the quality, range, and profundity of his philosophy. With the translation of his work by the renowned Marcilius Ficino (q.v.) in 1497, Proclus helped to make Neo- Platonism one of the dominant philosophies in European religion, mysticism, the occult, and literature for some three hundred years. (See: Pythagoras, Orphism, Plotinus, Boethius, Neo-Platonism, Ficino, Cambridge Platonists, Thomas More.)

Prodigies. Infants who exhibit mature powers of technical or artistic perfection. There is no normal explanation of this, although it is often advanced by the supporters of the theory of reincarnation (q.v.) as evidence of the experiences gained in former lives being carried over to the present consciousness. This theory may be countered by the fact of spirit possession, or mediumship. This view is strengthened by the fact that prodigies have sometimes been suddenly deprived of their powers in later life. (See: Ariola)

Prognostication. The act of making a forecast.

Progression (Spiritualism). The pathway of each spirit through the many phases or spheres of experience constitutes a progression, the ultimate of which we cannot conceive as yet. The rate of progression depends on the person's capacity to profit spiritually by his experiences, and in some cases, his deliberate refusal to learn.

Prolologoi. According to mystic principles, these are the seven primal forces that developed into archangels.

Promittor. In astrology, that which "promises," being a planet which in its travels through the Zodiac promises a person something that is to occur when a significant chart factor will be attained.

Proof. Mathematical proof is the only complete proof that is possible, since it does not depend on empirical fact but, rather, on logical assumptions and operations. The psychic investigator is concerned solely with proofs of identity, and this kind of proof, acceptable in everyday affairs, is called legal proof.

Prophecy. In the occult the power of true prophecy belongs only to those psychically attuned to the Akashic or Astral records (qq.v.). Failure indicates the adept has failed to read correctly the true Astral history.

Prophet. One who declares, who is a messenger of God, foreteller of the future, and, finally, an interpreter of God's will. Generally, the word "prophet" refers to the prophets of Israel—those mystics and preachers who rose up in the 8th and 7th centuries B.C.; and, particularly, the Major figures Isaiah, Jeremiah, Ezekiel, and Daniel. However, in Islam, Muhammad (q.v.) is deemed the greatest of all prophets.

Prostitution, Sacred. Prostitutes in the role of beneficent agents are and have been since ancient times a part of many religions. In India, for example, Hinduism—as practiced in the worship of one of the manifestations of Siva (q.v.)—looks upon sacred prostitution as a visible event of the union of man and God. In ancient Babylonia this prostitution centered around the worship of Mylitta (Herodotus identified her with Aphrodite). In Egypt sacred prostitutes were a basic aspect of the religious practices that were offered to several of their gods. In ancient Cyprus sacred prostitutes were in abiding service to a specific temple where the worship of some form of the Great Mother of the Gods (Aphrodite, Astarte, Mylitta, Cybele (qq.v.)) was performed. In Greece, in the cult of Aphrodite, this practice prevailed in the city-states of Ephesus and Corinth. In ancient Sicily, the Elyminian people established a famous temple for the worship of Astarte-Aphrodite-Venus where some authorities feel that sacred prostitution was almost certainly a permanent part of the religious ritual. Interestingly, in ancient Judea, though surrounded by the practice of sacred prostitution and with prostitution itself a common feature of their society, no sacred prostitution was ever permitted. There are two chief theories currently accepted for the prevalence of sacred prostitution: (1) the community's strong belief that the deflowering of a virgin was dangerous for a husband: a fear that made it necessary for every girl to go to a temple and there be deflowered by the first stranger who desired her; (2) the belief that sacred prostitution was an absolutely necessary means by which the society could obtain the essential life-sustaining fertility of land, of beast, of man.

Proterius. The ancient story of how the exorcist St. Basilius thwarted the Devil from ruining Proterius' daughter. Although Proterius had determined his daughter would enter a convent, she married a servant who had signed a pact with the Devil, which St. Basilius discovered and destroyed, permitting the couple a life of happiness.

Protevangelion. In the Christian Church, this is the so-called "First Gospel," for it represents the promise, given to Adam and Eve immediately after the fall, of a Redeemer who is to come: the Christ.

Proxy Sittings (Spiritualism). A device to eliminate the possibility of the sitter's mind being read. The would-be sitter appoints a deputy to sit, who knows nothing of the desired communicator. A record of this sitting is then sent to the inquirer for analysis. Success with this method has been attained, but the one who arranged the proxy must mentally do his best to influence the desired communicator beforehand, and there should be a willing band of co-operative spirits for this work attached to the medium.

Psalmomancy (Judaism). Divination by use of the Psalms of the Old Testament, particularly the great magic Psalm 119. This is known as the Celestial Decree and has been used in divination by the ancient Jewish mystics.

Pschagogues. This Greek term denotes a necromancer who raises the spirits of the dead.

Pseudopod. The modified tip of an ectoplasmic rod, adapted in the fashion of a rudimentary hand, for grasping objects, thus producing telekinetic phenomena.

Psi. Processes and factors in human personality, or in nature, which appear to transcend or deny the accepted limiting principles of science. A general term for parapsychological events such as psychic, ESP, and psychokinesis (qq.v.).

PSI Missing. In parapsychological research those individuals who score so consistently off target that it suggests unconscious faculties so motivated as to enable the person to use his psychic talent to avoid achieving paranormal success.

Psyche. Greek word for soul.

Psychedelic Drugs. The use of drugs such as L.S.D., mescalin, psylocybin, etc. to expand consciousness and achieve a profound sensory perception. On occasion extreme perceptual distortion and hallucination may result in feelings of euphoria or despair. Psychedelics have been used by Mexicans and American Indians in the form of peyote-called "peyotl" by its Aztec discoverers. Among the Indians peyote is usually a part of a religious ceremony, and has no untoward effects. It is interesting to note, however, that the study of "peyotl" by Western scientists first began toward the end of the 19th century—particularly, with the experiments of Weir Mitchell in America, Havelock Ellis in England, and Alexandre Rouhier in France. But after the first spurt of curiousity had expired, almost no significant research on peyote took place again until the last couple of decades. This contemporary interest was incited by the work of a number of American anthropologists along with a group of well known writers.

Psychic. Non-physical. Common term for a medium, metagnome or sensitive. Descriptive of supernormal phenomena. First used in France by Flammarion and in England by Serjeant Cox.

Psychic Art. See Automatic, Clairvoyant, Direct painting.

Psychic Breezes. See Breezes.

Psychic Evidence Society. Founded 1931 in London as a psychical research society for clergymen in Great Britain.

Psychic Lights. See Luminous Phenomena.

Psychic Music. See Music.

Psychic Phenomena. See Phenomena.

Psychic Photography. Although highly publicized in the early years of this century, psychic photography has suffered a huge decline in credibility and has almost vanished as a source of valid psychic information.

Psychic Power. See Power.

Psychic Rods. Rods and levers supposedly built from ectoplasm (q.v.) for the purpose of moving or holding objects, or the production of raps by striking objects. They are described extensible, rigid or elastic, according to the spirit operator's requirements.

Psychic Science. A system of knowledge which states: 1. That at the death of the body, man continues to function as a conscious being. 2. That he functions after death in a refined spirit-body or soul which has substance and weight, and which can be seen and photographed. 3. That this soul existed within the physical body during life, and is organic, having brain, nerves, blood-vessels, heart, etc. 4. That the soul can communicate in various ways with persons on earth both before and after death. 5. That the world in which the soul dwells after the death of the body lies immediately around the physical earth. 6. That a man while alive may leave his physical body, and by the use of his soul, explore spheres of refined physical states, commonly called the spirit world. This experience is not to be confused with "out-of-body" events for in this type of separation the episode generally occurs in the vicinity of the primary self.

Psychic Sounds. See Sounds.

Psychic Touches. See Touches.

Psychic Winds. See Breezes.

Psychical Research (Spiritualism). Systematic scientific inquiries concerning the nature, facts and causes of mediumistic phenomena. The claimed facts are first tested. If they are established, natural explanations are sought to account for them. If still unknown, the nature of the unknown force has to be investigated. If it shows intelligence, it has to be seen whether it can possibly be due to earthly intelligence. Only after all ordinary sources have thus been eliminated is a supernormal source of intelligence postulated and tested. Most countries have their Societies for Psychical Research (S.P.R., in America the A.S.P.R.), or kindred societies which perform much valuable work in testing phenomena and defining the mode of action in many cases. While the existence of phenomena is generally acknowledged, many researchers are still cautious about the "spirit hypothesis," though many great scientists have openly admitted their belief in it. The early research societies were founded in England, where the first of them, the Ghost Club, was formed in Trinity College, Cambridge, in 1851. In 1875, Serjeant Cox founded the Psychological Society of Great Britain, the S.P.R. followed in 1882, and the A.S.P.R. in 1885. (See: Parapsychology)

Psychical Research Foundation. Headed by William Roll, and based in Durham, North Carolina, this research group studies survival after bodily death. One of the Foundation's attested experiments has revealed that a sensitive is able to leave his body and visit the body of his pet cat.

Psychism. Psychical research.

Psychist. A psychical researcher or a student of psychology.

Psychoanalysis. Founded by Freud at the end of the 19th century. His work revealed the profound importance on human life of the unconscious, of dreams, of infantile sex, of repression, aggression, and the action of the libido. Psychoanalysis has been a revolution in the treatment of mental problems and in the understanding of the human psyche. It has influenced nearly every art and science, and also religion. Psychoanalysis, through the works of Freud and Jung has enlarged our understanding of such psychic phenomena as telepathy, clairvoyance, and astrology. Though Freud began as a confirmed materialist, he changed his mind about parapsychology, and in 1921 wrote in defense of occult phenomena.

Psycho-Energetics. A term adopted by some physicists and parapsychologists for the discipline that studies the reaction of material objects to psychic energy. This discipline is analogous in its perspectives to psychokinesis or psychokinetics (q.v.), which is often abbreviated to PK.

Psychode. A term for ectoplasm.

Psychogram. A spirit message.

Psychograph. An instrument designed to test psychical phenomena, consisting of a disc with an index rotating over the alphabet. The medium rests his fingertips on the disc. Also called a scotograph and radiograph. The supernormal appearance of some text or writing on photographic material.

Psychography. Direct Writing.

Psychokinesis. Term of parapsychology (P.K.). An influence exerted on a physical system by a person without the use of any known physical instruments or intermediating forms of physical energy. The term covers experiments in which mind influences matter.

Psychology. The scientific study of the phenomena of consciousness.

Psychometry. A faculty discovered by J. R. Buchanan in 1842, whereby an object when held by a sensitive person, produces a community of sensation conveying the nature and history of the object. Some mediums possess this faculty, though when demonstrating, it is commonly augmented by other mediumistic faculties, such as clairvoyance, etc. The material objects are viewed to be acting as catalysts for the psi faculty.

Psychophobia. A dread of destiny and a fear of what is not seen.

Psychoplasm. Term for ectoplasm.

Psychosomatic. Regarding the mind and the body as a single unit, from the medical point of view. Chiefly, however, it signifies the potent influence of the mind in creating a seeming illness when there is no actual organic impairment.

Psylli. In former times, persons who were believed able to charm snakes.

Ptolemy. The last of the famous astronomers of ancient times this Greco-Egyptian was also a noted mathematician and geographer. Until Copernicus, he dominated the world of astronomy with his complex system of an earth-centered universe. *Tetrabiblos,* his book on astrology, has been a major influence on the development of this discipline.

Public Demonstrations (Spiritualism). It is customary to include in Spiritualist services, a demonstration of clairvoyance by a medium. The purpose of this is to give individual proof to newcomers of the continued survival of their deceased friends and relatives. The means by which a medium accomplishes this, is by close rapport with a trusted spirit helper who acts as interpreter and regulator of communications. The actual impression may be visual (clairvoyance) or by hearing (clairaudience) or by sensing the actual physical condition of the deceased before passing. Public demonstrations of spirit healing are sometimes given, when disabled or incapacitated persons are invited on to the platform where a marked improvement of the affliction is often made obvious to the audience as a demonstration of spirit power.

Puharich, Dr. Andrija. Psychic investigator and researcher who has exposed such famous mediums as Edith Sitwell and, on the other hand, has sponsored such well-known psychic demonstrators as Uri Geller. He brought Uri Geller from Israel to the Stanford Research Institute (q.v.) for a long series of tests, and is the author of a book on Uri's mysterious powers and the outer space source of his special paranormal capacities. He has also written a book on the psychedelic effects of mushrooms. (See: *Uri,* by A. Puharich; and Uri Geller)

Pure Land Sect (Buddhism). Founded by Huiyuan (334–416), this has become the Judo sect in Japan and the Ching t'u in China. The latter stresses salvation through faith, devotion, and spiritual grace.

Purgatory. In the Roman Catholic Church that place of punishment where forgiven sins plus venial sins must be endured, to cleanse and prepare the soul for its entry into heaven.

Purification. A ritual that has been used the world over since ancient times, in which individuals or groups cleanse themselves of sin, or make an effort to propitiate the spirits or the gods toward some end. It has also been used, and still is, by those embarked on a cosmic or spiritual journey—as alchemists, Cabalists, Yogins, initiates in an occult or religious endeavor, or those consulting sorcerers or paranormal specialists like witchdoctors, etc. While water is most commonly used to purify objects or persons, fire, cutting the hair, changing clothes, sexual abstinence, cessation from activity, isolation, and body-painting have also been utilized to guarantee purification. (See: Scapegoat).

Purusha (Hinduism). The original eternal man, signifying "Person." Also, both the soul of the universe, and the Supreme Being. Further, it is a name of Brahma.

Purushottamas (Buddhism, Hinduism). Representing that which is the "Best of Men." However, when considered mystically, it refers to the soul of the universe, the Supreme Being. It is a title of Vishnu. (See: Purusha)

Purva Mimansa System (Hinduism). Jaimini's doctrine, oriented toward the achievement of the soul's freedom through strict observance of the Vedic rites, prayer, and worship.

Puthoff, Harold Parapsychologist who has worked at the Stanford Research Institute (q.v.) and has researched many paranormal studies. He is also a key supporter of scientology (q.v.). His experiments include such widely different investigations as the psychic relationship between two eggs when one of them is being broken, and the testing of Uri Geller's (q.v.) powers in telepathy, precognition, and psychokinesis (qq.v.).

PWCCA. The Welsh term for the Devil.

Pyramid. The ancient Egyptian pyramids have been an awesome mystery to students since they were built, and the most recent thoroughgoing scientific studies only heighten their wondrous scientific and cosmic dimensions. But traditionally, since the word means "a going out of the temple of the body to heaven," its symbology denotes a going out of the body, the dead—a going from life to death. In the occult, it represents Cosmic Man descending from heaven, since the pyramids seem to reflect in their measurements, cosmic laws, the human body, and man's union with the supersensible world.

Pyramidology. An occult system of prophecy based on various proportions and measurements of the Great Pyramid, which are held to correlate with important historical events. It is often asserted that the pyramid builders possessed scientific knowledge which was in some aspects superior to that of today. (See: Pyramids)

Pyromancy. Divination by the observation of fire.

Pythagoras (c. 572–497 B.C.). One of the giants of mathematics, philosophy, astronomy, physics and mysticism of the ancient world, whose range of knowledge enormously influenced Plato and Aristotle. Beyond these attainments, Pythagoras established a religious brotherhood in Southern Italy that proclaimed moral reformation and the immortality and transmigration of the soul, for the soul being the harmony of the body cured the confusion of the senses. Pythagoras' religious ideas reflected those of the Greek mysteries. Central to Pythagoreanism was the notion that the substance of all things was numbers; therefore Pythagoras stressed the symbolic relationship of numbers to mysticism—for example: one was identified with reason, two with the soul, odd was form, even was matter. The remarkable profundity of this thinker-visionary shaped the whole subsequent history of mystical-occult thinking in the West.

Pythoness. In Greek religion, the priestess of Apollo who demonstrated prophetic powers. But it refers to any woman who possessed oracular gifts. In biblical times a woman so possessed was considered a powerful intercessor for necromancers.

Quabala. See Cabala

Quadrants. In astrology, one quarter of the twelve houses of the Zodiac's circle.

Quadrupetal. In astrology, this refers to those symbols which are four-footed: Aries, Taurus, Leo, Sagittarius, and Capricorn (qq.v.). Ancient astrologers held that those born under these various signs exhibited the qualities of these zodiacal animals.

Quadruplicity. In astrology, any of a group of four, containing therefore such elements as the cardinal signs, the fixed signs, the mutable signs (qq.v.).

Quakers. See Friends, Society of.

Quaternity. Those concepts in the theories of Theosophy, Anthroposophy, and Eastern doctrine which perceive man as a union of four basic components; that is—physical body, etheric or life body, astral or soul body, and "I" the egoic.

Queen of Elfame. During the era of witchcraft trials in Scotland, this appellation was the name of the deity who directed the witches' Sabbat (q.v.). During the orgies of the sorcerers and witches, the Queen of Elfame was then said to have unrestrained sexual intercourse with male witches.

Queen Sabbath. (Judaism). *Shabbat ha-Malkah* "Queen Sabbath" was the name given by the Jewish Rabbinical Mystics to the Sabbath day, which in Jewish custom begins at sundown on Friday night. The Cabalists (q.v.) called the Sabbath the "over-soul," for they envisioned the Sabbath as an angel who lived in the Seventh Heaven in the divine presence of the Schechinah (q.v.) and who descended from heaven to earth every Friday at sundown. Queen Sabbath, therefore, imparted a holiness, a rapture and a benevolence to this weekly holy day.

Quelle Document. One of the earliest references to the life of Jesus, in a Greek translation from an earlier Aramaic writing. It gives a plain, simple teaching, and makes no reference to the miraculous.

Quetzal. The ancient Mayans and Aztecs worshipped this brilliantly plumaged bird, particularly in relation to their great god Quetzalcoatl (q.v.). The plumes of the Quetzal were treasured and made into capes for the rulers and priests.

Quetzalcoatl. Although chiefly a major god in the pantheon of the Mexican Toltecs and Aztecs, this god of good, of light, of peace, of the arts and crafts, and the progenitor of the Mexican civilization, was worshipped by one name or another, by many of the tribes of Northern South and Central America. A large complex of myths were woven around this human god, however the major legend tells of his sailing away to the Land of the Rising Sun, but promising like a Messiah to return one day in glory.

Quevent. In horary astrology (q.v.) the person who asks the questions of the astrologer.

Quid Quod Pro. Latin phrase meaning "something for something," which typifies much of the early relationship between man and his deities. The Greek Agamemnon offered his daughter Iphigenia in sacrifice to appease the goddess Artemis to favor the sailing of the Greek troops against Troy; and the Hebrew Patriarch Jacob prayed to God offering to him his absolute dedication in return for protection from his enemy, his brother, Esau (see Gen: XXIII). The ancient Hittite people were an extraordinary example of extreme devotion to this behavior pattern; and most ancient religions contained rituals in which the worshippers offered "something" to their divinities in return for something," such as: fertility, rain, protection, vengeance, personal gain, victory in war, or destruction of enemies, etc.

Quimby, Phineas Parkhurst. The originator of "mind cure," a system of healing which profoundly influenced Mary Baker Eddy, the founder of Christian Science.

Quinary. The mystical arrangement of five elements, which could be five colors, five planets, or five occult innovations.

Quindecem Viri. In ancient Rome the 15 priests who were the guardians and interpreters of the Sibylline Books (q.v.).

Quintessence. The name that Pythagoras (q.v.) gave to the fifth element—the first four being fire, air, earth and water. This fifth element is the celestial ether or astral light that fills the universal space, and owing to its power it is believed to contain the total secrets of ESP and the complete domain of the occult.

Quiradelli, Corneille. French 17th century Franciscan priest who was both an astrologer and the author of several works on astrology.

Q'umran Community. A Jewish monastic sect which existed from the end of the second century B.C. to A.D. 70. Their headquarters was a building at Khirbet Q'umran, on the edge of the valley Wady Q'umran. It was here that the famous Dead Sea Scrolls were written. From these writings, we may deduce that they were probably a branch of the Essenes who, like them, were ascetic, ritualistic, and practiced healing and community of ownership—rules which were strictly observed. Some have found reason to believe that Jesus was an Essene or a member of a similar sect. However, lacking direct evidence, and from what we do know of his character, this is not consistent. Some of his teachings regarding property are similar, but Jesus, a non-ascetic in eating and drinking, friend of prostitutes and sinners, by teaching that the Sabbath was made for man, diametrically opposed monastic ideas of his times.

Qu'ran (Meaning that which is uttered or recited). The sacred writing of Islam. The work of Muhammad under divine inspiration. The first "Sura" of the Qu'ran was revealed to him in fiery letters written on a cloth.

Qu-Tamy. Among the Chaldeans the priest who in mystic trance envisions revelations from the moon goddess.

Ra. In ancient Egyptian mythology, the creator of the world and of men; the world's soul, the god of the sun.

Rabdos. The demon who symbolizes the most potent object of magical power, the wand.

Radiations, Human. See Emanations.

Radical. In astrology, the horoscope at the moment of birth, called the radix or radical map. In the more complicated horary astrology it indicates the zodiacal map which judgment perceives is most likely to lead to the right answer to a question, called "birth of a question."

Radiesthesia. The theory that dowsing with rod or pendulum operates by the instrumental detection of subtle radiations from the hidden substance. Dowsing practice on these lines.

Ragnarok. In the ancient mythology of Scandinavia this is the world's ultimate destiny, being that event which is the twilight of the world.

Rahab (Judaism). The Archangel who is the Prince of the Sea, in the ten angelic "Hosts of Heaven."

Rahamin (Cabalism). Represents the sixth of the ten sepiroth (q.v.), meaning "the compassion of God."

Rahu (Hinduism). The greatly feared demon snake who is believed to have almost swallowed the sun during an eclipse. Rites are used to this day against this monster during a period of eclipse of the sun.

Rainbow. One of the impressive heavenly phenomena that has stimulated much mythological and religious symbolism. By many it was deemed a bridge between heaven and earth, particularly in Norse mythology; for the American Indians it represented a serpent; for the ancient Israelites it was God's promise never again to bring a flood upon the world.

Raja-Yoga (Hinduism). An advanced system of Yoga (q.v.) which enables the devotee to achieve a high state of consciousness through more developed meditation. The stimulation of the consciousness in the practice of Raja-Yoga reveals the difference between the true inner self and that which the individual believes to be himself.

Rakshasa (Hinduism). A kind of goblin or evil spirit.

Rama (Hinduism). Rama-chandra, which is the seventh incarnation of Vishnu.

Ramakrishna (1834–1886). Well-known modernist reformer of Hinduism. Swami Vivekananda was his disciple.

Ramanuja (Hinduism). Profound philosopher and religious thinker of the 11th century A.D. whose re-examination of Vishnuism and the Vedanta (q.v.) led him to the insight that the world and the soul was a transformation of God diversely exhibited.

Ramganny (Hinduism). A dancing girl who exercises her talents in some Hindu temples in order to excite desire in the spectators.

Rangi. In the mythology of New Zealand the divinity of heaven or the sky-space who was married to the Earth Mother.

Rap. Sounds produced by physical mediumship. They may simulate almost any known sound, and are said to be produced by beating actions of slender ectoplasmic rods.

Raphael (Judaism). One of the ten Archangels who is the Prince of Healing and carries on high to the Throne of Mercy the repentant prayers of man.

Rapport. An intimate community of sensation, such as exists between hypnotist and subject, control and medium, object and psychometrist, or in telepathy, sender and recipient.

Rashnu (Zoroastrianism). One of the three judges who weigh the souls of the dead when they are put on a scale.

Rasputin, Grigori Efimovich (1872–1916). In all the annals of mankind few have achieved such enormous political power as this uneducated Russian peasant—solely on the basis of his abilities as a mystic, psychic, and healer. Trained as a monk in his village in Western Siberia, he came to St. Petersburg in 1903, quickly won his way through his magnetic personality into aristocratic society as a mystic, and in 1905 was introduced to Empress Alexandria. His curative powers helped the hemophiliac Tsarevich Alexis, while his charismatic, hypnotic powers led the Empress to believe him a saint sent to save the royal family. For several years during World War I, he was the sole head of the Russian government for all domestic affairs. A notorious debauchee, and unquestionably corrupt, he was also the undoubted possessor of enormous psychic talents and curative powers. Fearing his absolute domination of imperial Russia's government, a cabal within the royal family murdered Rasputin in 1916.

Rati (Hinduism, Buddhism). The Venus of the Hindus, representing "Love, Desire," who is the goddess of sexual delight. She is the wife of Kama, the god of love. In Buddhism, Rati is the daughter of Mara (q.v.) the killer, death, the evil principle.

Rationalists. Those philosophers who oppose the Empiricists such as: Descartes, Spinoza and Leibnitz. The rationalists believe that logical reason can arrive at truths independent of sense experience.

Raymond. Son of Sir Oliver Lodge (q.v.). The famous book of that name provided evidence for his survival in the spirit world.

Rays. In the ancient Akkadian culture of the Near East, the power which all gods possessed. If one god was able to steal the rays of another, the latter's power was destroyed.

Receptivity. (Spiritualism) A mental condition necessary for mediumship. Only by quietude and the stilling of one's thoughts can the first faint beginnings of spirit communication be recognized. It is important to note that the ability to become receptive should be under control of the medium's will. A regulated channel, not an open one, is the ideal.

Rectification. In astrology that special skill which is used to correct the time of birth through compiling the history of a person's life and aligning it with the proper planetary positions, aspects, conjunctions, etc.

Red. As an auric color, red symbolizes passion and anger.

Red Pigs. Formerly in Ireland witches were believed able to turn straw or hay into red pigs which they then sold. But buyers driving them home found that when their red pigs crossed running water they became transformed to the original straw and hay.

Reese, Bert (1851–1926). American-Polish clairvoyant medium. Once when arrested for disorderly conduct, he proved his powers in court by reading sealed messages. He was acquitted.

Refranation. In astrology, in the branch called horary astrology, this describes the situation of two planets which are applying to an aspect (q.v.) of each other. When one turns retrograde before the aspect is completed, this is an indication that it is refraining its influence, and a sign that the situation being studied will not achieve a successful materialization.

Regurgitation. An imitation of physical phenomena produced by swallowing flimsy material before the seance, its subsequent regurgitation purporting to be ectoplasm. Adequate tests have been devised which makes this deception impossible under controlled conditions.

Reichenbach, Baron. The famous pioneer psychic researcher who in 1840 discovered and named an emanation of the human body as odic force. He also experimented with sensitives who could perceive radiations from magnets in the dark. Reichenbach wrote several important works which have been translated into English.

Reincarnation. The theory that the soul can return to earth many times. A fundamental doctrine widely accepted by Eastern tradition, Hinduism and Buddhism. It was also taught by the Essenes, with whom Jesus may have had some contact. Josephus, the historian, refers to it as a common belief among the Jews at that time. In modern times the Theosophists accepted it as a central doctrine. Allan Kardec (q.v.) of France based his "Spiritist" teachings on it. He explicates this doctrine in his *Book of the Spirits*, which is still widely read and accepted by South American Spiritualists and many other groups.

Religion. A system of faith and worship, usually of a God or gods, or of a Higher Power. It implies the binding of man to God.

Religion of Spiritualism. Spiritualism is an accepted religion in England and many other countries. It asserts that man is a spirit and part of the Great Spirit; that he honors and serves God by serving his fellow man. The faith of a Spiritualist rests on knowledge—the unshakeable conviction through personal evidence that man's spirit is indestructible and survives death. Organized Spiritualism has its churches and ministers, but no priesthood. The mouthpieces of the World Spirit, the mediums, are allowed to speak directly to the people, bringing solace and comfort.

Repulsion. The opposite of attraction, caused by mental disharmony. An inexplicable aversion to a person could be explained by the incompatability of the respective auras.

Rescue Circles. See Circle, Rescue.

Resurrection. In Christianity, it is based on the physical resurrection of Jesus. But the death and sometimes resurrection of a god is one of the oldest myths in human history and is generally related to fertility rites, chiefly of vegetation. A few examples are: the Egyptian Osiris, the Phrygian and Lydian Attis, the Hittite Telepinus, the Babylonian Tammuz, and the Cyprian Adonis (qq.v.).

Retrocognition. Knowledge of the past, supernormally acquired.

Retrocognitive Clairvoyance. Term in parapsychology for an extrasensory correspondence between a present mental pattern of A and a physical event which happened in the past.

Retrograde. In astrology, the apparent backward motion of a planet. This event can have a marked effect on a person's activities, for that planet's influence is considered to have become weak or on the wane.

Retroversion. The procedure during satanic rites of reciting backwards prayers—supplications, verbal rituals, and of writing backwards occult names and invocations.

Reuchlin, Johannes (1455-1522). Christian scholar and humanist whose Judaic knowledge enabled him to write both a Hebrew grammar and several notable compilations of Cabalistic works.

Revelation. A communication to man of the divine will. The multiplicity of means by which this has occurred include oracular pronouncements, dreams, visions, ecstatic experiences; through books, prophets, storms; or by the most ordinary of means, such as sudden intuition or long meditation.

Revivals. Revivalists of religious fervor and enthusiasm have been noted for a variety of psychic phenomena. It is recorded that strange music, healing, prophecy, the gift of tongues (xenoglossy), are characteristic upsurges of exaltation.

Rhabdic Force. See Dowsing, Rhabdomancy.

Rhabdomancy. Water-divining, dowsing.

Rhasis (c. 850-932). Arabian philosopher, physician, and alchemist, whose wide experiments in medicine and chemistry enabled him to discover a number of chemical compounds such as borax and orpiment. He wrote, it is said, some 226 books, on many subjects, but his works on medicine and alchemy exercised an important influence as late as the 17th century.

Rhine, Joseph Banks (1895-   ). Though he is famous as one of the early and best known experimenters in parapsychology, Rhine actually began his career as a botanist and a teacher of physiology. What drastically altered his career was the research in extrasensory perception of the eminent psychologist William McDougall (q.v.) whose work first inspired him to pursue the study of the paranormal. Then later, with the help of McDougall he set up the epoch-making laboratory in parapsychology at Duke University in 1928. Here Rhine's work in telepathy, clairvoyance, precognition, and psychokinesis (qq.v.) was immensely impressive to a large number of psychologists. So much so, that it served to establish a permanent interest in parapsychology both in America and Europe: particularly, research centers in England, the Netherlands, Czechoslavakia, and Russia. Equally important were his many notable books and his popular lectures on the subject, which stimulated and developed a very large public to a marked interest in paranormal phenomena. Despite the fact that his work contradicted the prevailing scientific and psychological doctrines of his time, parapsychology rather soon became a respected scientific discipline in many universities in the United States. In his research, Rhine utilized a deck of 25 Zener cards (q.v.) for most of his experiments in extrasensory perception. However, after the initially striking impact of Rhine's work became an every-day phenomenon of his fellow psychologists, there followed a sizeable critical reaction: much of the criticism focused on the questionable rigor of the scientific control that had been used to obtain his unusual results. With the years, however, the development of more sophisticated and stringent techniques that have been instituted by Rhine in his research (and, of course, by other parapsychologists) has given their discipline a far greater credibility, and, consequently, diminished the amount of criticism from the skeptical scientific community. Rhine has been keenly aware of the difficulties involved in carrying out his sensitive and multi-dimensional experiments in parapsychology (for example, the fact that there are very few subjects who are able to display paranormal talents for a long period of time; or the fact that it may frequently be difficult to repeat successful experiments in other laboratories). But he has never wavered in his defense of parapsychology's immense importance both to science and to man, and in his belief in the certainty that human beings do possess paranormal abilities. Thus, it has been the persistence of his interests despite the array of criticism, the success of his efforts to attract outstanding colleagues, and the radically challenging nature of his results that have played a remarkable part in making parapsychology a major adjunct of contemporary psychology and an enlightening subject to Americans and much of the literate world. (See: *Extra-Sensory Perception*, 1934; *New Frontiers of the Mind*, 1937; *The Reach of the Mind*, 1947; *New World of the Mind*, 1953; Co-author of: *Extra-Sensory Perception After Sixty Years*, 1940; *Parapsychology: From Duke to Fram*, 1965. See also these entries: Extrasensory Perception; Sigmund Freud; Wm. James; Parapsychology; Parapsychology in U.S. Colleges; Charles Richet; Gertrude Schmeidler; S.G. Soal)

Ric (Hinduism). The most important of the four Vedas which make up the Rig-Veda (q.v.). It is believed to have been compiled in the third millenium B.C., and to contain parts even older than the Aryan immigration into India.

Richard of Saint Victor (d. 1173). Scottish Christian mystic who was prior of the Abbey of St. Victor in Paris. His contribution to Roman Catholic mysticism was uniquely demonstrated in the unusual clarity of his presentation of the six stages of mystic contemplation developed in his books *Benjamin Major* and *Benjamin Minor*.

Richet, Charles (1850–1935). This eminent psychic researcher was Professor of Physiology at the Faculty of Medicine in Paris, Hon. President of the Society of Universal Psychic Studies, President of S.P.R. in 1895, and President of Institut Metapsychique Internationale. In 1875 he dealt a death-blow to "animal magnetism" by proving that hypnotism was psychological, and had nothing to do with magnetic fluids. Richet introduced card-guessing into paranormal experiments; these eventually developed into the famous Zener Cards (q.v.) now universally used by parapsychologists.

Richmond, Mrs. Cora L. V. (Cora Scott, Cora Tappan). (1840–1923). American speaker and healing medium, who was famous at sixteen years of age for her inspirational addresses and lectures. She was appointed pastor of the First Society of Spiritualists in Chicago, and assisted later in founding the National Spiritualist Association. Mrs. Richmond was a prolific author and a very popular lecturer.

Ridiah (Judaism). The Archangel who is the Prince of Rain, in the ten angelic hosts or categories.

Ridley, Miss Hazel. American direct voice medium. Her voices were whispers proceeding from the larynx with no movement of mouth, lips or tongue. In a test of her powers Dr. Wilson G. Bailey, physician of New Jersey, filled her mouth with liquids, but the voice was unaffected.

Rig-Veda (Royal Veda). Earliest Vedic book of sacred Indian literature, consisting of ten books containing over a thousand hymns in archaic Sanskrit. Its creation is generally dated between 1000-800 B.C., but it was not written down for many centuries.

Right-Hand Path. "The Path of Light," which throughout esoteric writings opposes the "Path of Darkness," the "Left-Hand Path." In ancient Greece, those in the Right-Hand Path mount to Olympus, those of the Left Hand take the path to spiritual death.

Ring-Pass-Not. This mystical concept describes the circle of bounds belonging to those whose consciousness is blinded by the illusion of separateness. After a certain level of the unfolding consciousness, there are those who are blocked by delusion from ascending to a higher stage.

Rishi. A venerable title which signifies an inspired poet or sage. That Rishi is a venerable appellation is confirmed by the legend that the great hymns of the Veda (q.v.) were first revealed to Rishis—the sacred "seven Rishis" who are designated the prajapatis, meaning the children born of the mind of Brahma (q.v.).

Rising Sign. In astrology this is the sign which is rising on the eastern horizon at the moment of birth.

Rochas, Eugene (1837–1914). A renowned French psychic researcher and author who studied human emanations, hypnotism, reincarnation and physical phenomena. Rochas founded the well-known theory of "exteriorization of motricity."

Rolle, Richard, of Hampole (c. 1300–1349). This unique English mystic who never completed his studies at Oxford University nor took priest's orders, was yet one of the most learned men of his time. He exercised an important influence on a number of religious communities while he lived and continued to attract religionists for centuries after his death. His works in Latin and English are models of interesting writing and are imbued with the persuasive emotion of an enraptured mystic who refers to his ecstacy as "fire, sweetness, and song." See: *The Commandment of Love to God, Form of Perfect Living.*

Ronach (Cabalism). That middle level of life which confronts the astral world (q.v.).

Rood. Generally a crucifix symbolizing the cross of Christ, though it may mean any cross or crucifix.

Rooster. Since ancient times a bird used by the Greeks and others in augury and occult manifestations. Its crowing before midnight in any vicinity was considered a certain omen of death in that vicinity. Further, as the herald of the dawn, it symbolized resurrection and rebirth.

Root Races. Theosophical doctrine asserts that mankind's evolution passes through a Round on earth, these embodying the seven Root Races. Each Root Race's development suffers a racial cataclysm when it has completed half of its cycle. Following this view, our own Fifth Root-Race will endure such a cataclysm about 18,000 years in the future. The history of the Root Races included the Adamic, Hyperborean, Lemurian, Atlantean, Aryan, and two more still to come.

Rose. Since ancient times the rose has generated many occult, religious, mythological, and mystical beliefs. In Hinduism, one of the wives of Vishnu was found in a rose; Eros in Greek mythology gave a rose to the god of silence; in Rome, on Rose Sunday, the rose was blessed; among Muslims in the Orient it is believed that a tear of Mohammed's created the rose; in certain parts of the British Isles, it is believed a red rose will not bloom over a grave; and, too, since the most early times roses were used as a powerful ingredient in love philters. The Rosicrucians view the "rosy cross" as a transcendent mystic symbol. In the occult there is a prevailing view that demons, witches, vampires, and werewolves cannot touch or smell a rose.

Rose of Lima, Saint (1586–1617). The patron saint of South America, she was the first person born in the Americas to be canonized by the Roman Catholic Church. Against extraordinary opposition of family and friends, she lived a life of seclusion, virginity, and mystical adoration of Christ, God, and the way of heavenly purity.

Rosenkreutz, Christian. Some believe that he was the founder of the spiritual and mystic Rosicrucian Order in the fifteenth century. Other authorities believe he was initiated into the doctrine and became its most important proponent, thus developing a spiritual program that had a very significant effect on later mysticism, aspects of Christianity, and the occult. (See: Rosicrucianism).

Rosicrucianism, A.M.O.R.C. A secret society which flourished in the fifteenth and sixteenth centuries, alleged to have been founded by a German, Rosenkreutz (q.v.) about 1430. They practiced healing, occultism and alchemy. There is an occult society of this name in existence today, with a metaphysical teaching designed to awaken dormant faculties. Their symbol is a rose in the center of a cross; they claim a traditional association with the "Great White Brotherhood" of Egypt, which was established in 1500 B.C.

Rowan Tree. According to a Scandinavian folk legend, the occult powers of this tree enabled it to shield one against malevolent influences.

Ruach (Judaism). The breath of God's ineffable soul which at the creation of man in his own image, God breathed into man's body. Thus, according to the Talmud, developed the notion "God the Father" that became of signal importance in Christianity. Ruach, however, is a transcendently important concept in Judaism, for it also refers to the Schechinah (q.v.); it made man related to God as his child; it was the immortal element of the body; and it was the Ruach which enabled man, finally, to attain Gan Eden, meaning Paradise. For the Cabalists, in the *Zohar*, the Ruach is a larger mystical symbol, describing it there as "The soul is the daughter of God."

Rudra (Buddhism, Hinduism). God of storms, father of the Rudras and Maruts, and sometimes called the god of fire.

Rule, Margaret. In the great New England witch trials, Margaret Rule admitted that she was possessed by both a "white spirit" and by the Devil himself.

Ruler. In astrology, this signifies the planet which is associated with a sign. For example, Mars has the rule of Aries (q.v.); Venus has the rule of Taurus and Libra (qq.v.); Mercury rules Gemini (q.v.); the Moon rules Cancer (q.v.); the Sun, Leo (q.v.); Mercury, Virgo (q.v.); Pluto, Scorpio (q.v.); Jupiter, Saggitarius (q.v.); Saturn, Capricorn (q.v.); Uranus, Aquarius (q.v.); and Neptune, Pisces (q.v.). However, some astrologers feel the old Ptolemaic concept no longer is valid in view of our greater knowledge of astronomy, the vast distances in space, and the incommensurate size of the bodies—for example, the Moon compared to the Sun.

Runes. Used by the Germanic peoples from about the 3rd century A.D., the word means a secret, a mystery. Early in history this Runic alphabet was an integral element of magic, and divination in the Germanic and Anglo-Saxon world. It was Woden who underwent a titanic ordeal upon the world-ash Yggdrasil (q.v.) in order to obtain the Runes for mankind. Runes have been held to possess the power to resurrect the dead, also to assist in fertility, love, and magic. The Druids (q.v.) were believed to be the wizards who most knew the profound secrets of Rune-magic.

Ruskin, John (1819–1900). This eminent English author, art historian and art critic was an adherent of Spiritualism.

Russian Paranormal Research. In recent years, following the lead of British and American work in psychic exploration, the Russians have devoted much effort in this area. Experiments with such subjects as Ninel Kulagina (q.v.) and Rosa Kuleshova (q.v.), and telepathy, etc. highlight their on-going researches. Russian interest in the paranormal is further demonstrated by the Laboratorie De Cybernetique, based at the University of Leningrad in Moscow, which is now engaged in organizing, world-wide, a universal parapsychological and psychotronic congress to pool paranormal developments.

Ruta. In the legend of Atlantis (q.v.) this was an island that belonged to the Kingdom of Atlantis (q.v.).

Ruysbroeck, John (1293–1381). This Dutch Brabrantine monk was one of the Roman Catholic Church's most evocative and influential mystics. Both by his character and religious wisdom he exercised a profound and lasting religious change in much of Northern Europe. To his hermitage at Groenendael, where he was prior of a small, select religious community, came numerous visitors, notably Gerard Groote. Through Groote, founder of the Brothers of the Common Life (q.v.),

Ruysbroeck's mystical message of the soul's ascent to God spread to many countries. His writings are among the finest in Christian mysticism. (See: *The Book of Supreme Truth, The Kingdom of the Lovers of God, The Adornment of the Spiritual Marriage*)

S.A.G.B. Spiritualist Association of Great Britain (q.v.).

Sabbatai Zevi (Judaism) (1626–1676). Cabalist-"Messiah"—one of the most sensational of the many self-anointed "Messiahs"—who had captured the hopes of the persecuted Jewish people over a long period of nearly 1700 years. Born in Izmir, Turkey, where he became an expert in the Cabala, mysticism, and esoteric messianic prophecy, at 22 he proclaimed himself the "Messiah." Sabbatai's youth, his good looks, his absolute assurance, swept up the tortured Jews of Europe and North Africa in a frenzy of adoration and belief, and when he announced in 1666 that he would topple the Sultan of Turkey (ruler of the Holy Land) and lead the Jews back to Mt. Zion, belief became glorious certainty. But Sabbatai was but another false Messiah, and he crushed the wild delirium of millions of Jews by succumbing to a threat of death by the Sultan and converting to Mohammedanism. He was the last of the "great" line of Cabalists, to crown himself with the title of "Messiah."

Sabbath (Judaism). Borrowed from the Sumerian "Shabattu" meaning "a calming of the heart," where it was observed as a holiday every seventh day beginning with the full moon festival for Nananar, the moon god. The Babylonians honored Shabbattu as a day of penitential reflection. Since these astronomically minded people discovered the lunar month of twenty-eight days, the quarter phases were probably black-listed for astrological reasons: the moon would be in square aspect to its full position, considered unpropitious for activity. This may provide a reason behind the traditional rest on the Sabbath, and the mystical powers of seven generally. It had a great influence, however, on Judaism.

Sabbath Lights (Judaism–Cabalism). In the Talmud the Jewish wife is commanded to usher in the Sabbath with the Kindling of the Sabbath Lights on Friday just before sundown. The Cabalists saw in this rite a mystical light of the woman's soul. They originated the custom of closing the eyes after lighting the candles so the woman could inwardly pray to God.

Sabbathi. The angel of the celestial hierarchies who is assigned the sphere of Saturn. Being the recipient from the Holy Spirit of the divine light, he gives it to the members of his Kingdom.

Sacerdotalism. Any religious system based on order, rather than human and spiritual values.

Sacra. Denoting sacred objects.

Sacra Privata. In ancient Rome the father of a household was a priest and his children acolytes in the religious ceremonials of the Lares, Penates, and Vesta (qq.v.).

Sacramental Meal. The ritual meal, a cardinal element of many religions, which symbolizes either identity with a divinity or absorption of the divinity into the worshipper's body. Christianity's paschal lamb (Christ crucified), the Eucharist's Holy Communion bread-and-wine which is eaten and drunk, and the glorifying of the sacramental meal (or mass) by making it the focal ritual, exemplify this tradition.

Sacred Writings. The most widely distributed forms are the chanted hymns of many religions.

Sacrifice, White Dog. Among the American Iroquois Indians the celebration of the New Year was observed by the ritual of sacrificing a white dog. The god Teharonhiawagon, who symbolizes life, stimulated this annual ceremony.

Sadhu (Hinduism). A holy person or religious teacher, who carries a bowl for begging, a staff, rosary, water pot, and brush. At death, he is buried in a sitting position, since he is believed to be merely in a trance.

Saggitarius. Astrological sign (November 23–December 22). Element— fire; Symbol—Centaur; Ruling planet—Jupiter. Qualities— highly endowed with mental gifts, discriminatory abilities; unusually honest, fearless, and bluntly outspoken; sensitive to suffering; a keen eye for the satiric and comic. Negatively, Saggitarius can be too suspicious, and when they must reflect on a situation can be too timid and cautious; have a hasty temper; and tend to respond in extremes to life's events. Being persons with highly complex natures and insights, they are often misunderstood.

Saint-Germain, Comte de (c. 1696–1784). One of the charismatic figures of 18th century Europe, whose fame as an occultist is celebrated in a voluminous history of biographical incidents, many of them, however, being quite legendary. His travels through much of Europe where he astounded many with his alchemical displays of turning base metals into gold and his skills as a magician and as a seer, plus his gifted diplomatic maneuvers for the French government—in Holland, England, and Italy, made him renowned.

Saint-Martin, Louis Claude de (1743–1803). French Rosicrucian, Cabalist, and mystic, his wide learning in the occult made him a master of many influences. From an early study of Rosicrucianism, he turned to the mysticism of the Spanish writer Martinez Pasquales, but it was the German mystic Jacob Boehme who most deeply influenced his mature conceptions. Under the name of *le philosophe inconnu* (the unknown philosopher) he wrote a number of important works, notably *The Error and Truth of Men*, and a study of the Tarot. His translations of Boehme, and his *Theosophic Correspondence* are significant aspects of his life-work.

Saint Paul. The story of Christianity is in large part the work of one of the greatest teachers and proselytizers in the history of religion. Coming from a well-to-do Jewish family, trained in the most advanced learning and best schools of his time, he was, nonetheless, a deeply religious person who had absorbed and dismissed the Greek skepticism of his age. As a learned, orthodox Jew, he saw every deviation as a grave threat to Judaism and acted zealously to prosecute heretics. Then came the shattering mystical revelation on the way to Damascus which completely altered not only the life of St. Paul, but the whole history of the Western world. He was a man possessed, in the finest and noblest sense of the word, and henceforth he spoke with the authority of a prophet and the style of a great writer. His memorable concepts and phrases have enriched the language of the West. If today we criticize his formalism, when compared to Christ's all-embracing humanism, he was, unquestionably, a profound and extraordinary religious teacher.

Sakti (Hinduism - Lamaism). That supernatural power which Hindus believe is able to protect one against the evil eye. It refers also to the female component or energy in the gods. In its use in art it is symbolized as a triangle that points downward. In Tibetan art, however, it demonstrates a unity of the male and female elements, being depicted by the sexual embrace of the god and his Sakti.

Samadhi (Hinduism - Buddhism). The eighth stage of Yoga; said to be the highest attainable earthly state. Samadhi is a deep trance of higher contemplation, and a complete temporary renunciation of earth life and the body's needs. Some yogis are alleged to have passed their remaining time on earth in this state, ending their days bricked up in a sanctuary by their faithful disciples. In Buddhism it represents the contemplation of reality to the point of spiritual ecstasy developed through the total erasure of all sense of separateness. In Hinduism, however, as described above, it is that exalted state which is achieved in Yoga practice through meditation.

Samadhi (Hinduism - Buddhism). Represents the ultimate goal and the last stage (the eighth stage) in the discipline of Yoga (q.v.). Samadhi in the Sanskrit means "to direct towards" with the idea that the mind is moving towards an object. In this stage—which is a deep trance of higher contemplation and the point at which the practitioner is merged with the "object" of meditation, the Yogi master achieves a remarkable polarity—he is at once totally within the self and totally outside the self. So complete is the achievement of "union" with the inner self and also with the cosmos that there is a mystic sense of absolute blessedness and serenity. This state tends to give proof of certain bold insights in the Upanishads declaring that the self is God (a view, by the way, quite embarassing to almost all Upanishad teachers and therefore suppressed; but see the Upanishads: Chandogya (6.8.7), and Barandaranyaka (2.5.19). Yet samadhi gives evidence of an actual union of one's self and one's inner god, along with an extraordinary receptivity to the cosmos and its processes. It has even been claimed that some Yogis have passed their time on earth in this state, and have ended their days sealed within a sanctuary. While the fact of the attainment of samadhi has been known and experienced by many devotees of Yoga throughout Asia, it is only in recent years, however, that the scientific community of both the East and West have begun to study and understand its profound importance for mankind. In doing so, they have discovered startling proof of the phenomenal control that can be achieved through the combined actions of belief, discipline, and will. The breakthrough occurred in 1957 with the work of the Indian physiologists Annand, Chhina, and Singh, and in the 1960s through the investigations of the Indian neurophysiologists Drs. Bagchi and Wenger on Yogis and Zen monks; and later in a number of universities in the United States and at the Menninger Foundation under a research team directed by Dr. Elmer Green who made studies of the Indian Yogi Swami Rama. Suddenly and dramatically, the tables were turned: all the claims Yogi Masters had been making for many centuries were discovered to be perfectly true—remarkably substantiated; overnight, holy medical dogma about the impossibility of controlling the autonomic nervous system was exploded, proven to be completely fallacious. Master Yogis could with the greatest of ease *control* their autonomic nervous systems. At will, with no strain, they could change their brain waves, their heart rate, their blood pressure, their body temperature, their respiration level, the electrical resistance of their skin; and, in addition, totally ignore all outside sense stimuli— loud banging noises, burning objects applied to the skin, and even freezing temperatures. These revolutionary studies, having destroyed long-held medical laws, opened the way in the late 1960s and 1970s for a flood of new information in the area of biofeedback (q.v.). Samadhi, then, as a result of the belated research done on this mind-body state has played an epochal role in freeing the Western mind. It is now an acknowledged fact that those who have mastered the highest stages of Yoga (an ability achieved, however, only after years of persistent practice) possess a technique and have reached a level of being which brings extraordinary benefits and enormously alters their states of consciousness.

Samana (Buddhism). The individual who labors to gain salvation.

Samanera (Buddhism). An initiate, considered a novice; a beginner on the path of spiritual development.

Samma (Buddhism). The supreme apex. Also describes each step of the noble eightfold path.

Samsara. Hindu term for the karmic chain of birth, death and rebirth on earth. Release from this chain is only to be gained by Yoga practices (identification of the Smaller Self with the Absolute Self).

Samuel, Rabbi. The twelfth century French-centered Cabalist, famous in legend for the Golem (q.v.) he was said to have created. Although he was unable to make his golem talk (as other golems reputedly could—particularly Solomon Ibn Gabriol's maid-servant golem in 11th century Spain, and the golem of Chelm in 16th century Poland), wherever Rabbi Samuel went his golem followed him both as bodyguard and servant.

Sand Painting. Ceremonial earth painting created by American Indians of the Southwest which are kept in strictest secrecy (though a few strangers have observed them). Some of them depict lightning and the gods. The Navaho, makers of the most notable sand paintings—some of which are ten feet wide—complete and destroy them within the same day. Only five colors of painted sand are used: red, white, yellow, black and gray-blue.

Sand Reading. A personal psychic assessment of the imprint of the client's hand in a tray of sand.

Sanga (Hinduism). The attachment to material and wordly things and cares which thwarts the achievement of *moksa* (q.v.).

Sankara. One of the greatest of Indian philosophers, he upheld Brahmanism. He died about 820 A.D. His famous commentary on the Vedanta (q.v.) established the doctrine of *advaita* (q.v.).

Sankhya (Hinduism). One of the oldest systems of Hindu philosophy, it was founded by Kapila in 600 B.C. It was dualistic, postulating a positive equilibrium of spirit and substance, eternal without prime cause. Plurality of selves was held to be the consequence of the balance being upset. It develops the concept that spirit (*purusa*, q.v.) and matter, the basic cosmic elements, must be joined in order to generate world evolution.

Sankhyas (Hinduism). Followers of the Sankhya (q.v.) school of Hindu philosophy. Buddhist philosophy has been strongly influenced by this teaching.

Sannyasin (Hinduism). Those Brahmans who have achieved the highest level of their religious lives.

Sapphire. This gem is a rare stone which has been widely used as a charm, for it is considered to possess powers which bring the owner good luck, health, and cures for a number of ailments.

Sarjent, Epes (1813–1880). He was an early American psychic researcher and editor. Epes studied mesmerism in 1837 and drew public attention to the famous Hydesville phenomena (q.v.). He wrote many works on Spiritualism.

Saros. In ancient astrology, the Chaldeans and Babylonians, by using the number 60 as a base figure, developed the concept of the saros; this was a lunar cycle of 6,585.32 days, equaling 223 lunations (q.v.) or 18 years, 11-1/3 days. These astronomical observations enabled the Chaldeans and Babylonians to make more accurate astrological predictions than had ever been made before. Further, it enabled them to predict eclipses. At the end of a saros the centers of the sun and moon return during this period to almost the same sequence they had had at the start of the saros.

Sarva (Hinduism). The deity of the Vedas who is "The Destroyer," which later became a name of Siva and one of the Rudras.

Sarvajna Vishnu (Hinduism). "All-Knowing Vishnu."

Sarvakartriva (Hinduism). The ground principle of the universe which in its dynamic creativity is the source of all that exists.

Satan. The principle of evil in a number of major religions, notably—Judaism, Christianity, and such ancient religions as Zoroastrianism and Manichaeism. Having been an angel in heaven, when he rebelled against God he and a host of minor angels, henceforth known as devils, were condemned to eternal damnation in Hell. Satan's activity on the earth is chiefly the destruction of souls, either through buying them by means of granting a term of magical powers, or through temptation by way of sexual gratifications. While Lucifer is the name for Satan sanctioned by doctrine, he is also called: Abaddon, Apollyon, Asmodeus, Beelzebub, and Belial; and also by such titles as Dragon, Serpent, Evil One, God of this World, Prince of Darkness, Prince of the Devils, Prince of the Power of the Air, Prince of this World, and the Tempter. Satan has been an enormously pregnant figure in much of the Western Occult, particularly in Necromancy, Sorcery, Witchcraft, Black Magic; and such religious movements as the Cathar, and the Albigenses (qq.v.). He is the reigning deity in the celebration of the Black Mass (q.v.).

Satanic-Occult Films. From the very start, the film medium provided film makers with the fluidity and range to explore the development of satanic and occult movies. George Méliès, French magician and the first film director who began making moving pictures in the 1890's, utilized fantasy and satanism, giant gods and devils, in his short films, and expanded his notions of the fantastic in his 1902 film "A Trip to the Moon." In America, the Edison and Biograph film companies, in 1909, did versions of the popular George Arliss play, "The Devil"; but the year before, 1908, "Dr. Jekyll and Mr. Hyde" was produced by the Selig Polyscope Company, a story that has become the most often produced of all horror stories. "Frankenstein" was screened in 1910 by Edison, and under the title of "Life without a Soul" and was again produced in 1915. Back in Europe, in 1913, "The Student of Prague" was a film with the story of a student pursued by his evil double; in 1915, came "The Golem" (q.v.) and in 1919, the production of that masterpiece "The Cabinet of Dr. Caligari." Meantime, in the United States, a steady stream of satanic-occult films continued with such popular productions, to name but a handful, as "Dracula" 1931, "The Cat People" 1942, "Werewolf" 1956, "The Devils" 1971, "Hex" a fine picture of witchcraft, magic, and mysticism, and "The Exorcist." a satanic blockbuster. Both of these recent films "Hex" and "The Exorcist" exhibit the skill, maturity, and fidelity to subject matter which is now invested in the creation of films that explore the world of the occult, the satanic, and also the paranormal.

Sataran.. In the religion of the ancient Sumerians this was the name of Tammuz (q.v.), a term signifying "The Serpent Goddess."

Satchidananda, Sri Swami. Revered Hindu spiritual leader and founder of the Integral Yoga Institute in the United States, he is also well known for his work in the world ecumenical movement as a director of the Center for Spiritual Studies. Born in 1914, and having worked in a number of occupations, at 28 he undertook his full spiritual quest, studied with a number of masters, and received sannyas (monkhood) initiation when he was only 35. He has been a Professor of Hatha and Raja Yoga at the Yoga Vedanta Forest University, and he has organized many Yoga centers throughout Southeast Asia. In 1966, during a global tour, he came to the United States, and won such an admiring response that his Integral Yoga Institute and its branch Ashrams have attracted many students. He is an ardent lover of modern music of all kinds, the author of *Integral Yoga Hatha*, and the recipient of the Martin Buber Award for outstanding service to humanity.

Sat-chit-ananda (Hinduism). The possessor of that blessedness resulting from an inner state of the highest qualities.

Sat-cit-ananda, Saccidananda (Hinduism). A Vedanta definition describing the highest reality; it is the Atman (q.v.) when it has evolved to complete realization.

Satellitium, Stellium. In astrology this signifies a cluster of sometimes as many as five planets in one sign or house (qq.v.). Although a cluster of five planets is an important satellitium, if the sun is present this increases its significance; and it is increased even more if the moon joins this type of multiple conjunction (q.v.). However, if there are only four planets, this cluster, too, is considered to be a major satellitium.

Sator Formula. In the long history of magic squares (q.v.), the Sator Formula ranks as the most famous. Its universal dominion is established in its omnipresence, for it has been found on ancient walls, on drinking vessels, etc. It is a formula for uncovering witches, obliterating fires, assuring the success of wishes, and a host of other uses. It is considered to be an anagram of *Pater Noster* and a formula of Alpha and Omega.

S A T O R
A R E P O
T E N E T
O P E R A
R O T A S

Satori. Zen Buddhist term for enlightenment produced by meditation.

Saturn. One of the most important planets in the history of mysticism and the occult. Among the ancient Hebrew mystics Saturn was the creator, through God, of the universe, and related, also, to the Archangel (q.v.) Oriphiel or Orichiel. In esoteric doctrine, it relates to the bone system in man, and to the whole physical organism. Violet is its color; it is the choleric temperament—fire; it symbolizes the Salamander. In Earth-evolution, the first stage is the Saturn epoch; in the week, it relates to Saturday. (See: Capricorn; Saturn Square; Saturn Chasing the Moon).

Saturn Chasing the Moon. In astrology, an affliction of the moon by Saturn (q.v.). Because their rates of progression can be relatively close, it is a very unfortunate aspect (q.v.) since it can often persist for a lifetime in a person's horoscope. But this infrequent type of affliction only results where the moon at birth is in conjunction, square, or opposition (qq.v.) to Saturn.

Saturn Square. A magic square (q.v.) which was used by the ancient Chinese to enlist the potent influence of Saturn (q.v.). Considered to be the oldest of all magic squares and described in the *I Ching* (q.v.), it is constructed of three rows of three figures because Saturn is the third sephira (q.v.). Through this instrumentality, God displayed his manifestation in creating the universe.

Saturnalia. A festival or period during which people engage in unrestrained freedom of behavior, widely different from their normal social actions. The famous Saturnalia in ancient Rome was a period of wild sexual license and a time in which the slaves and servants also behaved as the masters of their owners or employers. The name Saturnalia was derived from Saturn (q.v.), the creator of the universe and the vanquished ruler of the legendary Golden Age. Among African tribes, such as the Ashanti, the period of the Saturnalia enabled the people freely to speak out whatever grieved them or troubled their minds.

Saturnine. This term derives from astrology, meaning one with a dour temperament; in astrology it describes one with a strong Saturn accent.

Saul's Musical Cure (Judaism). When Saul, the ancient King of Israel, succumbed to a mental state of manic-depressiveness, the young David by his skillful harp playing drew the evil spirits out of the King and cured him. All through ancient Hebrew history music has been used by the professional school of prophets (the Hebrew soothsayers) to achieve a state of ecstacy in order to prophesy. Further, evil spirits were exorcised from victims by music, notably the seven sacred modes, each mode having a mystical affinity with a particular heavenly body and each mode curing a specific illness.

Savin. The Devil's herb, a plant used by European witches for the purposes of abortion and sterility.

Scapulomancy. Divination through the study of animal bones, particularly the cracks in the shoulder blade after it has been subjected to fire.

Scarab. In ancient Egypt a highly important amulet cut in the shape of a beetle. Derived from the god Khepara, who moved the sun across the sky as the beetle its ball, it was worshipped as a symbol of fertility and resurrection, used in funerary rites, and utilized by those of high status as a seal.

Scatcherd, Felicity. Writer and humanitarian, she was a keen student of psychical research, especially of psychic photography. (See: Skotograph)

Schelling, Friedrich Wilhelm Joseph von (1775-1854). One of Germany's eminent philosophers during the 18th and 19th centuries when German philosophy dominated Western thinking. Schelling was the founder of identity-philosophy, for he believed that man and the material world coincide in the Absolute (q.v.); that philosophy studies the development of spirit; that the world soul activates the whole; and, finally, that mysticism, the highest stage of human insight, brings man to a complete union with the absolute self in a mystic imperturbability.

Schiller, Ferdinand Canning Scott (1864-1937). The eminent British pragmatist philosopher who saw the creativity of the human mind as a basic factor in man's relationship to the universe. Schiller also believed that all matter was to some degree alive. For him, God was an omnipresent principal of goodness, who being finite was still struggling to develop. In addition to philosophy, Schiller (like William James q.v.)

was deeply interested in psychic phenomena and strove to further our knowledge of this human capacity. He was president of the S.P.R. (q.v.) in 1914 and author of "The Progress of Psychic Research" in the *Encyclopedia Britannica* 1920, and "Spiritism and Telepathy" in *Hasting's Encyclopedia of Religion and Ethics.* (See: *Problems of Belief,* 1924)

"Schlangenbalg." A notorious book of anti-semitism. The title means "Snakeskin," and the book was written by an apostate Jew, Samuel Friederich Brenz, in Germany in the 17th century. The author especially condemned the Cabalism and "golem-magic" practiced by the Jews.

Schmeidler, Gertrude R. (1912-). Professor Schmeidler along with J.B. Rhine, S.G. Soal, and Gardner Murphy, (qq.v.) was an academic pioneer in the study of parapsychology. She has taught psychology at Harvard, City College, and Barnard College. Her long experience in parapsychology has enabled her to write a number of illuminating articles and books on her experiments, notably "Rorschach Variables to ESP Scores," *Journal of the American Society for Psychical Research.* Another of her studies has revealed that people divide into two groups on the subject of parapsychology: those who believe in it, and those who doubt the existence of such human capacities. Dr. Schmeidler has made one of the most complete experiments to date on the personality traits of persons with greater-than-average psychic talents. See: *Extrasensory Perception*—1969; and with R. McConnell, *ESP and Personality Patterns*—1958.

Schneider Brothers, Rudi and Willy. Two outstanding physical mediums of recent times who were tested under the most stringent conditions. Of Willy's phenomena, over a hundred scientists declared conviction of its reality by demonstration under the most exacting tests. In 1924 he came to London and gave twelve sittings, demonstrating telekinetic phenomena for the S.P.R. Rudi was tested in the National Laboratory for Psychical Research, where a special "electric chair" device gave instant warning by light signals of the medium's movements. Under these conditions, breezes, levitations, telekinesis, and materialization of hands and arms were produced.

Schopenhauer, Arthur (1788-1866). Famous German pessimist whose philosophy describes the world as blind will; he counseled that the free man must subdue this blind will in himself through the Buddhist ideal of desirelessness. Schopenhauer, brilliant as both a writer and thinker, who very markedly influenced Western philosophy, described the Upanishads (q.v.) as one of the greatest books ever created. His own masterpiece is *The World as Will and Idea.*

Schrenck Notzing, Baron A. von (1862-1924). Distinguished German pioneer of psychical research. Physician and psychiatrist of Munich, authority on sexual anomalies and criminal psychopathy. He conducted experiments with every important medium of his time.

Schropfer, Johan Georg (1730-1774). One of Germany's historic occultists whose abilities as a necromancer (q.v.) made him the leader of a host of followers whom he initiated into the realm of occult lore.

Schuré, Edouard (1841-1929). French scholar and Theosophist who is best known for his classic work on the ancient mystery schools and the history of the occult—*The Great Initiates*. Often quoted by other writers, Schuré's book investigates the traditions in India, Egypt, and Greece, showing the evolution of esoteric developments in these cultures.

Schweitzer, Albert (1875-1965). A master of many disciplines, being a doctor of philosophy, of theology, and medicine, a world-renowned organist and Bach authority, he was also one of the twentieth century's most famous mystics. Born in Alsace, he early achieved fame as a theological scholar with his two books *The Quest of the Historical Jesus* (1906), and *Mysticism of Paul the Apostle* (1931). His ability as an organist and his biography of Bach made him a preeminent musician and musicologist. But he gave up numerous honors offered to him by the world's best universities when he was thirty to become a physician. In 1913, he opened his world-famous hospital, Lambarene in Gabon, Africa. His books on Africa are famous. His masterpiece, *Philosophy of Civilization*, sets out his theories on ethics, religion, and mysticism as he elaborates the grand theme that human progress depends on all men developing a dedicated "reverence for life."

Schwenkfeld, Kaspar (1490-1561). Coming nearly a hundred years before Boehme (q.v.), he was the first great Protestant mystic. He was a Silesian nobleman who saw the ritual of the church as a detriment to a direct and immediate awareness of Christ. Although denounced by Luther as a heretic, and the sect he influenced was persecuted, the group persisted. Eventually they became followers of Boehme and emigrated to the United States. The community they established near Philadelphia still flourishes.

Scientology. "The science of knowing how to know" according to the Hubbard Association of Scientologists. They employ a technique of "Dianetics" to uncover memories of previous incarnations.

Scopelism. A magical practice in which charmed bones are thrown into a neighbor's field, often to serve them warning not to cultivate the field if they do not wish to die by the malevolent arts of the bondthrower.

Scorpio. Astrological sign (October 24 - November 22). Element—water; Symbol—the Eagle and Scorpion; Ruling planet—Mars. Qualities—this sign has the widest range of the 12 signs. The natives possess intense loyalty to their abiding interests, are highly capable, enthusiastic, courageous, ultimately successful in their endeavors, and are generous and loyal to those they trust; however, they can be relentlessly revengeful, pugnacious, arrogant, violent in their moods and too wasteful of their emotional and sexual passions. Altogether, then, this is a highly capable and a difficult sign to understand.

Scot, Michael (c. 1175-1232). Scottish sorcerer at the Court of Emperor Frederick II, whose reputation was so widespread that the Italian poet Dante makes mention of his legendary powers.

Scriptograph. Messages alleged to have been written by deceased persons, often in their own handwriting, which appear on sensitive photographic materials without any exposure to light.

Scriptures. Sacred writings of various religions.

Scrolls, Dead Sea. See Dead Sea Scrolls.

Scrying. Divination through the art of crystal-gazing or water-gazing.

Seance. A session or sitting which is conducted by a spiritualist medium or where at least one of the participants possesses mediumistic powers. The purposes of the session may be to establish communication with the dead, or to obtain psychic manifestations, or to witness some form of paranormal phenomena.

Seance-Room. This should ideally be a room dedicated for this purpose and used for no other. It should be no larger than necessary, devoid of soft furnishings and draperies as far as possible, with plain wooden chairs and floor, facilities for soft red lighting and window shutters if required for physical phenomena.

Second Death (Spiritualism). Spiritualists believe that as the soul leaves the earth body for further development in a higher spirit sphere, it is most likely that there takes place a similar refinement of personality on passing to the next sphere above. This is a joyful occasion for the spirit people concerned. In occultism, the dissolution of the Kama Rupa (q.v.).

Second Sight. Supernormal perception, often symbolic, of the near or distant in space or time.

Seer. A natural clairvoyant or prophet.

Sekhmet. The profundly symbolical goddess of the ancient Egyptians who was depicted with a lion's head that bore the omnificent sun's disk and the uraeus serpent.

Sektet. Among the ancient Egyptians, this was the ship of the setting sun which was directed on its journey by the souls of the dead.

Selichot (Judaism). These are prayers in supplication to God for his forgiveness. Selichot are penitential prayers in which each individual as a sinner presents himself to heaven's judgment to implore God's clemency. They were inaugurated among the Jews in about the seventh century A.D. The penitent arises at midnight for ten days (from the high holy period of Rosh Hashanah to the Day of Atonement—Yom Kippur, the holiest and most soul-searching of all Hebrew holidays) to recite his midnight prayer of penitence. This period which corresponds to the great ancient ceremony of Yamim Noraim (q.v.) was especially sacred to Jewish mystics, to Cabalists, and the Hasidim (qq.v.). In many Jewish congregations Selichot are intoned in the synagogue before dawn for some two weeks preceding the holy days of Rosh Hashanah.

Sending. The practice of one with supernatural power in which he sends an object or a person to bring evil to a designated victim.

Senses (Astrology). Significators of the basic senses. The significators of the five physical senses are:

Mercury — sight
Venus — touch
Mars — taste
Jupiter — smell
Saturn — hearing

Sensing (Spiritualism). Term often used by mediums when describing a community of sensation with a control, deceased person, or psychometry article.

Sensitive. A person possessing psychic powers.

Sensitivity, Exteriorization of. See Exteriorization of Sensitivity.

Sensory (Passive) Automatism . Externalization of perceptions in inner visions and audition, from a source beyond the conscious will. A theory for clairvoyance, clairaudience, and crystal gazing which was developed by W.H. Myers.

Sentient Soul (Anthroposophy). That developmental stage of human consciousness typified by the Egypto-Chaldean period. Chiefly, it represents man's growth in perceiving the earthly world through the physical senses, which culminates in the sciences: mathematics, astronomy, alchemy, navigation, anatomy, etc.

Sephiroth (Cabalism). Throughout the history of ancient Hebrew mysticism the theory of the agency by which God acted culminated in the doctrine of "emanations." The Sephiroth are a formal structure of delegated powers from the Divine, the En Sof (q.v.), which is the fountainhead of Cabalism notably in the Zohar (q.v.). The ten Sephiroth are: (1) Kether Elyon,—supreme Crown; (2) Chocmah—wisdom; (3)

Binah—intelligence; (4) Hesed—love; (5) Geburah—power; (6) Tifereth—beauty, or compassion; (7) Netzah—lasting endurance; (8) Hod—majesty; (9) Yesod— foundation; (10) Malkuth—kingdom.

Seraphim of Sarov (1759–1833). Renowned Russian mystic whose ascetic life in the forest near Sarov, and his mystical and spiritual visions, won him a huge following. Forced to a monastery because of the crowds who sought him out, he became a famous healer of both spiritual and physical disorders. A man of profound love, of transcendant spiritual and prophetic powers, his spiritual light shone round him like a saintly nimbus.

Seraphita. The mystical Rosicrucian play of Honoré de Balzac, the great French novelist. Its theme is the triumph of love over desire. Strangely, the novel foreshadowed one of the most important events in Balzac's life. Written in 1834–35, it was dedicated to Countess Evaline Hauska, a woman for whom he was compelled to wait eighteen years before he could marry her.

Sergius of Radonezh (c. 1314–1392). Founder of the Monastery of St. Sergius, soldier, mystic, and "peasant saint," his shrine at Zagorsk is a famous shrine. His mystical doctrine has been extremely influential in Russia and even Dostoievski was profoundly touched by his teachings.

Serialism. A philosophic system by J. W. Dunne, based on his personal experiments with precognition in the dream state. It is also a theory of time and causation.

Serios, Ted. The Chicago bellhop whose ability to produce pictures inside a camera, using nothing but his mind and his "gismo," a small hollow tube, has made him the object of intense scientific study and the subject of many articles. Though some believe him a fraud, psychiatrists who have worked with him consider his psychic talents to be genuine.

Seven Deadly Sins, The. Ancient theologians are believed to have derived these from astrology, in this manner: Pride, Jupiter; Covetousness, Saturn; Lust, Venus; Wrath, Mars; Gluttony, Mercury; Envy, Moon; Indolence, Sun.

Seven Heavens, The (Judaism). In the pseudepigraphic Book of Enoch, there is a glorified description of the architecture and the inhabitants of the Seven Heavens. These details had a pronounced effect on the New Testament and, beyond that, on occultism.

Seven Principles (Spiritualism). Spiritualists have no fixed creed; the following principles have, however, been adopted by the Spiritualists' National Union, with the proviso that all members have liberty of interpretation. 1. The Fatherhood of God. 2. The Brotherhood of Man. 3.

Communion of Spirits and the Ministry of Angels. 4. The Continuous Existence of the Human Soul. 5. Personal Responsibility. 6. Compensation and Retribution hereafter for all the good and evil deeds done on earth. 7. Eternal progress open to every soul.

Seven Principles of Man (Theosophy). Derived from Hindu doctrine, these are: (1) Atma—Spirit; (2) Buddhi—Spiritual Soul; (3) Manas—Mind; (4) Kama—Feeling; (5) Prana—Life; (6) Lingasharira—Etheric Double; (7) Sthula-sharira—Physical Body.

The Seven Sleepers of Ephesus. A famous Christian legend of the seven young men who through the miracle of magic slept in a cave at Ephesus for a period of 200 years—from 250 A.D. to 450 A.D. This miracle saved them from the persecution that ravaged Christian communities in that epoch.

Sex. Seems to play both a mysterious and potent part in religious, occult and psychic phenomena. For example, there are more female mediums than male. According to some S.P.R. reports, some physical mediumship has been accompanied by sexual orgasm. Poltergeist activity usually occurs in the vicinity of boys and girls at the age of puberty, twelve to sixteen years. Yoga teachings emphasize the sublimation of sexual energies into ecstatic states. All through the history of religion sex has been a dominant partner of this phenomenon, notably in the temple prostitutes of early Near Eastern religion and in the symbolology of Hinduism. Christianity's unceasing vehemence against sex outside of holy marriage attests to its omnipotence. Much of the occult is entwined with sex, spectacularly in the lives of witches and in all forms of Satanism and Black Magic (qq.v.).

Sextile (Astrology). An apparent angle of 60 degrees between two celestial bodies, astrologically said to promote harmony between them. It has the meaning a 60 degree aspect (q.v.).

Sexual Union with the Devil. This is a key aspect of ancient witchcraft, and all during the history of witch evolution this has been an essential rite. In contemporary witch history, however, this is no longer a fact; moreover, there are witch covens (q.v.) today dedicated to beneficent activities, in healing, in psychic ministrations, etc.

Seybert Commission, The. For the investigation of Spiritualism, instituted by the wish of Henry Seybert, American Spiritualist, who left $60,000 to maintain a chair of Moral and Intellectual Philosophy at the University of Pennsylvania, March 1884, for investigation of all systems of morals, religion, philosophy and Spiritualism.

Shakers. Groups of early American religious sects who were sympathetic to the Quakers and to refugees from Cevennes. As many as sixty groups existed in 1837. They were very sympathetic to the North American Indians. The name "Shakers" was no doubt due to the slight trembling observed as they became inspired.

Shaktism, Saktism (Hinduism). The Hindu devotees of the Tantra (q.v.) who see Brahma as the absolute spirit, which embodied in shiva and shakti (the male-female principle) creates from the One in a series of 36 *tatvas* (q.v.), the Many. This process undergoes a continuous cycle of progression and retrogression.

Shaman. Although this originally referred to a Siberian medicine man, it evolved as a designation of a medicine man in any primitive society. A shaman's supernatural power resides in some spirit or deity with whom he is in contact, thus he possesses both beneficent and malefic powers. In certain Siberian tribes, the shaman lived as a woman. By a process of frenzied dancing, the shaman contacts the spirits of animals or dead humans, obtaining, thus, magical and divinatory inspiration.

Shamanism. Mediumistic practices of primitive tribes who believed in spirit communication. (See: Shaman.)

Shamash. The sun-god of the ancient Assyrian-Babylonion religion who produces the fertility of nature that occurs in the ushering in of spring.

Shang-Ti (1200 B.C.). Ancient supreme god of China. He was not a creator, but was said to be spontaneously evolved by the Yang and Yin interplay.

Shari'a (Islam). Meaning the law, which includes Allah's prescriptions for the proper human conduct. For Muslims this is the law of Allah, meaning the "Highway" of God's command and his overt assistance.

Shastra (Hinduism). Collective name for both the sacred and legal textbooks of the Hindus.

Shaw, George Bernard (1856–1950). Second only to Shakespeare as an English dramatist, and probably the greatest playwright of the twentieth century, he was also one of its most commanding personalities; but, characteristically, few understood that this life-long socialist and champion of communist Russia was also one of the most dedicated mystics of his age. In the tradition of many eminent mystics who exerted enormous influence in their own life-time, (Plato, Ruysbroeck, Cusanus, St. Bridget, Schweitzer, etc., qq.v.), he was a great platform speaker, a superb drama and music critic, a leading figure in the Socialist Fabian Society, a stellar political propagandist, the first dramatist of his time, the progenitor of a worldwide Shavian Cult, and, finally, the most widely known personality of his period. But he was also a believer in telepathy, faith healing, yoga; a deep student of the profound mystic William Blake (q.v.); the life-long champion of his own mystical notion of the omnipotent power of the "Life Force" which commands all life and all being; a long-time friend of the Mother Superior at Stanton Abbey in Ireland, and the writer of numerous plays and books, nearly all of them suffused with his rational mysticism and the philosophy of the overwhelming drive of the "Life Force." See: *Androcles and the Lion; Major Barbara; Man and Superman; Adventures of a Black Girl in Search for God; St. Joan.*

Shema, The (Judaism). A central tenet in Judaism which asserts, unequivocably, the doctrine of the Unity or Oneness of God. In Deuteronomy, the statement "Hear, O Israel: the Lord our God, the Lord is One!" is part of the prayer that is most often invoked by Jews.

Shen (Neo-Confucianism). The religious aspects of Shen are the spirits of heaven and absolute spiritual power. Philosophically, Shen is godlike power, spiritual and creative power, mystery, the divine man; and, too, vital force, the mind, and energy.

Shen Jen (Taoism). He who having achieved a mystical union with the universe is "The Spiritual Man."

Shepard, Jesse (Francis Grierson, 1849–1927). Phenomenal medium for music trance and xenoglossy (q.v.). His achievements on the piano were acclaimed as supernormal by Prince Adam Wisniewski, a personal friend of Liszt himself. Under the famous name of Grierson, Shepard wrote of his strange life.

Shilluk. These Nilotic people of the Sudan are ruled by a King in whom it is believed lives the divine spirit of the founder of their nation—Nyakang. This god within the King determines the fecundity and health of the Kingdom.

Shimbi. Among Africans in the Congo, the name of a fairy or a genie.

Shinto. Former monotheistic state religion of Japan (late eighteenth to nineteenth century), which tried to supplant Buddhism. Meaning "the way of the Gods," it centered around the divine authority of the sovereign Mikado, reminiscent of the older Roman ruler-worship. One of its sects, the Tenri Kyo, bears a remarkable parallel to the modern phenomenon of the founding of Christian Science in the West. Tenri Kyo grew out of the revelations of Maekawa Miki, a woman who became a faith healer, and also wrote two sacred books published in 1867 and 1875—the same years in which Mrs. Eddy's famous books were produced.

Ship of the Dead. The ancient belief of a phantom ship that carries away the souls of men. Generally, it is described as a cloud-ship or mist-shrouded as it floats across mountains and moors, while upon the sea it sails without benefit of the prevailing wind or tide.

Shrichakrasambhara Tantra (Buddhism). The sacred scripture which explicates the holy Mandala (q.v.) as portrayed in many temples.

Shrine. A place or object where sacred items are kept and to which worshipers or pilgrims come to show reverence or to obtain spiritual or other benefits. Often shrines are the sacred residences of gods or spirits. Among the numerous objects which have served as shrines are temples, trees, animals, pots, cenotaphs, stones, the homes of saints, and the homes of the great and the holy.

Shu. Based on the *I Ching* (q.v.), Shu signifies number, out of which all things become. To heaven belong the odd numbers (yang—q.v.), to Earth the even numbers (yin—q.v.)—the principles of increase and decrease. Both these numbers equal 55, and out of these, by changes and transformations, the heavenly and earthly spirits receive their movements.

Shu Shu. Represents the arts of divination and magic in ancient China. These also include astrology, almanacs, yin yang (q.v.) wu hsing—the Five Elements, fortune telling, dream interpretation, and a number of other supernatural disciplines.

Sibyl. In Greek mythology she was a prophetess, generally quite old. One of the most famous was the Cumean Sybil, consulted by Aeneas whom she led to the underworld. The Cumean Sibyl also sold to Tarquin the Sibylline books.

Sibylline Books. In ancient Rome the Sibylline Books, which contained inspired utterances of prophecy, were consulted in times of calamity. These books contained the prophetic writings about Rome's destiny, and were bought by Tarquin from the Cumean Sybil. (See: Sybil)

Sicun. Among the American Dakota Indians this was the essence of a deity. This Sicun was present during the birth of a human being.

Sidereal Light. The astral light which is deemed the Mysterium Magnum, being both the origin and form of the universe.

Sidereal Time. Astrologers in using the stars, which in a sidereal day seem to form a circle around the heavens, calculate from the highest point a star reaches each day. A sidereal day, therefore, runs until the time it takes the star to return to its highest point on the next day.

Siddha (Hinduism). Represents one of the 88,000 semi-divine beings of supreme holiness who inhabit the heaven between the earth and the sun. It also refers to supernatural power, or to one who has achieved this power.

Siddhartha (Buddhism). Buddha's first name, signifying the efficient one, he who has gained his object.

Siddhi. Superhuman physical powers attained by Yoga experts.

Sidgwick, Henry (1838-1900). Professor of Moral Philosophy at Cambridge, he was the first president of S.P.R.; he took a leading part in testing many famous mediums.

Sigil. In astrology, an indication of something important in a person's life, signifying that which is either beneficial or malevolent.

Sign (Astrology). A particular 30 degree segment of the tropical zodiac, named after one of the constellations, but not now coincident with it, due to the phenomenon of precession. Nonetheless, in the main, as used in astrology, it signifies one of the twelve signs of the zodiac: Aries, Taurus, Gemini, Cancer, Leo, Virgo, Libra, Scorpio, Sagittarius, Capricorn, Aquarius, Pisces (qq.v.).

Signatures. The concept that plants were created by God for man's use. Since the structure of each plant showed its proper function, the walnut, for example, because of its kernel's convolutions, was proper for brain diseases. The mandrake with its forked root resembling man was a plant of immense supernatural powers.

Signes Obscures. Mystical symbols which have been found on the walls of prehistoric caves in France and Spain. While the exact meaning of these symbols is not certain, it is believed that they represent outline drawings of animal traps which were traced some 10,000 to 20,000 years ago.

Silbert, Frau Maria. Austrian physical medium known for telekinesis, stigmata, apports and trance phenomena. An impressive feature of her mediumship was the supernormal engraving of cigarette-cases while her own hands were in full view.

Silence. According to the Society of Friends, the basis of worship, for it is in silence that God speaks to the Spirit.

"Silver Birch." The American Indian trance control who was admired by many mediums. He was a great orator and teacher from a higher sphere. Many books have been published of this guide's wisdom.

Silver Cord. Occultists see this inner cord, which is anchored to the vestigial pineal gland in the brain—named the "third eye"—as the vital link with the astral form (q.v.). This "cord" is cut at death. Most likely it takes the name of silver cord from Ecclesiastes XII:6—"Or ever the silver cord be loosed. . ." (See: Astral Cord).

Simeon Bar Yochai (Judaism). Rabbi, scholar, Cabalist, and mystic, of the 2nd century A.D., he plays an important role in Hebrew learning, particularly in the code of Oral Laws. Unyielding in his defiance of Roman rule, he was condemned to death by the Romans. Legend has it that he spent thirteen years hiding in a cave and during this period performed many miracles. Cabalists ascribe the authorship of the Zohar to Simeon Bar Yochai. Every Year thousands of Jewish pilgrims still visit his grave at Merom in Israel on the 18th of Iyar (which comes either at the end of April or the beginning of May in the Hebrew Calendar).

Simon Magus. The New Testament, Acts 8:5-24, records the power of Simon the Magician, a sorcerer, who had been converted to Christianity. He is the subject of many references by early Christian writers, particularly since his companion, Helena, a victim of the domination of evil angels, had reputedly been embodied in a number of persons, in successive times, including the legendary Helen of Troy. In Simon Magus' creed he describes himself as one who was the first emanation, the first existent primal deity, the Word, the Paraclete, and the Almighty.

Simon the Stylite (c. 390–459). The most famous of the pillar saints who lived on his column for 36 years. These pillars symbolized "holy mountains," or a place of spiritual elevation where divine manifestations could be more easily experienced.

Simony. The buying and selling of sacred things. The term comes from Simon Magus (q.v.) the Magician who offered to buy from St. Peter certain magical powers, among them the gift of tongues.

Simulacra. In ancient Egypt these were paintings and statuettes of slaves, persons, animals, and sometimes other beings, that were placed in tombs. These simulacra accompanied their masters into the other world to render them service and minister to their comfort.

Sin. Commonly understood as a transgression of divine laws, or as innate depravity consequent upon the fall of Adam.

Sinclair, Upton. Famous American novelist who experimented with the possibilities of telepathy. His wife was gifted with supernormal perception. His method was to make several drawings which were afterwards folded, then in a dark room his wife would select from them at random and write or draw her impressions of each one.

Singer, Isaac Bashevis (1904–   ). Distinguished American writer, celebrated for his stories and novels in Yiddish which are a complex mixture of Jewish folk life, Judaic sensibility to its vein of mysticism and Cabalism (q.v.), and an intense feeling for spiritualism, the occult, the satanic and the demonic in human life. Translated into many languages, and, of course, into English, his extraordinary artistry, command of language, fidelity to place and character, and the singular richness of his intellectual vision have made him attractive to critics and popular to readers of modernist literature. A few of his titles will show the range of his interests: *Gimpel the Fool and Other Stories, The Magician of Lublin, The Seance and Other Stories, Satan in Goray.*

Sinister. A term in astrology, meaning a left-handed aspect (q.v.). This is in contrast to the dexter aspect (q.v.).

Sio Humis. The great Rain Spirit of the American Hopi Indians.

Sistrum. In ancient times this was a rattle used in dancing; sometimes, as in Egypt, being part of the fertility rites. The sistrum was also used by the Aztecs, and all through South America; and it was a permanent feature in religious and profane dancing in Rome up to the 11th century A.D.

Sitter (Spiritualism). A member of a seance or sitting, other than the medium. The mental attitude of the sitter should not be over-emotional or prejudiced. This is most important for the successful production of psychic phenomena, and is due to the spiritual law of like minds attracting like.

Siva, Shiva (Hinduism, Buddhism). Siva is one of the three pre-eminent gods of Hinduism, "the great god" who embodies many diverse qualities and who is the third deity of the Trimurti (q.v.). Originally, he was the god Rudra, the Destroyer—the god of storms and the god of fire. But Siva also means "gracious," and the petitioner to Siva appeals to his benevolent side in order to stifle any outburst of his latent destructive faculties. To safeguard the continuance of birth in the world, Siva represents the divine reality in its negative aspect, as the destroyer of the worldly and ordered vision of the world. Another facet of Siva reveals him to be the powerful representative of yogi (q.v.), in his character of *Mahayogi*—the yogi who has achieved the height of perfection in meditation and in ascetic discipline. Still another aspect of Siva's character is his role as *Bhutesvara*, the lord of spirits and demons, the haunter of graveyards who wears a necklace of human skulls or is draped with living snakes. In this role Siva is the riotous wine lover who abandons himself in his lust for his *Sakti* (q.v.), his wife, who, incidently, in all his aspects is always at his side, so much so, that to teach the inseparable union of these two, Siva is on occasion portrayed as half-man, half-woman: above with a woman's breasts, below with a man's sexual organs. Perhaps the climax of Siva's godly powers is displayed in his representation as a dancer, and, most powerfully and expressively, in the famous "dance of Siva." This dance dramatically symbolizes his five activites of creation, maintenance, destruction of the world, the embodiment of souls; and the ultimate escape from the cycle of lives. He is that unique deity who by his dancing is able to control and to make dance the three great basic elements of the cosmos: energy (heat), mind, and matter. (See; Brahma, Vishnu)

Sivaism, Shivaism, Saivism (Hinduism). One of the major groupings of Hinduism, it is based on certain Agamas—those books outside the Vedic tradition. Shiva, as part of the trinity (Brahma and Vishnu) has inspired a whole religious outlook buttressed by a unique philosophical system.

Six Egyptian Commandments, The. The great Egyptian Book of the Dead (q.v.), created by the guild of priests about 1500 B.C. to guide the deceased safely in their journey to the other world, contained six famous commandments. The dead, in their supplication to Osiris, the god of the dead, to vindicate their right to eternal blessedness, uttered

the following ritualistic declaration:
1. I have not slighted God.
2. I have not slain.
3. I have not commanded to slay.
4. I have not committed fornication or impurity.
5. I have not stolen.
6. I have not spoken falsehood.

That Moses based his Ten Commandments on this Egyptian ritual is at once obvious. And when Judaism handed these down to the Christian world where it became a bedrock moral code, the stupendous importance of these articles of profession is immediately apparent.

Sixth Sense. This is a concept which has been postulated many times under many names. First used technically by Tardy de Montravel, he considered it the source and sum of all senses. Charles Richet (q.v.) used this term to represent telepathy, clairvoyance, psychometry, premonitions, predictions, crystal vision and phantasmal appearances, which he pronounced to be due to a perception of the vibrations of reality.

Skin Writing. See Dermography.

Skotograph. Name devised by Miss Felicity Scatcherd (q.v.) for spirit-writing on an unexposed photographic plate. Also known as "psychograph."

Sky Walker. The yogi who can transcend his body and travel in astral form (q.v.).

Slade, Henry. American medium of the late 19th century who was best known for his slate-writing phenomena. He was the subject of much stormy discussion and alleged trickery, although many vouched for his honesty.

Slater, John (1861–1932). American clairvoyant medium who for fifty years gave demonstrations of reading sealed letters and remarkable evidence of survival. In 1930 he was arrested in Detroit for making predictions, but he won his case and continued his work.

Slate Writing. Once a popular phenomenon of the seance room, but no doubt owing to the high probability of its fraudulent production, it has now become rare. Two slates were sealed with a fragment of pencil between them, and during the sitting it would be heard writing a message, subsequently disclosed when the slates were opened.

Sleep. In old dream interpretation, to dream that one is asleep and having a dream indicates that the chief incidents of such a dream or events quite similar will occur.

Sleep-State. (Spiritualism). The normal periodic state of unconsciousness, during which the physical body may separate from the spirit body, which can then travel unhampered, though still connected by a vital thread which sustains the physical body. These nocturnal experiences are sometimes remembered in the conscious state on waking (astral projection). An interesting theory is that communicators themselves have to enter a sleep-state in order to communicate. This may account for their memory difficulties when entering earth conditions.

Sleeping Preacher. Rachel Baker, famous in her day as the sleeping preacher, was born in Pelham, Massachusetts in 1794. When she was 17 she showed symptoms of somnambulism, and during these spells she delivered sermons of marked maturity. Her trance-speaking finally occurred daily, uninterrupted by change of locality. These trance-sermons made such an impression that they were transcribed and published.

Smagorad. A magic book of such supposed infinite power that its possessor could control the stars and the elements of the earth. It was claimed by Arnauld Gillaume, a French magician, to have been given by God to Adam. (See: Guillaume)

Smead, Mrs. (Mrs. Willis M. Cleaveland). Planchette medium who was noted in the early 1900s for her peculiar revelations of life and conditions on planets Mars and Jupiter which were interesting, but not considered convincing.

Smells, Psychic. All kinds, from delicate flower perfumes to noxious odors, many times have been supernormally simulated. This phenomena may well have a physical basis. Some chemical reaction may take place in the body tissues and the scent exuded from the skin. There are many instances of sulphur smells accompanying other phenomena (See: Swedenborg, Mirabelli, D. D. Home, and Mrs. Crandon.)

Smith, Christopher Neil. The Vicar of St. Saviour's in Hampstead, England. He is considered one of the most eminent of contemporary sorcerers. His method of casting out spirits utilizes the laying on of hands, and his reputed success as an exorcist keeps him in constant demand.

Smith, Helene. Notorious Swiss medium whose ability to contact famous controls such as Victor Hugo and Cagliostro (qq.v.), and her spurious claims of being a reincarnation of Marie Antoinette, of Lorenza Feliciana (Cagliostro's wife), and an Asian Indian princess made her a famous European psychic in the 1890's. She also demonstrated the ability to travel to Mars, and no less a psychic investigator than Professor Flournoy (q.v.) wrote a laudatory book on her Martian travels and her reproductions of the Martian language.

Smith, Justa. Dr. Sister M. Justa Smith, a bio-chemist and enzymologist, has become internationally recognized for her experiments proving that some persons have the vital psychic power to cure ill-nesses and make plants and seedlings grow along with distressed en-zymes. Working on the purely material level of enzymes, seedlings and plants and also wounded lab mice, she has eliminated all elements of possible fraud and proven scientifically the existence of psychic heal-ing. Dr. Sister Smith, a Franciscan nun, formerly head of the science department at Rosary Hill College in Buffalo, is now assistant director of education at Roswell Park Memorial Institute, a leading cancer research center.

S.N.U. The Spiritualists' National Union (q.v.).

Soal, Samuel George. An eminent English researcher in parapsycholo-gy, notably in the area of telepathy, he was a professor of mathemat-ics at the University of London, and Perrott student in Psychical Research at Trinity College, Cambridge. He was also a Fulbright Research Scholar in Parapsychology, and in 1951 president of the S.P.R. (q.v.). Utilizing his skill in mathematics, in 1937 Soal conducted statistical research on the incidence of telepathy; in the period 1934–36 he repeated the famous Zener cards (q.v.) experiments of J. B. Rhine (q.v.). He was awarded the William McDougall (q.v.) Memo-rial Prize for his book *The Mind Reader, Some Recent Experiments in Telepathy,* which was published in 1960. Although he was a cele-brated authority in psychic research through the 1930's to the 1960's, his integrity as a scientific investigator was absolute, and when he discovered the occurrence of fraud in his own already published ex-periments, he did not hesitate to make this discovery public. Soal was the author of a number of important papers in parapsychology, fre-quently lecturing on them to British professional audiences. (See: Parapsychology, J.B. Rhine; see: *Telepathy* and Allied Phenomena—co-author, Rosalyne Heywood, *Modern* Experiments in Telepathy—co-author, S. Bateman.)

Society for Psychical Research. This world famous British society, was established in 1882. Its objects and aims were summarized: "1. An examination of the nature and extent of any influence which may be exerted by one mind upon another, apart from any recognized mode of perception. 2. The study of hypnotism and the forms of so-called mesmeric trance, with its alleged insensibility to pain; clair-voyance and other allied phenomena. 3. A critical revision of Reichen-bach's researches with certain organizations called sensitive, and an inquiry whether such organizations possess any power of perception beyond a highly exalted sensibility of the recognized sensory organs. 4. A careful investigation of any reports, resting on strong testimony regarding apparitions at the moment of death, or otherwise, or regarding disturbances in houses reputed to be haunted. 5. An inquiry into the various physical phenomena commonly called spiritualistic: with an attempt to discover their causes and general laws. 6. The collection and collation of existing materials bearing on the history of these subjects." The results of their investigations are published regularly as "Proceedings of the Society for Psychical Research." They have so far established as facts: (a) the possibility of thought-transference, (b) a connexion between death and apparitions, (c) the existence of hypnotic states. On the question of survival they maintain that the constitution of the Society precludes a collective opinion.

Society for the Study of Supernormal Pictures, The. Established in London 1918. Members were mostly professional photographers. The report issued in May 1920 after testing thousands of pictures: "The members here present, desire to place on record the fact that after many tests and examination of thousands of pictures, they are unanimously of the opinion that results have been obtained supernormally on sensitive photographic plates under reliable test conditions. At present, the members do not undertake to explain how the results have been obtained, but assert that they have undoubtedly been secured under conditions excluding the possibility of fraud."

Socrates. (469–399 B.C.) The illustrious Greek philosopher whose life has served as an extraordinary model of wisdom, integrity, and courage since his death, believed it to be his mission to teach his fellows by asking them questions on their fundamental ideas. He never wrote anything so far as we know, but his famous pupil and admirer Plato immortalized him in his Dialogues. How much is the philosophy of Socrates in Plato's dialogues—where Socrates is speaking—and how much of it is Plato's remains one of the unsolved problems of Western philosophy. Socrates claimed a personal guide or daimon, who advised him unerringly in times of difficulty or emergency. Completely unperturbed by the animosity of his times, he refused offers to escape his judicial death-sentence of the drinking of hemlock poison, and affirmed his belief in immortality to the end.

Solar Equilibrium. In astrology this term refers to the Solar Figure which is drawn for the sunrise of a specified day with each House (q.v.) at 30 degrees.

Solar Plexus. An important network of nerves situated in the pit of the stomach. It is often associated with one of the psychic centers or "chakras" of Yoga. Sitters sometimes experience curious "drawing" sensations in this region during the production of phenomena.

Solar Semicircle. In astrology, these are the Signs or Houses from Leo to Capricorn (qq.v.) inclusive; they represent a semi-circle of the Zodiac.

Solipsism. A doctrine that the self of the philosopher comprises the whole of reality, therefore denying the external world an independent existence.

Solomon's Mirror. A sparkling steel plate, cleanly polished and carefully treated, for use in divination.

Soloviev, Vladimir Sergeyevich (1853–1900). Russia's foremost modern philosopher was also one of its most eminent moral-religious thinkers, and a noteworthy mystic. Soloviev was, in addition, a quite important poet. Because of his liberal religious and social views, he was several times forced to leave his job as a teacher at Moscow University and at the University of St. Petersburg despite his brilliance (he had been appointed an instructor when he was only twenty-one). As a lecturer in religion and philosophy he attracted enthusiastic audiences, which included such personages as Dostoyevsky and Tolstoy. During his lifetime he was transfixed by three illuminating mystical visitations, the first occurring when he was nine and the second and third when he was twenty-two. Before he was twenty-six, Soloviev was esteemed as Russia's first major academic philosopher. For him all the aspects of existence were of an organic nature whether it was religion, philosophy, morality, mysticism, art, science, mankind or man. For example, he described the three levels of psychic structure as spirit, intellect, soul, and held that they were related to such ideal objects as good, truth, beauty; and God the Father, God the Son, and God the Holy Spirit he held to be related by way of will, representation, and feeling to all the other organic aspects and structures of existence. In his famous lectures on "Godmanhood" he declared it necessary for each individual to develop himself spiritually to the point of identification with Christ. Soloviev's courage, erudition, kindliness, and social sensitivity won him a host of readers and admirers in his lifetime, and the continued relevance of his ideas engages a contemporary audience both in Europe and America. (See: N.A. Duddington's English trans. of *Justification of the Good: An Essay in Moral Philosophy*; P. Zouboff's trans. of *Lectures on Godmanhood*; also, Paul Allen, *Vladimir Soloviev: Russian Mystic*, 1978)

Soma (Hinduism). The historically important plant which when made into an intoxicating liquor supposedly gives to the drinker supernatural powers. Soma, one of the three great gods of the Vedic religion and described in the ninth book of the Rig-Veda, is associated with this plant.

Somatic. Pertaining to the physical organism in contradistinction to the spiritual or psychic.

Somnambules. Old term for sensitives who were thrown into mesmeric trances for the purpose of activating supernormal faculties.

Somnambulism. Spontaneous or artificial sleep or semi-trance, where the subconscious faculties operate on the body instead of the conscious. It differs from ordinary sleep since the muscular system retains its waking tension; further, the eyes are directed upward and inward, and there is insensibility to pain, taste and smell.

Sons of Faith (Cabalism). In the Zohar (q.v.) this refers to certain adepts of Cabalism.

Sons of the Prophets (Judaism). Throughout the tradition of Jewish mysticism, these were a holy group of men who kept alive the divine spirit of prophecy.

Soothsaying. One of the ancient world's important occult practices in which individuals called soothsayers predicted future events or foretold happenings in other matters. Schooled in a wide variety of techniques (the reading of natural events, bodies, and planets, or the drawing of lots, and many other divinatory skills), soothsayers were often akin to public officials, notably in Greece, Rome, and China.

Sophia-Achemoth. For the Gnostics (q.v.) she was the Divine Mother and the bearer of Divine Wisdom.

Sosom. The bull roarer god among the Kaya-Kaya of New Guinea.

Soul. In its usual sense it means the indestructible spiritual part of the personality.

Soul Aura. That part of the human aura which radiates the intensity of spiritual power attained by the individual. It lies outside of the physical aura, and may extend to some distance in the case of developed souls. It is perceived by clairvoyant vision as a golden light radiating from the entire body.

Soul, Celestial. A being in a highly evolved spirit sphere.

Soul Group. See: Group Soul.

Soul, Old. See: Old Soul.

Soule, Mrs. Minnie Meserve (Mrs. Chenoweth). American trance medium whose trance phenomena were outstanding. Many famous personalities, including Robert Browning, Mrs. Browning, Lord Tennyson and H. W. Longfellow are purported to have communicated through her.

Sounds, Psychic. See: Raps.

Space. (Spiritualism). According to communications, space in the spirit world presents no limitations, the mere wish to travel being sufficient to bring it about. The location of the spirit spheres is usually said to be concentric with the earth's surface, permeating it and extending to a great distance beyond. Others say that space is a condition imposed by earthly consciousness. The inhabitants of the spirit world assert that they perceive objects spatially, yet they seem to penetrate the substance of them also. They add that they are not dependent on senses as we are, that the light by which they perceive seems to proceed from objects themselves, not by reflected light. The mental states of spirits would seem to condition their surroundings to a considerable degree, even to the extent of cutting them off from communication with other spirits, should they be in the habit of self-sufficiency. How far their superphysical state is affected by this mental process, is difficult for us to determine.

Space-Time. The concept of the universe as a four-dimensional continuum of length, breadth, depth and time.

Speaking in Tongues. See: Xenoglossy.

Specter. An apparition (q.v.).

Spectral Flames. Supernormal lights which have been seen around churches and cemeteries (see: Luminous Phenomena).

Specularii. Name for scryers or crystal-gazers in the 16th century.

Speculum I. Any light-refracting, shining surface which can be used to focus the attention. The crystal ball is used as such by scryers.

Speculum II. (Astrology). A table in a horoscope detailing its astronomical data: the planets' latitude, declination, right ascension, ascensional difference, pole and semi-arc.

Spell in Black Magic (q.v.). Casting a spell on a victim requires the exercise of both a prescribed verbal and ritual routine. It has been and still is one of the most widely used of occult practices by necromancers, sorcerers, shamans, witches, etc. An ancient terminology is frequently used in the casting of spells which may be a recipe of religious and occult terminology, and is often unintelligible to the agent. Grimoires (q.v.) have been popular sources of potent spells, but each practitioner, whether sorcerer or witch doctor, shaman or black magician, depends upon a fixed formula that is most often inherited and of ancient parentage.

Spenta (Zoroastrianism). A designation of the helpers of the powers of Ahura Mazda (q.v.).

Spenta Armaiti (Zoroastrianism). An Amesha-Spenta (q.v.) opposing Angra Mainyu (q.v.) who thereby increases the divine power of Ahura Mazda (q.v.).

Sphere, Celestial. The sphere inhabited by beings far in advance spiritually of earth consciousness. A world said to be of light and harmony.

Sphere, Contemplation. Said to be a highly evolved sphere where the main occupation is contemplation of the spiritual universe.

Sphere, Lower (Spiritualism). The nearest condition to earth, a transition place through which all must pass at death. If there is an emotionally strong attachment for any particular experience of earth life, it may prolong the stay in this lower state until such time as the spirit wishes to progress.

Spheres. This notion has several meanings: on the one hand, it refers to the spheres from which we come, and, on the other, it signifies the spheres through which we pass to our ultimate destination when we die. All the great mythic, spiritual, religious, and many philosophic systems have elaborated various patterns of spheres which make up the universe—that dynamic matrix in which we are created, or which imprisons us, or is the ultimate abode in which we live an eternal life of torture or blessedness. Some of the names of these spheres are—(their meanings and connections will be explained below): Heaven, Hell, Nirvana, Brahma, Amenti, Hades, Elysium, Elysian Fields, Tartarus, Seven Spheres of the Archons, Valhalla, and The Happy Hunting Grounds. Chiefly, the main doctrine in most religions is a contrast between the sphere or spheres of heaven or the sphere or spheres of Hell. Most particularly, this notion is to be found in Mithraism, Zoroastrianism (Par3eeism), Christianity, and Islam. However, the concept of reincarnation (q.v.) introduces a more complex drama into the problem of life and death, of salvation and damnation.

Gnosticism was the clearest expression of the doctrine of spheres with its Seven Spheres of the Archons under the dominion of their ruler, the Demiurge (q.v.). These seven spheres encircled man on earth where in both body and soul he was a prisoner of both the Archons and the Demiurge; but in addition to body and soul man also possessed "spirit"—the spirit of the transcendent God who dwells beyond these imprisoning spheres. Gnosticism was a faith which taught the initiate the gnosis "knowledge of the way" to escape his imprisoning spheres in order to reach the neutral eighth sphere and from there to arrive at last to the blessed "Light" of God. In Hinduism and Buddhism, though all men embody the Atman (q.v.) (god within themselves) they can only obliterate the inexorable round of karma (q.v.) by living a life of purity, of goodness, and holiness. There are, however, a number of intermediate Heavens and Hells in Hinduism. The ancient Egyptians believed that at death the soul descended to the sphere of the lower world (Amenti) where it was judged—the good soul with a majority of good deeds in life was directed to the Elysian fields (Aahlu), the impure soul with a majority of bad deeds was sentenced to a trial of reincarnations in a series of animals and if it continued in wickedness it suffered death and cruel annihilation. In contrast, the souls in the Elysian fields after three thousand years of enjoyment returned to earth, rejoined their old bodies, and lived their lives again. The Greeks held that the sphere of the gods was mount Olympus; that the human dead went to the sphere of Hades where the fortunate and blessed were ushered to the sphere of Elysium and where the wicked were sent to be tortured in the sphere of Tartarus. The ancient Jews held varying views on the spheres of Heaven and Hell, believing vaguely in heaven (Gan Eden) and Hell (Gehinnon), but believed firmly that on the great Day of Judgment God would raise the dead. However, the Cabalists (q.v.) asserted a doctrine of four different spheres: the sphere of the preexisting souls in the sphere of emanations, the earth sphere, the spirit sphere, and the highest sphere—the blessed world of emanations coming from the En Sof (q.v.), God himself, in the sphere beyond the universe. Swedenborgians hold a theory of emanations which is structured into a divine sphere, a sphere of the spiritual world, and the sphere of the natural world. Since philosophy has played a leading role in the notions of spheres, particularly in the West, it is important to understand that Plato, Aristotle, Plotinus, Leibnitz, Spinoza, and Hegel—to name the most important, have all contributed concepts in the ongoing development of this doctrine. Plato is a central figure with his theory of the sphere of perfect Ideas: Aristotle's first cause—the Sphere of the Unmoved Mover, has had an enormous influence; Plotinus' concept of emanations has been widely influential; Liebnitz's doctrine of monads (q.v.) has been pervasively utilized; Spinoza's view of the divinity of both God and nature has been a highly attractive principle; and Hegel's all encomposing status of the Geist (spirit) has been extraordinarily fecund in enriching the doctrine of spheres.

Given the long history of the notion of spheres, it is understandable that modern Theosophy and the twentieth century spiritual science of Anthroposophy should have developed very sophisticated doctrines of spheres. Both are aware that spiritual growth requires dedicated discipline and many years. For H.P. Blavatsky (q.v.), mankind from the beginning was taught the Wisdom-Religion by guardians from "superior spheres" and a multiplicity of spheres has nurtured and developed these elect guardians who have constantly brought to mankind the "divine ethics." Keeping this in mind, a simplistic scheme of spheres in Theosophy would show an astral sphere, a sphere of eternal reality, and the earth sphere. Likewise, in Anthroposophy, a simplistic scheme of spheres would depict a sphere of Heaven—The Spirit World; below this are nine spiritual spheres containing the nine orders of spiritual beings; and, finally, the material sphere, or the earth; then below the earth there are also nine additional spheres. Importantly, the spiritual spheres are watched by two Guardians of the Threshold (q.v.)—the Lesser Guardian and the Greater Guardian. The doctrine of the Spiritualists holds that there are several successive spheres surrounding the earth where the spirit life dwells after death. The lower spheres interpenetrate the higher. And the growth of spiritual consciousness increases as one matures and then ascends into the next highest sphere. In recent years some types of spiritualist movement have called the sphere after death by the name of Summerland. This name is remniscent of the American Indians name of Happy Hunting Grounds, the sphere of the soul after death for warriors and hunters.

Spielgelschrift. Writing which is backwards, that is, mirror-writing, from right to left. Automatic writing (q.v.) is very often produced in this fashion.

Spinoza, Benedict (1632-1677). Dutch rationalist and determinist philosopher who aimed to construct, on the knowledge of God, a system of philosophy and morals by a rigorous mathematical method. He is known as the father of modern pantheism. Man as a separate being was trivial; for only by merging with God came understanding; and as a consequence of this concept Spinoza asserted that freewill was an illusion since all finite things are considered as part of a chain of consequences.

Spirit. In almost every mythic, religious, and spiritual system the notion of spirit is related—directly or indirectly, to gods or a God. Frequently, it also refers to *pneuma* (the breath)—the "divine afflatus" which, again, only symbolizes the "spirit" of the divine power or powers. It is the spirit in man which is the indestructible essence of self-conscious life, sensible of all things, limited only by its manifestation or "body." In Spiritualism the word spirit is often loosely used to describe a discarnate person as distinct from an earthly being. In this sense the spirit possesses a body of material analagous to, but not identical with material elements.

Spirit Body. See Bodies.

Spirit Children (Spiritualism). None are born in the spirit world, but children who die before maturity are considered to continue their growing and development in spirit life. Often they help in mediumship, acting in the capacity of controls or helpers. Many earth children are conscious of playmates in spirit, and talk to them freely. This faculty usually disappears as the child becomes more sophisticated and engrossed by earthly considerations.

Spirit Communication. See Communication.

Spirit Doctors (Spiritualism). Doctors skilled on this earth, who have passed over but who continue to administer to the sick from the spirit spheres by working through a dedicated medium known as a healer. It is worth noting that not all healers know that they are mediums.

Spirit, Great. God. Deity. Form of address often used by controls.

Spirit Guide. See Control.

Spirit Healing. See Healing.

Spirit Helper. See Helper.

Spirit Hierarchy. See Hierarcy of Spirit.

Spirit Hypothesis, The (Spiritualism). Psychic phenomena cover a huge field of supernormal manifestation. To attempt to explain their varied operations scientifically, all possible physical explanations are tried in turn. It is when an intelligence not of this earth obviously directs the phenomena, that one is logically forced to adopt the simple "spirit hypothesis"—that the intelligence is what it claims to be—the human mind of an entity who once lived on this earth. Most spiritualists agree that the fundamental conditions for its acceptance are: 1. The information must be supernormal, that is, not explicable by normal perception. 2. The incidents must be verifiable memories of the deceased persons and so representative of their personal identity. 3. The incidents must be trivial and specific—not easily, if at all, duplicated in the common experience of others.

Spirit Lights. See Luminous Phenomena.

Spirit Photography (Spiritualism). Reproductions on a photographic plate of discarnate entities, most often their faces, which is frequently invisible to the photographer who has taken the photographs.

Spirit Obsession. See Obsession.

Spiritoid. Messages which come from the sub-conscious mind, which are dramatized and personalized.

Spirit Operators (Spiritualism). Term for the workers in the spirit band, who are assisting the production of psychic phenomena for any specific purpose.

Spirit Spheres. See Spheres.

Spirit World. A collective term for all the realms of spirit, inclusive of the spheres or planes, but excluding the earth world. (See: Spheres)

Spiritis Rector. In Latin, this term signifies the ruling or master spirit, and it came to mean a subtle natural force in the physical body. For the alchemists, the substance designated Spiritus Rector, which was an ultimate distillation, was considered capable of transmuting base metals into gold; and the term also referred to an elixir with the supreme property of prolonging life indefinitely.

Spiritism. The belief that the spirits of ancestors or other spirits can both communicate with and be contacted by man. Further, that there are souls of matter, nature spirits, demons, celestial and angelic beings, and, finally, that there are deities. In an early form of Spiritualism, developed by Kardec (q.v.) in France, it meant the doctrine of compulsory reincarnation.

Spiritual Realism. A doctrine that self-forgetfulness leads to a supreme realization of personality; that spiritual activity makes causality; that only the truly good will is free.

Spiritualism. The science, philosophy and religion of continuous life, based upon the demonstrated fact of communication, by means of mediumship, with those who live in the Spirit World. Spiritualism is a science because it investigates, analyzes and classifies facts and manifestations, demonstrated from the spirit side of life. Spiritualism is a philosophy because it studies the laws of nature both on the seen and unseen sides of life and bases its conclusions drawn therefrom, when sustained by reason and by results of observed facts of the present day. "Spiritualism is a religion because it strives to understand and to comply with the physical, mental and spiritual laws of nature which are the laws of God." (Definition adopted by the National Spiritualist Association of Churches in America.) There is now a spiritualist seminary at Morris Pratt Institute in Whitewater, Wisconsin. But the most famous spiritualist center in America is the Lily Dale Spiritualist Camp in New York.

Spiritualist. One who has accepted as proven on adequate evidence given through mediumship, the fact that human spirits survive death, that they can communicate with us, that there is a hierarchy of spirit beings, that all spirits are part of a unified consciousness or God.

Spiritualist Association of Great Britain, The. Formerly the Marylebone Spiritualist Association, one of the two largest Spiritualist Associations in the world, founded in London 1872 for the study of psychic phenomena and the public dissemination of evidence obtained through mediumship. It engages only trustworthy mediums of proved ability, and provides facilities for investigation and discussion without bias under strict anonymous conditions. Its membership is open to all, irrespective of beliefs.

Spiritualists' National Union, The. The other of the two largest Spiritualist organizations in the world, founded in 1890 to promote the advancement and diffusion of the religion and the religious philosophy of Spiritualism on the basis of the Seven Principles (q.v.). It aims to unite Spiritualist churches into a brotherhood, to encourage research and to provide schemes for the certification of lecturers, exponents and healers. (See: Spiritualist Association of Great Britain)

Spodomancy. The art of divination by interpreting the cinders remaining in sacrificial fires.

Spontaneous Psi Experience. A spontaneous psychic experience which occurs involuntarily.

S.P.R. The Society for Psychical Research (q.v.).

Spunkie, The. In Scottish folklore, a goblin, believed to be a familiar of Satan. Lost travelers are lured by a light which continually recedes and as the victim proceeds he finally steps over a precipice or is trapped in a swampy bog by the devilish Spunkie.

Spurzheim, Johann Kaspar. A Viennese phrenologist who popularized phrenology in America when he gave a series of lectures in Boston in

1832. He had studied in Vienna with Dr. F. S. Gall (q.v.), phrenology's founder, and was quite adept in the science. Men like Daniel Webster, Andrew Jackson, and Walt Whitman were diagnosed as persons of distinction by the new discipline, and all of them endorsed its value.

Square (Astrology). An apparent angle of 90 degrees between two celestial bodies said (astrologically) to be productive of difficulty.

Squassation. A form of rope-hanging torture formerly used to force those accused of witchcraft to name their accomplices.

Sraosha (Zoroastrianism). One of the Yazatas (q.v.) who first taught the law, and, as a divine guard of the world, wakes at the third hour of the night, and later arouses the rooster to enable it to chase away the demon of sleep from humanity.

Srotapatti (Buddhism). The "entering of the stream" which at its farthest reach ultimately carries into the ocean of salvation and into Nirvana (q.v.).

Sruti (Hinduism). The oral tradition of the Vedic scriptures which bears such spiritual weight that the hearing of it makes it the revealed message. This most sacred part of the scriptures which are directly heard and deemed to be "revealed" are the Mantras, Brahmanas, and Upanishads (qq.v.). (See: Vedas)

Stanford Research Institute. Stanford University in California has become one of the world's most prestigious research centers in paranormal studies. It has engaged in research projects in psychic phenomena for the United States Department of Defense; made a film of Uri Geller's (q.v.) psychic abilities after an extensive study of his paranormal talents; and has provided facilities for a number of the most advanced students in psychic experimentation, such as Russell Targ, Harold Puthoff, Astronaut Edgar Mitchell, and Dr. Andrija Puharich (qq.v.). The Institute maintains a full staff of parapsychologists on its faculty.

Star of David. See Magen David.

Star of Bethlehem. The "wise men of the East" who came to seek Jesus, the wondrous babe born under the influence of the miraculous star, were astrologers. The star of Bethlehem is believed to have been a conjunction of Saturn, Jupiter, and Mars, an important satellitium (q.v.), at the cusp of the Tenth House (q.v.). By locating the geographical place at the time of this planetary conjunction, these Eastern astrologers knew they would find the babe destined to change world history.

Statue. In old dream interpretation to dream of marble statues is a sign that the dreamer will soon experience preferment.

Stead, W. T. (1849-1912). He was a brilliant journalist and editor, a prolific author, an enormously effective political crusader, an ardent advocate of spiritualism, and an altogether extraordinary personality and gadfly in English life over a period of some forty years. In his work in spiritualism he obtained proof of survival through communications from a Miss Julia Ames, an American editor friend who had died previously. Messages from the living were also obtained by him. Through the efforts of his control "Julia" a Bureau was opened in 1909, giving free sittings to people anxious to establish communication.

St. Elmo's Fire. A glowing light observed at the tips of parts of ships. Taking its name from the patron saint of Mediterranean sailors, it may portend such events as good or bad luck, a lost soul, or good weather.

Steiner, Rudolf (1861-1925). The founder of Anthroposophy or "spiritual science," Austrian educator and philosopher, he had an enormous influence in Europe and later America, owing to his keen human sensitivity and passion, his spiritual knowledge and insights, his educational theories and Steiner schools, his numerous lectures, and his nearly 50 books. He was, besides, an eminent psychic and clairvoyant. Influenced by Blavatsky's Theosophical doctrines (q.v.), a specialist on Goethe (the editor of Goethe's scientific works), he was also skillful in the arts (dancing, painting, architecture, speech, drama), in science (medicine, pharmacology, physics, mathematics), in economics, and the social order. Rudolf Steiner schools, flourishing in many countries today, have demonstrated the validity of his pedagogical concepts.

Steppenwolf, Der. This novel by the German writer Hermann Hesse, written in the 1920's, is a classic work in the realm of man's relationship to the occult forces of the universe. Widely read when first published in Germany, its power and richness of insight have made it a continuing international favorite, particularly with the young both in colleges and to those seeking new spiritual horizons. Hesse dramatizes through the book's protagonist, Harry Haller, the notion that man must learn to accept all aspects of his personality: that is, the part of him which is bourgeois and the part which is wolf, the side of life which depends on reason and the side of life which depends on occult myth.

Stevenson, Ian. Dr. Stevenson, Chairman of the Department of Psychiatry at the University of Virginia Medical School, whose 20 years of research on the evidence of reincarnation have covered some 1,300 cases and extensive trips around the globe, is undoubtedly the world's foremost authority on the scientific evidence for reincarnation. Stevenson's interviews with persons who have experienced out-of-body interludes, who have been close to death, and who have claimed to live in the astral world (q.v.) between incarnations, have convinced him that the evidence for reincarnation is definitely in the realm of "rational belief." Further, he asserts that a belief in reincarnation makes the responsibility for moral improvement wholly the problem of the individual, not that of his parents or of his society. Thus, to live a "good" life, in Stevenson's view, enables one to lose the fear of death.

Stevenson, Robert Louis (1850–1894). The British novelist, playwright, poet, and equally famous essayist. He studied engineering then dropped it for law and graduated from law school. But the latter profession he also abandoned. Early successful as a writer, his international popularity began with *Treasure Island* in 1883, and increased with *Kidnapped* and *The Strange Case of Dr. Jekyll and Mr. Hyde* in 1887. The latter story of a split personality harboring both a saintly and satanic character has the distinction (among its other numerous triumphs) of having had more film productions than any other work of literature. Stevenson frankly acknowledged throughout his life that a spirit dictated his stories. In fact, for more than twenty years he was a member of the Edinburgh Psychical Research Society. Stevenson once wrote that his spirit collaborator or "little people" did half his work "while I am fast asleep, and in all human liklihood do the rest for me as well, when I am wide awake. . . ." As a result of his many experiences with the mediumship of D. D. Home, Stevenson became one of the first Secretaries for the Scottish Spiritualist Association.

Sthenometer. An instrument devised by Dr. Paul Joire to prove that a kind of nervous force, generated by the medium's body, can be stored for a short time in wood, water and cardboard, in a similar way to light, heat and electricity.

Stigmata. Marks on the body which are spontaneously produced, and which usually resemble the wounds of the Crucifixion. They may bleed freely and severely incapacitate the person who is often of an hysterical disposition; this may also occur under the influence of a strong emotional experience or religious delirium. Authentic cases are legion with St. Francis of Assisi and Therese Neumann of Bavaria being notable examples. There are instances where stigmata has been recorded in its various stages, by the camera.

Stigmata Diaboli. The seal or mark of the Devil, known as "Devil's Marks." This is not the same as the "Witch's Mark" (q.v.), though it has frequently been confused with the former term. (See: Witch's Marks)

Stobart, Mrs. A. St. Clair. This unusual woman once confessed that she always acted on her intuition. During World War I a typhus outbreak in Serbia took her to a hospital unit there, where she was ultimately given command of a division and eventually led the retreat of the Serbian army successfully in the face of incredible hardships.

After World War I she became convinced of the truth of Spiritualism. She wrote several books on her findings relating Biblical events to psychic phenomena. With Rev. Vale Owen she became leader of the Spiritualist Community and devoted her remarkable talents to uniting all religions on a spiritualistic basis.

Stoicism. A system of Greek and Roman philosophy, which was founded about 315 B.C. Stoicism held that God was the fiery mind of the world, and that all things, as part of nature, are determined by fixed laws. The doctrine asserted, too, an endless cycle of cosmic conflagrations and eventual rebirths. Further, Stoics declared that virtue was the only good, that all men belong to a universal brotherhood, and maintained the indestructibility of the soul. In its time it attracted many eminent persons to its ranks, and even today still enlists admirers.

Stone Boat. A talisman or charm among Indian tribes in North America, which was a polished stone, in the shape of a canoe. It was often worn around the neck.

Stonehenge. One of the greatest of ancient European monuments, on Salisbury Plain in England, built by the Druids (q.v.) from 1800 B.C. through 1500 B.C. and used as a religious, occult, and astronomical temple. Built of massive stones, carried 150 miles from Wales, it is acknowledged one of the most remarkable achievements of prehistoric Europe. Arranged in an impressive circular design of concentric stones, topped by stone lintels, with a two-mile-long processional avenue, this remarkable structure was keyed toward determining the arrival of the midsummer sunrise, the summer solstice, when the sun enters the sign of Cancer.

Stone Throwing. See Poltergeist.

Strangler. A term describing the Devil, for in the sixteenth century, it was commonly supposed the Devil strangled people dying of apoplexy.

Subconscious Coloration (Spiritualism). In trance communications, the medium's subconscious mind is said to be used as an instrument by the unseen operators. The message is therefore liable to coloration by reason of the contents of the medium's mind. So much depends upon the skill of the spirit and the passivity of the medium. No amount of coloration can, however, account for knowledge outside of the medium's range being brought through.

Subconscious Mind. That part of the mentality of which one is not immediately aware. It differs from the conscious mind in that it appears to function without awareness of the stimuli, and it has an extensive control over the working details of the bodily organism. Spiritualists assert that spirit messages have revealed that the subconscious can be an instrument which entities can learn to manipulate in order to control a medium's organs, thus producing automatism phenomena.

Hypnotists and psychologists know that under hypnosis, the subconscious mind may be controlled by the hypnotist's suggestion. Some of the most astonishing revelations have come from the subconscious, as, for example, from the subconscious of Edgar Cayce (q.v.). And C. J. Jung (q.v.) has taught us that man is powerfully dominated by the racial inheritance that resides in his subconscious.

Subject. In Spiritualism, a creature of the earth, human or animal, as distinct from a discarnate entity.

Subjective Phenomena. That phenomena which arises within the mind, exclusive of external observation. (As distinguished from objective phenomena.)

Subjectivist Theory of Ethics. One of the chief theories of ethics, which would ascribe ethics to the results of environments and social conditioning alone, recognizing no influence outside of the natural world, and causation.

Subliminal. Psychological term for all mental processes below the threshold of consciousness.

Subud. A mystical movement established in 1947, and stemming from the teachings of Pak Subuh of Indonesia. It does not claim to be a religion, but aims at unity of all peoples in worship of God. It does, however, reserve certain "divine mysteries" as secrets. Pak Subuh was born in 1901 and claimed revelations in his twenty-fourth year; his coming is supposed to have been foretold by Gurdjieff (q.v.).

Sudre, Rene. Psychic researcher and French scientist, Professor L'Ecole des Hautes Etudes Sociales, Vice-President of the National Laboratory for Psychical Research, co-worker with Dr. Gustave Geley (q.v.) at the Institut Metapsychique 1921–26. A prolific writer on psychic subjects.

Sufism. A mystical development within Islam, mostly of Persian influence. Its doctrines summarized are: 1. God alone exists; He is in all things, and all things are in Him. 2. All things are emanations from Him and have no real existence apart from Him. 3. All religions are indifferent. They serve a purpose, however, as leading to realities. The most profitable in this respect is Islam, of which Sufism is the true philosophy. 4. There is no distinction between good and evil; for God is the author of all. 5. It is God who determines the will of man; therefore man is not free in his actions. 6. The soul existed before the body, in which it is confined as in a cage. Death is not to be feared, for it is then the Sufi returns to the bosom of the Deity. 7. Apart from the grace of God, no man can attain to this spiritual union; it may however be attained by fervent prayer. 8. The principal duty of the Sufi is meditation on the unity of God, the remembrance of the Divine names and progressive advancement in the tariquat, or journey of life so as to attain unity with God. However, Sufism is a more sophisticated doctrine than it appears, and its intense concentration on man's relationship to God has frequently led (as it has in Hinduism) to an awareness of the immanence of God; that is that one's self is God. Consequently, Sufism has always attracted a large number of Islam's most brilliant thinkers and writers whom it has stimulated to create some of the most profound philosophical insights and a body of great literature. (See: Ghayali, Rurni, Dervish)

Sufism. One of the very important spiritual-mystical movements of humanity. Sufism was a mystical development within Islam which since its beginnings during the 9th century, has evolved a highly sophisticated body of literature and has created several effective systems of meditation. At its inception, Sufism fed on certain strains of mysticism and pantheistic concepts in Muhammed's teachings, but over the centuries of its career it has added its own native insights and has also incorporated aspects of Gnosticism, Neo-Platonism, Pseudo-Dionysus, Cabalism and perhaps Buddhism. The diversity of its elements along with the purity of its purpose has made it an important species of mysticism that has always attracted a broad variety of persons. The heart of Sufism is the attainment of the soul's union with God. Some of its teachings are: God alone exists; He is in all things and all things are in Him; Absolute Being (God) is also Absolute Beauty; because Being is an emanation of Beauty, God produced the world and all that exists in the world; the soul existed before the body; except for the grace of God no man can attain spiritual union, though it may be attained by devotion and fervent prayer and meditation on the unity of God. Aside from the generally common devices of attaining mystical ecstacy (poverty, austerity, humility, fortitude, discipline, concentration), Sufism has also developed its own uniquely effective routines of meditation along with its famous devotional dances (the well-known whirling dervishes). Further, it has produced a number of special insights, such as: the self is God [see: Samadhi]; the universal man is the archetype of the universe; apprehension of the oneness of everything; the notion of one's nothingness which is beyond nothingness; also, in the teachings of the Indian Kabir (1435–1518) the awareness that Brahmanism, Vaishnavism, and Sufism have a fundamental similarity—that Rama, Hari, and Allah are but one and the same. Finally, Sufism has always attracted the greatest poets and writers of the Muslim world whose brilliant work has won many foreign readers. Some of the most admired of these writers are: Omar Khayyam (died c. 1123), Farid ad-Din Attar (died c. 1230), Jalal ad-Din Rumi (1207–1273), Hafiz (born Shams ad-Din Muhammad) (died c. 1389) and Mawlana ad-Din Jami (1414–1492).

Initially persecuted by orthodox Muslims (particularly since many Sufis preached pantheism and the notion that man was himself also God), it was Ghazali (q.v.) who made Sufism respectable by introducing Sufi mysticism into orthodox Islam. For more than a thousand years Sufism has continued to flourish; its monastic life has been very flexible with its convents, for example, at different periods containing full-time along with part-time residents. Presently, there are hundreds of convents, and the adherents of Sufism number several million. One of Sufism's most popular manuals of mystic instructions was written by Muhammad Amin al-Kurdi al-Shafti al-Naqshaband which contains such precepts as: to attain mystic unification with Allah imagine that you are dead and now all alone to face God's judgment; eliminate every desire of the heart and direct your perception toward God. At its best, Sufism with its spiritual doctrines, its programs of meditation, in addition to the meaningful symbolism, the lyrical beauty, and the basic wisdom of many of its poets and writers has made Sufism in recent years a fruitful source of knowledge for a host of persons in the West who are seeking a way of achieving spiritual enlightenment, and, too, self awareness, self development, and inner peace.

Suggestion. Defined by F. W. H. Myers (q.v.) as a "successful appeal to the subliminal self." Hypnotism provides the best examples of its power. As the subliminal or subconscious mind has control over the body far transcending the conscious, a successful suggestion may accomplish seeming miracles; affecting heart beats, circulation, inhibitions, memory, etc. It cannot, however, produce new knowledge.

Sukha-dukha (Hinduism). The pursuit of pleasure and the resulting pain bring the involvement in activity and thought which prevents the achievement of moksa (q.v.).

Sukya. Throughout Central America a sorcerer who practices the art of curing disease.

Sumeru (Buddhism, Hinduism). The ancient notion of the earth as a mountain which stands in the midst of the world-ocean.

Summerland. In Spiritualism it is the sphere of the spirit world most often referred to. Summerland appears to be a blissful land of rest and harmony, partly a creation of the inhabitant's own desires, but to what extent cannot be determined. Many descriptions seem to suggest the pleasures of earth life minus its drawbacks. In Summerland they would seem to have trees, animals, houses, lakes, gardens, rivers, also recreative activities, halls of learning and infinite leisure.

Sunya-vada (Buddhism). Meaning the world is a void or unreal. This doctrine belongs to the school of Mahayana Buddhism (q.v.).

Superconscious Mind. Term used by F. W. H. Myers to define the higher aspects of the conscious mind, as in intuition.

Superior Planets. Those farther in orbit from the Sun than the Earth's: Mars, Jupiter, Saturn, Uranus, Neptune, and Pluto.

Supernatural. Phenomena which violate natural laws. But · man throughout his history and everywhere has believed in the supernatural in all its relationships—the religious, the occult, the psychic, and the mystic. In fact, his devotion to this dimension of his existence was so widespread, constant, and intense that though the supernatural supposedly "violates natural laws," it was this same preoccupation that produced all the disciplines which have made it possible to understand the natural laws (astronomy, physics, chemistry and mathematics) plus all the rest of man's major creations—religion, philosophy, literature and architecture—and all the other arts.

Supernormal. Coined by F. W. H. Myers in substitution for supernatural, when describing psychic phenomena. Its modern equivalent is *paranormal* (q.v.), meaning not as yet within accepted experience of cause and effect.

Supraliminal. Psychological term for the mental content above the threshold of consciousness.

Supreme Spirit. A term often used in Spiritualism signifying God, or Unifying Consciousness.

Survival. The continuation of personality after death is the core of all forms of religion and of all spiritual doctrines. Given that man's unique distinction on earth is his soul, then it seems natural to perceive it as being a fragment of a divine spirit. And given, too, that this divinity is universally accepted as immortal, it follows that man's soul is also imperishable. But the leap from the imperishability of the soul to the imperishability of the body is quite a natural evolution in most religious and spiritual movements—particularly after the creation of this idea by the ancient Egyptians (See: Spheres)

Surya (Hinduism). Meaning the sun, the Sun-god.

Sutra (Hinduism-Buddhism). The earliest form of aphorism, embodying a philosophic or behavioral notion for guidance in the conduct of life. In Buddhism, a Sutra means any of the sermons of Buddha.

Svabhava (Hinduism). This fundamental concept has several meanings. On the one hand it signifies: the essence, natural state, innate nature. Secondly, some Hindu thinkers use the term to mean: the spontaneous interaction of the various world substances, for in their view this is the principle that governs the universe.

Swaffer, Hannen. Born in 1879, he was a popular journalist, author and spiritualist, and succeeded Sir Arthur Conan Doyle as President of the S.N.U.

Swastika. One of the most widely used symbols throughout both the ancient and modern world, it was used by the Hindus, the Egyptians, the Trojans, the Druids, American Indian tribes, etc. The Hindu Brahmin priests use it in the ceremony of the lightning stick, while the worshippers of Vishnu decorate their foreheads with swastikas. Fundamentally, the swastika symbolizes the sun, its hooks being the solar movements. Also, the good-luck swastika revolves sunwise, to the right; the bad-luck swastika turns to the left.

Swedenborg, Emanuel (1688–1772). One of those luminous geniuses who was not only a master of many disciplines but whose discoveries and inventions in all of these areas were nearly always years ahead of his time. The descendant of a long line of famous clergymen and scholars (his father was a distinguished Bishop and author), this universal man became the most eminent person in Swedish history. Proficient in mathematics, astronomy, chemistry, physics, physiology, philosophy, and religion—he wrote the first book in the Swedish language on algebra; he was the first to evolve the nebular hypothesis of planet formation; he formulated a vortex theory of particle movement in atoms which closely resembles the nucleus-electron model of contemporary physics; he was the first to discover the true nature of the cerebrospinal fluid; he was the first to discover that the motion of the brain synchronizes with that of the lungs; and he made notable contributions to philosophy. Then he dazzled his age in a completely contrary fashion: with unparalleled visions of the spiritual world and his apocalyptic views on the true nature of Christianity—which established him as a seer-visionary-prophet, the progenitor of a new Christian church. In addition to these superhuman achievements, Swedenborg, who served for some thirty years as assessor of the Royal College of Mines, made outstanding contributions to and important inventions in metallurgy, mining, shipping, and in various military areas. Up to 1745, Swedenborg's main labors and discoveries were in the physical and biological sciences. But in 1745 occurred a transcendant event in his life: he experienced a divine vision and call from God. This call he declared was a command to announce the second advent of God on earth. Henceforth, he dedicated his entire soul-illumined genius to preparing for this epiphany: to report, therefore, the return of the Messiah; to describe the reality of the spiritual world; to help build the creation of the new Jerusalem; and to describe the true meaning of the divine word to man. Further, it was necessary to cleanse Christianity of its false doctrines, to formulate a true Christian theology, and to establish the new age of truth and reason in religion. Swedenborg preached that all creation—including the universe and man's earth, has its origins in divine love and wisdom. All his prodigious output of theological works centered on the theme that God is the Divine Man who combines—as does every man—a trinity of love, wisdom, and activity. Swedenborg died in 1772, but in 1784 the Swedenborgian church was founded in England. Emmanuel Swedenborg's life and work has had an animating influence on the sciences, on literature, on spiritualism, and, of course, on theology. Some of his important books are: *Heaven and Hell; The Infinite and the Final Cause of Creation, Also the Intercourse Between the Soul and the Body; The Five Senses;* and *The Worship and Love of God.* Also, see: G. Trobridge—*Swedenborg, Life and Teaching,* 4th ed.

Sycomancy. Divination by using the leaves of the fig tree. Questions were written on the leaves. A quick-drying leaf was an evil omen while a slow-drying one was a good augury.

Symbolism. The art of representation by different means.

Synchronicity. A theory of acausal action, relating meaningful coincidences, put forward by C. G. Jung, (q.v.) after a study of the random symbolic methods of various divination practices. An avid student of astrology, Jung utilized his theory of synchronicity in several experiments to prove the merit of astrology.

Synthesis. In astrology, this is the art of combining the separate influences in a nativity and establishing a summary thereof. Only experienced astrologers possess the skill necessary to achieve a true synthesis.

Tabernacle (Judaism). A temple which Moses built, at God's instigation, for the wandering Jews in the desert as a holy place of prayer and worship. Authorities have envisioned it as a symbol of the universe: the 12 loaves symbolizing the 12 months of the year; the 70 branches of the candlesticks symbolizing the divisions of the planets; the 7 lamps being analogous to the 7 planets; finally, the tabernacle's veils in 4 colors being a symbol of the 4 elements. Cabalists, mindful that the famous Jewish historian Josephus described it in these terms, were strongly influenced by his judgment.

Tabernacle of Peace (Cabalism). In the ancient historic Jewish community of Safed, Palestine, this was an ascetic organization, devoted to Judaic mysticism, notably Cabalism.

Tabl. A drum used by the ancient Egyptians in many of their mystery ceremonies and medical practices, often played with a feathery, insistent rhythm. Made of a wooden shell with little depth, these drums, even to this day, are frequently orchestrated in pairs, and then they are called tabbalat arrakeb.

Table Turning, Rapping. Typtology. In the early days of 1850, it became almost a fashionable pastime to hold sittings for this purpose. The sitters would place their fingertips lightly on the table-top, just touching those of their neighbors, then with lowered lights the table would rock slightly, and by an agreed code, spell out messages. The table is rarely used today. Like automatic writing and planchette methods, it lends itself too readily to subconscious motivation.

Tables of Houses. In Astrology, this is the essential information by which to calculate the following information: the birth chart's Ascendant and Midheaven, the cusps of all the other houses, and the different latitudes and the varying sidereal time. Tables by Dalton, Raphael, and Hugh Rice are available in occult book stores. There are a number of systems used to calculate the cusps of the Intermediate Houses, but those considered the best are the Campanus, Regiomantus, Horizontal, and Placidus.

Tablet for Anointing. In ancient Egyptian burial rites this was an alabaster slab incised with seven hollows to hold the seven holy oils. Giving magical protection on the trip to a new life in the next world, the oils were administered to the body in one of the last ceremonies at the tomb.

Taboo. A practice found in most primitive tribes, based on a rule of prohibition, the violation of which brings an inviolable penalty that is imposed by the rituals of magic or religion. Mainly, the taboo is centered on a prohibition against violating that which was dangerous, unclean, or sacred; and, further, it was forbidden in general use.

Tadebtsois. The Samoyed tribes of Siberia believe these are invisible spirits who continually fly through the atmosphere threatening their existence. To mollify these spirits the Samoyed hires a professional Tadibe (q.v.).

Tadibe. Among the Samoyed tribes of Siberia a Shaman who possesses abilities as a sorcerer, medicine man, magician, and necromancer. These skills enable him to go into a trance by which he contacts the spirits (Tadebtsois—q.v.); he can also conjure, cure illnesses, and perform startling feats of magic. His office is hereditary but still requires much training; nevertheless, any tribesman who exhibits special aptitudes as a Shaman is permitted to enter the priesthood.

T'ai Chi. A highly important symbol in Chinese art which represented the Great Absolute. A circle half red—the yang (q.v.) and half black—the yin (q.v.) is bisected by a wavy or double-curved line; also, there are eight trigrams (see I Ching); finally, in many representations of T'ai Chi the twelve signs of the Zodiac are incorporated.

Taigheirm. In past times in the Islands and Highlands of Scotland, this was a magical sacrifice of black cats to the underground gods and the infernal spirits. Exorcists engaged in this ritual to obtain from the devils the gift of second sight.

Taleb. In the culture of the Arabs, one who is a holy or a learned man.

Talisman. An object which may be a stone, a ring, a pendant, etc., possessing occult powers (akin to a charm, q.v.). The supposed wondrous, magical powers of what is most often an engraved object sometimes belong to the owner even though the object may be absent. Talismans, like charms, may be a wand against evil.

Talmud (Judaism). A vast work in Hebrew-Aramaic compiled through some 800 years (300 B.C.–500A.D.), composed of some six orders which are subdivided into 63 treatises, representing both the oral tradition of Judaism and a commentary on the Old Testament. The *Mishnah*, the older portion of the Talmud, and the *Gemara*, a commentary on the *Mishnah*, embody the philosophy, history, ethics, sciences, folklore, etc., that occurred, developed and accumulated through these centuries.

Tamarisk. A tree flourishing in the Mediterranean world, bearing feathery branches and credited with extraordinary occult powers. The tamarisk is often planted close to sacred temples. There is a notable grove next to the Temple of Philae (island of the Nile) which legend reports as the burial site of Osiris.

Tamas (Hinduism). The principle of inactivity and indifference in matter or *prakti* (q.v.) elaborated in the Tamas, one of the three *gunas* of the *sankhya* (q.v.).

Tamate. Among the South Pacific people of Melanesia it means a spirit; for their neighbors in the New Hebrides, the term designates a secret society primarily dedicated to the spirits of the dead.

Tamburan. A sacred house in the culture of the people of New Guinea.

Tammuz. The Babylonian god of vegetation and springtime, beloved by Ishtar (q.v.), who descended into Hades when Tammuz was slain in order to bring him back again. The mystery of his life and resurrection was re-enacted each year.

Tamouanehan. A term used by the Aztecs of Central America which referred to the holy place of unborn souls.

Tane. The Polynesian creator god who was also the god of beauty. Kane was another name for this divinity.

Tanit. The Carthaginian goddess of the heavens and the moon, the virigin goddess identified with the Phoenician goddess Astarte (q.v.). In her temple at Carthage was the sacred veil, the city's protector, its most treasured palladium.

Tannaim (Judaism-Cabalism). Rabbinic sages who compiled later condensations and supplements of the Torah, the Talmud (q.v.), and the Bible canon following the first century A.D. One of the most popular of all the books which interpreted the canon of Jewish law was written by the Tanna (singular of Tannaim) Joseph Caro (1488–1575), the famous Cabalist of Safed, Israel. His book titled *The Shulchan Aruch* (The Set Table) still commands enormous authority among Orthodox world-Jewry.

Tantras (Hinduism, Buddhism). A large body of works, outside the Vedic (q.v.) tradition, which are dialogues between Siva and his wife. These discussions cover ritual, magic, salvation, witchcraft, charms, the obtaining of union with the divine, superhuman powers, power for good or evil over people, success in business, and the perfect ecstacy of sexual performance. The tantras were composed over a period from the 7th century A.D. to about the 15th century A.D. The paintings in Hindu and Tibetan tantrism of a male and female enjoying sexual intercourse are supposed to represent the mystic union of the godhead with itself out of which has occurred the creation of the universe. For the two central notions of the tantras (a body of some 64 treatises, mainly Hindu but some Buddhist) is salvation through union with the divine; and the teaching of the supremacy of the female principle as the divine energy. (See: Tantrikism)

Tantrikism (Lamaism, Buddhism). Worship of the divine energy (*Sakti*) in the female form. (See: Tara and Kali.) Believers perceive the bliss of Buddha and Siva is the result of union with their female partners, thus Nirvana can be obtained through sexual union. An abundant literature on erotic practices has been created on the subject with the *Tathagatagunyaka* the most explicit (q.v.).

Tao. Chinese word for Logos, the Absolute, or the course of nature; a conception of an impersonal deity. The Taoist doctrine implies a passive reaction to the world, in sharp contrast to the Confucian system of activity.

Tao (Taoism, Confucianism). In Taoism, it means the way, principle, cosmic order, nature. Though it is vague and hidden, deep and obscure, in it is all form, essence, reality. Tao produced all things. Its two great standards are "let alone" and "the Natural." Finally, it may be achieved but it cannot be seen; it may be transmitted, but it cannot be received. In Confucianism, it represents the moral order and life, truth, the moral law and principle; it also means following the Reason of things and the Reason which is in everything. The way determines the active principles—yang (q.v.) and the passive—yin. (q.v.)

Tao shu (Taoism). The essence of Tao (q.v.), the center at which all infinities and distinctions merge and disappear.

Tao Te Ching (Taoism). The basic book of Taoism.

T'ao T'ieh. In ancient Chinese art a symbol for the elemental concept representing the powers of life.

Tapas. Yoga exercises designed to free the spirit from the body.

Tara (Lamaism). Tibetan goddess, the female companion of Avalo-kitesvara, the preeminent bodhisattva (q.v.) of Mahayana Buddhism (q.v.). She is also important in Tantrikism (q.v.). The green Tara and the white Tara (the former worshipped in Nepal the latter in China) are incarnations of the two Buddhist wives of Sron-tsan-gampo who introduced Buddhism to Tibet.

Targ, Russell. Parapsychologist at the Stanford Research Institute whose unusual background has made him highly qualified to engage in paranormal research. His status as a senior research physicist at S.R.I. (10 years of experience in laser investigation), his skill as a magician, and his long years of interest in parapsychology, have given him the qualifications to do advanced work in his present profession. It was Targ who persuaded Geller (q.v.) when he came to S.R.I. to undertake the elaborate series of tests which attracted so much attention.

Target. A term in ESP (q.v.) and psychokinesis (q.v.). In ESP it means the mental or psychic aspects the subject is attempting to pinpoint by understanding or action. In psychokinesis it is the movement of objects according to psychic transference.

Targum (Judaism). A translation or interpretation in Aramaic of a portion of a book of the Old Testament. Some of the targumists introduced mystical notions into their interpretations which demand knowledge of the great mystical tradition of Judaism.

Tarot. The seventy-eight picture cards which have been used as a system of divination for thousands of years, based, many believe, on the ancient Egyptian Book of Thoth. The symbolic figures on the cards represent the stages in man's destiny, being divided into the major arcana of 22 cards, and the minor arcana of 56 cards. In the minor, are four suits: swords, pentacles, wands or scepters, 14 in each suit. However, the major arcana represent a far-ranging sweep of esoteric insight demanding close study. That the modern playing cards are derived from the Tarot deck is believed established by the close similarity in our present-day pack to—the swords are now clubs, the pentacles are now diamonds, the cups are now hearts, and the wands are now spades. Most recent archaelogical evidence traces the introduction of the tarot cards to Europe by way of the city of Marseilles in France. It is believed that they were brought either by Greek colonists who came to what is now Marseilles about 600 B.C. or by Phoenician colonists who had preceded the Greeks.

Tart, Charles. One of America's foremost parapsychologists. Tart, a professor at the University of California at Davis, has made notable studies in altered states of consciousness (q.v.) and the complex relationships between ESP and the brain's alpha wave patterns. Aware that parapsychologists are merely on the frontier of scientific knowledge in the domain of the paranormal, Tart has, nonetheless, written some of the most informative and challenging papers and books on the subject, notably—*Altered States of Consciousness*—1969. See also: "Hypnosis, Psychedelics, and Psi: Conceptual Models" in Cavanna and Ullman's book—*Psi and Altered States of Consciousness*—1968; *On Being Stoned: A Psychological Study of Marijuana Intoxication* —1971.

Tartini, Giuseppe (1692–1770). Italian violinist and the composer of *The Devil's Sonata*. Tradition has it that this "Sonata" was dictated to Tartini by the Devil during a dream.

Tashli Lama (Lamaism). In Tibet, the lama just below the Dalai Lamai. He is considered an incarnation of Amitabha Buddha.

Ta shun (Taoism). That total harmony resulting from profound virtue or that mysterious power which results from a mystic union with the universe.

Tasseography. Divination by reading tea leaves in a teacup.

Ta-Tcheseht. In ancient Egypt, a term for the underworld.

Tate, Sharon. The American actress who in 1969 was murdered in a ritualistic slaying, commanded by the "Messiah" Charles Manson, a devotee of Black Magic (q.v.). The Manson "family" (a floating group of some half dozen followers) lived under his total control. Three of this group who carried out the murder of Sharon Tate and six other victims were sentenced to death along with their Satanic leader, Charles Manson. (See: Charles Manson)

Tathagatagunyaka (Hinduism). One of the Tantras (q.v.) which elaborates the worship of the divine energy in female form, and explores sexual union and erotic practices and techniques in the most unrestrained manner. Convinced that the mystic union of Siva and his Shakti (Devi) is both a union of the Godhead with itself and the zenith of all bliss, the *Tathagatagunyaka* devotes itself to an examination of every human medus and nuance by which sexual experience can duplicate this ecstacy on earth.

Tattva (Hinduism). The 36 *tattvas*, created by Siva (q.v.), which represents an unfolding of the universe in the abstract conscious life as his mind awakened and recognized the relations determining reality.

Tat Tvam Asi (Hinduism). A basic concept of Hinduism, meaning: "That art thou"; that is, you and Brahman-Atman are one.

Tau Cross. Shaped in the design of a T, it is an ancient symbol of eternal life. The Druids (q.v.) would venerate and make sacred a tree by etching into its bark the shape of a tau cross. Among Christians it is hailed as the "Cross of St. Anthony," since the saint was allegedly martyred on such a cross. Freemasonry utilizes it as one of its symbols.

Tauler, Johannes (1300–1361). One of the most eminent of German mystics, he was greatly influenced by Eckhart (q.v.). Born in Strassburg, he joined the Dominican order, studied in Cologne, and became probably the most acute observer of the mind as it grapples with the immanent presence of God. His work on the ethical and religious aspects of mysticism has exercised a continuing influence in Western mysticism, and most notably on Martin Luther. His sermons have gone through many editions.

Taurobolium. In the ancient Persian religion of Mithras (q.v.) this was the blood baptism into the mysteries of the Mithraic cult, and also into the mysteries of the Great Mother goddess Cybele of Phrygia, Asia Minor. The Cult of Mithras became popular among the Romans, and most especially with the soldiers. Initiates were reborn into a new and purified life when the blood of a sacrificed bull flowed down upon them from a grating below the sacrificial platform.

Taurus. Astrological sign (April 21–May 21) Element—earth; Symbol—the Bull; Ruling planet—Venus. Qualities—strongly independent, forceful, enjoy the good things of life; are warm, friendly, affectionate, and comfortable with domesticity; extraordinarily receptive and able to assimilate the thoughts of others; and have great memories. On the adverse side, they are inflexible and stubborn; intense despisers of enemies, moody in their response to others; too lavish in their spending, and often overloaded with carrying the burdens of others. Self-control is the most pressing of the habits essential to the success of this sign.

Tawhid. In the Muslim religion a term for the oneness of Allah.

Tchama. In ancient Egypt a papyrus roll used for all important papers and compositions. The famous *Book of the Dead* (q.v.) is one of the best known tcahamas, being 123 feet in length.

Tefnet. Egyptian goddess, wife of Shu, and mother of Nut and Keb. She is represented as two-headed.

Telegnosis. That knowledge of another mind which does not depend on perception or physical relationships, but is nonetheless immediately perceived. (*See:* Telepathy)

Telekinesis. The movement of objects without any other means than the utilization of psychic energy. However, this capability is not always available to the psychic who has demonstrated this talent. Spiritualists assert that mediums achieve telekinesis by ectoplasmic extensions from the medium's body.

Teleology. The belief that divine causes can be inferred from a study of means and ends.

Telepathic Control. See Book Tests.

Telepathic Instructions (Lamaism). Tibetan instruction in mysticism, during which initiates are taught by the means of telepathy (q.v.); which uses silence, or signs and gestures without any speech.

Telepathy. The transmission of thoughts from one person to another and excluding any form of communication through any type of sensory perception. Most commonly this phenomenon occurs with those who have achieved some degree of attunement. Telepathy, however, does not refer to the clairvoyant perception of objective events. (See: Parapsychology)

Teleplasm. The material from which the voice box is made for production of direct voice phenomena. Ectoplasm from the medium is mixed by the spirit operators with "psychoplasm" to produce a palpable substance called "teleplasm," capable of being molded into various shapes.

Telescope in Dreams. In old dream interpretation, to dream that one is looking at the stars is a sign of coming advancement in the world; to dream that one is looking at the moon, and with great pleasure, is a revelation of future abundant wealth.

Telescopic Vision. A particular kind of clairvoyant perception, akin to viewing through a long telescope things not perceivable in the normal way.

Telesomatic. Term descriptive of materialization.

Telesthesia. Communication of sensation at a distance.

Tellurian. Characteristic of earth. An earthly inhabitant.

Telluric Force. Rhabdic force, which means the unknown force which activates the divining rod when dowsing.

Tellurism. A supposed magnetic influence permeating the earth and its creatures, formerly believed to be the cause of animal magnetism.

Templars. Christian order, formed at Jerusalem in 1119 by a group of French Knights to protect the Christian shrines of Palestine and the Christians from the attacks of Moslems. Spreading all over Europe, and governed by a Grand Master, their success and power drove the Roman Church to accuse them of heresy. In 1306, their Grand Master was charged in Paris by the Inquisition with anti-Christian practices specifically, of worshipping the Devil, Islam, "Baphomet" (q.v.), and of practicing vile vice. Their members were destroyed, their property confiscated, and their order everywhere suppressed; they finally disappeared as a movement by the end of the 14th century.

Tempon-teloris-Ship of the Dead. This ship is believed by the Dayaks of Borneo to carry the souls of the dead through the fire-sea to the shores of the Blessed.

Temporal. Pertaining to earth life, as measured by time. Transient, limited existence.

Temurah I (Cabalism). One of the three ancient methods used by Cabalists in the rearrangement of Bible words or sentences to derive the esoteric substratum and deep spiritual meaning of these words. *Gematria*, and *Notarikon* (qq.v.) are analogous devices.

Temurah II (Judaism). The art of word-changing in Hebrew mysticism by which a change of letters in a word creates a new meaning of a Biblical statement.

Ten. In religion and mysticism this number represents both totality and completion. For example; in the *Rig Veda* (q.v.) there are 10 books of hymns; Buddha is described as possessing 10 noble states and 10 powers; in Northern Buddhism, there are 10 Paramitas or sublime virtues; in the Babylonian myth of the flood, 10 Kings (10 ages) preceded the flood; in Judaism, the Temple of Solomon and the Temple in Ezekiel's vision are structured in their dimensions by 10, and 10 is the symbol of the Absolute and the law; in Pythagoreanism 1, 2, 3, 4 are the tetrad, while their union is the decad—10; for Plato, 1 to 10 was the form of the 10 archetypal principles upon which the world is created, and he described 10 princedoms in Atlantis (q.v.) upon which the world was based; Cabalism (q.v.) describes the 10 sepiroth (q.v.) as the Macroprosopus—the "Greater Countenance,' which foreshadows the archetypal man, Adam Kadmon (q.v.); finally, some occultists picture 10 as the regulator in the realm of numbers.

Tephramancy. Divination which studies the ashes of the fire remaining from the bodies of a sacrifice.

Teraphim (Judaism). A term in the Old Testament designating certain images, idols, or household gods that were the object of worship and utilized in divination by many Israelites.

Teresa of Avila, Saint (1515–1582). Spanish Carmelite nun, a noblewoman who forsook her privileged world and became a tremendous reformer of the Catholic Church. Acknowledged as one of the most renowned mystics, she was also a founder of a new Carmelite order and with St. John of the Cross (q.v.) founded convents for friars. Her spirituality, wisdom, wit, common sense, practicality, shrewdness, managerial genius, and the extraordinary depth of her mystic insight and literary work have marked her as one of history's foremost women. Despite long years of intense and powerful opposition within the Church, her remarkable gifts eventually proved her reform movement invincible. Her Discalced or Barefoot Carmelites with their strict religious devotion, after her death, spread from Spain all over Europe. Not only did she inspire a massive religious awakening in Spain, but her writings which are considered spiritual classics, have won her fame throughout Christendom and the world. (See:*Life; Spiritual Relations; The Interior Castle; Exclamations of the Soul to God*.)

Teshub. In the ancient Hittite religion, the god of thunder.

Testament of Abraham (Judaism). The apocalyptic book written sometime between the 2nd century B.C. and the 2nd century A.D. which narrates Abraham's death and ascent to heaven. This divine revelation reflects the Hellenized period of Jewish mystical writing in which a great number of such apocalyptic books were written, notably: *The Testament of Adam and Eve, The Testaments of Isaac and Jacob, The Testament of Solomon, The Testament of Job,* etc.

Testament of Solomon. A grimoire (q.v.) reputed to have been written somewhere between 100 to 400 A.D.

Tetrabiblos. One of the greatest of all works on astrology, which is recognized as truly the bible for astrologers, this four-volume book was written by Claudius Ptolemy (q.v.). Modern astrologers, however, must make corrections when Ptolemy is calculating by his geocentric astronomy, since, following Copernicus, modern astronomy is heliocentric.

Tetractys—Ten Symbolic Dots. In the system of Pythagoras (q.v.), this was the symbol of ten dots by which he determined there were ten planets in our solar system. Science confirmed his theory when, adding to the seven planets known by the ancients, Uranus, Neptune, and Pluto were finally discovered. The symbol

.
. .
. . .
. . . .

was used by Pythagoras to explain his conception of the truths of the universe. For by connecting these dots in ways that formed many rectangles and triangles, his complex mathematical system yielded logical deductive information foretelling the structure of nature.

Tetragammaton. For the Cabalists the mystical symbol of God, which has been part of the long Hebrew mystical tradition. The "ineffable name" of God by which all the powers of the universe could be controlled was composed of four letters, signifying Yahweh, pronounced in the Hebrew as "Adonai," and written, generally, JHVH. Sometimes it was written—JHWH, YHVH, or YHWH. In English, it becomes Jehovah.

Tetragammaton Elohim. The latter word, the Hebrew name for God, and the first word (q.v.), being a powerful term, this super-charged phrase was used as one of the nine mystic terms by which to call up demons.

Tezcatlipoca. The Toltec-Aztec god of gods, the sun-god, god of day and night. In the honoring festival each spring, a young man, impersonating the god, was ceremoniously wedded to four wives, then slaughtered; and along with him thousands of others were sacrificed in the belief that this river of human blood would insure that Tezcatlipoca would be forever alive.

Thangawalu. Among the Fijians in the South Pacific a term for one of the giant deities.

Thaumaturge. Although this is an ambiguous word with a long, evolutionary history, essentially it means a worker of miracles or wonders. With its roots in the prototypal Indo-European language, from whence it came to the Greek language, it bears an ancient heritage. As it clearly should, for almost from the birth of civilization there have been thaumaturges—shamans, Druids, medicine men, magicians (qq.v), etc. Moreover, the shaman, the Druid, the medicine man was always much larger than a mere "worker of miracles," for he was also an intercessor with the higher spirits and the gods, and, therefore, both in reality and in symbol, the exemplar and the authority of a religion. It was only in relatively modern history that a split in the function of thaumaturge occurred. In the earliest years of Christianity, the thaumaturge referred to an outstanding saint who was heralded for his miracles, but somewhere in the 13th century it lost its status and came to designate only the magician. One of the most remarkable thaumaturges in the early period was Simon Magus (q.v.) who, as formerly, exemplified in himself both the awesome miracle worker and the majestic saint; ambition, however, drove him to outsoar his lifetime's fame—he founded a new religion and installed Simon Magus as God. Two of the saints of Christianity who were prominent thaumaturges were St. Gregory, bishop of Caesarea (c. 260–330), famous for his miracles; and the charismatic, mystic St. Bernard (1091–1153), Thaumaturge of the West, so powerful that for many years he was the uncrowned Pope and Emperor of Europe.

Thaumaturgy. The performance of miracles and of magic by a thaumaturge (q.v.). A thaumaturgist who is a master utilizes beneficient powers, unlike an exponent of black magic (q.v.).

Thedoros of Lemmos. The legendary Greek witch, chronicled by historians, whose fame as a sorceress led to her condemnation and eventual execution.

Theocracy. The state governed by the law of God; that political organization governed by divine will. The ancient Hebrew and Muslim states, and Calvinist Protestantism in Geneva are examples of church and state functioning as one structure.

Theogony. A history and geneological account of the gods, which also reveals their origin.

Theomancy. In the ancient world this was divination by oracles believed to be divinely inspired. In Cabalism (q.v.) the utilization of these divine oracles was the proper method to win the power of God's omnipotence; in magic divination by theomancy was achieved through the recital of the arcane sacred names.

Theophagy. The widely spread practice in the ancient world of eating the body of the god. In Christianity, the Eucharist, in which the consecrated bread and wine is consumed in the ritual of Holy Communion, reflects this ancient practice of theophagy; for the early Christians ate of the paschal lamb, the burnt offering which symbolized the crucified Jesus.

Theophany. The miraculous evocation of a god to a human being; for example, of Jehovah to Moses; also, the supernatural change of Jesus on the mountain—*Matt.* 17:1–9. In ancient Egypt, the theophany referred to their gods, both animal and half-animal.

Theosophic Addition. The theosophic value of a number is obtained by adding together all the figures in a sequence; for example, 4 equals all the digits from 1 to 4 added together thus: 1 + 2 + 3 + 4 which together equal 10.

Theosophical Society. Mme. Blavatsky (q.v.), founder with Col. H. S. Olcott of the Society in 1875, defined its doctrines as being based on: "Wisdom Religion or Divine Wisdom, the substance and basis of all world religions and philosophies, taught and practiced by a few elect, since man became a thinking being." This elect, the supreme teachers, being the masters, adepts, mahatmas, or great white brotherhood (q.v.)—are ever-present and are still aiding in the evolution of the perfect man through the universally divine emanations of goodness, beauty, and truth. The activities of "astral shells" (q.v.) produce spirit messages (where the masters are strongly active), compulsory reincarnation, and the development of latent psychic powers. However, Mme. Blavatsky renounced the reincarnation doctrine (according to Dr. Carl Wickland) in a communication. The society's headquarters is established in Adyar, Madras, India. (*See:* Theosophy)

Theosophy. Historically, this term, meaning "divine widom," was coined by Ammonius Saccas (q.v.) to describe the philosophy, religion, and science from the Orient, the Greek mystery schools (q.v.), the Hebrew Essenes, etc., which form an accumulation of mystical experience, a deposit of divine truth. Evolving from the supreme religious teachers (Buddha, Confucius, Zoroaster, Manu, Pythagoras, Plato, the divine incarnations of Hinduism, Sankaracharya, and Jesus), it also embodies elements from the Gnostics, the Neoplatonists, Boehme, Paracelsus, Bruno, etc. (qq.v.). For Theosophy, genuine reality inheres in the spiritual world which creates the material world in a sequence of emanations that reveal the supreme godhead; therefore, man is a soul within several bodies—physical, astral, invisible mental; man lives a great number of lives. Since all existence is dominated by polarity, spirit and matter, then life also exhibits this quality. The soul, in an ovoid of luminous matter being an immortal entity, shapes the mental body—to think; the astral body—to feel; the physical body—to act. Finally, universal cycles, in body, psyche, soul and spirit develop—the minor one representing the reincarnation of soul in many human beings, the major one representing "the cycle of necessity" or the evolution of the spirit over immense periods of time. (See: Theosophical Society)

Therapeutae. A Jewish monastic order of monks and nuns which flourished near Lake Mareotis, south of Alexandria in Egypt, long before the advent of Jesus Christ. Distraught by the immorality and evil rampant in their time, many Alexandrian Jews sought to become "healers of their own souls" (the meaning of Therapeutae), and formed a monastery to live a life of holiness. Some of their godly devotions, however, resembled Dionysian ecstacy, particularly their dancing and singing during certain festivals. The Jewish Therapeutae were also ardent mystics whose knowledge of the mystery-cults of the Persians, the Chaldeans, the Gnostic anchorites, and the mystical Platonic philosophers enriched their own Hebrew inheritance of mystic tradition. Early Christianity in its monastic developments used the examples of the Therapeutae as a model for its own institutions.

Theresa, Saint (1873–1897). French Carmelite nun. At the age of 15 she joined the Carmelite convent at Lisieux, and though frail and tubercular, she is credited with many miracles. Perhaps her greatest miracle is the fact that she has become one of the most widely loved saints of the Catholic church, for she was but a shy plain nun, distinguished only by her godly goodness and beautiful holiness. Her autobiography and letters glow with the purity of naked humility and simplicity, teaching the achievement of goodness through doing the humblest tasks and actions, qualities that have made her books remarkably popular.

Theriolatry. In ancient Egypt the practice of worshipping the gods in the form of animals.

Theurgy. This Greek term meaning wonder-working refers to the occult art of achieving the agreement of divine or beneficent supernatural powers to desist from an action. Conversely, through the discipline of self-purification, sacred rites, and the understanding of signatures in nature (divine signals), the theurgist gains the assistance of supernatural, divine, or beneficent spirits in a desired action. (See: Thaumaturge)

Thiasoi. Communities of brotherhoods in ancient Greece who were initiates in the Orphic Mysteries, the cult worship of Dionysus or Bacchus established by Orpheus (q.v.).

Thief in Dreams. In old dream interpretation, a dream of thieves robbing your home is a prediction of honor and profit—the good fortune proportionate to the amount robbed. But to dream that you catch the thief and achieve his arrest signifies you will have trouble enjoying your good fortune.

Third Eye. An occult organ of psychic vision supposedly situated in the forehead. Attempts have been made to identify this fabulous organ with the pineal gland, at one time considered to be the seat of the soul.

Thirteen (Cabalism). The number analogous to unity.

Thomas the Rhymer. (c. 1220–c. 1297)Legendary Scottish soothsayer who achieved widespread fame as a prophet during his own lifetime and for centuries after. He was a man of wealth and owner of estates near Berwickshire and Roxburgh. Sir Walter Scott bought some of the land reputedly once owned by Rhymer. Many poets and writers, including Scott, wrote tributes to the prophet and supposed poet. His sayings and prophecies have long been cherished and influential among the people of Scotland.

Thomas, Rev. C. Drayton. English psychic experimenter who was notable for his book tests, experiments designed to exclude telepathy in mediumistic communications. By this method the communicator quotes a precise passage in a book or newspaper accessible to the experimenter, the appropriateness of which has a direct bearing on the matter under discussion. Excellent results have been obtained by this and similar methods (see Cross-Correspondence), which provide some evidence for survival.

Thompson, Mrs. R. English medium who having exhibited physical mediumship, was persuaded by F. W. H. Myers (q.v.) to give her services to the S.P.R. (q.v.) in 1898. There she gave trance sittings only. His belief in survival was mainly due to the many sittings he had with this medium. After his death in 1901, Mrs. Thompson, on an impulse,gave two sittings to Sir Oliver Lodge, who obtained characteristic communications from Myers.

Thor. Scandinavian god of thunder, son of Odin (q.v.). It was believed that lightning flashed from his mighty hammer, and that his rolling chariot caused thunder. Far up in the black clouds was Bilskinir, his mansion. He was a god of deeds, journeying through the world destroying giants, splitting mountains, and creating paths for precious streams of water. Our Thursday commemorates his name.

Thoth. Ancient Egyptian god of wisdom, inventor of the arts and sciences, speech and writing. Most frequently he is represented as an ibis or with an ibis head. In the Greek pantheon, Hermes was identified with Thoth.

Thought Forms. In the occult and in parapsychology thoughts are things which frequently possess more dynamic power and resultant force than material elements. For example, there are numerous cases on record in which psychics by viewing an object that belonged to a criminal have been able to help the police discover his whereabouts. For these objects seem to transmit to the psychic operator thought forms which have attached themselves to these objects. Thought alone has been known to produce an image on exposed photographic plate. In the East, a well known phenonemon is the building up of an objective image by the sheer power of thought concentration. Ages of fakirs (q.v.) have performed these extraordinary feats which are simply "thought forms." But the ability to create these seeming actualities takes years of careful practice.

Thought Power. The power of thought is far more subtle, potent and extensive than is generally realized. Recent tests in extrasensory perception conducted by researchers would seem to support this assertion. The ability of the mind to control a wide spectrum of phenomena has been one of the most frequently proven of human capacities. Skills of Yogin; of talented mediums; of witchdoctors, shamans, occultists, and seers; of hypnotists; of contemporary demonstrations of biofeedback (q.v.), psychokinesis, and telekinesis (qq.v.) demonstrate the long, uninterrupted history of both the exhibition and the documentation of thought power. (See: Thought Forms, Samadhi)

Thought Reading. Thought transference, or telepathy in reverse. It is often suggested that it may be the remains of a primitive faculty necessary before the time of articulate speech. Critics unacquainted with mediumship from first-hand experience often offer this as an explanation, but mediums rarely give what is expected of them. A communication is often from some person completely outside of the sitter's conscious thoughts and expectations.

Thought Transference. See Thought Reading, Telepathy.

"Thracian Rider" God. This popular Thracian god was worshipped under a number of names (Heros, Heron, Apollo, Asklepios, etc.) and is always portrayed mounted upon a horse pursuing an animal. Sometimes his statues depict him with several heads or several faces. The "Thracian Rider" god and such similar Greek deities (Poseidon of Hades, the Dioscuri, Boreas) reflect the dazzling impressive horse riding created when it was introduced into the Greek world about 1000 B.C.

Thracian Rites. Ancient Thrace, a vast Balkan area which contained a portion of northeastern Greece, was famous for its wild oriental practices of sorcery, magic, human sacrifice, and abandoned orgiastic rites. Nonetheless, from Thrace came Orpheus (q.v.) and Eumolpus, founder of the Eleusinian Mysteries (q.v.).

Thrasyllus of Alexandria (d. 36 A.D.). Astrologer who was both an eminent practitioner and author on the subject. One of his pupils was the strange Roman Emperor Tiberius.

Thread. Throughout the Middle Ages and even later a red-colored thread or cord was believed to be a sure mark of a witch.

Three. One of the key numbers in mysticism, the occult, and religion. In the occult 3 is the number of the higher worlds, for implicit in every duality is a hidden oneness, the Godhead, revealing that the 2 and the 1 in the completeness of 3 are the numbers denoting the Absolute, Brahman-Atman, Ahura-Mazda, God. Again, 3 is seen in the Sun, Moon, and Earth; in the Christian Holy Trinity; in the concept of body, soul, and spirit. Actually, many major religions possess a trinity in their godhead: Siva-Vishnu-Brahma (Hindusim); Druid means "3" (Druidism); and in Gnosticism (q.v.) all divinity and being are based on 3. Since 3 was the first perfect number, oracles were intoned from a tripod. Pythagoras saw all being as a product of the combinations of the 3 original forces of the universe—matter, soul, and spirit. The triangle has been a universal symbol in mysticism, the occult, and religion, since it possesses 3 points, 3 angles, and 3 sides.

Three Faces of Eve, The. The occurrence of multiple personalities in individuals is one of the best documented phenomena in the realm of psychic manifestations. Many trance personalities and controls are certainly revelations of subliminal personalities. Dr. Morton Prince's case study of "Christine L. Beauchamp" in which three personalities lived in the same girl is classic of multiple personality. The "sleeping preacher" (q.v.) is another famous example, as is the "Watseka wonder" (q.v.). (See: Mlle Cousedon.)

Three Gems (Buddhism). The Buddha. the Dhamma, and the Sangha. (qq.v.)

Throne. A term used by some astrologers to signify a planet in a sign of which it is the ruler (q.v.).

Thury, Marc (1822–1905). Professor of Physics and Natural History at the University of Geneva. He was the first to put forward the ectoplasmic theory, naming it "psychode" as the operating agency of "ectenic force." He believed it to be subject to the will of the medium, though admitted the possibility of wills other than man's being responsible.

Thyia. Legend portrays her as being the mother of one of Apollo's sons, and being the first to sacrifice to Dionysus and originate orgies in his honor. She gave the name of Thyades to the women of Attica who engaged in Dionysiac orgies each year on Mt. Parnassus.

Tiamat. In the Babylonian creation epic, Tiamat plays a seminal role, for not only does she embody the watery chaos but her union with Apsu (the divinity of sweet water) gives birth to all the gods. Even more, when Apsu is killed, Tiamat, surging with revenge, prepares to destroy all the gods. But Marduk (q.v.) thwarts her purpose by killing Tiamat and from her lifeless corpse fashions the world. Still other legends picture her as a monstrous serpent or a terrible dragon. She also played a dominant role in the cosmogony of the Assyrians, while the Hebrew cosmogonists were influenced by this Babylonian goddess in their theories of Gehinnon (q.v.).

Tibetan Book of the Dead. Written in three parts as a gospel for the dead, who must endure forty-nine days to experience his rebirth, the lessons try to fix attention on the nature of an individual's visions. The book is known as the *Bardol Thodol.* Part one (Chikhai Bardo) elaborates the psychic quality of the moment of death. Part two (Chonyid Bardo) pictures the dream state that succeeds death. Part three (Sidpa Bardo) is a panorama of the divine secrets of birth and the pre-life history. Seen by some as a veil disguising the mystical teachings of the ancient gurus, it is an instruction on the death and rebirth of the ego, stressing the winning of freedom by fixing the memory upon certain central teachings.

Tibetan Numbers (Lamaism). In Tibet the occult art of numbers concentrates on their metaphysical, religious, and mystical implications. For example, there are three precious things: Buddha, faith, community; there are three Gems: Buddha, Lamaism, and the Law; and there are ten space directions.

Tiki. Among the Polynesians, Tiki means a god, or the first man, and is also a term for statuettes.

Timaeus of Locris (c. 1st cent A.D.). Greek Pythagorean philosopher and astronomer, who is considered by occultists to have been the earliest known author on the doctrines of magic. Certainly, his book on cosmology which delineates the origin, constitution, and laws of the universe attributes to the material of the cosmos God's being, and sees in it the mathematical harmony of the Pythagorean system. Further, it elaborated the important theory of Emanations from God filling the universe with imperishable bodies and with the World-Soul—a theory central to much mystic and occult deliberations in the many succeeding centuries.

Time. Clairvoyant phenomena have a peculiar disregard for the normal time sequence, perception being sometimes of the future or of the past. Similar effects have been noticed in the Zener card (q.v.) experiments by Professor J. B. Rhine and similar parapsychological experiments of this nature. Sometimes the card forecasted has been the next or the next but one to be exposed in the future. Mediums' controls are vague and often erroneous in time estimates, saying that they have a different time sense or, "no time, as you understand it." Hypnotic experiments, however, reveal an enhanced time sense, the entranced person often being able to register a lapse of time to precise limits when suggested to do so. The faculty of psychometry (q.v.) also gives a sample of past time sequence in the history of the object. The fact of prediction alone, makes one wonder whether our time sense is illusory. J. W. Dunne (q.v.) has some interesting theories based on his own researches wherein he believes that we all travel through a preset experience in normal consciousness. When we sleep he says, our point of focus is expanded, and we are then conscious of a little more in advance of the "now" point, due to the enlarging of the field of focus.

Time in Astrology. Astrologers use various "times." These are: Greenwich Mean Time, Standard Time, True Local Time (or local mean time), Sidereal Time, and Daylight Saving Time.

Time Pattern Research Institute, Inc. Horoscopes manufactured by a computer, one every two minutes, is the business of this corporation. Given the computerized epoch in which we live, and the fees charged for such "readings," this industry should proliferate enormously. But most knowledgeable persons are agreed that a professional astrologer is far more reliable.

Tincture. Among alchemists tincture signified a substance which colors, dyes, or stains, but even more it is the active principle native to a substance which the alchemist could distill and release through his art.

Tiresias. Most famous of Greek soothsayers, blind from the age of seven, who is so prominent in the mythical history of Greece that he has been connected with most of its important events. The blind seer's powers were still active after his death in the realm of the lower world. Throughout literature, from the time of ancient Greece to the present, Tiresias has symbolized prophetic wisdom.

Tirthankara (Jainism). A great saint or teacher of Jainism who is a "perfect soul," of which only 24 are described. Reputedly he is also totally self-contained, totally unattached, totally desireless, always open-eyed, never needing sleep or food, fearless, and full of pity. Further, his levitated body, casting no shadow, faces in all directions.

Titans. The most ancient divinities of Greek mythology who were potent powers before the Olympian divinities won complete domination. They were the offspring of Uranus (q.v.) and Gaea (q.v.). The Titans' revolt against Zeus led to their overthrow and captivity in a cavity below Tartarus, sometimes considered to be Hades. The great Titans were 12 in number, 6 sons and 6 daughters, among them legendary Cronus and Oceanus.

Tiv, Tiw, or Tyr. The ancient Scandinavian god of victory and the bravest of all the gods. Tuesday is derived from his name.

Tizane, Police Commandant. The French investigator who made a study of four hundred cases of reported ghosts. But the report of his extensive research issued in 1951 was a most indecisive statement.

Tlazolteotl. The Aztec mother of the gods.

Tomczyk, Mlle. Stanislawa (Mrs. Fielding). An outstanding Polish medium, who was photographed several times at her demonstrations in daylight. Invisible threads were found to extend from her fingers, capable of supporting a pair of scissors. In 1910 she was tested by the Physical Laboratory in Warsaw, and produced remarkable phenomena. Both Baron Schrenck-Notzing and Professor Charles Richet (qq.v.) wrote descriptions of her mediumship.

Ton. Among the Dakota Indians the belief that Ton is a power. Since the gods possess Ton, this enables them to perform supernatural feats.

Tonacatecutli. A major divinity in the Aztec religion.

Tonalamatl. One of the Aztec divinitory books which was based on the Tonalpohualli (q.v.).

Tonalpohualli. The Aztec section of a calendar period which encompassed a span of 260 days. (See: Tonalmatl)

Tonatiuh. For the Aztecs the omnipotent, life-giving Sun God.

Tongues, Talking in. See Xenoglossy.

Torah. Mosaic Law. The Pentateuch.

Torah Reading (Judaism). Among all Jews, the world over, this is a ritual of great religious, social, historical, and mystical implication. (See: Yad).

Tornait. Spirits who assist the shamans (q.v.) of the Greenland Eskimos. In Alaska, however, the Tornait are strange monsters, wandering mountain giants, the Half-People who are malevolent and harmful. Nonetheless, they are under the control of more elevated, powerful spirits.

Tornak. The guardian spirit of a shaman among some Eskimo tribes. Inhabiting bears, stones, or human beings, the guardian spirit warns the shaman of approaching danger.

Totem. See Totemism.

Totem Feast. To achieve the renewal of power, both of the tribe and their totem (q.v.), the tribe yearly engages in the symbolic rite of eating the totem.

Totemism. A widespread mystical custom among many people, ancient and modern, in which an object becomes the great sacred factor in their existence. This object may be an animal, a plant, or a mineral, but always the supreme mystical relationship between it and its worshippers is absolute. For it gives them their name, is their emblem, is treated like one of their own, is almost never killed or eaten, and is on occasion taken out and rubbed against in order to gain its power.

Totem Pole. A pole or post containing totemic figures, often brightly painted, installed in their communities by Indians on the Northwest coast of America. (See: Totemism)

Touches (Spiritualism). This phenomena is usually present at seances where objects are moved (telekinesis), and would appear to be caused by a similar agency. They may be soft, hard, warm or cold, and imitate the sensation of contact with any known substance. It is said that they are produced by spirits operating rods of ectoplasm.

Tovodun. Ancient Dahomean gods. This term is the root of the word vodun.

Trance (Spiritualism). The mediumistic trance is a sleep-like condition which enables the subject's body to be used by a discarnate spirit. It is a state which has usually resulted from a sustained cooperative effort over several years of development, in collaboration with a spirit helper, to fulfill a missionary purpose. The depth of unconsciousness reached, and the degree of control, varies greatly in individual mediums. In the lightest state, the medium is conscious to the extent of hearing any words through her own lips, while in deep trance no memory is retained of anything which transpires. F. W. H. Myers (q.v.) recognized three stages in trance. First, the subliminal self obtains control; secondly, the incarnate spirit whether or not maintaining control of the whole body, makes excursions into, or holds telepathic intercourse with the spirit world. Third stage—the body of the medium is controlled by another discarnate spirit. For hypnotic trance, see Hypnotism.

Trance Personalities. See Control.

Transcendental Meditation. Based on the ancient and modern techniques of Hindu and Yoga meditation practices, the International Meditation Society was founded in 1958 by Maharishi Mahesh Yogi (q.v.). What most distinguishes his approach from all past methods is the phenomenally short time it takes to teach students to acquire the skill to engage in transcendental meditation—about six hours, taught in six lessons. Teachers of the method are trained by Maharishi Mahesh Yogi in a number of centers in India, Italy, Switzerland, Spain, Belgium, the United States, etc. The Students' International Meditation Society concentrates on teaching school and college students at a nominal cost. In the United States there are now numerous teaching centers located in almost every city and state. (See: *Maharishi Mahesh Yogi.*)

Transcendental Music. Beautiful, unaccountable sounds of instruments or singing, a phenomenon which has been noticed at deathbeds and funerals.

Transcendentalism. A term much used by philosphers, for example, in the doctrines of Kant, Hegel, Sartre, etc. The celebrated Kant who gave the term its modern philosophic meaning, held that space, time, quality, quantity, etc. were concepts in the mind, beyond things and which enabled man to understand his material world. But the root meanings of transcendentalism are the knowledge of the Absolute (q.v.). The immanence of the Absolute in the finite or material world is the doctrine of pantheism (q.v.), but spiritual and religious transcendentalists criticize this notion, believing it to be merely an illusion. What the famous American movement of transcendentalism (Emerson, Thoreau, Bronson Alcott (q.v.) and others) preached as their doctrine were the notions of idealism, individualism, self-reliance, and social reform—but underlying these concepts was the fundamental view that nature was a living process, an organic enterprise in the moral service of man, and man by working with nature could create the future. (See: Maya)

Transfiguration (Spiritualism). A form of physical mediumship whereby a recognizable likeness of a discarnate person is built over the medium's features. It depends on the production of ectoplasm which is fashioned by the spirit operators into a mask. In good subjects the vapory material can be seen in the process of forming. This phenomenon usually takes place in a dim light owing to the sensitive nature of ectoplasm.

Transformation. A change of body, most often utilizing magic, as humans transformed to animals or inanimate objects, or gods into animals or humans. Many tales of folklore in every part of the world portray this phenomenon.

Transit. In astrology, the movement of a planet through a sign or house (qq.v.) is its "transit" of these. It is this transit which enables planets to form conjunctions and aspects (qq.v.).

Translation. Ecstatic experience of the higher spheres before death. It sometimes occurs during periods of meditation.

Transmigration. One of the most widely held beliefs as mankind developed—both East and West—was the notion that at death the soul entered another body or was reborn in another body. The soul, therefore, being imperishable, could enter a plant, an animal, another person—even a demonic or divine being. In the domains of Hinduism, Buddhism, and Theosophy, for example, this transmigration of souls is a progress in moral perfection. (See: Metempsychosis)

Transportation. The supernormal conveyance of human bodies through doors and walls, and to great distances is rare, but there are a few cases where evidence seems to have substantiated this phenomenon. Some mediums are said to have achieved this phenomena before witnesses, notably Mrs. Guppy (q.v.), Indride Indridason, and the Pansini brothers. The exploits of the latter were certified by Dr. Joseph Lapponi, medical officer to the Pope, in 1906.

Transposition of the Senses. A peculiarity of some trance states, whereby the senses of sight, smell, or taste, may be experienced at the fingers, toes, ear lobes or forehead. Yogis also claim this faculty by development.

Transubstantiation. A change of substance usually referring to the doctrine of the Eucharist sacrament of the Lord's supper, where the bread and wine were declared symbols of the body and blood of Jesus.

Transvection. The almost universal pictorial symbol of the witch's night-flight astride a broomstick, a forked stick, a spinning stick, pole, etc. Researchers believe that in early times when female sorcerers were employed to restore fertility during a drought, their frenzied dance gyrations stirred up clouds of dust, and seemingly the old women were riding upon the whirling dust clouds with the sticks or brooms with which they beat and swept the dry ground.

Travelling Clairvoyance. See Clairvoyance.

Travers-Smith, Mrs. See Dowden, Hester.

Tree of Life (Judaism-Cabalism). The Tree, which the Hebrew Patriarchs described as the "Tree of Eternal Life," grows in Gan Eden (q.v.), where the saints and the righteous in the radiance of God's Shechinah (divine presence) eat of the fruit of that bliss that is found only on this Tree. The Cabalists picture the Tree as a symbol of the foundation pattern of the universe and its basic unity. Further, it is a model of God, the universe, and man. Its three triangles, two being polar forces with the third acting as the mediator of balance and reconciliation, are underlined by a sephira—an ancient Hebrew unit of measure. It is interesting to note that tree worship has also been a prominent feature in the religion of the Greeks, the Romans, and nearly all the subsequent nations of Europe. Still a witness of this ancient heritage is the May Day celebration of the Maypole: the May Day Queen being a symbol of that ancient fertile spirit of vegetation.

Treta-yuga (Hinduism). An epoch of 1,296,000 years, representing the second age of the world.

Trevisan, Bernard (1406-?). The Italian alchemist famous for his extraordinary devotion to alchemy and his experiments on the discovery of the philosophers stone (q.v.). He was a wealthy nobleman of Padua. Having traveled all over Europe and Asia and spent vast sums of money in pursuit of his passion, it was not until the very end of his life that he is reputed to have achieved his life-long aspiration. His book *The Natural Philosophy of Metals*, in French, shows his love of experiment.

Triglav. Among the ancient Slavs of Central Europe, he was the supreme divinity.

Trigon. In astrology, the three signs of the same triplicity. (See Trigonocrators)

Trigonocrators. In astrology, this term means the ruler of trigons (q.v.).

> Fire.......Sun, Jupiter, Mars
> Earth......Venus, Mercury, Saturn
> Air........Mercury, Venus, Saturn
> Water......Moon, Mars, Mercury

Trika (Hinduism). A sivaite doctrine, founded in the 9th century A.D., which asserts that the recognition of Siva (q.v.) as one's inmost nature dissolves the plurality of existence, and the threefold (*trika*) being of Siva, into a oneness, thus turning around the unfolding of the universe through the 36 tattvas (q.v.).

Trika. A doctrine of Saivism which asserts that the recognition of Siva (q.v.) as one's inmost nature dissoves the plurality of existence into a oneness. The threefold *trika* of Siva (represented by his three greatest powers) are thus unified, and the in this way is halted the unfolding of the universe through elements of the tattvas (q.v.). (See: Trimurti)

Trimurti (Hinduism). Brahma-Vishnu-Siva, the trinity of gods, representing creation-maintenance-destruction in the universe.

Trimurti. The omnipotent triad of the three greatest of the Hindu gods, Brahma, Vishnu, and Siva (qq.v.) The complex variety of qualities and powers inherent in this mini-pantheon is most often portrayed in one body with three heads: a symbol of the union of the cosmic-human significance of these three deities. For without their agreement there can be no creation, nothing to maintain, and nothing to destroy. All Hindus, with the one exception of the Jains (q.v.), worship the Trimurti.

Trine. An observed angle of 120 degrees between two bodies in the ecliptic, said (astrologically) to be helpful for the two principles concerned.

Tripitaka (Buddhism). The three baskets: the basket of discipline, the basket of (Buddha's) sermons, and the basket of metaphysics.

Trithemius (1462–1516). Born in Germany, the magician and alchemist studied in France where he adopted his Latinized name. Upon his return to Germany, he served as an abbot in a monastery at Spannheim and later at St. James of Wurzburg. His fame as an occultist rests upon his works on geomancy, Cabalism, necromancy, sorcery, a book on guardian angels who govern the world (translated into English in 1647), and a work on alchemy. His book on sorcery contains the first record of the famous folk story of Dr. Faustus. He is credited with having revealed to Emperor Maximillian a vision of his deceased wife.

Troll. In Germanic and Scandinavian mythology the trolls had originally been giants, fiends, demons, or ghostly monsters. But in later ages they became either dwarfs or giants dwelling in caves or hills.

Troll-drum. The shamans (q.v.) of the Lapps employ this instrument in their repertoire of magical procedures.

Tropical Signs. Astrologers mean by this: Cancer and Capricorn (qq.v.).

Trowbridge, W. R. Professor at Princeton University whose interest in the occult, in magic, and psychic phenomena made him an indefatigable investigator in these areas. His writing on Count Cagliostro (q.v.) gave a balanced view of this noted occultist, but his investigation and expose' of Eusapio Palladino, the famous medium (q.v.) in New York in 1909 almost destroyed her gigantic reputation.

True Black Magic, Book of the. This Grimoire (q.v.) is merely a slightly altered version of the Key of Solomon (q.v.).

Trumpet. A megaphone of cardboard or metal, used for direct voice phenomena. It was first used by Jonathan Koons (q.v.), an early American medium. The volume of the voice is amplified by its use. Voice phenomena without the trumpet is termed "independent voice."

Tsakol. Among the Guatemalan Maya-Quiche Indians, he is the "Creator-God" and the companion of Bitol, the "Maker-God."

Tsatsa. A term rich in occult, religious, and spiritual significance among the Jivaro Indians of Ecuador and Peru, where tsatsa refers to a shrunken head. Since the head is the seat of the soul and manu (q.v.), and the capture of an enemy's head confers sanctity, power and status to the warrior, the practice of maintaining the severed head for a long period of time has been and still is an especially widespread art. But the Jivaro Indians are particularly noted for their method of removing and curing the head through a unique process of shrinking and curing.

Tso wang (Taoism). The state of absolute freedom in which the distinction between self and others, life and death, self and things is erased and all becomes one, with man becoming one with the universe. Therefore Tso wang means sitting in forgetfulness.

Tsong-Kha-Pa (1357–1419) (Lamaism). One of Tibet's most eminent religious reformers, he became a Buddhist monk, concentrating his reform on restoring the primitive religious practices. Tantrism and animism (qq.v.) he strongly opposed. In order to rejuvenate Buddhism and restore its original integrity, he founded a monastic order in Lhasa—the "yellow hats" (q.v.), which today is the dominant organizational entity in Tibet.

Tuatha De Danann. The gods of early Celtic Ireland, who, the legend runs were vanquished by the Milesians, ancestors of the Irish, but who continued on in the hills and subterranean world where they metamorphosed into fairies and sorcerers. In their glory as gods, they were led by Lugh, the sun god, and Lir, the god of the sea.

Tuchulcha. An oriental demon that the ancient Etruscans represented as being a torturer in the underworld.

Tumbler and Letters. An improvised method for obtaining spelled communications, on the lines of the ouija board or planchette. The medium and sitter place their fingers lightly on the upended tumbler within a circle of letters. Those letters which are touched by the glass's movements, may spell messages.

Tummo. A method of biofeedback which raises the heat of the body in cold conditions, practised by Yogis and Tibetan lamas. These adepts have been known to live in caves in high latitudes without fires and a minimum of clothing. (See: Samadhi)

Tunisa. A term describing Burmese diviners.

Tusita (Buddhism). Before his incarnation Buddha was domiciled in this heaven—and it is here that Maitreya abides until the fortunate moment of his incarnation.

Tutelary. That divinity, saint, or spirit acting as the guardian of an individual, a place, or thing.

Tuttle, Hudson (1836–1910). Early medium of Ohio, U.S.A. Possessing no education and of poor parents, under the guidance of his control it is claimed that he wrote books of great learning and erudition on natural science and philosophy. He was the author of many books on Spiritualism.

Tvastri, Twasthtri, Tvastar (Hinduism). A Vedic god who is the ideal artist and artisan, the endower of life. He shapes life in the womb, and thus both the gods and men owe their existence and appearance to his genius. Also, he bestows fruitfulness of offspring through granting sexual potency. In the later literature he is named Visvakharma.

Twain, Mark (1835–1910). Despite his skeptical attitude toward many aspects of his culture, Twain, like many eminent persons of his period (Wm. Lloyd Garrison, Abraham Lincoln, Horace Greeley, Wm. James) believed in psychic phenomena, and he also believed in survival after death. Twain's support of the reality of psychic events was rooted in the many experiences he had had of such a nature: so startling, that it was he who first coined the term "mental telepathy." Interestingly, Professor J.H. Hyslop (q.v.) was convinced of Mark Twain's return through his experiments in cross correspondence with Mrs. Hutchings, Lola V. Hays and Mrs. Chenoweth (Ada Besinnet). Details are to be found in the Journal of the A.S.P.R., July 1917.

Twelve Nidanas (Buddhism). The 12 Nidanas are the causes which bring the "spiritual being of man into earthly incarnation."

Twin Soul. Occult term for a psychic affinity. Twin souls are said to incarnate together over many lifetimes.

Tyche. The goddess of good luck in ancient Greece and Rome. In acknowledgment of the flimsy nature of good fortune, the goddess was represented with various symbols: with a rudder, she signified the guide of the world's affairs; with a ball, the slippery quality of fortune; with the horn of Amaithea, the fruitful gifts of fortune. All through the Middle Ages and the Renaissance in Europe, this goddess was a very popular figure in art and literature.

Typhon. The fire-breathing giant, the malevolent Satan of the Greeks. He was the monster with a hundred heads, burning eyes, and terrible voices, who was sometimes portrayed as a ravaging hurricane. Zeus subdues Typhon with a thunderbolt for daring to gain sovereignty of the gods and men. Being the father of the winds, he was also the father of the savage Harpies, the predatory monsters with women's heads and the bodies and claws of a vulture. The Harpies were the instruments of divine vengeance.

Typtology. Communicating with spirits by the technique of rapping, utilizing various patterns. By using the alphabet (verbally or as printed), the rappings join letters which form a message or an anwer. Again, one rap may indicate "yes," two, "no"; the sitters creating whatever codes they desire. (See: Table Turning)

Tzitzimitl. The Aztec deities who in the form of monsters prey on human beings whenever there occurs an eclipse of the sun. They were the rulers of evil.

Tzu hua (Taoism). The following of a thing's own principle of being which enables it to create self-transformation without any divine or external agency. This is Tao (q.v.).

Uu

U. An important mystical letter for both Pythagoreans and Cabalists, since converted into numbers (3 x 7) it equals 21, the position of "u" in the alphabet. Again, alchemists considered it a potent letter in the process of alchemy.

U F O. The acronym which means Unidentified Flying Object. In recent years reports of the sightings of UFO's have increased in number from many quarters on the earth.

Uijatao. Philipine tribesmen used this term for their priest-king.

Ukoback. One of the interior demons of Hell who works at keeping its fires burning.

Ukteni. The American Natchez Indians believed this water snake, Ukteni, "teacher of wisdom," to be the possessor of the mana (q.v.), which gave it great magical powers.

Ultor. In Roman mythology Ultor was "the avenger," the surname of the war-god Mars, one of the three tutelary divinities of Rome.

Ultra Perceptive Faculty. A capacity for obtaining information concerning an object or an individual by the employment of a perceptive faculty other than those of the recognized senses of sight, touch and hearing. This supposes that a psychic "imprint" can be left on an article after handling.

Umbral Eclipse. In astrology, the entrance of the Moon into the Earth's shadow; partial eclipse when it is not wholly shadowed; total eclipse when completely immersed. In an eclipse of the sun, the moon must be fully positioned within the shadow of the sun

Unanimism. A mystical concept created by the French writer Jules Romains (1885–1972) to mean a belief in a certain element of reality which is of a spiritual nature. For Romains the soul can enter into direct, immediate, and intuitive communication with the universal soul.

Under the Sunbeams. In astrology, a planet less than 17° distant in longitude from the Sun (though if it is within 3° arc of the Sun its influence from the sun is at its most intense), and once pictured as being an unfavorable situation. But modern astrologers, by taking both a more analytical and broader consideration, are more flexible in their interpretation of this planetary position.

Underhill, Evelyn (1875–1941). The English writer, poet, and mystic whose own mystical experiences and her study of the Christian mystics enabled her to express the mystical ecstacy with commanding skill. Especially revealing are *Mysticism, Concerning the Inner Life,* and her intensely felt volume of mystical poetry, *Immanence.*

Underworld. One of the universal notions found in many religions which refers to a domain below the earth where the souls of the dead sojourn. Generally, a guide or a severe test conducted by judges effects entrance to this nether region. (See: *Book of the Dead;* and Spheres)

Undine. One of the elementals (q.v.), being an elemental spirit of the water, a nymph. Later, undines became fairies, but in the occult this elemental was a fertile spirit.

Unfoldment. Term descriptive of the development of personal psychic or spiritual powers.

Unfortunate Signs. In astrology, this term refers to the negative signs: Taurus, Cancer, Virgo, Scorpio, Capricorn, and Aquarius (qq.v.).

Unger, Georg. German mathematician, physicist, and Anthroposophist who founded the Mathematical-Physics Institute at Dornach, Switzerland. He wrote the book *Flying Saucers, Physical and Spiritual Aspects.*

Unguents. These salves through the millenia have served for many purposes, but in the occult they have been used to gain visions and, by the Devil, to injure mankind. Witches are reputed to have used a satanic unguent as an aid to flight on their way to the Witch's Sabbath (q.v.).

Unicorn. In mythology, religion, and the occult this mythical figure (a horse with a single twisting horn on its forehead) has symbolized a number of meanings. First mentioned in the Old Testament (Deut. 33:17), it later came to represent chastity or purity. During the Middle Ages, it became emblematic of the Holy Spirit as the polar destructive-creative evocation of the divine power. In alchemy, it symbolized Mercury and the Lion. But the Unicorn Horn—that is, the supposed material of the unicorn's horn; was used medicinally and as a talisman (q.v.).

Unidentified Flying Objects. See Flying Saucers.

Unio Mystica. The Latin term for mystical union wherein the individual consciousness either mentally or emotionally merges with a transcendant consciousness.

Union of Opposites. One of the most universal of concepts, variously operating in the mystic, the occult, the spiritual, and the religious realms. In the mystic: the great pervasive notion of the union of the individual finite with the infinite; in the occult: the alchemists' many polar categories (union of temporal and spiritual, of masculine and feminine principles, the androgyne, sexual intercourse); in the spiritual: union of the soul with the cosmic soul; in the religious: the various sacraments of grace God grants to evil humanity.

Union of Spiritualist Mediums. This group was founded by mediums in London, 1956, for the purpose of raising the standard of presentation of mediumship and the status of mediums and public speakers presenting Spiritualist philosophy. It also engages in the training and encouragement of young workers in the movement. An Advice and Information Bureau is maintained.

Unitarian. A member of a Christian sect which believes in the unity of the divine nature, as opposed to the doctrine of the Trinity.

United States Parapsychology Foundation. One of the early nonacademic organizations founded by a group with diverse professional backgrounds to further the study of paranormal phenomena. Its work on *psi* experiments has produced some unusually fine data in the field of ESP (q.v.). The Foundation was at one time headed by Eileen Garrett (q.v.). Because of its scrupulous scientific procedures and the importance of its findings, this organization has been influential in helping to create the wide academic acceptance of this difficult area of human capabilities.

Univercoelum, The. A publication founded by Andrew Jackson Davis (q.v.) in 1847 in the United States to promote a "Reorganization of Society" as a consequence of a new divine revelation. This revelation was to supersede those of the Old and New Testaments, of Swedenborg (q.v.), and Fourier. Articles in the magazine covered subjects on prophecy, clairvoyance, somnambulism, trance phenomena, and also the teaching of an "interior and spiritual philosophy." This latter philosophy asserted that God was an infinitely intelligent Essence embodied in all that exists.

Universalism. A doctrine that all men will eventually be saved.

Universal Mind. Term used by Spiritualist author J. A. Findlay, to describe mind substance as the result of etheric vibration. It is, he says, the creative power in the universe.

Universals. Philosophical term for the essential idea of a thing, as distinguished from the discrete thing itself. This extraordinarily fruitful concept which was developed by Plato (q.v.), has been a dominating notion in philosophy since his time. Equally, it has exerted a massive influence in the theoretical writings of Jewish, Christian, and Islamic theologians. Even more, it has constantly furnished macrocosmic-microcosmic insights for most occult, mystical, alchemical, and spiritual thinking in both the Asian and Western world. (See: Neo-

Platonism). Plato believed that knowledge of Universals was really a process of relearning what was known in a preexistent state.

Universities. Occult schools and universities have flourished for thousands of years, notably in ancient India, China, Egypt, Iran, Judea, Greece, Rome, etc. In relatively more modern times, for example during the Middle Ages, Salamanca, in western Spain, was a noted center for occult schools; in France, Jechiel, a Jewish Rabbi, supervised such an institution; Paracelsus (q.v.) lectured on alchemy at the University of Basel as did many other alchemists and occultists. In ancient Mexico there were the Calmeac, Aztec schools that prepared the sons of nobles in the occult arts and for the priesthood. Such a school flourished in Paris in the 19th century according to M. Figuier's book *Alchemy and Alchemists.* That such schools exist at present is quite evident from reports—coming only from England and the United States, of many societies of witches, and Satanists. (See: Aleister Crowley; Charles Manson.)

Unknown Father. A figuration of Gnostic mysticism—the demiurgos who was next in power to the omnipotent godhead. In the Gnostic religion itself—the progenitor of creation.

Upanishads (Hinduism). One of the extraordinary collections of treatises (more than 100), written in prose and verse, that were composed between the 8th and 6th centuries B.C. In range of subject matter they are one of the most remarkable set of writings created by humanity. Not only do they antedate all other philosophic works, but their ethical, spiritual, social, religious, humanistic, and literary revelations and qualities also preceded such developments in other great world cultures. The term relates to the method of teaching: the pupil sat opposite (upa-ni-sad) the teacher. Though these books have had, understandably, an incalculable influence in India and the East, their emergence into Western consciousness has made them markedly significant both to eminent thinkers and a vast, expanding public. The Upanishads deal with such topics as the essential nature of the Divine Principle and the life-discipline that is required for salvation; the revelation of an individual soul (atman q.v.) which is centered through its union with the universal Atman—the impersonal Supreme Being (Brahma q.v.); and believe that this universal Atman is the source and goal of all human beings. However, in the radical *Chandogya Upanishad* there is the daring declaration *tat tvam asi* (q.v.) "that art thou": that is, "you, too, are God." Futher concepts discussed are the nature of eternal life, transmigration (q.v.), and the crucially consequential notion of *maya* (q.v.).

Upasanakanda (Hinduism). The part of the Veda that elaborates the aspect of worship.

Uraeus. In ancient Egyptian religion the sacred asp, symbol of immortality, which adorned the headdress of royal personages and divinities.

Urakabarameel. In the apocalyptic book of Enoch one of the leaders of the fallen angels.

Uranian. In astrology, an individual who is erratic, independent, and one who possesses original ideas because of the influence of a strong Uranus birth receptivity.

Uranian Astrology. A system of Astrology developed by Alfred Witte of the German Hamburg Astrology School. Mainly, it diverges from traditional Astrology in its use of Planetary Patterns; its sole reliance upon "hard" angles; and its delimiting of personal points.

Uranus. In Greek mythology the word means heaven, and also the divinity Uranus, who is the ruler of the world and the father of the Titans, the Cyclops, etc. through his marriage to Gaea (Earth). Hating his children, he banished them to Tartarus (Hades), eventually suffering for this by being castrated and dethroned by Cronos. The Gigantes sprang from the drops of his blood, and out of the foam draping his limbs in the sea sprang the beautiful love-goddess Aphrodite.

Urim and Thummin (Judaism). One of the magical devices of the ceremonial prayer service used by the priests in the early Israelite worship of God. For the Urim and Thummin was a jeweled breastplate which the priests, being mediators between man and Jehovah, used as an object for divinatory purposes.

Urmensch. The primordial man of many religions who is often the progenitor of the race (Adam and Eve), and may become the supernatural prototype of man as Gayomard in Iran, Purusha in India, or Christ as the Logos, or Anthropus in Gnosticism. Moreover, the Urmensch legend as in the Indo-Iranian cosmogony of Yama and Yima may first be represented as the primordial archetypes, then the progenitors of the race, and, finally, with death, these two become the rulers of the dead.

Uroboros. One of the esoteric symbols of the occult and alchemy, the tail-eating serpent, which the ancient Greek alchemists saw as a representation of the unity of sacrificer and sacrificed. In later times, this symbol took on meanings of cosmic birth, death, and the phoenix legend.

Urvan, Urvanem (Zoroastrianism). In the Avesta (q.v.) this signifies the life-spirit or Buddhi.

Usanas (Hinduism). The planet Venus.

Ushabti. In ancient Egyptian religion these were statuettes placed in tombs in the form of mummies. According to Chapter VI of the *Book of the Dead* (q.v.) the Ushabti will answer, that is, be responsible if the owner of it is called on to work in the next world. These statuettes were a significant aspect of the magic ritual of the burial ceremonies.

U. S. M. Union of Spiritualist Mediums (q.v.).

Utnapishtim. The Babylonian Noah whose story undoubtedly was the source of the *Genesis* legend in the Old Testament.

Utsanati. The American Cherokee Indians believed this rattlesnake was the "wise one" designed to be the helper of man.

Uttara-Mimamsa (Hinduism). Another term for Vedanta (q.v.).

Vv

Vac (Hinduism). In Vedic religion this is the Logos, meaning *Word*—and amplified, means cosmic reason. It is similar in concept to the term as conceived by the Greeks.

Vadhaghna (Zoroastrianism). The evil ruler whose power Angru Mainyu (q.v.) promised to confer on Zarathrusta, if he would curse Ahura Mazda (q.v.).

Vairagya (Hinduism). Achievement of *moksa* (q.v.) by way of the action of renouncing worldly things.

Vaitarini, Vaitaraini (Hinduism). The abominable river choked with blood, excrement, and garbage which must be crossed to reach the underworld.

Valentine, Basil. An important German alchemist of the 15th century. He was only known as the prior of the Abbey of St. Peter at Erfurt until the chance discovery of his alchemical works revealed him to have been an accomplished master of his subject. He has been credited as the discoverer of antimony, whose medicinal virtues he extolled. His alchemical writings were published in the 17th century. *Apocalypsis Chymica*, and *De Microcosmo degue Magno Mundi Mysterio et Medecina Hominis* are two of his important books. Two additional works— The *Triumphal Chariot of Antimony* and *Practica cum 12 Clavibus* (known as "The Twelve Keys" to the alchemical process) were much appreciated by Paracelsus (q.v.). The latter based certain of his hermetic and esoteric notions on Valentine's concepts.

Valentinus. Founder of a mystic sect of Gnostics in the second century A.D. His doctrine asserted that the great sacrament was the heavenly marriage of Sophia (wisdom) and the Redeemer. The sect carried the name "Valentinians."

Valhalla. In ancient Scandinavian mythology, the haven of dead heroes which was the "hall of the slain" in Odin's palace in Asgard. Each morning the heroes emerge from the palace—through its 540 gates, to engage in warfare; with the coming of night they return to enjoy a feast with the gods, being waited upon by the Valkyries (q.v.) (See: Spheres)

Valiantine, George. American semi-literate direct voice medium. His most outstanding accomplishment was the alleged return of Confucius in a sitting with Neville Whymant, an authority on Chinese history and ancient literature, who vouched for the accurate pronunciation and recital of standard works in old Chinese. A gramophone record was made of the voice of 'Confucius' in London, 1927.

Valkyrie. In Norse mythology, the beautiful maidens of Odin who attend the fields of war, choosing those who are to be killed; further, they then choose the heroes whom they conduct to Valhalla (q.v.). Originally, the Valkyrie were sorcerers and witches.

Vampire. This Slavic term describes a night-wandering blood-sucking ghost or a dead person who returns from the grave with the malefic desire to suck the blood of sleeping persons and so cause their death. A vampire may also be a living sorcerer who metamorphoses himself and engages in the same behavior. Different Slavic nations have different versions of vampire legends; for example, Ukrainians believe they are wizards or sorcerers; Bulgarians and Serbians believe they are corpses over which a dog or a cat has jumped; Grecians use a Slavonic name meaning werewolf (q.v.). C.F. de Schertz in *Magia Posthuma* (1706), and Calmet in *Dissertation on Vampires* have explored the subject. By the way, the four best methods to kill a vampire (according to legend) are: behead the suspected corpse or take out the corpse's heart; pierce corpse with either a white-thorn or aspen stake; or burn it.

Varaha Muhira. The Hindu astrologer and mystic who wrote a work on astrology about 500 A.D.

Varshneya (Hinduism). A name of Krishna.

Varuna (Hinduism). One of the most ancient of the Vedic divinities, he may originally have been a sky god, who evolved into the universal encompasser. He is the divinity of the night and the waters, the god of the subconscious level of the soul which harbors the creative power for everything which later becomes visible.

Vassago. The spirit of the crystal which is called on by the crystalgazer to bring him success in his search.

Vasus (Hinduism). These represent the eight evil deities who serve Indra (q.v.). In their cosmogonic identification they represent personifications of cosmic phenomena.

Vaughan, Diana. Early American Satanist who claimed she was the chosen bride of the evil spirit Asmodeus, and had had an affair with Lucifer. Diana Vaughan in her notorious book *Memories of an ex-Palladist* declared she was a member of a Satanist group in Charleston, South Carolina, who worshipped Lucifer (q.v.).

Vaughan, Thomas (1622–1695). The English alchemist and Rosicrucian who translated *The Fame and Confession of the Brothers of the Rosy Cross*, and wrote *Anthroposophia Theomagica*.

Vaulderie. A French term signifying that one is in league with the Satanic powers. This epithet derives its name from Robinet de Vaulse, a hermit, one of the first persons accused of this anti-Christian crime. In the fifteenth century the French Inquisition burned a number of persons who were accused of *vaulderie*.

Veda (Hinduism). The Vedas represent the oldest and the most important texts of Hinduism. Created by the Aryans who invaded Northwest India about 1500 B.C., this collection of sacred literature is a mixture of the Aryan nature-fire-soma religion and the religion of the native Indian people whom they conquered. This large body of sacred works was composed over a period of some 1000 years (1500 B.C. to 500 B.C.); and it is divided into five samhitas (collections) separately designated: Rigveda (q.v.), Yajurveda, Samaveda, Artharvaveda, the Upanishad (q.v.). While the Rigveda is the oldest and the most important of these texts with some 1028 hymns in praise of the soma-fire-nature gods which announce all the basic notions that were to be more fully elaborated through more than 3000 years, the four companion books have also had a profound impact on the beliefs of the Hindus and other cults, and, too, on the philosophies of the Indian people. Each of the major treatises is accompanied by sacred prose works known as Brahmanas to which are added commentaries known as Aranyaka and Upanishad. The veneration in which the Veda is held is reflected in their description as *Sruti* (that which is revealed orally by Brahmana (q.v.) to the *Rishis*, the inspired seers. The Yajurveda contains the Veda of prayers and sacrificial formulas. The Samaveda is the Veda of songs. The Artharvaveda is the Veda of the priests; it consists of a highly developed system of magic, spells, and divination; but for a long time this samhita was refused acceptance into the holy canon. Skipping over the Upanishad for a moment, the Brahmanas contain the rules and the explanations of the ritual sacrifices: these rules were used by the priests in their worship of the fire god, Agni, and the sun god, Surya; as for the actual fire that was burning during the religious ritual—this fire served as a means of communication between man and the gods. The Aranyakas are known as the "forest texts," because they were recited in the forests in deference to their esoteric and magical nature. However, the chief purpose of the Aranyakas was to give the devotee instruction in the techniques of substituting symbols for the ritual sacrifices and by the use of meditation to perform them mentally. This tradition and its training formed a transition to the later development of the mystical, spiritual, and boldly speculative teachings of the Upanishad; further, it stimulated the eventual creation of the various systems of Yoga (q.v.). Returning now to the Upanishad, it is at once apparent that unlike the Brahmanas and the Aranyakas, the commentaries which came to be known as the Upanishad were elevated into the Veda and made a part of the five sacred *Sruti*. The Upanishad is the Veda that most fully elaborates one of the most fundamental principles of Hinduism—the view that all the gods are but an outgrowth of Brahman, the universal soul; and then in an epochal cosmic leap from heaven to earth declares that the same process applies to man: that each human soul, the atman (q.v.), merges with and is one with this Brahmanic universal soul (see Tat Tvam Asi, Upanishad). One of the early major deities of the Rigveda was the god Varuna—the all-seeing god of justice and the guardian of the cosmic order or *rita*: From this attribution of Varuna evolves another fundamental notion of Hinduism—that order controlled not only the macrocosm but also the microcosm (qq.v.)—and therefore for man there were the controlling laws of samhara, karma, and moksha (qq.v.). While there have been many cults that have developed out of the Vedic tradition and which split away from the Hindu religion (Jainism; Saivism; Tantrikism; and, in an important sense, even Buddhism (qq.v.); etc.) all, nonetheless, adhere to certain common beliefs and most worship the same gods embodied in the Vedic tradition. Finally, the immense richness and continuing profundity of much in the Vedic literature has made it one of the major religions of mankind, but beyond this achievement, in the last several hundred years it has won numerous adherents in the Western world—among philosophers, artists, religionists, mystics, spiritualists, and the lay public. And this interest has accelerated in our contemporary period to the point where scientists, too, notably many in the field of psychology have begun to study the whole Vedic evolution to learn what it can contribute to our present-day cultures. When it is realized that the great ancient religions of Egypt, Babylonia, Assyria, Greece, Rome (to name only some of the famous ancient religions) are dead, and that even Judaism no longer serves as a fecundating force outside of its own religionists, the continuing importance of the Vedic tradition is clearly a striking phenomenon. (See: Anthroposophy, Bhagavad-Gita, Samadhi, Soma, Theosophy, Transcendentalism, Trimurti, Vedanta, Yoga).

Vedanta (Hinduism). The most literal meaning of the Vedanta is "the end of the Veda." Practically, however, it refers both to the teaching of the Upanishads (q.v.), the last treatise of the Veda (q.v.), and to the knowledge of ultimate meanings. These ultimate meanings deal with man's relationship to the existence of Brahman (q.v.), to his relationship with the world, to his fellow man, and to his own inner self. After about 300 B.C.—the end of the Upanishadic formulations, an intense study of the Upanishad led to the development of a number of philosophic schools with opposing interpretations of its central meanings. An exemplary summary of the Upanishadic doctrines (known as either the *Brahma Sutra* or the *Vedanta Sutras*) became the focus of sharp discussion. The best known and the most influential of the diverse schools of Vedanta is that of Sankara (q.v.) (*c.*788–*c.*820), who was a Saivite Brahmin (qq.v.) and famous for his commentary on the *Brahma Sutra* and the ten most esteemed Upanishads. For Sankara, the Upanishad presents an organic unity when understood in its totality. As a non-dualist, Sankara sees Brahman as pure reality, pure consciousness, and pure bliss. And since the world is a creation of Brahman and completely dependent on it, and since Brahman is unchanging and indestructible, the seeming change that men discern in the world is merely illusion or "maya" (q.v.). Further, Brahman exists as the Absolute (q.v.) without qualities—however, in Brahman's existence as a personal god, Ishvara, in this embodiment there is now an inherence of qualities. Finally, Sankara holds that ultimate enlightenment can not come by way of devotion to duties and ritual practice but rather by way of the eradication of ignorance, of maya, and through the higher knowledge of Brahman and the self. Critical of Sankara's views were the two important schools of Ramanuja (1017–1137) and Madhva (1197–1276). Ramanuja, who was a worshipper of Vishnu (q.v.), believes that Brahman in its cosmic aspect posseses qualities which are divine; that there is an actual world of separate souls who are, of course, dependent on God; and that the path to salvation is by way of Bhakti (q.v.). Madhva, too, agrees with Ramanuja that there is a world of pluralities: a world of permanent reality, of separate souls, and of God—who is Vishnu. Despite the conflicting viewpoints among the interpreters of the Vedanta, this metaphysical-religious outlook continues to exercise a dynamic influence on the intellectual and religious life of India. There are a number of modern Indian Vedantists (S. Radhakrishnan, Swami Vivekananda, Aurobindo Ghose) whose works have had a marked impact on their readers—both in India and in the West. On another level, such Western writers as Aldous Huxley and Christopher Isherwood have popularized the fundamental insights of Vedanta and stressed their relevance for modern man. (See: Veda. See too: *The Perennial Philosophy* Aldous Huxley (1946); *Vedanta for Modern Man* Christopher Isherwood (1951). (This is the Harper Bros. ed. and title. The book has been published and reissued by several publishers under different titles.)

Vegan. A strict vegetarian who renounces all meat consumption, including animal products (butter, cheese, etc.).

Vegetarianism. The renunciation of flesh-eating for various reasons. One group of vegetarians asserts that meat-eating forms toxins and poisons the body. Ethical objections are raised by others on the grounds that animals are in the same evolutionary scale as man, and possess souls. The possibility of cruelty in the killing of animals is another argument used. Extremists who renounce animal products as well, such as milk, eggs, etc., are termed Vegans (q.v.). In the Hindu religion it is this belief in reincarnation which is a compelling reason for the practice of vegetarianism; and, too, it was a belief in reincarnation that made vegetarians of the ancient Pythagoreans and the ancient Theosophists. Modern Theosophists and Anthropsophists (qq.v.) are also vegetarians for the very same reason.

Vehicle of Life. An occult concept denoting the Etheric Body (q.v.) of man on earth. Pythagoras (q.v.) defined it as the "Septenary Man" whose constituent elements were earth, water, air and fire catalyzed by a three-fold soul, thus "Septenary"—the sum of seven.

Vele. A type of black magic (q.v.) employed in the South Pacific Islands of Guadalcanal, Savo, and Russell.

Veleda. A prophetess of the Germanic tribes whose eminence as a seeress and goddess gave her oracular messages prodigious weight among both the ancient Germans and their enemies the Romans. It has been claimed that even the Romans sent her valuable gifts in exchange for her oracular counsels and that in Emperor Vespasian's reign she was honored as a goddess.

Venfica. A witch who specializes in dispensing philtres and poisons.

Verdelet. A demon of hell, master of ceremonies there; also, he is responsible for transporting witches to the Sabbath.

Vernal Equinox. In astrology, that period when the sun enters Aries (q.v.), the first day of spring.

Vervain. A sacred herb used by the Romans to cast out evil spirits, and by the Druids (q.v.) in many supernatural activities. Later demonologists and sorcerers believed that wearing vervain was essential to the act of evoking demons. This powerful herb was used by witches, or, oppositely, to drive away witches. It was also used to cure ulcers, inflame love desire, to purify, and to ease childbirth.

Vesme, Count Cesar Baudi De. Noted Italian psychic researcher and author, he was born in Turin in 1862. He experimented with prophecy and games of chance; his *History of Experimental Spiritualism* was honored by the French Academy of Science.

Vespertine. In astrology the setting of a planet in the west after the sun. (See: Matutine)

Vestments of Witches' Mass. These vestments have been variously described: sometimes as a bishop's pontificalia, black and ragged; sometimes merely a plain black cape (a long mantle worn by ecclesiastics); sometimes a cape of white silk; and sometimes any priestly vestment such as the eucharistic chasuble, stole, maniple, girdle, alb, or an amice. Sometimes these priestly vestments are decorated with mutilated crosses, a black goat rampant, or the heraldry of hell.

Vibration (Spiritualism). A regularly recurring unit of frequency in a given time. A misleading word frequently used by Spiritualists to denote a phase of mental attunement. To reduce the spirit world to time and space concepts is to make it of the same order of existence as the physical world; different only in degree and still operating in time and space. Yet the spirit people tell us constantly: "we have no limitations of time and space;" that their world is of a different order; that it is of a non-time-space order—the world of ideas. Accordingly, spirit beings, to contact our environment, do not have to do anything mysterious physically, like "lowering their vibrations." They contact us as spirit—"behind" our sense impressions of space and time.

Vibrations. The theory of vibrations was a very significant occult preoccupation in the 19th century. As a result of the discoveries by scientists of the motion of light, sound, electricity and magnetism, and the ancient occult theory of emanations plus the Pythagorean theory of the music of the spheres, and the spiritual and Theosophical theory of aura (q.v.) "vibrations" became very popular. Indeed, the modern notion of "brain waves," is an important constituent of ESP and telepathy and psychokinesis (qq.v.), for they depend on "energy waves." Numerologists, who assign a rate of vibration to each number, assert we react differently to a five, an eight, or a twenty. During the 19th century, however, each person was claimed to possess a basic rate of vibration because his name could be formulated in a number which produced a unique vibration. Those who lived in harmony with their vibration-number were successful and happy.

Vidar. The old Scandinavian god, son of Odin, and next to Thor (q.v.) the strongest of the gods. He endowed men with the gifts of silence and caution and was, particularly, the god of the forests.

Viduus. A divinity in ancient Rome responsible for parting the soul from the body at death.

Vidya (Theosophy). That knowledge by which one of the Pathan determines the true from the false in order to direct his efforts efficaciously. Opposite of *Avidya*.

Vihara (Buddhism). A domicile, but metaphorically a state of life or condition of heart. The houses given Buddha for use of his Order; now the most common name of a Buddhist retreat or monastery.

Vijnana (Hinduism). Represents consciousness which expresses itself through awareness of the particular in human experience.

Villanova, Arnold de. Physician and alchemist of the Middle Ages whose fame in both areas made his services attractive to the sovereign of Naples and then later to Pope Clement V, whom he served as personal physician. Despite his anti-clerical statements, his reputation as an alchemist, and his reputed commerce with the Devil, the Inquisition could not touch him because of the Pope's protection. Some of his works are: *Rosarium, Philosophorum, Speculam Alchemioe,* and *Perfectum Magisterum.*

Villars, l'Abbe de Montfaucon de (1635-1673). French priest, author, and mystic who first made his reputation as an eloquent preacher. Increasingly, however, his literary and mystical interests dominated his life, and with the publication in 1670 of *Comte du Gabalis*—a fine novel suffused with satirical and mystical qualities antipathetic to religious dogma, the opposition of other priests led him to leave the church. Nonetheless, his succeeding novels, and his philosophical and religious writings won him both a popular and sophisticated readership. His bizarre murder on a public highway in 1673 is to this day veiled by mystery.

Villiers De L'Isle-Adam, Phillipe Auguste Mathias, Comte de (1838-1889). French novelist and Satanist. His book of Satanic stories, *Les Contes Cruels* (1883), was followed by *Tribulat Bonhomet* (1887) whose hero exemplified a passion for the sadistic life of evil. Written in the romantic mode, his work is often suffused with the fantastic, and a cold hatred for both beauty and the basic normalities of life. He also wrote a sensational play, *Axel,* and the novel *L'Eve Future.*

Vinnana (Buddhism). The normal consciousness by which one apprehends the physical world and thus accumulates the experience of life. Vinnana has the same meaning as the term "Vijnana."

Vintras, Eugene. A simple, devout Norman peasant who in 1839 suddenly became a remarkable visionary as a result of tricks played upon him by a religious mystical society, The Saviours of Louis XVII. Believing he had been visited by a heavenly messenger with a divine message, his religious visions became so remarkable he soon won a large following as a new Christ, enlisting to his group even some priests, while his miracles were certified by physicians. Then one of his votaries accused him of practicing Satanism; however, when he was condemned by the Pope, Vintras countered, declaring he himself was the Pope. But shortly afterwards he was imprisoned, and on his release five years later set up his cult in London where it flourished for years.

Violent Signs. In astrology, these refer to: Aries, Libra, Scorpio, Capricorn, and Aquarius (qq.v.).

Viraj (Hinduism). That which is the male half of Brahma, and, by extension, that which symbolizes all male creatures.

Virgo. Astrological sign (August 24–September 23); Element—Earth; Symbol—the Virgin; Ruling planet—Mercury. Qualities—Excellent conversationalists, very logical, discriminating, enormously persistent; interested in social welfare; altogether, a sign of intelligence, possessing loyalty, frankness, acumen, and integrity. These individuals can, however, be overly critical, hypersensitive, overly conservative, too slow in making decisions; they can sometimes be too self-centered, and too proud; they must be careful not to permit a tendency to extreme nervousness to drive them into dissipating their energies in the search for excitement.

Virgula Furcata. The Latin term which means forked rod. Popularly used for centuries by dowsers as a divining rod.

Vishnu (Hinduism). Hindu deity, one of the Trimurti (with Brahma and Siva) and one of the most ancient of Hindu gods; "The Preserver," a beneficent god, said to have had a number of subhuman and human incarnations or "avatars (q.v.)." Incarnated as Krishna, the charioteer, he is the divine-human spokesman of the Bhagavad–Gita (q.v.). Many worthy people of recent times have been considered incarnations of Vishnu by the Hindus.

Vision. May be divided into two classes, objective—perception of material objects in accordance with optical laws, from a definite point in space, and subjective—independent of space, objective existence and optical laws. Clairvoyance or etheric vision should be classed in the latter, although it may yet prove to be "objective" in a different order of existence.

Vision, Clairvoyant. See Clairvoyance.

Vision, Crystal. See Crystal-gazing.

Vision, Induced. See Double.

Vision Questing. The practice of some North American Indians in puberty rites of sending a boy to the woods almost naked (winter or summer) and armed only with bow and arrow. The rite demanded of the boy that he not to return home until he had heard from a supernatural power. If on the first venture he failed, he was often sent out again. Despite the value of success, some boys never experienced visions on these quests. (See: Gertrude Schmeidler)

Vision, Spontaneous. See Apparitions.

Vision, Telescopic. See Telescopic vision.

Visionary. A term which encompasses a number of meanings: speculative, impractical, idealistic, illusionary and a dreamer. It also has the meaning that indicates the experience of visions. All civilizations have witnessed individuals who have reported remarkable spiritual, cosmic, and religious visions.

Visions of Career. The life-vision, which the American Crow Indians believe is the vision that when it is once seen determines one's unique career, and certain success. The power of the vision compels in spite of one's inclinations.

Visistadvaita (Hinduism). The doctrine of the Vedanta (q.v.) which observes that the Absolute (q.v.) is personal; further, that the world and individuals are both real and separate; finally, the attainment of salvation occurs through the grace of God, having been earned with the devotion of *bhakti* (q.v.).

Visitants. Spirit communicators. Apparitions.

Visuddhimagga (Buddhism). A famous treatise by Buddhagosha which means "The Path of Purity."

Visva Devas (Hinduism). The lesser deities.

Vital Body. The double or etheric body.

Vital Force. See Emanations, Psychic force.

Vital, Hayim Calabrese (1543–1620). One of the foremost interpreters and exponents of Cabalism (q.v.), he was an eminent disciple of Isaac Luria (q.v.). His work the *Shaare Kedusah*, "The Gates of Holiness" is both an introduction to the Cabala and an important exposition of the long tradition of the ethics involved in Judaism's mysticism and Cabalism. *Shemonah Shearim*, "The Eight Gates," and *Etz Hayim*, "The Tree of Life" are massive treatises of the secret doctrine which is the foundation of the Lurianic Cabalism.

Vitalism. Theories of life ascribing its phenomena to other than merely physical principles. Non-materialism.

Vivarta (Hinduism). That process of turning and whirling which produces the illusory Many.

Vizaresha (Zoroastrianism). Those demons of darkness who ruthlessly drag souls into hell.

Vladimir, Saint (c. 955–1015). The grand prince of the Kiev and of all Russia, Vladimir in his early years was a successful soldier. Until about the age of thirty-three he was a fervent pagan (with some 800 concubines and numerous wives) but in 988-9 he converted to Greek

Orthodox Christianity (most likely to secure a new wife, the sister of the Byzantine emperor). He easily installed his adopted religion as the official faith of Russia. Strangely, he spent the remainder of his life doing good works for the church. With time, a compendious legend of his saintly behavior and mystical experiences became attached to his memory. His mystical awareness of Christ, in its cosmic sun-spirit nature, has made him known as the "Beautiful Sun" in Russian mystical and occult tradition.

Vocal Signs. In Astrology—Gemini, Libra, and Aquarius. (qq.v.)

Vodun or Voodoo. A religious-magical system composed of African occult practices and elements of Roman Catholicism. Coined in the United States by Haitian Negroes in Louisiana, the word is probably from Dahomey in West Africa. The gods of Vodun are a complex of sacred divinities and supernatural entities whom sorcerers communicate with in their practice of black magic (q.v.), spells, necromancy, charms, hexing and jinxing.

Voice, The. Abbreviated expression for "the direct voice phenomena."

Voicebox (Spiritualism). An instrument fashioned by the spirit operators from ectoplasm, for the purpose of producing the sound of a human voice. It is similar in construction to the human mouth, tongue and larynx, sometimes with a tube leading to the medium's ear or nose. It has often been photographed, and appears as a mass of white substance lying usually on the medium's shoulder. Sometimes it is built inside the trumpet.

Voices, Subjective. See: Clairaudience.

Voices, Supernormal. The direct and independent voice, also voices from materialized forms. Voices heard only by oneself would be clairaudience.

Void of Course. In astrology—the Moon or another planet that will reach the following sign without having formed any aspects (q.v.); that is, it is temporarily void of influence. In horary astrology, it signifies a person who engages in actions which are aimless.

Voodoo. (See: Vodun.)

Voodoo Serpent. In the Voodoo occult system (q.v.) the mammoth Voodoo Serpent superintends and controls the world's power, for it is the master and owner of all the secrets of nature.

Vow. In the occult sphere, to commit oneself to a supernatural power or design of action that necessitates certain prohibitions. Alchemists, for example, believed that only the purest discipline could bring the rewards they sought. Mystics often achieve their ends by obeying a vow of strictest obedience to a program of austere abstinence. Satanists may take a vow to consecrate themselves to the Devil. Sorcerers, witch-doctors, and shamans either profess or understand that a vow is involved in their relations with demons.

Vyahritis (Hinduism). The three, great, primal mystical words said to have been milked by the "Lord of Creatures" (praja pati) from the Vedas (q.v.). These are: *bhur*—which became the earth; *bhuvah*— which became "this firmament"; and *swar*—which became "that sky."

Ww

Wai Tai (Taoism). This occult term has many meanings in Taoism. Basically, it refers to external alchemy which teaches the art of nourishing life by enabling the practitioner to attain Tao (q.v.), immortality, and the transmutation of mercury into gold. But Wai Tai also reveals the secrets of medicine, of charms, of magic, and the occult secrets of making one's body disappear and also of changing its form.

Wakan. An occult power described by American Indian tribes as being an innate supernatural force that suffuses the world, maintains cosmic order, and reveals itself in prophecies, visions, magic, etc. It is analogous in some measure to the Polynesian concept of *Mana* (q.v.).

Wakonda, or Wakan. The Sioux tribe of American Indians attributed this supernatural, impersonal, and mysterious power to certain objects; for example, to stones, to spiders, etc.

Walburga, St. (c.710–777). Saint Walburga, from whose name, ironically, was derived the notorious Walpurgis-night (q.v.), was born in England, the daughter of a King of the West Saxons. But in her middle years she emigrated to Germany where she joined a monastery at Heidenheim. Here her life of exemplary holiness attracted numerous pilgrims to her shrine when she died. Saint Walburga has been one of the most popular saints in England, Germany, and the Low Countries; moreover, her shrine at Eichstadt, Germany is to this day a venerated memorial.

Walker, William. English spirit photographer who is reputed to have been the first man to obtain psychic extras in color.

Wallace, Alfred Russell (1832–1903). The famous naturalist and codiscoverer with Darwin of the principles of evolution. Wallace was a definite materialist before he was introduced to Spiritualism. But after testing many of the most prominent mediums of his time, he concluded that the phenomena of spiritualism were quite valid. "They are proved quite as well as any facts are proved in other sciences," he wrote.

Wallis, E.W. (1848–1914). Outstanding British trance medium, healer, lecturer and author. Founder and editor of the psychic newspaper "Two Worlds" until 1899, then was editor of "Light." His wife was also a well-known trance medium, and together they wrote some excellent books on mediumship.

Walpurgis-night. One of the four great nights for the assembly of witches which occurs on the evening preceding May Day. On Walpurgis-night (also called *walpurgisnacht*) witches engaged in a Bacchanalian orgy, in japery, and Satanic rituals. (See: witch; Sabbat; Walburga, saint.)

"Walter." Walter Stinson, the famous control of the Margery mediumship (Mrs. Crandon (q.v.)). He was a deceased brother of the medium, who had died in a railway accident at the age of twenty-eight. With his medium he was responsible for some of the best attested physical phenomena ever produced.

Waninga. Among the Australian Aborigines this object is similar to a Churinga (q.v.). Fashioned of spears and bound with human hair, it is covered with colored feathers.

Warlock. A skilled demon conjurer whose attraction to Satan and his legions of demons enables him to practice the arts of black magic, sorcery, fortune telling, and wizardry with great effectiveness. Closely aligned to the practitioners of witchcraft, he participates in the assemblies of the Sabbat (q.v.).

Warner, Sylvia Townsend (1893–   ). English novelist, poet, and occultist. Although Miss Warner made her mark as a novelist, because of the multiplicity of her talents—the assured style of gentle fantasy, irony, wit, satire, and scholarly integrity—she is also an extraordinarily skilled occultist. See: *After the Death of Don Juan, The Corner that Held Them.*

Water Divining. See: Dowsing.

Water Signs. In astrology these are the signs: Cancer, Scorpio, and Pisces (qq.v.).

Water-bearer, Waterman. In astrology, a term and symbol for the zodiacal sign Aquarius (q.v.).

Water Sprinkling. A phenomenon fairly common in psychical circles. Small drops of water or perfume are often sprinkled on the sitters, walls and furniture. It has also been noticed in connection with poltergeist phenomena.

Watseka Wonder. A case of multiple personality which occurred in 1865. Laurancy Vennum, a 19-year-old girl, was changed during hypnosis (to cure her of nervous seizures) into a girl who had died some twelve years before. This new personality knew so many details of the dead girl's life and behaved so absolutely like her that the dead girl's family and friends were amazed. Though this "new" personality disappeared in time, through the years she occasionally reappeared and took possession of Miss Vennum. The Vennum-phenomenon attracted much attention; and was attested as a genuine case of multiple personality and spirit possession by the A.S.P.R. (q.v.). The newspapers coined the expression the "Watseka wonder."

Wax Molds. See: Molds.

Weak Signs. In astrology, these signs are: Cancer, Capricorn, and Pisces (qq.v.).

Weigel, Valentin (1533-1588). Notable in the tradition of Germany's eminent mystics, Weigel, however, during his lifetime as a Lutheran clergyman and pastor of the church at Zschopau, displayed only the bourgeois characteristics of a kind, loving, and highly responsible churchman. But after his death, some twenty-one years later, when his posthumous work was published, the world discovered that he had been an avid disciple of Tauler and Paracelsus (qq.v.); that he was, in reality, an impressive mystic and spiritual adept.

Weil, Simone (1909-1943). Weil was a saint; and she was also one of the most extraordinary, brilliant, and visionary philosophers of the twentieth century. The uncompromising purity of her insights, her selflessness, and her ethical integrity were reminiscent of such figures as Socrates and Spinoza. Jewish by birth (her family had wealth and intellectuality), her mystical experience of revelation and union with Christ when she was twenty-nine, and her attraction to Roman Catholicism, led her to the adoption of Christianity. As a result of her ideals and her particular genius for empathy with the world's dispossessed, at thirty-four she died of starvation because she had refused to dress or eat better than victims of Fascist and Nazi oppression; in earlier years she had followed the same restrictions in sympathy for the starving Chinese and also the French workers. Although she never devoted herself to a large work on philosophy, she wrote many articles for small radical periodicals; she also wrote essays on aesthetic subjects, notably Greek literature; and she wrote several memorable pieces on mysticism and religion. She was absolute in her dedication to the search for truth, for social justice, and to her love of God. Repeatedly she asserted that the workers needed poetry and spiritual light more than the bare constant demand for increased amounts of bread. Given the brutal fact of evil in the world and within ourselves, she argued that man's unquenchable expectation of goodness is the sacred part of the human person. "We must love God through the evil that occurs"; and, too, we are delivered from evil if "we project a part of pure evil on something perfectly pure" (for example, "The words of the Lord's Prayer"). But the two concepts which are fundamental to Weil and which she constantly asserts are these: ". . . it is only necessary to be honest with oneself to realize that there is nothing in this world to live for." and . . . one "has only to refuse his love to everything which is not God." Life at its highest was for her the way of the mystics; and one achieved the goal of divine love by destruction of the self, by attention, waiting, transparency, inner emptiness, silence, and ultimately, certainty. Since her death, the beauty of her moral example, and the prophetic truth of her insights have won her an impressive audience and a steadily mounting reputation. (See: *Waiting for God, Gravity and Grace, Notebooks* (2 vol.), *Opression and Liberty*, and *Selected Essays*.)

Werewolf. This old Germanic term is a compound of words meaning "man" and "wolf." The mythologies of northern Europe related tales of persons who for a short time, or permanently, were transformed into wolves, or had the occult power to assume the form of the animal. Werewolves relished human flesh and hunted their prey in the night. The Elizabethan dramatist John Webster in *The Duchess of Malfi* reveals a character who feels himself to be a wolf. In ancient times this belief was prevalent in the whole Mediterranean Basin and in many Asian cultures. In China the word for werewolf was werefox. It is claimed that even today, in certain remote areas, there remains a belief in werewolves. (See: Lycanthropy.)

Westcott, William Mynn. Formerly the Supreme Magus of the Rosicrucian Society in England, Westcott was also a physician, an eminent Cabalist, and the founder of the Order of the Golden Dawn. (See: Aleister Crowley.)

Wheel of Life (Hinduism, Buddhism, Lamaism). This fundamental concept in Eastern religions, notably Hinduism, Buddhism, and Lamaism reveals the endless series of births, deaths, and rebirths in the transmigratory cycle, in metempsychosis, in reincarnation (qq.v.). In Lamaism this is most graphically illustrated by a vivid painting of a wheel in which is portrayed the six worlds, the twelve signs of existence, and, upon the hub of the wheel a cock, a pig, and a snake. These animals signify lust, greed, and anger—the great sins of man which chain him to the merciless wheel of life that is full of evil, sin, sorrow, and death continually repeating itself. This symbolic wheel is the traditional pictorial representation of the Eastern doctrine of reincarnation. The rim of the wheel symbolizes immortality; the three hub excrescences—ignorance, lust, anger. The six spokes—gods, demigods, tortured souls, human beings and animals.

Whipping. A widespread ritual in both ancient and modern religions and social groups which was used to achieve purification or exorcise spirits. As a ritual, some societies practice it when they officially install officers. It is also popular in the ritual of initiation rites.

White Brotherhood, The Great. Believed by some occultists and spiritual groups to be the true seat of inner world government by a hierarchy of Masters or Adepts.

White Fire (Cabalism). A term to express, in certain esoteric relationships, the ineffable, the infinite, the unknowable, hidden First Cause. Analogous to the mystic Ain Sof (q.v.).

White Spirit, The Great. A spirit's name for Deity.

White Stone, The. The Christ-like development of the individual, one who in esoteric Christian doctrine has achieved the higher ego (q.v.). The White Stone is a symbol and mark of this initiation. Some occultists believe that the white cornelian of the Rosicrucian Alchemists is an analogous symbol.

White Witches. A new breed of witches who practice a benevolent assistance program. Based on a pre-Christian, Druidic, or Celtic doctrine of witchcraft, they minister to their communities as good samaritans. These groups have sprung up in England and the United States in many areas. (See: John Wier)

Whole Signs. In astrology, these signs are: Gemini, Libra, and Aquarius (qq.v.). Some astrologers include Taurus (q.v.).

Whore. In old dream interpretation, for a man to dream of copulating with a whore is a sign that he is certain to suffer losses and disgrace. However, for a chaste girl to dream she is engaged in prostitution is a favorable omen. This means she will very shortly be married, and, even more, she will love her husband.

Wickland, Carl (1861–?). Dr. Wickland was the director of the Psychopathic Institute of Chicago for the treatment of mental patients. Through the mediumship of his wife, he was able, over a period of thirty years, to effect many cures by ridding patients of obsessing spirits. He travelled to California and founded the National Psychological Institute for treatment of obsession. He stated in his book *Thirty Years Among the Dead* that the spirit of Mme. Blavatsky returned and retracted the reincarnation theory. (See: *Thirty Years Among the Dead* (1924), Nat'l. Psychological Inst., ed.; London Spiritual Press, ed. (1968))

Wild Fire, or Strange Fire. The fire that was stolen from a family hearth or fire place in the belief that it possessed a power for malign witchcraft. (See: Ignis fatuus.)

Will-o'-the-wisp. A flittering phosphorescent light that hovers over marshy ground (*ignis fatuus*). In many mythologies, the will-o'-the-wisp is regarded as a demon who is a harbinger of death or ill fortune.

Will Power. Many instruments have been invented in attempts to prove that the human will is capable of exerting dynamic energy. However, despite the importance of this quest, these early efforts proved fruitless because the wrong question was being asked. Recently, a number of investigators have discovered that certain individuals are gifted with a special energy that measurably affects inanimate as well as animate objects. The failure of Western science until the last few decades to accept the reality of the range and specificity of such phenomena impeded a clearer understanding of the energy dynamics of many famous mediums and psychics. (See: Wm. Crookes, Eusapia Paladino, Samadha, Justa Smith, Mme. Tomczyk, Will to Believe, Olga Worral and Volometer)

Will to Believe. This phrase created by William James (q.v.) in 1896 has become a seminal notion in modern thinking. Disturbed by the narrow limits which scientists had set on valid experience and existence, James proclaimed the need for a greater scope in man's awareness of his potential and his cognitive-consciousness dimensions. He emphasized strongly that man had the right and necessity to believe where evidence is not complete. James in a large sense was one of the fathers of today's flourishing movement in parapsychology.

Williamson, Cecil. English impresario who inaugurated in Bocastle, England, the very popular museum named the Witches' House. It has the distinction of housing the most comprehensive collection in Europe of the artifacts and history of Black Magic (q.v.). An avowed sorcerer, he claims that by using ritual magic he has produced spirits.

Wilson, Jack. An American Paiute Indian prophet named Wovoka who during an illness in 1888 experienced a visionary revelation. His messianic vision proclaimed that the Indians would soon be transcended and enjoy union with the dead; that they would soon recover their rightful inheritance; and that they should prepare themselves for the glorious events by practicing various ceremonies. Wilson's prophecies greatly influenced the ritual of the ghost dance.

Windigo. Among the Ottawa and Chippewa Indian tribes of the northern United States and Canada, the Windigo is a mythical cannibal tribe. Some Canadian Indians regard the Windigo as a giant cannibal man. The name of this fierce monster is commonly used to frighten children.

Winds, Psychic. See: Breezes.

Wisconsin Phalanx. A Spiritualist association that was formed near Ripon by Warren Case in 1844. During the six years of its existence, it was a highly successful Spiritualist group.

Wise Men of the East, Magi. Known also as the Three Kings who emerged from the East, these masters in the art of astrology came to Bethlehem to witness the newborn glory of mankind—Jesus. Called in the Bible Caspar, Melchior, and Balthazar, these magician-priests brought precious gifts to the lowly manger of Christ. Their great knowledge of astrology had taught them that the appearance of an extraordinary star in the heavens foretold Christ's reign on earth.

Wise of Heart (Cabalism). The *Book of Zohar* (q.v.) emphasizes that these Cabalistic masters, The Wise of Heart, represent the great tradition of Hebrew mysticism: its strong tradition of ethical concern, and the wisdom of a true sense of God's external splendor.

Witch. The witch has a very ancient history and has been a universal phenomenon among mankind. Moreover, the similarity of behavior patterns in such widely separated worlds as Asia, Europe, Africa, and the Americas attests to a common genesis. Some researchers believe that ancient fertility rites—the need for rain during periods of drought (in which older women were utilized as the embodiment of the fertility principle—to sweep the dry, dusty ground with brooms)—are the source of the witch character. For in most countries drawings of a witch reveal her flying on her magic broom. Universally, again, witches (male and female) are evil sorcerers with immense occult powers. They eat human flesh, drink human blood, alter the forces of nature, foretell the future, transform themselves and others, copulate with anyone their lust fancies (Satan, demons, man, and beast); in addition, they can accomplish almost any supernatural feat. Nearly always, the witch possesses a magic rod, and upon her or his body, concealed, is a birthmark or other sign as proof of her or his compact with the infernal demons. There is no foul practice they have not committed. Their skill in mixing love philtres (along with poison philtres) has made them a magnet for lovers. Masters of Black Magic (q.v.), necromancy (q.v.), out-of-body powers; dispensers of every type of unguent, potion, philtre; casters of spells and charms; gluttons of loathsome food in their ceremonies; worshippers of Satan—witches, accordingly, have been feared and condemned by church and state. Witch hunts, witch trials, and witch burnings have been notorious throughout history. But the witch still flourishes. More remarkably, she has evolved into something of a popular figure. For your modern witch swings with the times. She wears some of the old style, but she can present herself in a completely new fashion. Some contemporary witch groups are devotees of Black Magic; oppositely, there are others who engage in benevolent activities. (See: Witch's Marks, Witch's Sabbat, Witch's Foot, White Witches, Witchcraft Covens, etc.).

Witch Doctor. Magician, highly trained, who was important to primitive tribes in the function of a shaman or medicine-man (qq.v.). Mainly, his skill in the use of spells, charms, incantations, and herbal prescriptions was utilized to cure disease, discover witches, and to frustrate evil magical influences.

Witch-Hunt. Historically, from the most ancient times, all primitive societies attacked and purged those who used poison, sympathetic magic, or who by occult instrumentalities injured a member of the tribe. Thus "witch-hunt" has both a universal and a very ancient past. However, during the Middle Ages in Europe, the church, Catholic and Protestant, attacked the cult of witchcraft with a blind, ruthless passion which persisted through more than a three-hundred-year crusade—in fact, from 1450 to 1782. Persons accused of witchcraft, on the flimsiest evidence, were tortured mercilessly until they confessed to the most heinous heresies and crimes. Thousands of innocent men, women, and children in every nation in Europe were tortured bestially, burned, and put to death. In America, hysterical witch-hunts in New England and Virginia followed the same European inhumanity. To read the *Malleus Malleficarum*—the "Hammer of the Witches" (q.v.) is to understand the raging animus that inflamed church and state against anyone accused of witchcraft. (Read: *Witchcraft in Western Europe* by M.A. Murray.)

Witch of Endor. The witch King Saul consulted when he was assaulted by a formidable Philistine army at Endor. The witch of Endor evoked the spirit of Samuel—the great judge, prophet, and hero who had anointed Saul at his coronation. The witch prophesied his defeat and death, an event which occurred in the battle on Mt. Gilboa—1 Samuel 10-31. This Biblical story strongly excited the imagination of seventeenth-century devotees of witchcraft.

Witch Plays. Three interesting plays on witches written by English dramatists bore the name "witch" in their titles. These plays are: *The Lancashire Witches* by Thomas Shadwell (1681); *Witch of Islington* (1597), and *Witch Traveler* (1623). The last two are also on record as having been acted, but their authors are unknown. Like most drama, English plays began as "miracle plays"; that is, they were religious in origin. Accordingly, in early English drama the "Hell-mouth" or Hell was a prominent part of the stage scene. While Satan is one of the most featured characters in these miracle plays (represented as black, with goat's horns, ass's ears, cloven hoofs, and an enormous male organ), his infernal companions, in the form of demons and monsters, surrounded by fire, appeared frequently from the hole of the "Hell-mouth."

Witchcraft. See: Witch.

Witchcraft Covens. See: Coven.

Witches' Bath. Trial by water for those suspected of witchcraft.

Witch's Bridle. A vile device of iron with four sharp teeth; two were used to pierce the tongue, the other two to pierce the cheeks.

Witches' Broth. A devilish potpourri concocted of infants' flesh and the flesh of hanged men, of frogs, black millet, and a magic powder. Drinkers of this broth purportedly could fly through the air.

Witch's Foot. A talisman popular throughout the Middle Ages in Europe and during the Renaissance to ward off evil spirits. It was a symbol in the shape of a pentagram (a five-pointed star) (q.v.) which was painted within the house.

Witches' Holy Water. At the witches' mass the holy water was generally urine, either the Devil's or one of the celebrant's. This "Holy water" was sprinkled upon the devotees just before the Celebration of Mass.

Witches' Ladder. The string of nine knots the witch hides near an enemy to cause his death.

Witch's Marks. Those protuberances—extra breasts or nipples on a witch's body—for her familiars to suck.

Witches' Sabbat. A congress of witches, warlocks, magicians, sorcerers, and necromancers (qq.v.) which gathered four times a year in dark forests, secret caves, moldering ruins, and sometimes holy places. But more local celebrations occurred at various intervals conducted by area leaders. At these Sabbats, orgies, necromancy, foul sacrifices, vile rituals using urine, and the carnal adoration of infernal demons and Satan saturated the night. February 2 (Candlemas), May-eve (Roodmas), August 1 (Lammas), and November eve (Hallowe'en) were the great sabbats. These dates seem to have been evocations of primeval and Celtic periods of seasonal and occult celebrations.

Witching. That which has the demonic power to be used in sorcery or occult practices.

Wizard. Among the ancient Druids (q.v.) a wizard was a man of deep wisdom and knowledge. It has also denoted a sage or a wise man. But conversely, wizards have also signified men who were adepts in the occult arts, men who were magicians and sorcerers, and men who were professional practitioners of witchcraft. Interestingly, it still bears metaphorical connotations of these meanings today.

Wolf. In old dream interpretation, to be chased by a wolf in your dream is an omen you are due to be cheated in a trade or agreement. If a girl has a dream of being frightened by a wolf, it reveals her present lover is an evil person. But if she has no lover then it signifies that some villainous man will try to win her affection.

Wonder Workers (Judaism–Cabalism). Name given to the practical Cabalists in the 16th century in Europe, but most especially, it referred to those in the Cabalist wonder-working center in Safed, Galilee, which was known as "The Lion"—the name for the famed Caba-list ARI (Rabbi Isaac Luria (q.v.)). The title of "Wonder-workers" was inherited by the Hasidic Rabbis (called Rebbes or Tzaddikim) who were known as the holy "wonder-workers." (See: Cabalism; Hasidim.)

Words of Power. Cabalists, certain mystics (notably in the Judaic tradition), shamans, necromancers, sorcerers, witches, Black Magic adepts, diabolists, wizards, witch doctors, many oracles, priests, (qq.v.) etc., have utilized words of power to produce or demolish cer-tain events or effects. So deeply enshrined is this belief in mankind's psyche that there is hardly a person who does not use, on occasion, "Words of Power." Often, these "words" are called prayers or wishes, but unconsciously and often consciously they are magic for-mulas uttered to produce or demolish certain events or effects.

Worlds, The Four (Cabalism). The Four Worlds of the Cabalists (q.v.) are described as: *Atziluth*, which designates the archetypal; *Briah*, the creative; *Yetzirah*, the formation; *Assiah*, the material. These Four Worlds through the power of God (in his ten spheres of emanation—the Sepiroth (q.v.)) come into being by way of degree; that is, in a de-scending order. The birth of the highest "World" is followed by the next highest, and finally culminates in the material "world"—the most limited of these divinely inspired creations.

World Soul. A philosophic-religious-occult view of an intelligent, dynamic, immanent principle of the cosmos. The World Soul is con-ceived as an organizing power and source of universal motion. The concept of a world soul has been held by most men from the beginning of their spiritual wondering; also, by Plato, Stoicism, Neo-Platonism, Bruno, Hinduism, Buddhism, and Christianity; also, such modern phi-losophies as have been essentially doctrines of Idealism.

World Traveler. Those psychics who during the trance state can pro-ject their astral bodies to far-distant places. Edgar Cayce (q.v.) it is claimed, was an eminent example of a "World Traveler."

Worrall, Olga. Spiritual healer and lecturer. Her powerful biological energy which she transmits to sick persons by the process of laying on of hands, has produced notable results in her patients. Practicing in a suburb of Baltimore, Maryland, her marked therapeutic powers have won the praise of many doctors. They have sent her patients from such distant places as Alaska, and doctors in increasing numbers have come to her lectures and discussed spiritual healing with her. (See: Will Power)

Wraith. An apparition of a living person which is widely believed to be a sign of that person's death. Seemingly, it is possible to see one's own wraith; and the legend goes that Queen Elizabeth, Shelley, and Cath-erine of Russia experienced such premonitory visions.

Wroe, John (1782–1863). English prophet, and founder of the sect of Christian Israelites, Wroe was famous for his visions and his trance revelations. His travels in the British Isles, in Europe, in the United States, and Australia made him a world figure. He wrote many works of mystical and visionary revelations, notably his *Panacea Society*.

Wu (Taoism). This concept, the essence of Tao (q.v.), is the notion of "Eternal Non-Being." This first principle declares that material objects have no being.

Wu hua (Taoism). The great Taoist Chuang Tzu (q.v.) affirmed that all things could be transformed into other things; that is, that there is an identity that unifies all that exists—most particularly: the self and the non-self, man and things.

Wu Wei (Taoism). Spontaneity and the state of nature are essential to man's wise existence, for Wu Wei (no activity) permits man to eliminate artificiality; and, also, that wisdom and morality which is superficial. Nonetheless, despite man's passivity and inactivity everything still gets done. Spontaneity in all of its aspects (conscious and active)—for example, accepting nature, and not interfering with *Tao* and heaven brings complete attainment. Such is the way of nature and the cosmos, and such should be the way of man.

Wyrd. The goddess of death among the Teutonic Germans.

Wyvern or Wivern. The legendary dragon, which in various forms was famous in Asian and European mythology and occultism. But the wyvern was a product of European mythology and esoteric perception which developed from the viper to become a fabulous two-legged creature resembling a dragon. It was a species of cockatrice or basilisk (qq.v.). All these creatures embodied profound occult and esoteric ramifications related to death and resurrection, to the cosmic within temporal existence and to alchemical spiritual transformation. An important strand of this multi-dimensional symbolism is the mythology of the deathless phoenix (q.v.).

Xaphan. Famous in the war of the angels against heaven for his desire to set fire to heaven. When Lucifer and the rebellious angels were hurled into hell, Xaphan became one of the lesser demons; his job was to start the blazing fires of hell.

Xavier, Francis de (1506–1552). Roman Catholic saint and one of the greatest Christian missionaries, he was among Loyola's (q.v.) original group of converts. Born in Spain of a noble family, in 1541 he began his missionary work in the Portuguese colony of India; from here he continued his phenomenally successful campaign in the East Indies, Ceylon, and Japan. His incredible missionary successes and conversions in the East were an outstanding example of the Jesuit training by Loyola (q.v.). He was buried in Gao, India, where his tomb has been the center of many reported miracles.

Xenoglossy. In spiritualism this phenomenon is the sudden speaking in tongues which are unknown to the medium. Certainly there is no validity in the view that the fact of xenoglossy can be dismissed as an evocation of subconscious memory, unless, of course, a medium has in the past been exposed to the language or languages used. In Christianity the Gift of Tongues has an ancient history. When Christ ascended into heaven (celebrated as Ascension Day—Holy Thursday) those who witnessed this event in the upper room at Jerusalem were endowed by the Holy Ghost with the power of extolling God in many languages completely unknown to them. It is believed, however, that during the first century of the Christian Church this Gift of Tongues continued to flourish. But following the emergence of Protestantism, there have been a number of small sects of Protestants who have claimed for their members the reemergence of this "Gift." Today, Pentacostals and born-again Christians in the hundreds of thousands now declare that the power of the Gift of Tongues has emerged again among the rededicated members of their Christian movement.

Xenophanes (c. 570–c. 480 B.C.). One of the important pre-Socratic Greek philosophers. The reputed founder of the significant Eleatic School of Philosophy, he introduced into Western thought the profoundly evocative concept "all is one." For Xenophanes the multiplicity of Greek gods was a wrong orthodoxy since he explained God as being both immovable and omnipresent. His philosophy has had a continuing influence from his own time until the present period—in philosophy, in religion, in mysticism, and in the occult.

Xibalba. Among the Mayan Quiche Indians of Guatemala, the underground world of the dead.

Xipe. In the Aztec religion the god of young vegetation, particularly young corn. During the ceremonies of his annual festival, prisoners-of-war were mutilated and their flayed skins decorated the bodies of Xipe's worshippers. At the conclusion of the festival the skins were buried. Symbolically, the skins signified winter vegetation; their burial the emergence of new life to replace the old.

Xiuhcoatl. In the Aztec religion the "Fire Snake," one of the cults of Quetzalcoatl (q.v.). It was also known as a cult of the "Plumed Serpent." Xiuhtecuhtli, the god of fire, is served by Xiuhcoatl.

Xochipilli. In the Aztec religion the "Flower Prince" who was the god of flowers. He was also the deity of the dance, and sport.

Xochiquetzal. In the Aztec religion, the goddess of love. She had the reputation of beguiling holy men during their spiritual hours of consecration. Women desiring children prayed to Xochiquetzal. During her sacred month, many young women were sacrificed—a number of whom were prostitutes.

X-Ray Vision. Some healers have claimed this power, which enables them to see the affected organs within the body. Some sensitives have also professed this faculty, by which they have claimed to be able to read sealed messages.

Xylomancy. A form of divination which involved tossing sticks or twigs on the ground and reading prophetic meaning from their position.

Yad (Judaism). The silver or golden pointer which is used to point to the text of the Torah when it is read in the synagogue during the Sabbath ceremonies, for no one is allowed to touch the open Torah. The ritual of reading the Torah throughout the year in the synagogue is very elaborate, and it was the famous Cabalist Joseph Caro of Safed (q.v.) who established the exact procedure of this dramatic ceremony, which has since been followed in the Western World by all Jews. It was another Jewish mystic, Simeon bar Yochai (q.v.) who lived in the 2nd century A.D., who described the mystical significance of the Torah-reading ceremony: "When the scroll of the Torah is taken out of the Ark (q.v.) in the presence of the congregation to read therein, the heavenly Gates of Mercy open and divine love awakens."

Yagi-gyemo (Tibetanism). One of the four pagan female divinities who preside over the seasons of the year in Bon mythology. Represented in the color blue, Yagi-gyemo is the queen of the summer. Bon mythology was the religion of Tibet that preceded the introduction of Buddhism.

Yajurveda (Hinduism). The second Veda (q.v.) which contains sacrificial prayers and material explicative in nature. It is divided into two samhitas: the Black Yajus (esoteric) and the White Yajus (exoteric). The major source of the Yajurveda is the Rigveda (q.v.).

Yaks (Lamaism). In Tibet yaks often wear papers containing prayers as they graze. These yak-papers are addressed to the Yi-dam (q.v.), the tutelary deity of the yak-owner.

Yakshas (Buddhism-Hinduism). These are supernatural spirits of vegetation who are companions of Kuvera, the god of wealth.

Yama (1) (Hinduism). The first grade of training in the discipline that leads to attaining the object of Yoga (q.v.), which includes ahimsa (q.v.), and brach macarya (q.v.). The ten rules of this initial training are: non-injury, truthfulness, non-stealing, continence, forgiveness, endurance, compassion, sincerity, sparing diet, and cleanliness.

Yama (2) (Hinduism–Lamaism). In the Veda (q.v.), Yama symbolizes the god of the dead, the ruler of the underworld, and the lord of ghosts, being also the judge there of souls who inhabit this nether world in a state of partial existence. Following a reading of a person's earthly deeds, Yama pronounces a sentence on this soul, sending it to Pitris (Manes) or to one of the 21 hells for purification. The god is represented as green, robed in red, and riding upon a buffalo. In Lamaism, the Shin-Kyong, as skeletons, are companions of Yama. And even in death in Tibetan art these bony Shin-Kyong are often represented in a mystic embrace of passionate and violent sexual intercourse, which reflects Lamaism's Tantric (q.v.) orientation. (See: Spheres)

Yamabusi. In the Japanese religion the Yamabusi were a sect of monks known as Hermit Brothers. They were noted for their mystical doctrines.

Yamin Noraim (Judaism). Since most ancient times this has been known as the period of the "Days of Awe." It represents a period of ten days preceding the solemn holy day of Yom Kippur. This very ancient custom was observed by the Jews by rising at midnight during the "Days of Awe" in order to hasten to the temple for the recitation of the prayers of Selichot (q.v.). This custom has been very important to all Jewish mystics.

Yang-Hsaio. In the technique of the *I Ching* (q.v.), Yang-Hsaio is a continuous line which plays against the divided line *yin-shiao* (q.v.) to form the trigrams. Yang-Hsaio represents the male or positive principle.

Yang sheng (Taoism). The art of preserving one's vital powers—which includes one's sexual powers. The technique embraces breath control, physical exercises, and a healthy diet.

Yasha (Zoroastrianism). In the Zendavesta (q.v.) that portion (seventy-two chapters) which contains the *Gathas*, the great hymns of Zoroaster. These Gathas are the oldest and most sacred part of the Zoroastrian book of worship, the Zendavesta.

Yashts (Zoroastrianism). In the Zendavesta (q.v.), the twenty-one chapters of the Yashts are invocations of divinities and angels.

Yatha ahu vairyo (Zoroastrianism). These are the sacred first words of one of the holiest of all Zoroastrian prayers.

Yawn. In the popular belief of many Christians, especially during the Middle Ages and up to relatively modern times, to yawn was dangerous, for it permitted demons to enter the body. To make the sign of the cross with the thumb over the mouth before yawning averted this satanic peril.

Yazatas (Zoroastrianism). Higher beings, some of whom are heavenly and invisible, led by Ahura Mazda (q.v.); and the earthly Yazatas, who are led by Zarathustra. The Amesha-Spentas (q.v.) belong to them. The number of Yazatas is exactly 100,000.

Year-cycles (Lamaism). In Tibet time is calculated in cycles of sixty years. These are very important in the calculation of birthdates, and for the most important actions and events, such as the selection of a new Dalai Lama, the building of a monastery or temple, the birthdates of young people to be considered for marriage, etc. In fact, in Tibet, nearly all of life's actions are governed by astrology; and astrology's dependence on time is almost as important as the sanction of the Dalai Lama or some other high Lama (the Tashi Lama, for example) and the tutelary deities. (See: Yi-dam)

Yeats, William Butler (1865–1939). One of the most eminent of modern poets, this Irish playwright, statesman, many-sided man of letters, and gigantic public figure, was also a Nobel Laureate (1923), and one of the most informed occultists of the 20th century. Beginning with his fascination with old Irish legends and magic, and later with Theosophy and Rosicrucianism, he went on to marry a woman whose gift of automatic writing enriched his occultism and enabled him to form a unique type of paranormal vision which was integral to his dramatic work and his superlative poetry. Many of the major English poets of our time such as Eliot and Auden have ranked him as a preeminent poet. Yeats was also a member of the Order of the Golden Dawn (q.v.), with the name *Daemon est Deus Inversus* (The Devil is God Reversed). See his plays *Mosada, The Hour Glass, Deirdre,* and his poems *The Wild Swans at Coole, The Tower,* and *Last Poems.*

Yellow. In old dream interpretation to dream of getting a yellow object was a sign the person would soon possess gold. For a girl to dream that her beloved is giving her yellow flowers was a presage of marrying a wealthy man.

Yesod. Cabalistic idea of an archetypal world, somewhat akin to the astral sphere.

Yetzer (Judaism). The immanent impulse or inclination which each man possesses at birth. This "Yetzer" is enormously important in the development and salvation of the Jewish individual. (See: Yetzer-tob and Yetzer-ha-Rah.)

Yetzer Tob and Yetzer Ha-rah (Judaism). The Judaic concept of good and evil, which emphasizes that these forces are not supernatural but reside within man. Their struggle to control mind and soul depends for its continuing resolution on the will and moral exercise of each individual. Though Cain after the murder of his brother Abel retorts to God's severe rebuke that it was God himself who put evil (the *Yetzer Ha-rah*) in his heart, later Jewish sages and Rabbis saw this "evil" as a negative force working for eventual good. They also explained that God's gift of the Torah to the Jews was the act of Grace, for if they studied the Torah it would dissolve their urge to do evil.

Yezidis. A religious sect centered in Kurdistan who worship a unique blend of Christian, Islamic, and Near Eastern religions. Their chief divinity is the angel Yazid, who along with six assisting angels rules the universe. Nonetheless, this Yezidis pantheon is subordinate to the supreme God who no longer concerns Himself with the universe He created. Their primary doctrine is a belief in a manifest oneness: there is no evil, sin, a devil, or hell—since God pardoned the devil after he repented and placed him again at the head of his angels. Yazid is worshipped in the form of a peacock. Interestingly, the Yezidis believe they are uniquely created and are not descended from Adam; hence they keep themselves separate from the people among whom they dwell. They are scattered over Southeast Turkey, Northwest Iran, and North Iraq. Their religious center is at Shaik Adi, north of Mosul, which contains the tomb of their foremost saint.

Yggdrasill (Ydrasil). In Scandinavian mythology this is the colossal evergreen ash tree, the three gigantic roots of which bind together Asgard, Midgard, and Niflheim—heaven, earth, and hell. The branches of Yggdrasil canopy both earth and heaven.

Yhva. Jehovah, the early tribal god and special protector of the Jews in the Old Testament.

Yi-dam (Lamaism). The tutelary gods. In Tibet every sect, order, and monastery is protected by one or a number of divinities. However, each person lives his life constantly protected by his own personal Yi-dam. This tutelary deity may be selected by the individual, but generally his guru will have selected it for him.

Yi-das (Lamaism). In Tibet locusts are believed to be the reincarnation of Yi-das, creatures who live in the lowest of the six worlds, just above hell. Yi-das have large bodies, but tiny mouths and throats so that they can only swallow a crumb at a time. However, because in their earthly lives they were covetous, gluttonous, uncharitable, they are tormented with constant hunger and thirst. When they have expiated their evil Karma (q.v.), they often return to earth as locusts, since the hunger of these insects is never satisfied.

Yigdal (Judaism). The famous thirteen articles which represent the essence of Jewish belief as the eminent Jewish philosopher Maimonides codified them. But it was Daniel Ben Judah, the Jewish poet, who in the 14th century turned these thirteen articles into verse calling it "Yigdal." Immediately popular among all Jewish sects, it has become a permanent part of Jewish liturgical worship.

Yi-king. A pre-Confucian writing in ideograms, with a commentary attributed to Confucius. May have been used for divination purposes, as it contains astrological references.

Yin and Yang. The primal passive and active principles of the universe which are central to the doctrines of Taoism (q.v.) and in popular Chinese Neo-Confucianism. Yin is the female principle, Yang the male principle; Yin is the negative force, Yang the positive force. But these forces are always both contrasting and yet completing each other. These principles, "souls," or "breaths" are productive of the universe, and are expressed in heaven and earth, man and woman, hardness and softness, good and evil, white and black, upper and lower, great and small, odd and even, life and death, love and hate; in fact, in all of existence and all of its relationships and dynamics. A great number of good spirits (shen) inhere in Yang, while evil spectres (Kwei) inhere in Yin. In trigram (q.v.) or kua symbols of the Great Ultimate, Yin and Yang produce all things. Interpretation of any possible Yin-Yang experience is worked out by a divination technique known as the I Ching (q.v.). Yin and Yang was the name of a school that utilized popular Chinese geomancy, astrology, magic, etc.

Yin-hsiao. In the I Ching (q.v.) this is the divided line which acts with the undivided line (yang-hsiao) (q.v.) to form the trigrams (q.v.). This is the female or negative principle.

Ymir. In Scandinavian mythology the great giant, the primeval man, from whose body Odin, Wili, and Ve created the world.

Yod (Judaism). The first letter of God's sacred name YHVH (q.v.). Yod represents a point, and in the Cabala (q.v.) it signifies the first "mark" made by God. Out of this first mark was generated all subsequent letters, all human beings, and all that exists.

Yoga. Ancient Hindu system of self-discipline and psychic training (first defined in the Bhagavad-Gita (q.v.), Chap. VI, 10-19), with the object of uniting the Lower with the Higher Self and thus attaining freedom from the otherwise inexorable round of rebirth and Karma (q.v.). Considerable mastery over the subconscious activity and direction over the physical body and its organs can be achieved, and strong psychic powers developed, although these, it is stressed, should not be sought for the sake of power. Many modified systems of Yoga are now popular in the West, using it primarily as a system of physical culture; an objective for which Yoga was never intended.

Yogacara (Buddhism). The Mahayana Buddhist (q.v.) school which directs its believers to the discipline of Yoga (q.v.) and the discipline of ethical conduct. This school is also called Vijnana-Vada, emphasizing that both Yogacara and Vijnana-Vada assert that consciousness is the essence of reality.

Yogin. One who practices Yoga (q.v.). Loosely applied term for any ascetic. Originally confined to men only.

Yomael. In the apocalyptic book of Enoch, Yomael is one of the ringleaders of the rebellious angels. The fiery Yomael is described as taking an oath of allegiance to the great chief of the fallen angels, Samiaza.

Yomi. Japanese term for the spirit world.

Yoni (Hinduism). A representation of the female sexual organ in the shape of a triangular prism depressed on the upper part to permit the insertion of the lingam (q.v.). Yoni also symbolizes: source, origin, first cause.

Young. In old dream mythology for an older or even middle-aged individual to dream that he is young was a dread omen of death. Even if a young person had a dream of being a child, the dread omen was the same.

Yu (Taoism). Being, existence, which comes out of Non-Being. Yu is the mother of all that exists. It also means desire, and in this aspect it corrodes the good life.

Yuga (Hinduism). One of the four ages of a world cycle with each succeeding age shorter and less spiritual and righteous than the one preceding. These four ages are termed: the Krita Yuga—which lasts 1,728,000 years; the Treta Yuga—which lasts 1,296,000 years; the Dvapara Yuga—which lasts 864,000 years; and the Kali Yuga—which lasts 432,000 years. The Krita Yuga (the Golden Age) is considered to have been in the Lemurian Age (q.v.); the Treta Yuga (the Silver Age), was mostly in the Atlantean Age (q.v.); the Dvapara Yuga (the Bronze Age) began 6000 years before the first Post-Atlantean Epoch; the Kali Yuga (the Dark Age) was inaugurated in 3101 B.C. The vast cycle of the four ages covers 4,320,000 years and is designated a manvantara (q.v.). At its end occurs a pralaya which initiates the "Night of Brahma," a period encompassing a thousand cycles. This "Night of Brahma" expires when Brahma awakens and then renews the cycle of the Ages. The period of one night and one day of Brahma constitutes a Kalpa— which is a complete cosmic cycle from inauguration to destruction of a world system. Finally, A Yuga is 1000th part of a Kalpa.

Zachaire, Denis (1510?- ?). French alchemist, born in La Guyenne, who was a student of law and later of science. However, Zachaire forsook both for his passionate interest in alchemy. His book, *Opuscule de la Philosophie de Metaux, Traitant de l'Augmentation et Perfection de Ceux* (1567), has been often reprinted and was signally honored by being translated into Latin. So rich in occult and alchemical insight is this work that it still commands a contemporary readership.

Zacornu (Islam). A grisly tree that grows in the Islamic hell, the fruit of which are the heads of devils.

Zahir (Islam). Among Muslims the designation Zahir encompasses the concept the Logos, meaning both the "reason" that governs the universe and the divine word.

Zalmoxis. The god of the dead among the ancient Getae, the people of Bulgaria, Moldavia and adjacent regions. Every four years, in a peculiarly barbarian ritual, the Getae made a special individual "immortal" by throwing him upon spear-points and instructing him with messages which he was to deliver to the lower world.

Zanoni. A book suffused with an occult background which was written by the English novelist Bulwer-Lytton (q.v.).

Zarathustra (c. 630 B.C.–c. 553 B.C.). He was the creator of a new religion and one of those radical mystics and prophets who from time to time are able to make their visions prevail, thus enriching the spiritual life of mankind. Zoroaster was the founder of Zoroastrianism (q.v.), which supplanted an earlier nature religion of Iran with a monotheistic conception. However, the new doctrine won its way slowly, and it was only after Zarathustra's death that his new religion finally spread throughout Iran (Persia). But in the process of establishing its dominance, Zoroastrianism was corrupted by elements of the older religions and by the Magi (q.v.), who introduced such notions as a continuing conflict on earth between good and evil forces—the result of the conflict between the great god, Ahura Mazda, and the devil, Ahriman (qq.v.). Even so, despite its ultimately wide acceptance, it did not become the official religion of Persia until the advent of the Sasanian dynasty in 224 A.D. Most authorities hold that Zarathustra's own genuine writings are those contained in the Gathas (hymns or songs) which are a part of the Yasna, one of the five books of the Zoroastrian Bible, collectively entitled the Avesta or the Zend-Avesta (qq.v.). In the tradition of Moses and the much later prophet Muhammad, Zarathustra endowed his people with a more humane, a more ethical, and a purer faith than they had known. Zoroastrianism in its later, contaminated form had a pronounced effect on Greek philosophy, Judaism, Christianity, and Islam; and it was a splinter sect of Zoroastrianism, Mithraism (q.v.), that almost won out over the state religion in ancient Rome, and then became Christianity's great pagan rival in the struggle for religious victory. Present-day adherents of Zoroastrianism in India and elsewhere are known as Parsi or Parsee. When the eminent philosopher Nietzsche looked for a superior man—a prototype of the superman, it was Zarathustra he chose to illustrate so complex a person in his world-acclaimed masterpiece Thus Spake Zarathustra.

Zazen. A method of Zen Buddhism in which enlightenment is achieved by way of meditation in the crossed-legged position. The doctrine stresses the identity of practice and enlightenment, each being contained in the other. While no additional enlightenment is to be pursued beyond the exercise of Zazen, enlightenment may also come, in a sudden burst of vision. Dogen (shoyo Daishil) was the founder of Zazen. (See: Zen)

Zebaot (Judaism). The name applied to the Hebrew God when he engages in both the role and act of making war upon evildoers. Among the Jews God has many names, symbolizing his numerous powers. A few of his well-known names are: Elohim, El Shaddai, Yahveh, and Adonai (qq.v.). But Zebaot is also part of the immensely important phrase "Yahveh Elohai Zebaot," which in Hebrew means "Yahveh, the God of armies," but in the English is translated "Lord of Hosts." (See: Tetragammaton, En Sof.)

Zedechias. A French Cabalist who in the eighth century, during the reign of Pepin the Short, is reported to have evoked the appearance of the elemental spirits called "sylphs." Zedechias aimed to enlist mankind into joining these beneficient Elementals. But despite the awesome array of splendor produced by the sylphs in their armies and aerial navies, in their spectacular creation of the aurora borealis, the French considered these friendly spirits to be only evil sorcerers.

Zeernebooch. In the Teuton and German mythology, Zeernebooch was a god who presided over the realm of the dead.

Zemi. In the Antilles (the West Indies Islands of Cuba, Hispaniola, Jamaica, Puerto Rico, and a few smaller surrounding islands), the Zemi is an idol fashioned of stone or wood and worshipped by the Taino Indians of this area.

Zem-Zem. The sacred well near the Great Mosque at Mecca, which legend proclaims miraculously overflowed for Hagar and Ishmael and saved them from dying of thirst in the desert.

Zen. The creation of Zen Buddhism, first in India and migrating from there to China and Japan, involved a time-period exceeding a thousand years. Zen Buddhism came to the West primarily from Japan. But Japanese Zen was derived from the ch'an schools of Chinese Buddhism (which were themselves a product of the Yoga (q.v.) practice of Indian Buddhism, where meditation and moral discipline brought transcendental wisdom (prajna) and Samadhi (qq.v.)). In Japanese Zen the emphasis is upon the essence of Buddhism—experiencing the great enlightenment (Bodhi) (q.v.) achieved by Buddha. Toward this end, it eliminates all intellectual and traditional orthodoxy. For it embodies the Chinese quest for prajna that is ultimately experienced through an instantaneous intuition. The two leading figures in the history of Japanese Zen are Eisai (1141-1215) and Dogen (shoyo Daishi) (1200-1253). Eisai introduced the Rinzai school—the teaching that enlightenment will come by way of training by Koan (the method of paradoxical statements—culminating in satori (q.v.)); Dogen introduced the practice of Zazen (q.v.), a method of quiet meditation in the cross-legged position. Again, it was the Chinese ch'an practice from which the Japanese learned not to theorize or to explain, since enlightenment must come from within the individual himself. However, as it early evolved in medieval Japan (1200-1700), Zen incorporated a very complex pattern of existence that included religion, government, art, literature, and social ceremony; along with the gaining and practicing of transcendental wisdom and Karuna—love. Contemporary Zen Buddhism is now more restricted. Today in Japan, Zen disciples are trained in a dojo—a training hall. Here the novice is initiated into the following monastic discipline: a life of humility, of labor, of service, of prayer, gratitude, and meditation. Westerners throughout the modern era have been indoctrinated, for the most part, into this type of Zen discipline, and guided toward the knowledge of sudden enlightenment through the training in Koan or the method of Zazen.

Zend-Avesta. The sacred writings of the Zoroastrians (q.v.). (See: Avesta)

Zener Cards. Used for experiments in telepathy. A pack of twenty-five cards comprising five sets of five diagrams (circle, plus sign, rectangle, star, wavy lines), used by J.B. Rhine (q.v.) and others in extra-sensory perception experiments in card-guessing. Later, packs were used that contained random distributions of the five symbols, which simplified statistical evaluation of displacement phenomena. (See: Parapsychology)

Zenith. Astrologers consider this pole of the horizon, which is directly overhead, a very powerful influence. For the closer a planet is to the zenith, the greater its potency.

Zeus. In Greek mythology Zeus was the supreme god, which made him the chief of the Olympian divinities. Zeus achieved his power with the help of his brothers after they overcame their father, Cronus (a Titan); and since Zeus means "sky" he was awarded the domains of the heavens and the upper regions. Beyond his celestial hegemony, Zeus dictated the destiny of mankind: everything good or bad in men's lives came from Zeus since he apportioned good or evil to mortals. But the career and influence of Zeus extended far beyond Greek borders, for he was identified with the Roman Jupiter and Dyaus Pita of the Hindus; and only Zeus of all the Greek gods is definitely known to have had an Indo-European origin and to have been worshipped as "Father" over an area from India to much of Europe.

Ziggurat. Babylonian and Assyrian temples that rose in square terraced stages to a lofty shrine at the summit in which was housed the god of that temple. These massive structures had inclined ramps; the inside of the temple was made of plain bricks, the outside of colored enameled bricks. The summit of the ziggurat was also utilized as a place for the famous astrological observations (important in the religious ritual) which were destined to be profoundly influential in the development of Western astrology.

Zion. In Judaism and Christianity, Zion has had an overwhelming significance. To the Jew it was the holy land of Jehovah, the soil consecrated to God, the place where his soul would rise when the Messiah appeared announcing the resurrection. For the Jewish Cabalists, the return to Zion signified the union of man with God. Large numbers of Cabalist rabbis during the 16th century settled in Jerusalem, Behron, Safed and Tiberias, of whom Isaac Luria, Joseph Caro, and Moses Cordovero (qq.v.) were the most famous. For Christians, in the apocalyptic writings, Zion or the "New Jerusalem" represents the capital of Christ's Kingdom at the Millenium.

Ziruph (Cabalism–Judaism). Divination by utilizing various combinations and various transformations of letters which was assiduously practiced by the Cabalists and Hebrew mystics for thousands of years. (See: Temurah)

Zoanthropy. A delusion that a person has been turned into an animal and acts like one. In the Bible in *Daniel* 4 there is a story of Nebuchadnezzar's zoanthropic monomania.

Zodiac. The circle or belt set along the ecliptic (q.v.), which contains the twelve divisions of the heavens. This belt is 18° wide, includes the path of all the principal planets except Pluto, is divided into twelve constellations or signs (qq.v.), and astrologers give to each 30° of longitude. The position of any planet or star both within and without the Zodiac is calculated by drawing a perpendicular to the ecliptic.

Zodiac, Sidereal. Those particular constellations which lie along the sun's path through the sky (ecliptic).

Zodiac, Tropical. The ecliptic (sun's path) extended laterally to seven or eight degrees and divided from the vernal equinox point into twelve equal segments (signs) named after, but not now coincident with the constellations of the same names.

Zodiacal Aspects. In Astrology these are the distances between planets as they move through the zodiac, with the calculations of the promittor and significator (qq.v.) playing key roles in their relation to each other. But these key roles depend on the further study of the "progressed horoscope" and the mundane aspects (qq.v.).

Zodiacal Man. The twelve signs of Astrology have long been credited with ruling separate parts of the body. These twelve signs rule the following body elements: Aries—head; Taurus—neck and throat; Gemini—arms and lungs; Cancer—chest; Leo—back and heart; Virgo—gastrointestinal tract; Libra—loins and kidneys; Scorpio—sexual and elimination organs; Sagittarius—thighs; Capricorn—knees; Aquarius—legs; Pisces—feet. Occultism has been deeply influenced by this astrological doctrine.

"Zodiacus Vitae." The Zodiac of Life. An old school text which was written by Marcellus Palingenius Stellatus, sometime about 1574. This book on astrology was widely popular in Shakespeare's England. Palingenius was a mystic who considered the twelve signs of the zodiac an allegory of the twelve labors of Hercules, which, again, symbolically, taught the evolution of the human soul through the mounting stages of mental and spiritual enlightenment.

Zoether. Supposed nervous aura, bearing the same relation to spirit that gravitation does to matter.

Zohar (Cabalism). One of the two major classics of Cabalism (q.v.), since its publication by Moses de Leon of Granada, Spain (d. 1305). It has profoundly influenced the lives of millions of Jews, numerous Christians, and a multitude of occultists. Titled the *Sepher Hazzohar* ("The Book of Brightness") Moses de Leon claimed it had been written by Simon-ben-Yochai (q.v.), but most authorities agree the book is the creation of de Leon. The *Zohar* explicates the nature of God, the divine emanations of the Sepiroth (q.v.), the creation of angels and man, and the esoteric message of the revealed law. Because the *Zohar* along with other major Cabalistic writings affirms that its mystical-occult concepts were derived from the canonical Hebrew scriptures, Christian theologians saw the *Zohar* as providing proof of the divinity of Christ and a host of other New Testament doctrines. Being a source of immense occult, esoteric, mystic, and prophetic material, the *Zohar* has maintained its continuing influence, authority and popularity up to the present moment. (See: Cabalism, Emanations, Sephar Yezirah, Sepiroth, Ain Soph, Messiah, Ziruph, Temura, Gematria, Simon-ben-Yochai, Joseph Caro, Isaac Luria, Moses Cordovero)

Zoism. A doctrine found in many parts of the ancient and modern worlds which advocates a reverence for animal life and a belief in their occult powers and influences.

Zollner, J. C. F. (1834–1882). Professor of Physics and Astronomy at Leipzig University. His investigation of the phenomena of Henry Slade, and his favorable reports of his psychic abilities subjected Zollner to the scorn and ridicule of his scientific colleagues. Zollner held a special theory, involving the fourth dimension, to explain psychic phenomena as normal happenings.

Zombi. Originally this term in the African tribes of the Niger-Congo, Kimbundu, and Tshiluba meant a god, and among the Kongo people, a good-luck fetish, but the notion of Zombi became a potent necromantic power in voodoo when transplanted to the West Indies. In voodoo West African magic, Zombi is the deity of the python. In the voodoo cults of Haiti and the southern United States the snake deity also bears the name "Zombi." But in the West Indian voodoo cults Zombi is a magical power that can enter into and reanimate a dead body. The Zombi is also a person who becomes a will-less robot, through the agency of the voodoo magician, and is controlled by him to behave in a state of speechlessness, doing the magician's bidding. Zombi has become part of the American language, being a description of one who is strange in appearance, mind, or action; or who somehow resembles the effect of the walking dead.

Zopyrus. The famous Greek physiognomist, one of the ancient forerunners of a psychic art, who is remembered in history for his judgment on Socrates' character based on a reading of his physiognomy.

Zoroastrianism. The doctrine of Zarathustra (q.v.), which is also

known as Mazdaism, Bah Din, Parsiism, and Fire-worship. Profoundly
ethical and envisioning both the universe and humanity on earth as
engaged in a struggle between good and evil, light and darkness, it ex-
horts mankind to choose between Ahura-Mazda and Ahriman (q.v.).
The former is the God of light, of truth, and right; the latter is the
Devil, god of darkness, falsehood, and evil. Although Ahura-Mazda
will ultimately triumph, man can gain eternal bliss or suffer eternal
agony by virtue of the life he chooses to live. The *Zend-Avesta* (q.v.)
warns man that at death his soul must pass over the "Bridge of the Re-
quiter" which will lead him to heaven or plunge him to hell according
to the way he has lived. (See: Amesha-Spentas; Atar Gathas)

Zosimos of Panopolis. Gnostic mystic, and alchemist of the third or
fourth century, he was the author of an encyclopedic treatise on
alchemy, which is the oldest surviving text on this subject. However,
his writings show him to have been versed not only in the Egyptian,
Greek, and Arabic lore of alchemy, but also in Christianity, for his
book describes a series of mystical visions in which both Christian and
pagan constituents are interlaced.

Zotzilha Chilmalman. The Mayan god of light and darkness, who eter-
nally struggles against Kinich Ahav, symbolizing the epical battle between day and night. This was a fundamental concept in Mayan religion, for the sun was the source of all existence.

Zraene Vile. Among the southern Slavs these are evil spirits who live
in the air. Once their tempers flare up they are inexorable in the
hounding of their victims.

LEARN MORE ABOUT
YOUR REAL SELF THROUGH
THE THEORIES OF EDGAR CAYCE

MORE HELPFUL READING
FROM WARNER BOOKS

BIORHYTHM: A PERSONAL SCIENCE
NEW UPDATED EDITION
by Bernard Gittelson

(F30-228, $3.95)

Now, with this new edition, you can chart your biorhythms through 1982! Discover how human performance is determined by three cycles which you can compute and predict in seconds, without math or machinery. This book means the difference between failure and a full, rich life where you control your own destiny according to the laws of science.

THE DREAMER'S DICTIONARY
by Lady Stearn Robinson & Tom Corbett

(F36-365, $3.50)

If you have different dreams, chances are you'll find their meanings here. Lady Stearn Robinson and mystic Tom Corbett have gathered 3,000 dream symbols and arranged them alphabetically for bedside reference. THE DREAMER'S DICTIONARY is the most complete and revealing guide to interpreting your dreams ever published.

PEOPLE READING
by Dr. Ernst G. Beier & Evans G. Valens

(J93-642, $2.95)

We control each other by words and gestures, by how we dress, what we eat, even by the jobs we choose. Here is where you'll find how to recognize and control the unwanted signals that may be ruining your life.